GOVERNANCE
AND
THE POSTCOLONY

GOVERNANCE
AND
THE POSTCOLONY

VIEWS FROM AFRICA

EDITED BY
DAVID EVERATT

WITS UNIVERSITY PRESS

Published in South Africa by:
Wits University Press
1 Jan Smuts Avenue
Johannesburg 2001

www.witspress.co.za

Compilation © Editor 2019
Chapters © Individual contributors 2019
Published edition © Wits University Press 2019
Images and figures © Copyright holders

First published 2019

http://dx.doi.org.10.18772/22019083443

978-1-77614-344-3 (Paperback)
978-1-77614-345-0 (Web PDF)
978-1-77614-346-7 (EPUB)
978-1-77614-347-4 (Mobi)

Project manager: Catherine Damerell
Copyeditor: Catherine Damerell
Proofreader: Lisa Compton
Indexer: Marlene Burger
Cover design: Hothouse
Typesetter: Newgen
Typeset in 10 point Minion Pro

CONTENTS

FIGURES AND TABLES

ABBREVIATIONS AND ACRONYMS

ANC	African National Congress
ANCYL	African National Congress Youth League
APSA	African Peace and Security Architecture
APRM	African Peer Review Mechanism
AU	African Union
BLF	Black First Land First
BRICS	Brazil-Russia-India-China-South Africa network
CCSA	Constitutional Court of South Africa
CoGTA	(Department of) Cooperative Governance and Traditional Affairs
Cope	Congress of the People
Cosas	Congress of South African Students
Cosatu	Congress of South African Trade Unions
DA	Democratic Alliance
ECOWAS	Economic Community of West African States
EFF	Economic Freedom Fighters
EVD	Ebola virus disease
GCRO	Gauteng City-Region Observatory
GDP	gross domestic product
GLS	Green Leadership Schools
Gear	Growth, Employment and Redistribution
HDI	Human Development Index
IDP	Integrated Development Plan
ILO	International Labour Organization
IMF	International Monetary Fund
MDG	Millennium Development Goals
MP	member of parliament
NCOP	National Council of Provinces
NDP	National Development Plan

NEPAD	New Partnership for Africa's Development
NGO	non-governmental organisation
NIE	new institutional economics
NMF	Nelson Mandela Foundation
NSFAS	National Student Financial Aid Scheme
OAU	Organisation of African Unity
OECD	Organisation for Economic Development and Cooperation
Outa	Opposition to Urban Tolling Alliance
PAC	Pan Africanist Congress of Azania
PAP	Pan-African Parliament
PHEIC	Public Health Emergency of International Concern
Posib	Protection of State Information Bill
PPP	purchasing power parity
RDP	Reconstruction and Development Programme
REC	regional economic community
RM	regional mechanism
SACP	South African Communist Party
Sadtu	South African Democratic Teachers Union
SALGA	South African Local Government Association
Sanral	South African National Roads Agency (SOC) Limited
SCA	Supreme Court of Appeal
SHD	sustainable human development
TAC	Treatment Action Campaign
UN	United Nations
UNDP	United Nations Development Programme
UNESCO	United Nations Educational, Scientific and Cultural Organization
WAHO	West African Health Organization
WCED	World Commission on Environment and Development
WHO	World Health Organization

Governance in the Postcolony: Time for a rethink?

David Everatt

POWER, CONTEXT AND APPLICATION

Notions of governance have spread globally across disciplines and sectors like an ugly but undiagnosed rash: governance pops up everywhere but is commonly undefined, and while content (or diagnosis) is assumed, it is rarely articulated. These notions range from theories such as network governance, regulatory governance, multi-level governance, adaptive governance, and so on, to sector-specific applications including internet governance, multiple iterations of corporate governance, humanitarian governance, non-profit governance, and more. But too often it is a label, almost an incantation, without substantive definition or clarity. It may be that multiple applications are an attempt to provide content to a 'catch-all' category, but then the challenges of context, power and application all apply. Seen from the global south, governance is most commonly applied as a simplistic, normative imposition; its tools are in place to decide on reward and punishment, flowing from a narrow, a-contextual and ahistorical application. It is used to delineate the good from the bad, to call to order, or to call for order and rules (to be written or to be obeyed). The problem is not the lack of a single, 'perfect' definition – although some greater definitional precision would certainly help – but the failure to locate governance in relation to power, context and application.

When governance is analysed in relation to power, context and application, it is not reducible merely to citing (in)efficiency in delivering services. Rather, it talks to fairness and transparency when power is exercised, and the creation of meaningful space for all relevant actors (uneven in many respects – membership, organisational coherence, and so on) to influence wherever power is located and the point at which it is exercised. It does so locally and globally.

The key issue is power. Governance is only rarely articulated explicitly in terms of and in relation to power, and the more prevalent this silence becomes, combined with the endless calls for 'good governance', the less value the term connotes or contains. Governance is ultimately concerned with the contestation between stakeholders wherever power is being exercised. Precisely because power is at stake, the rules of the game need to be clear, fair and known to all; sites of decision-making need to be transparent and accessible to all relevant players; and the similarly repeated-unto-death 'level playing fields' are non-negotiable. The chapters in this volume investigate how often or how rarely such conditions prevail.

In highly unequal global and local contexts, rule-based contestation is to be expected and welcomed – if the rules are fair, and the match is not rigged. It is in this space that governance operates. However, seen from the postcolony, precisely because it lays bare the unfairness of the rules, it is discomfiting. Governance is inseparable from context but is frequently an agenda-loaded tool used by the global north to rig fights and ensure victory. This is exactly why dislocating governance from the context, and the localised use and abuse of power, is so dangerous – and so common. Thinking contextually does not remove other key aspects of governance: the need for mature political and social institutions, democratic elections, the rule of law, and so on. Instead, it locates these in a global historical context of power relations. In the postcolony, these institutions and instruments of democracy are often an uncomfortable 'fit', produced for the colony by the imperial power, so nuance and contextual understanding are key.

Some shared content is required for governance to be an effective concept, let alone a useful set of tools, for all. This is especially true when good governance is most commonly a package of rules and tools created in the global north and imposed on the global south, in an assumed – yet self-evidently fallacious – context of equal sovereign nation states and neutral, fair-minded multilateral institutions. This is the moment when the democratic impulse should be at the heart of governance but is too often removed. Thus Fukuyama, for example, could observe that what matters is state capacity, not state behaviour. By stripping governance from power, context and contestation, he asserted: '[…] I am excluding democratic accountability from the definition of governance', arguing that the 'current orthodoxy in the development community is that democracy and good governance are mutually supportive', which, he argued, is merely theoretical and not 'an empirically demonstrated fact' (Fukuyama 2013: 6). By 2016, Fukuyama (2016) seemed to have moderated this rather extreme position, but the ideological impulse had been made visible to all.

The mere proliferation of the term 'governance' – whether coupled to 'good' or not – is one of the challenges this book tackles. If governance is to be an efficacious concept that helps highlight inequalities and unfairness (whether in the delivery of services or in global trade) it must have a minimum threshold of shared content. When that is in place, its sectoral application flows seamlessly. The danger we face is that the more governance is invoked, the greater the danger of its content being hollowed out. Governance then becomes incapable of helping us diagnose, analyse and understand challenges, or offering us remedies to improve performance (regardless of which sector or part of the state is at issue). If governance does none of these things, it is of little value, particularly viewed from the global south.

It is difficult to avoid the conclusion that governance is in some trouble in finding purchase as a transformative and liberatory notion, one that lays bare the site of power, the rules of the game and the motives of players. Rather, it is being commodified into a global consultancy industry, littered with dashboards, indicators and toolkits, loaded up with World Bank jargon, and is more a means of maintaining the status quo than calling to account the northern powers (economic and political) who benefit from that status quo. This theme is explicit in many chapters of the book, and implicit in all.

Many governance theorists bemoan the absence of a shared definition, and most start by reminding readers of the Greek etymology of the term ('to steer'), then the Latin, then the French and, later still, the English use of the term – even though use of the term governance only really became ubiquitous after the 1990s, with a self-evidently different and contextually driven lineage and content. While some bemoan the term as lacking any content because of contestation around its meaning, others find it coterminous with public administration.

In this volume, governance is less the performance of state machinery than the sequence of democratic moments where the exercise of power by the state is open to contest, challenge and counter, in an open and transparent manner, and in a meeting of equally legitimate entities. This borrows heavily from network governance theory, but focuses more on the democratic energy in the contestation: state and large power blocs must allow, facilitate and accept change or reversal from the full sequence of interchanges among themselves and with all non-state actors.

Fukuyama is generally known for arguing strongly that governance is best measured by how efficiently and effectively the state machinery can deliver services – literally, govern-ance (Fukuyama 2013, 2014, 2016). Few would quibble that this lies at the heart of governance – but most authors in this volume argue that context is vital, and some go further to see governance as an intrinsically active, democratising moment where contending forces with legitimacy struggle over what service will be delivered, to whom, at what cost, in what form, at what time, and so on. Seen from the global south, or from the postcolony, there is an inherent democratising impulse that animates and gives purpose to governance – at global and local levels.

The postcolony at one level 'identifies specifically a given historical trajectory – that of societies recently emerging from the experience of colonisation and the violence which the colonial relationship involves' combined with 'a series of corporate institutions and a political machinery that, once in place, constitute a distinct regime of violence' (Mbembe 2015: 102). As Young (2015) notes, the postcolony is not a given or a singularity – Mbembe's characterisation can be nuanced to include many former colonies seeking to throw off the colonial inheritance but which are not automatically as dysfunctional as Mbembe's description (many had decolonised considerably earlier than the African experience Mbembe wrote about); former settler colonies and their tortuous (flowing from previously murderous) relations with indigenous populations; and postcolonies that 'remain or have become dysfunctional', the latter closer to Mbembe's definition (Young 2015: 137).

Postcolonialism is a contested if important notion, and is the unavoidable framing and context for our various examinations of governance, given that virtually the entire African continent was successively colonised over centuries, with independent African states largely a phenomenon of the 1950s and 1960s, but stretching to the 1970s when the Portuguese left, the 1980s when South Africa was forced out of Namibia (then South West Africa), and 1990, when the settler colonial apartheid regime came to an inglorious end. Unlike 'the scramble for Africa' and the 1884 Berlin Conference that divvied up the spoils, colonialism is not a distant memory but a lived one for most Africans. Our independent states in turn are products of colonial power, with borders incorporating distinct, frequently hostile ethnic groups, religions, linguistic groups, and our governance arrangements authored by the departing imperial powers – or the settler colonialists who remain resident within the former colony.

Searching for the 'level playing field' in the postcolony – let alone among and between former colonies – is a rather fruitless exercise. So too is the glib assumption that as the imperial flag was finally lowered, so former colonies were immediately free and equal states, ignoring the fact that power transferred from one (colonial) elite to another (domestic) elite, both of whom had a shared goal: 'the national middle class is easily convinced that it can advantageously replace the middle class of the mother country' (Fanon 1963: 120) and from there '[t]he national middle class discovers its historic mission: that of intermediary' (1963: 122). Without a genuine rupture at the point of decolonisation, without an attempt to find a new national identity, voice, and set of values and newly designed institutions, that in Mignolo's (2007) terminology are 'delinked' from the colony, decolonisation birthed a post-colonial local and global structure of power, institutions and violence. Somehow, governance needs to find purchase in this morass. Ignoring context and assuming a global level playing field seems inconceivable, yet it is the current consensus.

Postcolonialism is challenged by former colonial powers, for obvious reasons, as an inability to 'get over it' and join the plurality of free nation states. Pointing to dysfunctional, violent and corrupt former colonies that have never achieved political legitimacy, the former colonial power forgets that talking about colonialism,

> [...] may seem to be calling up specters from the past, but in global terms colonialism itself represents the most widespread form of oppression in human history; its harsh power relations have resulted in the word 'olonial' becoming a metaphor for the imbalance of power itself (Young 2015: 149–150).

The postcolony has survived predictions of its demise, although many have been premised on the notion that a new, global platform of struggle should replace postcolonialism and unite global class forces, rather than lock them into 'old' binaries: often eco-socialism is offered as a new narrative for uniting class forces around the anthropocene and against imperialism. Dabashi (2012), for example, heralded the Arab Spring as signalling 'the end of postcolonialism' (the subtitle of his book). For Dabashi and others, postcolonialism had the effect of locking former colonies into outdated binaries – coloniser and colonised, imperial project and subject nation, 'the west vs. the rest' – which were unhelpful analytical lenses for examining power relations in the globalised twenty-first century (Dabashi 2012: xvii).

As with many proponents of decoloniality, Dabashi predicted that with postcolonialism out of the way, a new, cosmopolitan struggle culture would emerge, which would supersede old binaries. As Mignolo and Walsh (2018: 223) put it, the task of decoloniality (which cannot be undertaken by postcoloniality) is to 'delink from modern/colonial praxis of living and knowing, and to walk toward re-existing

5

in the borderland and the borderlines in decolonial praxis of living, knowing, sensing, and of loving'. It is the kind of language that would reduce management consultants to tears as they sought to operationalise it in a dashboard and measure performance.

The postcolony and postcolonialism have been roundly criticised by proponents of decoloniality. Despite the fact that both are taking aim at imperial/modernist domination, proponents of decoloniality repeatedly insist they are not seeking to depose one hierarchy in order to put in place a new one (for example, Ndlovu-Gatsheni 2013; Mignolo and Walsh 2018). Nonetheless, they have turned on postcolonialists as 'informed by a deep misunderstanding' (Ndlovu-Gatsheni 2013: 14, referring to Mbembe and Appiah). Postcolonial scholars have fought back, calling for a move away from what they regard as nativism or chic radicalism, and issued challenges for scholars in the south to take on 'the Western archive'. As Mbembe put it (n.d.: 24):

> Our capacity to make systematic forays beyond our current knowledge horizons will be severely hampered if we rely exclusively on those aspects of the Western archive that disregard other epistemic traditions.
>
> Yet the Western archive is singularly complex. It contains within itself the resources of its own refutation. It is neither monolithic, nor the exclusive property of the West. Africa and its diaspora decisively contributed to its making and should legitimately make foundational claims on it.
>
> Decolonizing knowledge is therefore not simply about de-Westernization.

For Ndlovu-Gatsheni, this was less a challenge than a failure to understand that Africans (in this argument) were seeking 'to regain lost ontological density'; like academics everywhere, however, he went on to add that the approach was 'mischievous and dishonest' and smacked of 'intellectual laziness' (2013: 14).

Mignolo and Walsh (2018: 228) make a robust argument for decoloniality, namely:

> Decoloniality's goal and orientation [...] are epistemic reconstitution. Epistemic reconstitution cannot be achieved by setting up a 'new' school of thought within [the] Western cosmology. It requires two simultaneous tasks: to open up the richness of knowledges and praxis of living that the rhetoric of modernity demonized and reduced to tradition, barbarism, folklore, under-development, denied spirituality in the name of reason, and built knowledge to

control sexuality and all kinds of barbarians. Second [… it] requires delinking from the bubbles of modern thoughts from the left and from the right.

From the outside, there may be an assumption that de- and postcolonialists should be coming at the same issue from different angles, with perhaps different points of emphasis. This is particularly true given the repeated assertion that the goal is to dismantle domination, not replace it. Given their hostility to intellectual domination, based on direct experience of colonialism and coloniality, alliances and partnerships between and among may be expected. After all, decolonialists are clear that the challenge is to shift epistemology from a Western to an open system, and reclaim knowledge from the dominant paradigm that Grosfoguel described as 'European/capitalist/military/Christian/patriarchal/white/heterosexual/male' (2011: 9). Grosfoguel (2011: 17) goes on to suggest that this may be because of different academic disciplinary backgrounds:

> With very few exceptions, most post-colonial theorists come from fields of the humanities such as literature, rhetoric, and cultural studies. Only a small number of scholars in the field of post-coloniality come from the social sciences, in particular from anthropology.

Clearly, expectations of some kind of anti-imperialist unity is naïve, and relations are fraught. The fratricide among what appear to be partners in the battle against coloniality is an unfortunate reminder of how easily a school of thought in the academy can turn on 'rival' schools of thought with just as much heat as it had reserved for its original target – in this case, global imperial domination – especially when those struggles are occurring primarily in the common room and the pages of journals.

Governance is (we argue) facing a substantial risk of losing urgency and relevance as it drowns in multiple definitions, forms, applications, and is used more as a method of reprimand than a tool to unleash local and global democratic energies. Intellectually, governance has to navigate context, power and application in the global south, where the postcolony is under attack from decolonialists and others. These are not irrelevant academic debates: they cut to the core of how the global south is defining its place, function and future. Two concepts come together in this volume: first, governance was the prime focus, but writing about governance from the global south makes the postcolony unavoidable; and second, writing simultaneously about both (in some chapters, very consciously; in others, the postcolony is implicit) allows for new perspectives on both.

GOVERNANCE IN THE POSTCOLONY: WHAT THE AUTHORS ARGUE

The opening chapter of this volume (David Everatt) argues that governance is at risk of being given too much content, by being applied to multiple contexts and locations. It is treated as both an object of theory and as various sets of tools (depending on where and how it is being applied). That is a challenge in itself, but is compounded by the fact that governance is rarely if ever analysed in reference to the contextualised exercise of power that is the intimate heart of governance. The same point applies to space: the imperious, 803-page *Oxford Handbook of Governance* (2012), for example, makes one reference to Africa – 'and Europeanisation' – while the African Union (AU) manages two mentions (no African country gets a mention at all). Brazil and India get four mentions, while China gets just two (Levi-Faur 2012). Many northern scholars of governance are engaged in a debate about the best indicators, and the best database, and who can best measure governance, while firmly avoiding geography, context and power when analysing the story those indicators tell.

Susan Booysen offers a notion of 'adversarial network governance', which she defines as 'contrariness' within the interdependence of network governance – in effect, a reluctant state apparatus forced to change direction (or cease acting in a specific domain). Three current South African case studies show how an adversarial network can force a government (a democratically elected government with a substantial majority, in this case) to reverse policies, or not to implement policy decisions, or to hold off from signing into law a deeply contested piece of legislation. For some, this may be the routine function of democratic opposition (civic, political or other), but it is important in highlighting governance at the point of contestation. This is useful in reminding us that 'the state' is not a uniform entity acting with a single purpose: in South Africa, for example, while former president Thabo Mbeki was questioning the science of HIV and Aids, the provincial government in Gauteng was ignoring remedies recommended by national government (such as the African potato and beetroot) and rolling out antiretroviral treatment. The state can oppose the state, and subvert it, just as non-state actors can do.

Mbembe noted (2015: 7) that for the global north looking at the postcolony generally, and Africa in particular,

> [i]t is enough to postulate, somehow, in a form totally timeless, the necessity of 'freeing' the economy from the shackles of the state, and of a reform of institutions from above, for this economy, these institutions, to function on the basis of norms decreed and universal.

Governance is currently a core part of the set of norms 'decreed and universal' handed down from the north, most commonly by the World Bank with its good governance fixation. This is not in any way to excuse the crassness of malfeasance or poor governance when or where in the south or north it occurs. But – to take the Fukuyama approach – merely *governing* in the south, and the postcolony in particular, is challenging enough. In a continent of colonially created borders that often divide existing communities (of language, culture and identity), attempts to develop both national identities and mature organs of state, rule of law and accountability (the Fukuyama approach) have been complemented by similar efforts at continental scale. Salim Latib analyses the 'shared values' governance frameworks developed by the AU to bolster these efforts, and to develop African governance rules, not simply swallow those handed down.

As Latib notes, the World Bank tends to sidestep political matters and prefers to focus on corruption, inefficiencies in procurement or implementation, and lack of accountability. Citing Ake (1991), he reminds us that political issues in African states are commonly regarded merely as engineering matters open to technical solution – a fundamental error, and not one that imperial powers assume to be true of themselves. Latib traces the evolution of formal African governance, including a range of AU instruments – the Charter on Human and Peoples' Rights, the Charter on the Rights and Welfare of the Child, the African Peer Review Mechanism, and others. All now fall under the broader umbrella of Agenda 2063, which articulates Africa's hopes to lift border restrictions on the movement of people – harking back to an Africa prior to 1884 and the lines drawn by imperial powers – only some 130 years ago. As Heath (2010) reminds us,

> Neither the Berlin Conference itself nor the framework for future negotiations provided any say for the peoples of Africa over the partitioning of their homelands. The Berlin Conference did not initiate European colonization of Africa, but it did legitimate and formalize the process. In addition, it sparked new interest in Africa. Following the close of the conference, European powers expanded their claims in Africa such that by 1900, European states had claimed nearly 90 percent of African territory.

While 1884 may not be 'within living memory' and lived experience, colonialism certainly is since decolonisation ended for Namibia in the 1980s, and for South Africa in the 1990s (while for the majority of African countries, decolonisation stretched from the 1950s to the 1970s). When governance operates within the postcolony, the rules of the game and of good governance have been written by the former colonial powers, after centuries of destructive extraction, racist violence and slaughter. The imperialist good governance project has a clear agenda, and the postcolony is a key target.

Patrick Bond's chapter resonates here, as it is based on the argument that 'the interplay of Pretoria officials and Johannesburg business managers in global governance' is in essence 'sub-imperial practices disguised by anti-imperial posturing'. The postcolony in this view is not an abject body waiting to be acted upon: it includes segments – whether in Pretoria or Arusha or Nairobi – more than happy to act as sub-imperial agents for an agenda that is set elsewhere, but includes massive personal self-enrichment, corruption, disruption of state and judicial processes – everything that goes against developing mature organs of state, in effect – and ongoing poverty for the mass of postcolonial denizens. Many chapters in the book note that understanding governance may require looking for its antagonists and understanding their agendas. Without subscribing to a particular conspiracy theory, the ongoing disruption of states, organs of state and key pillars of governance to permit enhanced plunder of natural resources is scarcely a new insight into the way African states have been treated since independence (always with willing local elites in tow).

Caryn Abrahams looks at food networks in Lusaka, noting that global regimes directly threaten food security in Zambia, and observes that the poor do not need assistance but need to be able to get closer to the levers of power if they are to have impact; the same is true of national governments, who face multinational companies, a profoundly unequal trading environment, and climate change. She offers the notion of 'deliberative governance planning' as a mechanism for drawing in all key players to chart an appropriate governance framework and concrete mechanisms for governing and regulating (in this case, food). Her case study highlights the complexity of these issues by outlining overlapping rationalities across different actors, and their resistance to behaving in predictable fashion. She echoes the challenge implicit in most of the contributions to this book, namely: 'what, in the end, is the purpose of governance thinking if it is not also to guarantee a set of just or equitable outcomes' for those affected?

Too often the proponents of postcolonialism and decoloniality are seen to be apologists for the state of the global south as judged through the eyes of the north. This is both a silly notion and a means of sidestepping the realities of those seeking to realise governance in the postcolony. Anthoni van Nieuwkerk and Bongiwe Ngcobo Mphahlele, in their case study of African crisis leadership, suggest ways in which West African states (Liberia in particular) have enhanced local governance by suffering a crisis – the Ebola outbreak in this instance – and have learned the importance of local responses, informed by local realities, assisted but not driven by any external/multilateral agenda. The chapter also shows other African states reacting to the same Ebola outbreak, where this lesson was perhaps not as well learned.

Pundy Pillay uses a very different approach, looking at the relationship between governance and development, and notes the current paradigm (which strongly echoes Fukuyama and many northern scholars) that poor countries are poor because they have bad governance, and wealthy countries are wealthy because they have improved governance. This simplistic paradigm ignores context, and the extent to which one part of the world improves its lot at the expense of the other. Governance in this worldview is a static moment in time, using preferred indicators and data sources to score nations on a yardstick, and it simply does not look beyond the output of such an exercise.

Pillay, as with Latib and others, points to the AU's Agenda 2063 as an attempt to develop a specifically continental approach to governance in a continent so deeply marked by colonialism and its after-effects. He also points to the need for govern-ance to be broken down into sectors (such as health and education) and localised, to the point where governance involves local stakeholders, non-state and state actors, who engage over the best use of limited resources for the best local outcomes.

The second part of the book has a more sector-specific set of perspectives. Mike Muller's chapter on 'governance versus government' starts by discarding Washington Consensus notions of good governance to try to understand how gov-ernance can help manage one of the most fundamental assets in any society – water. He rejects the global policy consensus that water service matters are best delegated to the lowest level, because they require national coherence. He also warns against non-state actors who may rightly campaign for this or that specific community, but by taking their fights to court they may win gains for some – at the expense of others. Muller argues for stakeholder network governance which allows all state and non-state actors space to contest nested within a coherent legal and policy frame-work, and he concludes with some support for Fukuyama's approach to governance.

What all in the postcolony share is that the colonial power in most instances drafted the constitution and left behind a version of its legal system; its language became the dominant local language; its education system took root (ironic given that the first degree-awarding institution is generally understood to be Morocco's University of Al Quaraouyine in Fez, founded by a woman). But, by the twenty-first century, the collective of the postcolony had been fully drawn into the modern uni-versity '[…] whose universal language is English' and which is '[…] a neo-liberal structure in which the university's primary function has become not so much the pursuit of knowledge but to compete with other universities', in Young's view (2015: 141). However, academics have agency within the academy, and must take responsibility for allowing themselves to mimic these contestations, in exactly the way we have seen postcolonialism and decoloniality taking the fight to one another.

Darlene Miller, Nomalanga Mkhize, Rebecca Pointer and Babalwa Magoqwana analyse conditions in the postcolonial academy through a decolonial lens, and argue that from the architectural design (separateness), to the pedagogic approach (the lectern as a symbol of power), to the language of instruction, the postcolonial university in South Africa continues to privilege white men above others, as well as a particular Western approach to learning and teaching. Through the case studies they use, the authors argue for an ecologically grounded and more spiritually centred approach that recognises the humanity and equality of all in the academy.

Kirti Menon and Jody Cedras take a different approach to governance and the academy by focusing on how decisions are made. They find the simultaneous exercise of the bureaucratic, the collegial and the political models in South African higher education institutions. In this context, the student protests (under the banner #FeesMustFall) – which demanded free, quality, decolonised education in South Africa – were a reminder of the easy way in which the postcolony has slid out of the past; and that universities have remained spaces that offer education and reward work unchanged from the past. Universities, as Young (2015) noted earlier, have perhaps become far too involved in chasing rankings and funding, and forgetting the humanity of their staff and students.

While Menon and Cedras find evidence of too much state intervention in universities, Chelete Monyane questions whether another key player in governance, the judiciary, has overstepped generally agreed interpretations of the separation of powers. Using the recent turbulent history of South Africa, he argues that the failings of government and politics, and the use of 'lawfare' to settle essentially political disputes, has had the effect of drawing the judiciary way beyond its comfort zone by having to deal with elements of 'state capture' and the looting of state coffers by elected and unelected officials alike.

While judicial independence is a continuum in imperial and postcolonial discourses, Monyane illustrates the pressures brought to bear on the judiciary by groups seeking to enhance governance, and the fact that elected officials regard their mandate as superior to the constitutional guarantees of judicial independence. The rules of this game, which emerge from the colonial past, assume that players in the game all want to play by the rules, a self-evident inexactitude. Contestation around these core tenets of governance is to be welcomed; but Monyane warns by implication that if the judiciary (this, his example) is drawn beyond the bounds of what its role is commonly understood to be, even if in pursuit of good governance, it will be very difficult to revert to the status quo ante, assuming the legislative and executive branches of government revert to less rent-seeking behaviours.

William Gumede's examination of state-owned entities in South Africa shows the limits of governance prescripts when faced by a relentless onslaught of rent-seekers. He traces the legal requirements enshrined in a succession of Acts of parliament, the successive King codes of corporate governance (which have fed into state govern-ance), but concludes that these ultimately serve little purpose beyond helping trace the collapse of municipal entities and state-owned entities, narrated annually by the Auditor-General and others. In effect, it seems that the more a sector is loaded with formal governance requirements, the less space is opened for democratic contest-ation over power and how decisions are made, and the easier it is to simply sidestep governance.

David Everatt's final chapter on quality of life argues that governance failures can be traced back to the natural inclination of government to avoid 'wicked' problems and seek easy wins. In post-apartheid South Africa, this has entailed an ongoing process of basic needs delivery, much of which has had the effect of locking black South Africans into apartheid-created (and race-based) spaces and ways of living. The emphasis on water reticulation, sanitation, electrification, and so on are vital – but as South Africa emerges from apartheid, which itself was only the last 42 years of 400 years of settler colonialism, the true challenges are far more complex, deep-seated, and profoundly difficult to 'solve' through 'delivery'. The psychosocial mix of received racism and violence (whether as victim or per-petrator) lives on in the minds of people whose locale has been 'developed'. The decolonial literature speaks strongly to the need to return to a human-centred mode of governing and governance. When one gets beneath the overbearing lan-guage of epistemological and ontological continuities and ruptures, the hegemonic architecture of knowledge and 'rules of knowing' (see, for example, Mignolo and Walsh 2018: 212), the real issue at stake is rediscovering humanity by delinking from the notion that there is one correct way of being and doing. That is simply stated but fundamentally challenging to governments in the postcolony, which may explain why few, if any, can bring themselves to tackle more than the low-hanging fruit available to them.

The danger is that by endless repetition, governance loses the sharpness and rele-vance it ought to have in a postcolonial context, and rather becomes a set of rules with attached penalties and sanctions wielded by former colonial powers to keep the postcolony in its place. In that sense, the postcolony is in itself a definitional site of governance at work: the tussle between the governed and those governing, mimicking a global struggle between imperial and postcolonial powers.

In the postcolony, governance is of singular importance. It is similar for decoloniality, which seeks to dislocate the current global power structure and replace 'the centre' with multiple, equal centres. But governance is not simply that which is handed down from the north/west. It is not a set of rules that advanced economies author in order to maintain their globally privileged position based as it is on centuries of colonial plunder.

At a global level, governance sees a substantial tension between imperial and postcolonial societies (amongst others); at a local level, governance is similarly about contestation and struggle, by partners with equal legitimacy (if different mandates and constituencies), where transparent rules and processes allow for a robust engagement over the best outcomes. The entire opus of development literature tells us that well-delivered and well-maintained services flow from genuine local participation. Governance should be both the means of drawing in and empowering all appropriate players, and agreeing on the best outcome: seen in that light, it is of profound importance across the postcolony, and between former colonies and imperial powers, and creates the conditions for the much-needed postcolonial rupture.

ACKNOWLEDGEMENTS

My thanks to Caryn Abrahams for her extremely useful comments on this chapter; and to the anonymous reviewers, whose comments were similarly useful.

REFERENCES

Ake, C. 1991. Rethinking African Democracy. *Journal of Democracy* 2(1): 32–44.
Dabashi, H. 2012. *The Arab Spring: The end of postcolonialism.* London & New York: Zed Books.
Fanon, F. 1963. *The Wretched of the Earth.* London: Penguin Books.
Fukuyama, F. 2013.What is governance? (mimeo). Center on Democracy, Development and the Rule of Law (CDDRL). Stanford, CA: Stanford University.
Fukuyama, F. 2014. *Political Order and Political Decay: From the Industrial Revolution to the Globalization of Democracy.* London: Profile Books.
Fukuyama, F. 2016. Governance: What do we know, and how do we know it? *Annual Review of Political Science* 19: 89–105. https://www.annualreviews.org/doi/abs/10.1146/annurev-polisci-042214-044240 (accessed 19 February 2018).

Grosfoguel, R. 2011. Decolonizing Post-Colonial Studies and Paradigms of Political Economy: Transmodernity, Decolonial Thinking, and Global Coloniality. *Transmodernity: Journal of Peripheral Cultural Production of the Luso-Hispanic World* 1(1): 2–38.

Heath, E. 2010. Berlin Conference of 1884–1885. In: Gates Jr, H.L. & Appiah, K.A. (eds) *Encyclopaedia of Africa*. Oxford: Oxford University Press. http://www.oxfordreference.com/view/10.1093/acref/9780195337709.001.0001/acref-9780195337709-e-0467 (accessed 8 August 2018).

Levi-Faur, D. (ed.) 2012. *The Oxford Handbook of Governance*. Oxford: Oxford University Press.

Mbembe, A. 2015. *On the Postcolony*. Johannesburg: Wits University Press.

Mbembe, A. n.d. Decolonizing Knowledge and the Question of the Archive (mimeo). Johannesburg: Wits Institute for Social and Economic Research (WISER). https://wiser.wits.ac.za/system/files/Achille%20Mbembe%20-%20Decolonizing%20Knowledge%20and%20the%20Question%20of%20the%20Archive.pdf (accessed 10 August 2018).

Mignolo, W.D. 2007. DELINKING. *Cultural Studies* 21(2–3): 449– 514.

Mignolo, W.D. & Walsh, C.E. 2018. *On Decoloniality*. Durham, NC & London: Duke University Press.

Ndlovu-Gatsheni, S.J. 2013. Why decoloniality in the 21st century? *The Thinker* 48: 10–15.

Young, R.J.C. 2015. *Empire, Colony, Postcolony*. Oxford: Wiley Blackwell.

PART I

GOVERNANCE IN SUB-SAHARAN AFRICA IN THEORY AND PRACTICE

1

Governance: Notes towards a resurrection

David Everatt

INTRODUCTION

Governance is a concept rich with democratic potential, and it has become a ubi-quitous part of the political, academic and other discourse since the early 1990s. Because of its inherent demand for power to be held accountable at every level, governance is potentially threatening to those with power, and to those who may wish to abuse power. In a country where the former president is (at the time of writing) facing over 780 counts of corruption, major parts of the ruling African National Congress (ANC) have fallen into a squabbling, thuggish entity feeding from the trough of public resources, and the country has witnessed a decade of 'state capture' engineered by willing buyers in the private and state-owned enter-prise sector and willing sellers in the state, the need for governance is self-evident. All major domestic policy documents, such as the National Development Plan (NDP) (National Planning Commission 2011), speak to 'good governance', and the worse the situation becomes, the more governance is hailed by its enemies. Like virtue, governance is apparently most often observed in the breach of it.

THESIS

This chapter argues that power is the central concern of governance – power and the ability to hold it to account. Power may be located in government, or may have been delegated to its local agents – MPs or school principals or librarians – or it may be located within non-state actors (NSAs) or non-governmental organisations (NGOs) or markets or multilateral institutions or corporations, themselves with power and resources from multiple sources. Ranged 'against' (not automatically in opposition), these holders of power are those with what may be termed 'legitimacy', by representing the people, communities, groups and collectives most affected by the decisions taken by these various agencies. The tension between them – the struggle against impunity and for accountability – is where governance should be sought.

To mediate this possibly Manichean separation, it is worth noting that corrupt political factions – across the political spectrum – are actively involved in forming or supporting the creation of their own NGOs, foundations, and support groups of various types. No easy assumptions should be made that either side is automatically on the side of the angels or the devil.

Governance is a process, punctuated by many local 'moments'. At each point there exists a dynamic tension between those who have delegated power (or authority) to make decisions or to act according to regulatory or rule-based guidelines, and those citizens/residents (hereafter, 'citizens' for ease of reference), citizen groups, special interests or others whose interests lie in a transparent process where laws, regulations and rules are fairly and equitably applied. Governance is about power – and holding power to account. This is why in this chapter, the antonym of governance is impunity. It is also why the strength of local organisations is of critical importance – as true of 'Sweden or Denmark on a good day' as of South Africa.

In South Africa's law and many policy documents, this more activist interpretation of governance seems to be the common understanding. Governance is not an act, or sequence of acts; nor is it obedience before rules; nor is it is the preserve of government, courts, or other regulatory authorities. All of these have a place in governance, as the Constitutional Court has argued:

> Our constitutional democracy can only be truly strengthened when: there is zero tolerance for the culture of impunity; the prospects of good governance are duly enhanced by enforced accountability; the observance of the rule of law; and respect for every aspect of our Constitution as the supreme law of the Republic are real (Constitutional Court 2016).

The National Development Plan (National Planning Commission 2011), which is intended to guide South Africa's trajectory until 2030, hinges on what it terms 'the engaged' or 'the active' citizen. Setting aside the implicit exclusionary implication of 'citizen' rather than 'resident', the matching of a constitutional call for 'enforced accountability' via 'the engaged citizen' sets out how governance is understood. It is reflected in legislation such as the Municipal Systems Act (No. 32 of 2000) and the Municipal Structures Act (No. 117 of 1998), which seek to embed local accountability at the lowest possible (manageable) level – that is, wards (commonly clusters of 4000 households, grouped into an administrative unit primarily for vote casting and counting purposes). The Integrated Development Plan (IDP), required from local up to provincial level, is then meant to be based on demand-driven development, where communities and individuals set out their needs, and monitor the extent to which those needs are or are not met over time. This is what the Constitution means when it refers to 'developmental' local government in Chapter 7:

> Developmental duties of municipalities: A municipality must – (a) structure and manage its administration and budgeting and planning processes to give priority to the basic needs of the community, and to promote the social and economic development of the community [...] (Constitution 1996: Chapter 7).

But local mimics global. Power is rarely happy to be held to account, and even these constitutional imperatives, and the legislation that embodies them in practice, have come up against a risk-averse public service, and rent-seeking has proceeded apace (Everatt, Marais and Dube 2010). The challenge, as Chabal (2014) has argued, is to focus on the core question – which is not seeking the best definition, the largest dataset, the most nuanced indicators, and the like. It is to ask, and help answer:

> How do ordinary people resist the totalising tendencies of the state and of the political elite that preside over their destiny? How do they create and main-tain the social, economic, cultural and political space they need to operate in the societies in which they live? How do they express their opposition to what they perceive as the oppressive environment that constrains their lives and activities? (Chabal 2014: xii)

It is from this bottom-up perspective, which puts the needs of the poor first and asks how the tools of governance can help lift them out of poverty, that governance ought to be understood and enacted in Africa.

EVOLUTION

Multilateral institutions produce documents littered with references to 'good governance', but many fail to define their terms – or prefer listing the multiple aspects and/or alternative definitions of the term, inviting the author to do the work.[1] This was not always the case. As early as 1997, the United Nations Development Programme (UNDP) nailed its colours to the mast, making it clear that governance was about action, about the healthy tension between power and accountability, between government and citizen:

> Governance is the exercise of political, economic and administrative authority in the management of a country's affairs at all levels. Governance comprises the complex mechanisms, processes and institutions through which citizens and groups articulate their interests, mediate their differences and exercise their legal rights and obligations. Good governance has many attributes. It is participatory, transparent and accountable. It is effective in making the best use of resources and is equitable. And it promotes the rule of law (UNDP 1997: 1).

Earlier, in 1994, the World Bank had noted (echoed by the UNDP) that governance is 'the manner in which power is exercised in the management of a country's economic and social development' (cited in Olowu 2002: 4).

Since then, almost every component of the UNDP formulation has been pared down and challenged – precisely because the UNDP and World Bank formulations place power and contestation at the centre of governance. This in turn (implicitly, at least) begs the broader question: how should good governance be understood at a global level, where the playing field is self-evidently tilted in favour of the global north, whether via the historical legacy of colonialism, the ongoing reality of coloniality, or the unfair trade pacts and the like which lock the south into poverty? The continuing bellicosity of the global north, with successive wars fought across the Middle East and in Africa, regime change, and the like ensure that states created in Berlin in 1884 have little or no chance of meeting the tenets of governance as defined in the UN/World Bank formulations. And to ensure that governance is a label rather than a tool, it has been separated from public participation, which would bring to the fore issues of power, mobilisation, accountability, and the like in a very direct form. Remarkably, participation now has its own governance rules – and by separating it from governance, and separating citizen action to ensure they can exercise their rights from governance, the governance industry (both academic and practitioner) has successfully transformed a vibrant tool into a worthy idea whose time has come and gone, but which we need to resurrect in more vibrant form.

For all the immediacy of the issue, governance in South Africa – as with other developing countries – needs to be understood in perspective and in context: not to be excused or apologised, but explained and understood. In a context of global political, economic, military, cultural and normative inequality, governance struggles to be an absolute measure. That said, however, the motive force that drives governance – the meeting of power and accountability – is being systematically eviscerated by the governance industry, driven from the global north. The larger the literature base, the dataset size and the number of indicators, the less effective governance has become, and the more extreme politics has become in encouraging rent-seeking, tampering with elections, enhancing the rich at the cost of the poor, and protecting the north at the expense of the global south.

Governance has been neutered and is in danger of being rendered a compliance-driven tick box exercise. It is on life support after consultants, specialists from multiple sectors, academics, individual and multilateral donor agencies, and others have defined, refined, finessed and repeatedly redefined the concept. It has been filled with a multitude of indicators, found in various local, regional and global databases that compete for being 'the best' governance measurement tool. It has generated academic debates about exactly what it does or should mean, and each debate seems to remove the concept further from its real habitat – watching power being exercised and holding it to account, thereby protecting the interests of those without power.

Governance has been variously conjoined to and separated from participation, democracy, delivery, institutions, leadership, states and sectors. It is applied willy-nilly to virtually every type of activity from internet governance to NGO governance to participation governance and beyond.[2] As a result of being pumped so full of content and spread across so many areas, governance has come to mean very little; more charitably, it means very different things to different people and to different institutions, but at substantial definitional cost.

A major stumbling block is the difference in worldview among those working with governance. For some, nation states and their *potential* to operate with equal efficiency is a given – they are objects of study, all of which (in this view) share the same attributes and should be able to operate with similar levels of efficiency. Some may be richer or poorer, more or less efficient, with more or less functional public services and tax collection efficiency, and the like; but at base they have been similarly (formally) constructed, and governance is a lens for dissecting their performance (more precisely, the performance of their governments). For others, the inequality inherent in the global architecture makes this argument untenable; governance in this view should be a lens for understanding those global inequalities, and the way they play out on the domestic stage, because they are what stop nation states in the developing world from being able to realise their potential. Governance should do the same within the countries – it is not simply a global lens – but in each instance (be it national or sub-national), the focus is on power, its use and abuse, and the countervailing force required to hold it to account.

When governance is detached from power and accountability, globally and locally, it loses both purpose and meaning. Yet much of the literature stemming from the global north seems set on delinking governance from accountability. For Francis Fukuyama (2013: 3), for example, talking about governance and account-ability muddies the waters because it locks us into a debate about 'predatory states' and how they may be 'roving' or 'stationary' bandits, in Mancur Olson's formulation (Olson 1993: 568). For Fukuyama (2013: 3), what matters is state capacity – not state behaviour – and governance theorists in his view should be primarily concerned with 'the question of where state capacity comes from in the first place, or how it increases or decreases over time'. Indeed, if Fukuyama asked his question through a lens of political economy, the result may be rather less neutral than expected: state capacity evolves with the nature and behaviour of the state, and if that state is a colonising power, for example, its capacity is bolstered by looting colonies to expand the domestic fiscus, with the reverse being true in the colony. But he does not, and so ends up with a remarkable conclusion: '[…] I am excluding democratic accountability from the definition of governance', observing sniffily that the 'current orthodoxy in the development community is that democracy and good governance are mutually supportive' which he argues is merely theoretical and not 'an empiric-ally demonstrated fact' (Fukuyama 2013: 6).

Seen from the global south, states from the global north[3] (using Olson's termin-ology) are self-evidently operating as both the 'rational, self-interested leader' of a stationary state who offers services at home with limited rent-seeking – but simul-taneously as the 'roving bandit' who maintains instability, regime change and war to prop up (already shaky, recent, and not organically evolved) postcolonial states from which to extract massive surpluses and route these from south to north. State capacity, in the south, is directly linked to global inequality and the continued dom-inance of the north – not as a *result* of poor governance and limited state capacity in the south, but as a *cause* of poor governance. That is where governance offers a useful lens, in highlighting the misuse of power, whether at global or more local scales. It is the logical conclusion of both Fukuyama's argument and those he criticises, though few are willing to venture into the arena of global inequality (including Robert Rotberg [2015], for example, who argues strongly for contextualising governance – but the context is repeatedly local, occasionally regional, and never global). The use and abuse of power is central to governance. It is redolent with democratic potential, which is why for many it seems that governance needs to be kept in check.

The neutering of governance is the natural self-protecting instinct of those with power – whether that be the local librarian or police chief, mayor, a provincial premier, a president, the global north, the Bretton Woods institutions, or capital, and so on. Democratic impulses – particularly when embedded in powerful concepts such as governance – are systematically defanged to ensure that accountability is replaced with measurement; the consequences that should flow from accountability are buried in indicator charts or expert reports; and, ultimately, governance survives as little more than a set of descriptions about what states need to deliver services to citizens more efficiently – a tick box exercise, and a sterile academic debate.

This chapter seeks to set the tone for the rest of this volume by arguing that governance ought to be key to making power accountable – wherever that power is located. It is a means of injecting democratic impulses into planning, decision-making, implementation and delivery by ensuring that accountability is locked into those decision-making processes; and should be key to effective monitoring and to evaluation, which are natural allies (and tools, supposedly with teeth) of governance. All are about better understanding and continually observing the use of power in setting agendas, delivering services, and improving the quality of life of all residents; and identifying abuse of power, rent-seeking, and the like, and triggering remedial action. The role of residents, and the strength of their organisations, is key to governance. In that respect – a rather robust cynicism about the willingness, ability or agility of the state in serving the poor and rich equally – the chapter is certainly closer to Olson than Fukuyama. In insisting on using governance to generate a global perspective, it goes further than Olson, Rotberg, Andrews, or other leading governance authorities seem willing to do.

GOVERNANCE AND CONTEXT

Governance has been rendered anodyne when it should be feared and embraced in roughly equal parts as a measure of the appropriate and responsive exercise of power to provide citizens with what they need, when they need it, where they need it, and at an affordable cost. The issue at stake is not merely efficiency or effectiveness of delivery as defined by a robust state, nor (merely) an analysis of the strength or weakness, power or powerlessness of a particular state; it is about delivery to the satisfaction of citizens, in particular the most needy or vulnerable. One need not assume, as Fukuyama does, that focusing on accountability is to be blind to the role of the state or 'begin with [... the] assumption that states are predatory' (Fukuyama 2013: 3). The simple fact of risk-aversion in the state at all levels is enough incentive to hold them to account, in a democratic nexus where power needs legitimacy to act in a democratic fashion.

When Fukuyama (2013: 1) stated that he was deliberately excluding democratic accountability from the definition of governance, he did so because the power of the state is pre-eminent in his concern with 'the quality of states'. That is a legitimate approach – but begs for context. For many others, as here, the quality of a state is measured in large part by its democratic credentials, which can only be understood in local, regional and global contexts, both historical and contemporary. Global inequality did not emerge by unhappy accident, but was forged by war and conquest. The 'quality of a state' cannot exist outside its (at least recent) history. But the challenge comes when we start asking: what is governance?

Governance has taken centre stage in discourse since the early 1990s, in a quite breathtaking rise. However, its ubiquity has occurred in tandem with governance coming to mean less and less. Precisely by being repeatedly parsed and applied in multiple contexts with different indicators, governance has been given too much content – which is why it now has very little at all. Instead of being a dynamic moment where power is held accountable, it has been watered down to mean little beyond obeying financial rules – 'good governance' – or a state supplying services efficiently to citizens – literally, govern-ance. Power is removed from the picture.

Context, whether local, regional or global, is largely gone. Context has some champions, such as Rotberg, Andrews, and others, but they consistently veer away from uncomfortable aspects of context that talk to global inequalities: Rotberg is happy to explain why Malawi is poorer than Kenya, for example, but not why Malawi, just over 50 years old, formerly Nyasaland colonised by the British, is as poor as it is compared to, say, Austria or the USA. Presumably these authors are not those castigated almost a century ago by W.E.B. DuBois for the 'belief that black folk are sub-human' (DuBois 1920: 39), some kind of racially essentiality augment?

Inequalities, conquest and conflict that prefigured or underlie the conditions in which governance now operates have disappeared from any mainstream[4] discussion about governance. Rather, the search is on for a single, global set of indicators by which 'everyone' can be measured, thereby assuming that 'everyone' is equal and has an equal chance of a perfect score, that 'everyone' can and should be measured in the same way – and that 'everyone' wants to be measured against the same set of indicators (and if not, what do they have to hide?).

In large part, this reflects ongoing ruptures in global political and academic discourse, regardless of topic. One set of mainstream Northern/Western academics and entities generates normative studies, indicators, benchmarks and global scorecards, buttressed by a particular set of values, setting up, in the words of Matt Andrews, a 'one-best-way' model – 'Sweden or Denmark on a good day, perhaps' (Andrews 2008: 379). Another group of scholars, primarily from the global south – in governance as in virtually any other field of social sciences, development, political economy, economics, law, and the like – argues for context, for an understanding and valorising of indigeneity, and thus of multiplicity in place of a normative global standard generated by the wealthy side of the world. It is remarkable that Olson (1993: 568), whose work has been important in the development of governance, could note: 'Since history is written by the winners, the origins of ruling dynasties are, of course, conventionally explained in terms of lofty motives rather than by self-interest', but not relate the observation to the global 'winners' of history, the Western/Northern powers who tore some 12 million Africans from their homes to become slaves in the 'new world', on top of the approximately 17 million who had the same treatment at the hands of Arab slave traders, destined to, inter alia, build Europe.[5] The Euro–US rise to global dominance is based on the economic value added by such state-sponsored violence; by the same token, the ongoing struggle to develop and maintain governance in many African countries fails in part due to the inherited effects of these acts, the psychosocial damage done to people and the social fabric, the violence of conquest and invasion, coupled with the shaky foundations on which modern African nation states are based – namely, the 1884 drawing board, and ongoing destabilisation, invasion, war, support for civil war, regime change, and the like. Governance is currently being primarily narrated by these 'winners'.

Postcolonial and decolonial discourse talk straight past mainstream discourse (and often each other) with neither, it seems, hearing the other. Mainstream Northern/Western practitioners and academics seem to see little value in engagement. The language of global north/south is of course clumsy, and the divide is not simply geographical location or origin. Guy Mhone and Omano Edigheji, for example, define governance simply in terms of how 'the apparatus of the state is constituted, how it executes its mandate and its relationship' to society generally and to specific constituencies, echoing Fukuyama; no broader context is cited, other than globalisation (Mhone and Edigheni 2003: 3, 4). Onkar Prasad Dwivedi claims that it is 'a paradox of history that the empire builders of Europe who started their business in Asia and Africa with naked corruption ended up handing over a relatively clean administration to the leaders of those newly-independent colonies' (Dwivedi 2002: 39), a claim justified by pointing to the 'cesspool of corruption and bad governance' (2002: 40) in contemporary African states, echoing a plethora of commentators who bemoan the state of Africa.

The issue is not about African exceptionalism, nor is it trying to hide or explain away corrupt leaders. The issue, however, is about context in both historical and immediate terms – understanding how Africa came to be as it is, via narratives and analytics that are generated by Africans, using indigenous metrics. In this perspective, the issues at stake for Adebayo Olukoshi are similar to those Fukuyama talks to, but seen through a rather different lens:

> Accountability in any political community occurs at multiple levels. Considering the key role and the enormous powers of the state, it is not surprising that considerable attention is focused on exacting accountability from it. And yet, it is equally important to acknowledge that the African state has undergone quite a major evolution over the years from the 1880s when the current configuration of countries was carved out at the Berlin Conference by competing European powers. From the different types of colonial states to the varieties of postcolonial states that emerged, we are challenged [...] to interrogate the idea of the state, what it means not only with regard to citizen and identity formation but also the mobilisation of development and security. If we consider all of the indicators of what makes for a properly functioning state, how many on the continent would effectively qualify to be described as such? [... This is] with regard to the essentials for a political community with legitimate institutions that serve a public purpose, which are invested with the powers to deliver that public purpose, and that establish a workable reciprocal relationship with domestic social forces (Olukoshi n.d.).

Sabelo Ndlovu-Gatsheni notes that at stake in the 'rather ironic but animated debate' about colonialism, post- and decoloniality is 'a simple reality that coloniality constitutes the foundational problem lurking at the centre of the modern world system' (Ndlovu-Gatsheni 2014: 32). He goes on to quote Ramón Grosfoguel:

> The heterogenous and multiple global structures put in place over a period of 450 years [of colonialism] did not evaporate with the juridical-political decolonisation of the periphery over the past 50 years. We continue to live under the same 'colonial power matrix' (Ndlovu-Gatsheni 2014: 32).

When we begin to appreciate the lingering power of coloniality, and the ongoing value of colonial extraction to northern interests, the 'cesspool of corruption and bad governance' begins to gain a context within which it can be understood – and challenged. It also provides a perspective from which Fukuyama's question about where states get their power has a rather different set of answers than if that question were posed in Europe or North America, for example. Without such context, the issue becomes racial and essentialised – bluntly, it boils down to 'look what happens when you let the natives govern'.

Governance in this highly political context can be used as a tool to question the global inequalities inherited from the past – a past of racism, slavery and colonialism – or can be used (more or less overtly) to prop up normative values and standards emanating from 'the winners' – those who benefited directly and materially from this violent past. Raising these issues most commonly triggers exasperation or frustration, exemplified in the words of former US Secretary of State Hillary Clinton addressing a forum on US diplomacy in Africa in 2010:

> For goodness sakes, this is the 21st century. We've got to get over what happened 50, 100, 200 years ago and let's make money for everybody. That's the best way to try to create some new energy and some new growth in Africa (Quinn 2010).

Governance is a victim of this unitary blindness, and rather unseemly rush to put the very recent past (far) behind us. In much mainstream literature, governance is taken to mean little more than measuring government delivery of services, in an a-contextual, increasingly technicist exercise. Recent African literature is moving in a different direction: talking far more to context, focusing on the local sphere, insisting on the issues of accountability and consequence, and the need for organised local citizen groups to hold power to account (Oloruntoba and Falola 2018). (We return to this shift in focus later.)

A more sophisticated sidestep than 'look how bad African leaders are' or 'get over the past' is needed to deal with the destabilising and often malignant presence of the past in the present. Matt Andrews (2008) goes some way towards acknowledging context, by noting that measuring effectiveness alone is of limited value if those effective states – even if, for example, they are all located in Europe – differ significantly from one another. Andrews stops short of the logical next question: if European states differ to the point where comparison is of limited value, how much more will countries across the world differ, emerging from radically different trajectories of conquest and occupation? And if so, how do we understand, analyse and assess their governance?

Instead, Andrews goes on to note that what are regarded as currently effective governments were themselves formerly developing countries, 'and they would surely have scored poorly on the current indicators' (2008: 380). At this stage, Andrews faces a challenge – to delineate the very different ways in which today's nation states came into being (as Olukoshi did), or avoid the issue; sadly, he chooses the latter path. Today's efficient states, he notes, made it from developing to developed by happenstance, from which today's developing countries could learn a lot, apparently:

> The effectiveness of these past governments is reflected in the progress of their countries over the past century, and the story of how they muddled through from the past to the present may be of most value for developing countries today (Andrews 2008: 380).

This quite remarkable quotation illustrates worldviews gliding past one another. For those living and operating in the developing world, there is no question about the fact that the developed world did not 'muddle through' – they built their 'effectiveness' and wealth and business interests and global economic, military, political, cultural and juridical dominance on the back of conquest, war, slavery and colonialism. If the developing world were to take Andrews literally, their future lies in conquering and colonising the developed world who did it to them previously – lest we forget, this included Latvia, Spain, Portugal, France, England and Scotland and then Great Britain, the Netherlands, the United States, Japan, Denmark, Norway, Sweden, Russia and Malta (and South Africa).[6] Based on the resources and bodies gained by conquering and plundering the north and west, the global south could then 'muddle through' into exemplars of effective delivery.

After the slave trade ended, including the Slavs ('Slav' is the root of 'slave'), an entire black-focused racial narrative was created to justify and explain away slavery, and then later colonisation as a 'civilising mission', rather than continental rape (Mbembe 2015; Kendi 2016). No 'muddling through' here: war, conquest, slavery and colonisation, and an ongoing deep-seated racist narrative that saw and still sees Africa (in particular) as having 'civilisational' problems in the words of then recently elected French president Emmanuel Macron, and unable to manage itself, its people, or its appetites. According to a report in *The Guardian*, Macron noted that '[…] part of the challenge facing the continent was the countries that "still have seven to eight children per woman"' (Anyangwe 2017), repeating the centuries-old racist tropes about promiscuous black women (Kendi 2016). The explanatory narrative – the civilising mission needed to rescue the natives from themselves – remains alive and well.

Andrews criticises others for insisting on a 'one-right-way' model – quite correctly – but then avoids the logical conclusion of his own argument, which is a multiplicity of models, voices, analytical frameworks and conclusions. His argument should oblige him to explain how to attain effective government and good governance if we (now) assume that war, conquest, slavery and colonisation are not options, despite their massive help in filling northern state coffers and allowing states to 'muddle through' on the backs of the colonised or enslaved. Rather, he drops into a-historicism and encourages developing countries – not all, but 'countries that are perhaps one or two steps higher on the effectiveness ladder but more contextually connected – adjacent, culturally and politically similar, for example' – to 'learn a lot' from developed nations (Andrews 2008: 391). Governance here seems to be a social Darwinist construct.

'Learn a lot' means 'learn the right things' – obey normative standards while muddling through a fundamentally unequal world. Stripped to its bones, Andrews' argument is ultimately no different from those he criticises. Northern academics, policy consultants and multilateral institutions insist on their 'one-right-way' models, because they share underlying values and assumptions about the past, the need to 'get over' it, to 'get over' slavery and colonialism, and the ongoing reality of coloniality in the present. In so doing, they turn a blind eye to the global disparities in power and economics built on the basis of slavery and colonialism, compounded by ongoing coloniality – in attitudes, in policy, in armed insurrection and regime change, and the like – which make the attainment of 'good governance' virtually impossible for the developing world, and, ultimately, repeatedly ascribe it to a racist subtext. How on earth did governance become complicit in such a situation?

GOVERNANCE AND MEANING

The chapter began by bemoaning the poor health of governance, which is so replete with content that it is in some danger of bursting, while meaning less and less. Contestation is useful up to a point; but when a concept is so repeatedly stuffed with, and then stripped of, contested interpretations – all by erstwhile supporters of that governance – something is going substantially wrong. Virtually all academic (and many non-academic) texts dealing with governance start by noting the plethora of definitions, the confusing welter of approaches: is governance about outcomes or outputs? Do quality of life or customer satisfaction or expert surveys 'count' as evidence, or are they biased or too flimsy? Is governance concerned with efficiency and effectiveness in delivery, or the nature of the state, or civil society, or all of the above? Is it centrally focused on the exercise of power, or on account-ability? Is it essential to democracy, or a defining aspect of democracy, or nothing to do with it at all?

The literature – after a quick reprise of the etymology of the term governance (which rarely elucidates whether it derives from the Greek origin of 'steer', or four-teenth- to sixteenth-century European writing about the shift of power away from absolute monarchy) – often bemoans the differences in datasets that exist, each with its own take on governance and thus its own measurements of what governance is, and when it is 'good' or 'bad'. Governance literature is often merged with discussions of failed or fragile states, with political science, commentaries on deliberative and participative democracy, and so on. Authors then diverge in multiple ways – into governance as process, measurement, system, as more or less proximate to political projects, taking different forms in different sectoral applications, and so on.

After the etymological tour, much governance literature emphasises the close approximation of 'govern' and 'governance', the latter seen as an extension of the former (for example, Tamayao 2014). Governance in this view is taken to be the performance of its duties by a government, measurable by the delivery of goods and services to citizens. Scholars then fall out with one another over how to measure this version of governance, both broadly (overall categories) and narrowly (specific indicators). The end result, in most cases, is that governance is reduced to a set of indicators – usually of 'good' governance – which are stripped of context, and fail to address power, complexity and competition.

Many cite Weberian bureaucratic modernity as key – a professional public ser-vice is vital to deliver goods and services to citizens – while others argue that meas-urement without a theory of change is of limited value. For Fukuyama (2013: 8), this Weberian 'ideal' is offered as an 'ideal type to which we hope highly corrupt, neo-patrimonial states will eventually conform', indicating in both tone and a-contextuality the normative values that Western notions of 'good governance' contain. Rothstein (2011) prefers emphasising the 'impartiality' of the state, because impartiality can be seen 'by groups with very different conceptions of "the good"'. Multiple governance-measuring databases and projects exist: Rothstein's Quality of Government Institute at Gothenburg; Freedom House's 'Freedom in the World'; the Index of African Governance; the 'Varieties of Democracy' project; and the largest of them all, the World Bank's Worldwide Governance Indicators.

At one level, proliferation is fine – rather many voices than only one. Earlier, we drew a parallel with monitoring and evaluation. In both cases – governance, and monitoring and evaluation (being commonly conjoined though distinct activities) – there is a multi-level focus. At one level, at issue is the delivery of services – are the right services being delivered, efficiently and effectively, to the people who need them, at the right time and cost, and in the right place? If not, what remedial action is needed? Evaluators can be deployed to find answers from the field, or if sufficient data exist they can be analysed to identify the problem and thus inform possible remedial action. In both instances, governance frameworks should identify policy or political blockages, and different types of remedial action can ensue.

At another level, however, both focus (or should focus) on power. Who has the power to make decisions – about the services to be delivered; about the intended beneficiaries; about budgetary allocations; and so on? In evaluation, it is legitimate to ask: who is paying for the evaluation, with what impact on the entire endeavour (similar to history being written by the winners)? Who defines the questions to be asked, and who gets to hear the answers? What are the power dynamics at play, whether in a local context (from micro to national), or across countries or continents? Who carries out the evaluation? In Africa, based on the (often correct) argument that the continent 'lacks capacity', donor agencies, multilateral institutions, and others commonly parachute in their selected consulting teams to design and analyse, while locals may be allowed to gather data. The consultants report back to the commissioning agent, and in many cases the target audience – whether the directly impacted beneficiaries or the host government – either do not receive feedback or have to wait their turn.

While this is happening on the ground, monitoring and evaluation (M&E) – as potentially powerful tools of accountability – have gone through a similar experience to that suffered by governance. M&E is a global industry, also drowning in a sea of consultants, definitions, dashboards, toolkits, indicators, best practice manuals, and the like. The danger is that the act – the monitoring system or the evaluation – becomes an end in itself, rather than operating as a tool for empowering the user/ beneficiary group and holding to account whichever agency (government or others) is delivering services. It is difficult to avoid the conclusion that whatever tools emerge from social or management sciences as mechanisms for accountability and redress are systematically hollowed out and rendered at best compliance-driven, and at worst symbolic.

THE BUSINESS OF GOVERNANCE

Governance has become a business. Business likes stability, can tolerate differences over detail, but flounders in the face of ideology, politics and the clash between power and accountability. I have argued previously (Everatt 2003) that poverty became a business, spawning thousands of consultancies, measurement experts, programme designers, theories of change, ZOPPs (the German 'Goal Oriented Project Planning'), logframes and the rest, with the World Bank (again) the biggest player on the block. The urgency of actually attacking and defeating poverty became enmired and arguably lost in the business of poverty analysis and sanitised debates over the efficacy of subjective or objective indicators, which variables to weight and by how much, and who had the biggest and best index. Governance is in substantial danger of a similar fate, for similar reasons: the underlying causes, of poverty as of poor governance, demand that power, politics and context are all simultaneously foregrounded and understood, and measured and remedied, and not pushed aside by consultants and their neat dashboard indicators. The point is to help states understand where governance is weak, why governance is weak – at micro-, meso- and macro- (sub-national, national and global) levels – and debate what to do about these factors, both endogenous and exogenous.

This sense of urgency is singularly lacking in much governance literature. A growing trend comprises arguments about what should be measured, and how. Fukuyama's removal of democratic accountability from the definition of governance is based on the notion that if accountability is included in the definition of democracy, then it cannot be a separate category. Academically defensible, certainly, but for those living under the yoke of appalling governance, fuelled by global inequality and the instability engendered by war-talk, a permanent US armed presence in Africa, and the renewed European fervour for including military aid in development packages (Merkel 2017), the nit-picking of categorisation is of scant comfort or value.

This parsing approach to what is unavoidably a political matter characterises much of the literature. The notion that governance can be understood without accountability taking centre stage is remarkable for its lack of politics and consequent lack of insight or domestic purchase in the developing world. When Rotberg takes issue with Fukuyama, there is a glimmer of something more useful – 'governance is tangible. It acts. It is not something stylistic or artistic' (Rotberg 2015: 8) – but their tiff boils down to disputation over input versus output measures, and why the Rotberg index is better than others. Many of his insights into the weaknesses of other index measurement tools are useful; but if we take him at his word – that we need 'to judge how well states deliver the key political goods that are their justification, it is important to parse governance, to break out the fundamental responsibilities and delivery expectations of governments into categories of analysis' (Rotberg 2015: 8) – then this surely can only occur in the context of global political economy, which is precisely the source of constraints on developing world states. Sadly, he does not make the link.

Many authors (for example, Fukuyama 2013; Rotberg 2015) understand governance as very close to quality of life studies – preferably without the subjectivity inherent in quality of life, customer satisfaction or expert surveys (al though some disagree with this observation, rather strongly in Rotberg's case). In other words, the evidence of governance is not a democratic state per se, or the satisfaction of citizens with what they receive, but rather the delivery of goods and services citizens, with as little rent-seeking as possible. In this, for Fukuyama, the quality of public administration is key to measuring effective governance – a professional public service on Weberian lines is a key indicator, regardless of the politics that guides and informs that public service. Andrews, sceptical of the notion that all countries should aim at 'Sweden or Denmark on a good day, perhaps […]' (Andrews 2008: 379), argues as we saw that a more appropriate comparison for developing countries would be developed nations when they too were developing; when they had a youth bulge, not an ageing population; when their socio-economic indicators looked more like today's developing nations. Each country would thus be understood on its own terms – a long step beyond all being compared with Denmark or Sweden – but still sidestepping the awkwardness of how the developed world 'muddled through' its developmental phase.

Mark Bevir's 'very short introduction' to governance notes that governance comprises all the processes of governing, whether by a government, a market or a network (and others), and includes family, formal or informal organisations, territory and the laws, norms, power and language of an organised society (Bevir 2013). At the descriptive level, this approach is fine – domestically, less so, since it again avoids any macro-level players or perspective but merely sets the scene, failing to explain how all these different actors interact, struggle, exchange, differ and finally allow decisions to be made, and governing (whether macro, meso or micro) to occur. In this sense, Hufty (2011: 405) takes a step closer, noting that governance relates to 'the processes of interaction and decision-making among the actors involved in a collective problem that lead to the creation, reinforcement, or reproduction of social norms and institutions'.

When authors do venture into global governance, such as Hyden and Court (2002), some note the discourse disconnect – 'academics and practitioners often talk past each other', they note, and pin the difference on those who see governance as steer and those who see it as the rules of public management. However, while they move into international relations and its various schools of thought, they again get caught up in definitional disputation. They lean towards the notion of governance as defining relations between state and society, ask (rhetorically) who sets the rules for judging 'good governance', and criticise definitions used by multilateral institutions for 'watering down its [governance's] political character' (Hyden and Court 2002: 19) and their assumed normative power. In so doing, their analysis is very useful: locally, by reminding us of the ongoing sequence of local interactions where governance is seen in situ; and the extent to which governance speaks to civil society and social capital in ensuring that the state does deliver as informed by organised citizens. But the global question (the intended focus of their input) fades away.

Domestic reciprocity, trust in institutions, transparency, accountability, and others are all cited as important – but power is absent, whether local or global. Remarkably, they conclude (closely echoing Dwivedi earlier) that '[i]t is a paradox of history that the empire builders of Europe who started their business in Asia and Africa with naked corruption ended up handing over a relatively clean administration to the leaders of those newly independent colonies' (Hyden and Court 2002: 39). As with so many authors, the spectacle of African corruption drives away a historical perspective, and the underlying notion of 'Blacks as "humans apart"' (Mbembe 2017: 86) raises its ugly head. Only African authors seem to be aware of the challenges of governance in nation states that were not merely colonised and bankrupted, but which had their boundaries drawn up in Berlin in 1884, creating a set of internal ethnic and other challenges that continue to play out today.

Rotberg, we have seen, takes issue with Fukuyama's approach which focuses purely on the state executing its duties, but gets involved in an argument about whether outputs are dependent or independent variables. Rotberg prefers Andrews' approach because (he argues) governance needs to focus on points of engagement between state and citizen, and thus outcomes are 'the true indicators of governance' (Rotberg 2015: 11). Rotberg uses his preferred approach (and set of indicators) to compare African countries – important, certainly – but fails to lift his gaze beyond the regional to question the global norm-setting, or historical cause and effect relationships. Pierre and Peters (2000: 7) similarly walk the reader through the definitional blurriness around governance, the competing schools of thought, and conclude that 'governance refers to slightly different phenomena in the United States and Western Europe'. But they miss the irony that it seems to mean very much the same when the gaze is directed southwards (whether from the US or Europe): African definitions of governance, or indicators and datasets (such as the Mo Ibrahim Index of African Governance), seem not to exist.

While academics debate the best way forward as they see it, practitioners are happy to weigh in. Daron Acemoglu claims that '[a]cademic research progresses slowly and according to its own dynamics, which often reward ideas that are contrarian even if they have little empirical evidence' (Acemoglu 2008: 2) – no doubt a witty aperçu, but in truth meaning 'stand aside and let the consultants decide on what matters'. A worse fate for governance is scarcely imaginable. That said, he at least (unlike many academics reviewed here) insists that history is not destiny, and that policies are rooted in domestic political economy problems – arguably a far more useful lens through which to study governance than institutional theory and the like. He is aware that setting rules for governance – such as central bank independence in his example – makes little sense in institutionally weak societies, since the local political economy will continue to distort such actions. Sadly, he too refrains from stepping back to ask why Africa is so institutionally weak, and precisely what the political economy challenges are that the continent and its countries face. Rather, he draws a distinction between 'elite rights' (for the north) and the distance developing countries have to travel to meet 'doorstep conditions' (Acemoglu 2008: 15). Context again vanishes.

At the risk of tedious repetition, it is notable that Dani Rodrik, writing in the same monograph as Acemoglu, opens by observing that for governance to have a genuine impact 'you must change "the rules of the game" – the manner in which trade policy is made or fiscal policy is conducted' (Rodrik 2008: 17) – but then posits this as an entirely domestic affair. This may be news to, for example, former colonies of France – Benin, Burkina Faso, Côte d'Ivoire, Mali, Niger, Senegal, Togo, Cameroon, Central African Republic, Chad, Congo-Brazzaville and Gabon – whose national reserves, by (colonial) law, are held in Paris, and have been since 1961. With a complicated formula, France 'allows' these countries to access only 15 per cent of the money in any given year. If they need more than that, they have to borrow the extra money from the French Treasury at commercial rates. These are not incidental quirks of history, or French 'muddling through', but fundamental governance challenges leaving power in the hands of former colonising powers while judging Africa as repeatedly wanting in the area of governance.

GOVERNANCE AND AFRICA

The common theme in most of the magisterial overviews of governance (only a few of which have been reviewed here) is that the issue of power and its misuse are ignored – not at local level, where the literature (as we have seen) is rich with adjectives describing the cesspools of African corruption; but at regional and global levels. If governance is to be decolonised, the issue of race needs to be tackled head - on. Achille Mbembe has recently described the challenge with regard to race:

> [...] the process of racialisation to mark population groups, to fix as precisely as possible the limits within which they can circulate, and to determine as exactly as possible which sites they can occupy [...] The goal is to sort population groups, to mark them simultaneously as 'species', 'classes', and 'races' through a generalised calculation of risk, chance, and probability [...] Race, from this perspective, functions as a security device based on what we can call the principle of biological rootedness of the species. The latter is at once an ideology and a technology of governance (Mbembe 2017: 35).

Mbembe's quotation hints at the challenge facing definitions of governance that has been drawn out already: the absence of power, or of struggle. The broad, generalised descriptions are not without value – governance is after all about the act of governing (just as performance is about performing) – and it is important to remember the complexity inherent in law, regulation, rule, by-law, authority, judgement, decision-making, and the like. But governance is also the process through which these are enacted.

The emphasis is on action, not stasis or a-contextual assessment; on vibrancy and challenge, not passively listing and following a prescribed set of rules; on a series of moments of democratic tension that ensure transparency and accountability sufficient to hold those with power to account, not merely listing outputs and drawing conclusions about the efficiency of the public service. Governance is the series of spaces and actions through which power is held accountable. In Mbembe's view, the struggle for Africans to hold global power to account is one that has repeatedly been lost.

Seen from a continental perspective, a growing chorus of African scholars reject the normative judgements of the global north, based as they are on the notion that 'decolonisation [w]as the proudest moment in African history' (Ndlovu-Gatsheni 2014: 36), after which it has all been downhill. Ending colonial rule did not equate with freedom or democracy, and as the rhetoric of good governance has proliferated, so too have African states who hold regular elections, have formally encoded separation of powers including an independent judiciary, and enjoy all the other attributes a modern state should have – but which have been hollowed out and are meaningless. As Dele Olowu has noted:

> Most African states were autocracies in 1975, and one should wonder why this is the case for states that have just emerged from the repression of colonial rule. One explanation is that African countries have been disarticulated since colonial times from their indigenous institutions of problem solving. Instead of Africa's postindependence governments redressing these anomalies, they

have further aggravated them by reproducing local despotism at the national level [...] (Olowu 2002: 55).

African scholars and practitioners have been crowded out of the debate about governance, and how it might be configured in Africa. This is slowly being addressed, but there is precious little space left for African voices to reimagine the global rules of the game, which ensure that neocolonial forces remain the writers of those rules. It is also clear that democracy is not a template, but the governance literature has created a tick box list which requires compliance rather than fulfilment.

CONCLUSION

If a state can tick the boxes of elections, the rule of law, freedom of speech, and so on – however unrealised in practice – they can make an argument for preferential trade deals, enhanced aid packages, and the like. The cynicism of northern governments conniving in this sham is a norm in itself. If a state showed signs of trying to strike out on a new path in its immediate postcolonial era, assassination or well-funded military coups were always a useful response, as Sankara, Lumumba, Nkrumah, and many others discovered. Governance has to become a two-way meeting of equals to have any traction in the global south.

When pliable leaders in Western-created states are installed, they behave accordingly. Their countries may have been 'business friendly' towards the West – but, as Olukoshi asks, what kind of accountability is expected when postcolonial leaders (and post-regime change leaders) 'function more like delegated latter-day colonial governors-general [...] with the sole duty of keeping their restive people "quiet" for the world to enjoy some semblance of order' (Olukoshi n.d.)? Governance as argued here is a mechanism for engendering accountability: for action, for empowerment, and for change. It is frustration with the failure to effect change that fed the Arab Spring, the #MustFall movements and many more, precisely because the lack of governance may have suited global vested economic interests, but were self-evidently antagonistic to the needs of the local population.

NOTES

[1] See various pages at http://www.worldbank.org.
[2] A Google search generates 175 000 000 hits for 'governance' in 0.60 seconds, and lists at least: Governance as process; Public governance; Private governance; Global governance;

Governance Analytical Framework; Nonprofit governance; Corporate governance; Project governance; Environmental governance; Land governance; Internet governance; Information technology governance; Regulatory governance; Participatory governance; Contract governance; Multilevel governance; Metagovernance; Collaborative governance; Security sector governance; Fair governance; Good governance.

3 This is awkward terminology for which I apologise, but the 'global north' and 'global south' are common enough placemarkers for an argument about global inequalities, and coloniality. The phrasing is used with an awareness of its clumsiness.

4 Again, an apology for clumsy language, but there is clearly a 'mainstream' academic discourse emanating from the global north (North America and Europe, usually with Australia and New Zealand thrown in), while southern-generated theory and discourse is generally much harder to find in journals, in curricula, and so on (with apologies to Raewyn Connell).

5 Numbers of course vary, with estimates ranging between 10 and 13 million. See, for example, https://www.gilderlehrman.org/history-by-era/slavery-and-anti-slavery/resources /facts-about-slave-trade-and-slavery (accessed 7 November 2017); http://originalpeople. org/the-arab-muslim-slave-trade-of-africans-the-untold-story/ (accessed 7 November 2017); http://newafricanmagazine.com/slavery-atlantic-trade-and-arab-slavery/ (accessed 3 June 2017).

6 Amongst a plethora of possible sources, see, for example, http://exhibitions.nypl.org/ africanaage/essay-colonization-of-africa.html (accessed 10 July 2017).

REFERENCES

Acemoglu, D. 2008. Interactions between Governance and Growth: What World Bank Economists Need to Know. In: North, D., Acemoglu, D., Fukuyama, F. & Rodrik, D. (eds) *Governance, Growth, and Development Decision-making*. Working Paper. Washington, DC: World Bank.

Andrews, M. 2008. The Good Governance Agenda: Beyond indicators without theory.*Oxford Development Studies* 36(4): 379–407.

Anyangwe, E. 2017. Brand new Macron, same old colonialism. *The Guardian* Opinion, 11 July. https://www.theguardian.com/commentisfree/2017/jul/11/slur-africans-macron -radical-pretence-over (accessed 13 September 2017).

Bevir, M. 2013.*Governance: A Very Short Introduction*. Oxford: Oxford University Press.

Chabal, P. 2014. Foreword. In: Obadare, E. & Willems, W. (eds) *Civic Agency in Africa: Arts of Resistance in the 21st Century*. Woodbridge, UK: James Currey.

Constitutional Court, South Africa. 2016. Judgment in *Economic Freedom Fighters v Speaker of the National Assembly and Others; Democratic Alliance v Speaker of the National Assembly and Others* (ZACC 11) (accessed 31 March 2016).

Constitution of the Republic of South Africa, 1996 (No. 108 of 1996).

DuBois, W.E.B. 1920. *Darkwater: Voices from within the veil*. New York: Harcourt, Brace & World.

Dwivedi, O.P. 2002. On Common Good and Good Governance: An Alternative Approach. In: Olowu, D. & Sako, S. (eds) *Better Governance and Public Policy: Capacity Building for Democratic Renewal in Africa*. Bloomfield, CT: Kumarian Press.

Everatt, D. 2003. The politics of poverty. In: Everatt, D. & Maphai, V. (eds) *The (Real) State of the Nation: South Africa after 1990*. Johannesburg: Interfund.

Everatt, D., Marais, H. & Dube, N. 2010. Participation – for what purpose? Analysing public participation in governance in Gauteng. *Politikon* 37(2–3): 223–249.

Fukuyama, F. 2013. *What is Governance?* Working Paper No. 314. Washington, DC: Center for Global Development.

Hufty, M. 2011. Investigating Policy Processes: The Governance Analytical Framework (GAF). In: Wiesmann, U. & Hurni, H. (eds, with an international group of co-editors) *Research for Sustainable Development: Foundations, Experiences, and Perspectives:* 403–424. Bern, Switzerland: Geographica Bernensia.

Hyden, G. & Court, J. 2002. Comparing Governance Across Countries and Over Time: Conceptual Challenges. In: Olowu, D. & Sako, S. (eds) *Better Governance and Public Policy: Capacity Building for Democratic Renewal in Africa.* Bloomfield, CT: Kumarian Press.

Kendi, I.X. 2016. *Stamped from the Beginning: The Definitive History of Racist Ideas in America.* London: Penguin Random House.

Mbembe, A. 2015. *On the Postcolony.* Johannesburg: Wits University Press.

Mbembe, A. 2017. *Critique of Black Reason.* Johannesburg: Wits University Press.

Merkel, A. 2017. Speech at meeting with African leaders ahead of G20 summit, Berlin. http://www.dw.com/en/merkel-calls-for-greater-investment-in-africa-ahead-of-g20-summit/a-39220029 (accessed 12 June 2017).

Mhone, G. & Edigheni, O. 2003. Globalisation and the Challenges of Governance in the New South Africa: Introduction. In: Mhone, G. & Edigheni, O. (eds) *Governance in the New South Africa: The Challenges of Globalisation.* Cape Town: University of Cape Town Press.

National Planning Commission. 2011. National Development Plan 2030. Pretoria: The Presidency, Republic of South Africa.

Ndlovu-Gatsheni, S.J. 2014. Global Technologies of Domination: From colonial encounters to the Arab Spring. In: Obadare, E. & Willems, W. (eds) *Civic Agency in Africa: Arts of Resistance in the 21st Century.* Woodbridge, UK: James Currey.

Oloruntoba, S.O. & Falola, T. (eds) 2018. *The Palgrave Handbook of African Politics, Governance and Development.* London: Palgrave.

Olowu, D. 2002. Governance, Institutional Reforms, and Policy Processes in Africa: Research and Capacity Building Implications. In: Olowu D. & Sako S. (eds) *Better Governance and Public Policy: Capacity building for democratic renewal in Africa.* Bloomfield, CT: Kumarian Press.

Olowu, D. & Sako, S. (eds) 2002. *Better Governance and Public Policy: Capacity building for democratic renewal in Africa.* Bloomfield, CT: Kumarian Press.

Olson, M. 1993. Dictatorship, Democracy, and Development. *American Political Science Review* 87(3): 567–576.

Olukoshi, A. n.d. On theorising African political economies and global conceptual prejudices. Expert meeting on accountable governance. Mimeo. http://www.gsdpp.uct.ac.za/Olukoshi (accessed 3 June 2017).

Pierre, J. & Peters, B.G. (eds) 2000. *Governance, Politics and the State.* London: Macmillan Press.

Quinn, A. 2010. Clinton: Africa must launch tough economic reforms. *Reuters,* 14 June. http://www.reuters.com/article/us-africa-usa/clinton-africa-must-launch-tough-economic-reforms-idUSTRE65D61920100614 (accessed 6 June 2017).

Rodrik, D. 2008. Thinking about Governance. In: North, D., Acemoglu, D., Fukuyama, F. & Rodrik, D. (eds) *Governance, Growth, and Development Decision-making.* Working Paper. Washington, DC: World Bank.

Rotberg, R.I. (ed.) 2015. *On Governance: What it is, what it measures, and its policy uses.* Waterloo, Ontario: Centre for International Governance Innovation.

Rothstein, B. 2011. *The Quality of Government: Corruption, Social Trust, and Inequality in International Perspective.* Chicago: University of Chicago Press.

Tamayao, M.J.M. 2014. What is governance? *Law, Politics, and Philosophy,* 21 August. https://tamayaosbc.wordpress.com/2014/08/21/what-is-governance/ (accessed 25 September 2017).

United Nations Development Programme (UNDP). 1997. *Governance for Sustainable Development: a UNDP policy document.* http://www.pogar.org/publications/other/undp/governance/undppolicydoc97-e.pdf (accessed 20 November 2017).

2

African Shared Values in Governance for Integration: Progress and prospects

Salim Latib

INTRODUCTION

By the twenty-first century, African countries have, by and large, established modalities that facilitate political dialogue, civic participation, and a level of democratic inclusivity in governance. This stands in contrast to the period between the 1960s and the 1980s, where over 30 of the 54 African countries were under military rule or subject to protracted internal conflicts at some stage. Military coups d'état are seldom heard of and only a few geographical territories still experience violent conflicts (Matlosa 2014). In most countries, regular multiparty elections have emerged as a shared norm (African Union Commission 2010: 2). There is a wider commitment on the continent to the rule of law, and public services are being delivered to citizens. This journey of democratic governance progress has not been easy or without challenge. There is uncertainty about whether the advances made are sustainable and if the current modalities of democratic governance will suffice for the future (Matlosa 2014: 25). The treatment of elections as a zero-sum game, the growth in popular uprisings against democratically elected governments and a propensity to amend constitutions to allow for political leadership continuity are indicative of the fragility of governance institutions.

Since the release of the 1989 World Bank Report *Sub-Saharan Africa: From Crisis to Sustainable Growth,* which contended that underlying Africa's slow development is a 'crisis of governance' (International Bank for Reconstruction and Development 1989: 60), a number of multilateral institutions, bilateral donors and civil society initiatives emerged to support and encourage the democratic governance momentum. Interventions from these organisations varied in orientation and approach. They are broadly inclusive of initiatives directed at improved governance by way of support to political level structures, towards those that focus on the more technical aspects of enhancing implementation capacity (Carothers and De Gramont 2013). The differences are driven by a combination of the mandate of the organisation and the manner in which governance is defined. An understanding of the broad governance definition and approach differences is essential for an appreciative engagement with the African-specific governance thrust. The overall consequence of continental momentum has been the adoption, by the African Union (AU), of a range of governance-centred legal instruments and the establishment of institutions to support compliance efforts.

AFRICAN GOVERNANCE

Over the last two decades, governance has been a catchword for policymakers and academics in both the global north and south. The varied contributions have often led to different and contradictory definitions of the 'governance' construct (Kjær 2014). It is not possible to refer to a single coherent African perspective of what governance is, or is constitutive of, from within the AU and its institutions. It may also not be intellectually prudent or practical to have an African definition, even as the construct is used without a firm definition in a range of AU documents, including the African Charter on Democracy, Elections and Governance. The meaning intended is often contingent on the context in which the construct is used. In its earlier construction, 'governance' was directed at explaining the practice of social steering (Peters and Pierre 1998: 225). It has since evolved within public sector deliberations, to refer to the exercise of building and managing state institutions for the delivery of public value. The trigger for a technical state-centred perspective of governance was the World Bank publication *Sub-Saharan Africa: From Crisis to Sustainable Growth.* In line with the non-political approach of the Bank, the report focused on issues of corruption, implementation inefficiencies and the lack of accountability. Its prescriptions emphasised institutional reforms, inclusive of better financial management, privatisation and economic deregulation (International Bank for Reconstruction and Development 1989).

The state-centric economic approach of the World Bank has been criticised by many within African civil society and academia. The overarching perspective is that the good governance programme as it emerged from the World Bank was, in essence, an attempt to transfer Western liberal economic approaches to African countries with little regard to context and political reality (Kjær 2014). The criticism of the World Bank institutional approach to governance gave rise to perspectives on governance that incorporated issues of politics and power, as in the definition by Gören Hyden in 1999: 'Governance is the stewardship of formal and informal political rules of the game. Governance refers to those measures that involve setting the rules for the exercise of power and the settling of conflicts over such rules' (quoted in Kjær 2014: 24). Such broader definitions invariably bring into focus issues of elections, participation and human rights, as has been at the centre of civil society concerns in Africa. For many, the term 'governance' also implied recognising that the delivery of public services goes beyond institutions of state (Mkandawire 2007: 681), and is inclusive of the work that unfolds within a wider set of institutions that are broadly established to serve a public purpose, including voluntary and not-for-profit institutions.

To assess the adequacy of AU-level interventions and the spread of governance instruments, a broad conceptual net of the constitutive elements of 'governance', in the light of the varied definitions, is still needed. The inspiration for a governance approach that would be relevant for evaluative purposes comes from the analytical model that Francis Fukuyama uses in *The Origins of Political Order* (2011). According to Fukuyama (2011), societies that achieve a higher level of success than other societies do so on the basis of the evolved maturity of three institutions: namely, *the state*, *the rule of law*, and *accountability*. In other words, societies that get it right have succeeded in having a state sector that is fit for purpose, accountability that is inclusive, and a legal system that is predicated on the rule of law. Decay and the necessity for change sets in when institutions are not fit for expected purpose, or do not meet new realities and transformative pressures (Fukuyama 2011: 7). It is not improbable to conceive of interventions that lead to better institutions and higher levels of prosperity, even though change is complex and subject to a range of broader contingencies. Prosperous societies are the ones that are able to combine all three sets of institutions in a stable balance, the achievement of which represents the miracle of modern society (Fukuyama 2011: 16). To understand the African governance space, and specifically the related policy and institutional interventions on the part of the AU, we would then need to see what has unfolded in each of these areas within the overall system.

EVOLUTION OF GOVERNANCE IN AFRICA

During the 1980s, the World Bank orientation to governance, with its preoccupation with state institutions and capacity, served as the dominant state-level policy approach across the continent. Whether voluntarily agreed to or as a self-imposed orientation, the underlying logic was that market-friendly strategies and reforms would lead to economic growth. The overall orientation was that in order to receive further bank loans or development aid, these countries would have to comply with specific governance requirements. In the instance of the World Bank, conditionalities mainly focused on institutional and regulatory changes that purportedly would make a country more market-friendly. While many bilateral donors followed suit and introduced similar conditionalities, some, such as the Danish, Swedish and Americans, emphasised issues of democratic governance reforms and related efforts (Carothers and De Gramont 2013: 92). During the 1990s, governance support grew massively as an area of focus, and a range of UN agencies began to introduce programmes to support African countries with governance reforms. The challenge with these was that they often had to be carefully positioned as technical support interventions since states were frequently still very wary of programmes and support activities that entered the realm of politics. In addition to conditionalities, many bilateral national donors incorporated political-level governance support initiatives that focused on providing resources to democratic governance-related civil society institutions, political parties and legislative structures (Carothers and De Gramont 2013: 136–139). Such support has always been a matter of some sensitivity in African countries.

African scholars were generally critical of the World Bank's approach and its influence on the policies of governments across the region. Claude Ake (1991), amongst others, articulated the notion that officials in the finance institutions hold the view that political issues can simply be treated as engineering problems. By the early 1990s, the efforts of African civil society served to assign a more political orientation to governance issues on the agenda on the African continent. Many development agencies also began to change their engagement strategies to explicitly incorporate political-level support initiatives or related conditions in their efforts. The changed orientation in the 1990s coincided with the global spread of liberal democratic practices. Authoritarian collapses accelerated dramatically during this period, and the developing world experienced the most intensive levels of democratisation since decolonisation (Carothers and De Gramont 2013). The momentum also spurred a new wave of democracy champions within African multilateral structures. By the launch of the AU in 2002, most African states had introduced constitutional guarantees with provisions for periodic elections, as well as mechanisms for the transfer of power and the renewal of political leadership. Shared values in governance were introduced to the provisions of the AU Constitutive Act, in that it contains a direct reference to upholding human rights and promoting 'good' governance (African Union Commission 2010). The Act builds on previous declarations and treaties, such as the 1991 Abuja Treaty, the Lagos Plan of Action, and the Conference on Security, Stability, Development and Cooperation in Africa (CSSDCA) (Abass and Baderin 2002: 7).

The CSSDCA Solemn Declaration, adopted in 2002, detailed a range of core governance values, together with the commitments to give effect to these. In addition to requirements on the need for civil society participation, there are provisions relating to peace, security, democratic governance, human rights and anti-corruption (Adisa 2002). In addition to the CSSDCA-related momentum on governance within the African continent, Member States of the AU also launched the New Partnership for Africa's Development (NEPAD). The founding document of NEPAD emphasised issues of governance, incorporating elections, human rights, anti-corruption and state capacity. The overall significance of the NEPAD for governance efforts was the founding of the African Peer Review Mechanism (APRM) as an African-specific approach to governance improvements through peer-level interactions between African Heads of State and Government (Gruzd 2014: 10).

By the January 2011 AU Summit on Shared Values, governance standards were disseminated in a range of AU instruments and declarations. Legal frameworks, such as those covering humanitarian issues, youth, gender and culture, also incorporated elements on governance. As a result of the growing momentum, including amongst sub-regional organisations in Africa, the Declaration of the 2011 AU Summit placed attention on the need for a more coordinated approach to governance for more profound impact through the establishment of an 'African Governance Platform' (African Union 2011). This platform, with participation from all AU institutions and regional economic communities (RECs) with a governance mandate, was officially launched in 2012, and has since established a series of structures to facilitate a more coordinative approach to governance (Wachira 2014). To understand the journey taken, it is crucial to engage with the African instruments and institutions that have emerged within the governance space.

AFRICAN UNION GOVERNANCE INSTRUMENTS AND INSTITUTIONS

The AU has over 40 formal instruments, and a range of declarations and decisions that incorporate governance considerations. Almost all instruments make general reference to the shared values of democracy, accountability, transparency and participation (African Union Commission 2010). However, only a selection of these relates to the core governance considerations of accountability to society, the adherence to the rule of law and the modalities for the organisation of the state. These instruments incorporate, in a very direct manner, the principles and provisions related to governance that Member States are expected to adhere to as part of their commitment to African integration and shared standards of conduct and practice. The adopted instruments are listed in Table 2.1, together with a brief explanation of their overall orientation. To facilitate further analysis, the instruments are categorised according to the three identified governance areas: the rule of law, accountability and the state. The provisions in many of the instruments would often cover more than one of the governance areas. The separation is nevertheless useful as it allows for a discussion on the adequacy of instruments in shaping national-level governance practices.

Taken together, the adopted instruments and their provisions cover the broad spectrum of consideration that would feature in more encompassing perspectives on governance. The challenge with these new 'norms' for the continent is the level of implementation and the optimality of AU monitoring practices that seek to ensure active compliance on the part of Member States. There are three stages before a Charter or Convention enters into force and hence becomes legally binding on countries that have ratified: adoption by Summit, including the registering of any reservations, signature by a Member State intending to ratify, followed by ratification and the depositing of the instrument. Each instrument has to be ratified by a minimum number (usually 15) of Member States before it enters into force. When an instrument enters into force, it is legally binding only on countries that have ratified it (African Union Commission 2009). The Charter on Values and Principles of Public Service and Administration and the Charter on Values and Principles of Decentralisation, Local Governance and Local Development are not yet in force. These core governance instruments, together with the date of adoption by Summit and the number of Member States that have formally ratified them, are captured in Table 2.2.

Table 2.1: African Union (AU) governance instruments

Governance area	Governance instrument	Orientation
Rule of Law	Charter on Human and Peoples' Rights	The Charter is directed at promoting and protecting human rights and fundamental freedoms on the African continent. It incorporates the right to participate in government and related protections from arbitrary state action.
	Charter on the Rights and Welfare of the Child	This Charter sets out rights and defines universal principles and norms for the status of children in 48 articles. It covers the whole spectrum of civil, political, economic, social and cultural rights. It further sets out the obligations of state parties to protect children.
Accountability	Charter on Democracy, Elections and Governance	This Charter is central to governance as it sets down requirements related to elections, participation and accountability to society. It incorporates issues of constitutionalism, the separation of powers, and adherence to the rule of law.
	African Peer Review Mechanism (APRM) – Questionnaire	The APRM has been described as being more of a process than an instrument. Its questionnaire nevertheless embodies instrumental elements in so much as it poses a range of normative questions on the optimality of governance and accountability in countries.
State Capacity	Convention on Preventing and Combating Corruption	The Convention outlines the obligations of African states in the areas of corruption prevention, criminalisation, international cooperation and asset recovery. It covers a range of offences, including bribery, diversion of property by public officials, trading in influence, illicit enrichment and money laundering.
	Charter on Values and Principles of Public Service and Administration	The aim of this Charter is the modernisation of service delivery by public institutions within Member States. It incorporates provisions relating to the development of state capacity and the protection of the right of public servants and citizens in the delivery process.
	Charter on Values and Principles of Decentralisation, Local Governance and Local Development	This Charter is primarily focused on promoting decentralisation, local governance and local development in Africa. It incorporates provisions directed at protecting local government institutions as vehicles for local democracy and delivery.

Source: Author

Table 2.2:   Adoption and ratification of African Union (AU) governance instruments

Governance instrument	Date of adoption	Ratifications
Charter on Human and Peoples' Rights	June 1981	54
Charter on the Rights and Welfare of the Child	July 1990	48
African Peer Review Mechanism	June 2002	36
Convention on Preventing and Combating Corruption	July 2003	37
Charter on Democracy, Elections and Governance	January 2007	30
Charter on Values and Principles of Public Service and Administration	January 2011	16
Charter on Values and Principles of Decentralisation, Local Governance and Local Development	June 2014	3

Source: Author; adapted from information on the AU website (www.au.int)

Each instrument contains provisions relating to the reporting period for Member States who have ratified (State Parties) and the overall channel for further 'action' by relevant policy structures. Most instruments require that Member States provide comprehensive reports every two years from the date of ratification. In some instances, such as in the Convention on Preventing and Combating Corruption, it is anticipated that state parties would report at least once a year. The assumption behind reporting is that this should provide a basis for oversight and for 'encouraging' compliance on the part of AU Member States. Each instrument provides that the relevant policy structures (Executive Council and the Assembly of Heads of State and Government) may initiate follow-up action on reports. The types of follow-up actions anticipated are not specified in the instruments and are generally presumed to be some form of sanction in the case of non-compliance. In support of its work, the AU has established a number of elected oversight structures, together with related supportive institutional entities in the governance fold. These are as follows:

1. African Union Commission (Commissioner of Political Affairs);
2. Commission on Human and Peoples' Rights;
3. Advisory Board on Corruption; and
4. African Peer Review Mechanism Panel.

Each of the adopted instruments embodies guidance on the institutions responsible for implementation and the roles and responsibilities of particular Organs of the Union. In most cases, final authority rests with the Assembly of Heads of State and Government. In the core governance instruments, the implementation responsibilities are diffused between specially elected bodies or individuals, and related support structures. In addition to the listed elected structures, the AU has established the African Court on Human and Peoples' Rights and the Pan-African Parliament (PAP). The current focus of the Court is on all cases and disputes submitted to it concerning the interpretation and application of the African Charter on Human and Peoples' Rights and any other relevant human rights instrument ratified by the states concerned (Udombana 2000). It is anticipated that over time, the Court would engage with cases brought forward on the basis of other ratified governance instruments. PAP currently only has consultative and advisory powers within the AU and is consequently primarily focused on securing the full participation of Africans in the development and economic integration of the continent. It is anticipated that after the ratification of a new PAP-related protocol by Member States, it would have legislative powers and may become the principal custodian of governance compliance oversight (Dinokopila 2013).

AFRICAN UNION GOVERNANCE IMPLEMENTATION CHALLENGES

The shift towards African-owned approaches in the early part of this century was, in part, a response to the challenges that confronted externally imposed governance modalities. Of particular importance in the African response was the establishment of the New Partnership for Africa's Development (NEPAD) after the democratic transition in South Africa. In the founding documents and utterances on NEPAD, the championing African Heads of State and Governments placed particular stress on African ownership and the imperatives of African leadership over internal governance issues and related crises (Achieng 2014: 54). The adoption in the first decade of the twenty-first century of the various governance-related instruments and the establishment of related institutions was hence testimony to the African commitment to governance development, and ownership over compliance oversight. The move from commitment to action has, however, taken time and the implementation of adopted instruments has been slow. Actual ratification of governance instruments can be a complicated process and is often reliant on actions on the part of officials within ministries, and related processes within each system of government. The slow pace of instrument ratification has spurred a broader momentum within the AU and other stakeholders on the popularisation of instruments. Without pressure from civil society and active follow-up work on the part of the AU implementation institutions, Member States continue with the ongoing business of government and are often unaware of non-ratification.

When an instrument is in force, Member States are reliant on communication from relevant AU implementation institutions to initiate internal reporting processes. The responsible AU institution would typically engage in a further round of consultations on the reporting structure, the process to be followed, and the manner in which reports are engaged with. While the APRM provides for country reviews and outlines the process to be followed, other instruments are predicated on an official-level clarification follow-up, or a hearing based on country-generated reports. There is presently no standard approach to monitoring compliance within the AU system. The tradition is that the responsible AU institution will design a framework for reporting, which often includes a series of questions to be responded to, together with guidelines on the structure and length of the report (Matlosa 2008). The gap between reporting expectations and actual capacity to implement is wide. Given current resourcing levels, including support from donors, it is unlikely that the necessary capacities for full monitoring of compliance of separately compiled reports will be available in the immediate future.

Some of the instruments provide that the Assembly will take appropriate measures aimed at addressing the governance issues raised in reports. Even if the AU succeeds in developing punitive actions for non-compliance, it is very hard to imagine that such measures would feature in recommendations. At most, Summit is likely to note measures to be taken by Member States in respect of identified weaknesses. The instruments would thus only really serve to affirm more formalised peer review-type compliance processes. In this case, one would have to look towards the APRM for inspiration and lessons learnt. It would also mean appreciating that in its current form, the peer review practice is fraught with challenges, as Heads of State and Government have insufficient time to engage fully on reports and related Member State responses.

As governance standards are established on the basis that adherence would secure internal harmony and development, it would be prudent to look at the use of governance standards for accountability during periods of actual or emergent crisis. This process has been slow for the AU. In the main, the dominant approach is one of mediation and engagement in times of conflict rather than one of securing compliance with established governance standards (Apuuli 2012). While mediation or peace negotiations are centred on softer dialogue on weaknesses in upholding African and global standards, other instruments are predicated on more forceful engagements on terrains where countries have not complied with adopted governance standards. Despite some positive progress on governance, many countries continue to confront challenges with respect to internal governance issues. These include problems related to the capacity and resources available for better governance, as well as challenges relating to the willingness of dominant elites to comply with the norms and values embodied in various regional and national instruments. In particular, difficulties have arisen in situations where there have been constitutional amendments to extend presidential term limits. During 2015, for example, changes to extend presidential term limits created challenges in Rwanda, Burundi and the Democratic Republic of Congo.

A more significant challenge for many AU Member States is the increasing levels of inequity and growing levels of youth activism. Many people and organisations are beginning to question the value of governance interventions and progress in light of the widening gap between rich and poor. Political inclusivity and participation have, for many, not resulted in economic inclusivity. While many economies on the continent are reportedly growing, the benefits are not distributed widely or equally. This concern with equity is beginning to inspire many to focus attention on economic governance issues. Included in this is a focus on the distribution of wealth that emanates from the extraction of natural resources (Bond 2009).

GOVERNANCE PROSPECTS

By the January 2011 Summit of Heads of State and Government on Shared Values, there was recognition that although there has been substantive progress across the continent, there are still many challenges on the route to shared values in governance for effective integration. Significant success has been registered in governance peer review exercises through the APRM. Over 30 countries signed the required Memorandum of Understanding as a commitment to a review, and over 15 have already undergone review (Gruzd 2014). There is now zero tolerance of unconstitutional changes in government, and the AU Peace and Security Council has demonstrated a capacity and willingness to intervene during governance-related crises. The AU has adopted a number of policy instruments on governance and a range of institutions have been established to exercise oversight. The instruments generally cover all of the more significant areas in governance, and collectively represent a comprehensive governance approach by the AU. Established institutions are beginning to monitor progress and are shaping programmes to support Member State efforts.

Even with the progress registered thus far there is an acceptance that there are governance challenges that have to be engaged with on the continent from within the overall AU system. Of particular concern to the 2011 January Summit of Heads of State and Government was the slow pace of implementation and the capacity to implement by Member States (African Union Commission 2010). In addition, there is growing uneasiness with the fact that there are many instruments and institutions in governance with minimal coordination and a lack of resources. In response to this, the AU has established the African Governance Platform (AGP) as part of the overall African Governance Architecture (AGA). The platform is meant to be a structure that would facilitate information sharing amongst all the organs and institutions involved in governance issues, including those within regional economic communities. It is anticipated further that the structure would enhance the impact through more coordinated oversight over existing instruments (Wachira 2014).

The continuing difficulties associated with implementing mandates had, by 2017, resulted in broader delivery concerns and conclusions of a 'chronic failure' within the AU institutional system. This reality and the related imperative for change are articulated in the Report on the Proposed Recommendations for the Institutional Reform of the African Union, presented to the January 2017 AU Summit of Heads of State and Government by the incoming chairperson of the AU, Paul Kagame. The report asserts that 'we have a dysfunctional organisation in which member states see limited value, global partners find little credibility, and our citizens have no trust' (Kagame 2017: 20). A key recommendation of the report is that APRM could be strengthened to track implementation and oversee monitoring and evaluation in crucial governance areas of the continent. How this will unfold to secure higher levels of active compliance with shared values in governance amongst AU Member States is yet to be defined or be engaged with in detail.

Coupled with the AU-level implementation challenges, emerging and ongoing debates on presidential term limits in some countries, and the adequacy of electoral processes for democratic consolidation, suggest that there might be a push towards rethinking adopted norms and standards within the AU. However, there are unlikely to be reversals at the level of the AU as it takes a very long time to change an adopted instrument, and it is very likely that many will be reluctant to address such changes. The same cannot be said of individual Member States. Arguments for changed approaches and norms are, in part, driven by notions that African states need to be developmental and emulate those in Asia (De Waal 2013: 153). Central to this is the need for a high level of political continuity with respect to developmental policies and leadership. Governance changes and lapses in practice may also be driven by concerns that existing arrangements are deepening inequality and do not allow for equitable and sustainable development. We may well witness some measure of regression at the level of some Member States. On the other hand, others might experiment with different modalities of inclusion, including the establishment of wider compacts with civil society, decentralisation through federal structures and a greater focus on local governance.

CONCLUSION

The trajectory of governance in Africa has been positive over the last two decades. However, this path is by no means certain. While liberal forms of democracy have taken root, related electoral systems struggle to find legitimacy in a context of deepening inequality and growth that is not beneficial to all. These emerging realities, and the growing gap between the promise of better governance and actual performance, call for research on governance modalities that would facilitate economic inclusivity. An exploration of these is unlikely to change the content of existing governance instruments as they are broad in focus and generally contain the most fundamental governance principles.

Even though the regional integration agenda establishes a momentum for shared values and therefore compliance with particular governance standards, African countries will continue to find ways of preserving their autonomy over governance issues. Such autonomy safeguards will be for the purposes of dealing with internal particularities, such as in the case of the role of 'traditional leaders', but may indeed also serve as a basis for avoiding adherence to commonly approved standards. As a result, commonality may well take time to achieve. As the momentum within AU institutions is further established, Member States are likely to pull back in the initial period. Such a pullback is, however, not sustainable since the democratic space has already established the power of civil society and peoples on the continent. If particular modalities of governance fail, people will exercise power and initiate changes that will drive more profound progress and innovation for better and more appropriate governance modalities.

REFERENCES

Abass, A. & Baderin, M.A. 2002. Towards effective collective security and human rights protection in Africa: An assessment of the Constitutive Act of the new African Union. *Netherlands International Law Review* 49(1): 1–38.

Achieng, R.M. 2014. Can we speak of African agency? APRM and Africa's Agenda 2063. *African Sociological Review* 18(1): 49–64.

Adisa, J. 2002. Making the mechanism work: A view from the African Union. *African Security Review* 11(4): 110–114.

African Union. 2011. Assembly/AU/ Decl.1 (XVI) Declaration on the Theme of the Summit: Towards Greater Unity and Integration through Shared Values. Addis Ababa: African Union Commission.

African Union Commission. 2009. Procedures for ratification of treaties in Member States of the African Union, harmonisation of ratification procedures and measures to speed up the ratification of OAU/AU treaties. Addis Ababa: African Union Commission.

African Union Commission. 2010. Towards Greater Unity and Integration through Shared Values. Discussion Paper. Addis Ababa: African Union Commission.

Ake, C. 1991. Rethinking African Democracy. *Journal of Democracy* 2(1): 32–44.

Apuuli, K.P. 2012. The African Union's notion of 'African solutions to African problems' and the crises in Côte d'Ivoire (2010–2011) and Libya (2011). *African Journal on Conflict Resolution: Special issue on the African Union* 12(2): 135–160.

Bond, P. 2009. Removing Neocolonialism's APRM Mask: A Critique of the African Peer Review Mechanism. *Review of African Political Economy* 36(122): 595–603.

Carothers, T. & De Gramont, D. 2013. *Development Aid Confronts Politics: The Almost Revolution*. Washington, DC: Carnegie Endowment for International Peace.

De Waal, A. 2013. The theory and practice of Meles Zenawi. *African Affairs* 112(446): 148–155.

Dinokopila, B.R. 2013. The Pan-African Parliament and African Union human rights actors, civil society and national human rights institutions: The importance of collaboration. *African Human Rights Law Journal* 13(2): 302–323.

Fukuyama, F. 2011. *The Origins of Political Order: From Prehuman Times to the French Revolution*. London: Profile Books.

Gruzd, S. 2014. *The African Peer Review Mechanism: Development Lessons from Africa's Remarkable Governance Assessment System*. Research Report 15. Johannesburg: South African Institute of International Affairs.

International Bank for Reconstruction and Development. 1989. *Sub-Saharan Africa: From Crisis to Sustainable Growth, a Long-term Perspective Study*. Washington, DC: World Bank.

Kagame, P. 2017. The Imperative to Strengthen Our Union. Report on the Proposed Recommendations for the Institutional Reform of the African Union. http://www.gsdpp.uct.ac.za/sites/default/files/image_tool/images/78/News/Final AU Reform Combined report_28012017.pdf (accessed 3 May 2018).

Kjær, A.M. 2014. Debate on Governance in Africa: An Emerging Political Economy Paradigm. In: Mudacumura, G.M. & Morçöl, G. (eds) *Challenges to Democratic Governance in Developing Countries*: 19–35. New York: Springer.

Matlosa, K.T. 2008. *The African Charter on Democracy, Elections and Governance: Declaration vs policy practice*. Policy Brief 53. Johannesburg: Centre for Policy Studies.

Matlosa, K. 2014. *Pan-Africanism, the African Peer Review Mechanism and the African Charter on Democracy, Elections and Governance: What does the future hold?* Occasional Paper 190. Johannesburg: South African Institute of International Affairs.

Mkandawire, T. 2007. 'Good governance': the itinerary of an idea. *Development in Practice* 17(4–5): 679–681.

Peters, B.G. & Pierre, J. 1998. Governance without Government? Rethinking Public Administration. *Journal of Public Administration Research and Theory* 8(2): 223–243.

Udombana, N.J. 2000. Towards the African Court on Human and Peoples' Rights: Better Late than Never. *Yale Human Rights and Development Law Journal* 3(1): Article 2.

Wachira, G.M. 2014. *Consolidating the African Governance Architecture*. Policy Briefing 96. Johannesburg: South African Institute of International Affairs.

3

Governance and Human Development in Sub-Saharan Africa

Pundy Pillay

INTRODUCTION

The primary purpose of this chapter is to reflect on the importance of good governance for development in sub-Saharan Africa. First, there is an attempt to define governance, 'good governance' and its importance or relevance for development. In this section, the debates questioning the role of governance in development are also raised. These debates suggest that growth and development enhance governance, rather than the other way around. Second, the chapter focuses on the concepts of 'sustainable development' and, more narrowly, on 'human development'. Third, the state of human development in sub-Saharan Africa is analysed. Finally, the chapter examines the issues of governance in the education and health sectors, mainly because education and health outcomes are primary determinants of a nation's development status.

According to the United Nations (UNDESA, UNDP, UNESCO 2012: 3), governance 'refers to the exercise of political and administrative authority at all levels to manage a country's affairs. It comprises the mechanisms, processes, and institutions, through which citizens and groups articulate their interests, exercise their legal rights, meet their obligations and mediate their differences'. In some instances, reference is made to democratic governance as 'a process of creating and sustaining an environment for inclusive and responsive political processes and settlements' (UNDP 2011). In this view, the institutional and human capacities for governance determine the way in which the effectiveness of public policies and strategies is attained, especially in service delivery.

International agencies such as the United Nations Development Programme (UNDP) and the World Bank thus view governance as the exercise of authority or power in order to manage a country's economic, political and administrative affairs. The 2009 Global Monitoring Report (UNESCO 2009), for instance, sees governance as 'power relationships', 'formal and informal processes of formulating policies and allocating resources', 'processes of decision making' and 'mechanisms for holding governments accountable'.

Broader definitions of governance encompass politics, policy, public administration, the interaction of these with civil society and the private sector, and the effects the various institutions have on socio-economic outcomes (WHO 2014).

Table 3.1: Dimensions of governance according to various institutions

Institution	Dimension/indicator
World Bank Institute (Worldwide Governance Indicators)	Voice and accountability Political stability and absence of violence Government effectiveness Regulatory quality Rule of law Control of corruption
United Nations	Participation Rule of law Transparency Responsiveness Equity Effectiveness and efficiency Accountability Strategic vision
Overseas Development Institute/World Governance Assessment	Participation Fairness Decency Accountability Transparency Efficiency
Mo Ibrahim Foundation/ Ibrahim Index of African Governance	Safety and rule of law Participation and human rights Sustainable economic development Human development

Source: WHO 2014: 9

These definitions include many functions, activities and interventions that apply to, and cut across, all sectors. The scope of governance summarised in Table 3.1, for example, captures most of the components found in the literature with the exception of human rights (WHO 2014).

Based on these broad definitions, tools for assessing good governance have been developed by several international agencies. For example, Worldwide Governance Indicators, published annually by the World Bank, scores countries on six dimensions (voice and accountability; government effectiveness; regulatory quality; control of corruption; rule of law; and political stability and absence of violence) and aggregates these scores into a single index (WHO 2014).

In the development literature, the term 'good governance' is frequently used. In particular, donors promote the notion of good governance as a necessary pre-condition for creating an enabling environment for poverty reduction and sustainable human development (SHD). Good governance was also accepted as one of the targets of the Millennium Development Goals (MDG). The good governance agenda often stems from donor concerns with the effectiveness of development efforts.

There are divergent views on the relationship between governance and development. To a great extent the view that governance should play a stronger role in development efforts has been strongly supported by donors and multilateral agencies such as the World Bank and the UNDP. As Baland, Moene and Robinson (2009: 3) put it, '[this] current paradigm puts issues of "governance" at the heart of an understanding of development. Poor countries are poor because they have bad governance and countries that grow or are rich are those that have improved their governance'.

In this view, effective governance institutions and systems that are responsive to public needs deliver essential services and promote inclusive growth, while inclusive political processes ensure that citizens can hold public officials to account. In addition, good governance promotes freedom from violence, fear and crime, and peaceful and secure societies that provide stability needed for development investments to be sustained. Governance thus can enable the achievement of a range of critical development objectives.

Some commentators have also pointed out that a key to understanding Africa's growth story since the early 2000s is assessing the quality of governance. According to this view, 'both economic theory and some cross-country comparisons suggest governance is a key factor in economic development and it correlates with faster growth, higher investment, and increased poverty reduction' (Asian Development Bank 2013).

Olukoshi (2011: 14–15) draws attention to the fact that during the structural adjustment years of the 1980s, the notion of 'good governance' was

> [...] introduced as one of the panaceas for achieving effective economic reform on the continent and for helping to underwrite the processes of political transition that were beginning to take place. Up to that point, the World Bank, even though it was heavily immersed in politics and in the politics of economic reform, had taken the view that its constitution and rules prevented it from dabbling in political questions. However, with the introduction of the notion of good governance, it was able for the first time to openly engage with political institutions and political questions. But there was difficulty in defining exactly what the notion could be extended to, even including defining what a good governance system is or could be. The notion of good governance was subordinated in the first instance to the larger project of how to save the structural adjustment project itself. After a decade of implementing structural adjustment and of the difficulties in getting results out of it, the search was on for what could be the missing link that could make adjustment deliver the results the authors of the programme promised in the first place. Thus, African countries appeared to be mired in deeper crisis and new contradictions appeared to have developed, even in countries defined as good adjusters that had accepted all the IMF [International Monetary Fund] and World Bank prescriptions.

Olukoshi (2011: 14) goes on to say that 'governance became instrumentalised in the hands of the Bretton Woods institutions to serve not necessarily democracy but the economics of the reform agenda that was itself questioned on the grounds that it was anti-democratic'. When asked how good governance would translate in practical terms, the World Bank and the UNDP and others ultimately came to define good governance in terms of, inter alia, property rights, the rule of law, judicial independence, and transparency. Olukoshi (2011: 14) also makes the point that the rationale for 'good governance' is often 'to strengthen the environment for business'. Moreover, it was also 'intended to strengthen the capacity of the Bretton Woods institutions to have access to information from governments and make them transparent in order to be able to carry out their intervention in the African countries. Good governance is clearly not an option, because it is not democratic governance. It was probably never meant to be equated with democratic governance' (Olukoshi 2011: 14). Olukoshi (2011: 15) gives the example of East Africa,

[...] where reforms on land and access to and use of land were pursued vigorously, [but] those reforms were not subject to domestic debate or to effective parliamentary scrutiny, despite the fact that legislation was being pushed through to effect the change desired. The power of the ministries of finance, the so-called independence of the central bank, whose governors were appointed to positions not open to scrutiny and for which they could not be called to account either by public opinion or even by elected governments, constituted the effective making of a technocracy and of the associated insulation of policy and public officials. This was perhaps one of the most anti-democratic experiences of the 1990s across the African continent, whose consequences continued to play out in terms of the nature and form of policy making on the continent.

Olukoshi's important point is that 'we cannot talk meaningfully about democratic governance and accountability if citizens cannot take an active part in policymaking and be confident that their active citizenry will help shape public policy' (2011: 15).

However, not all scholars agree with the view that poor development is caused by poor governance. In their useful analysis of the relationship between governance and development, Baland *et al.* (2009: 6) point out firstly that the literature on governance should be thought of as part of the broader literature on the 'relationship between institutions and economic development'. They found that income differences between rich and poor countries can be explained by differences in these institutions (taken to include broadly institutions such as property rights and the constitution, as well as economic policy). Second, they point out that in order to understand governance and why it varies, one has to study the political economy of development, for the reason that the outcome of political decisions 'will reflect the political institutions and sources in society which mould the political process' (Baland *et al.* 2009: 7).

Various other social scientists are also sceptical about whether good governance influences development. For example, Sundaram and Chowdhury (2012) argue that donors have chosen to prioritise 'good governance' reforms despite little empirical evidence. These authors are critical of, for example, the World Bank's Worldwide Governance Indicators, cited earlier. Sundaram and Chowdhury (2012) argue that the World Bank data are at best partial, and at worst misleading. In contrast to the World Bank view, these authors suggest that growth and development improve governance, rather than the other way around.

Khan (2006) also argues that good governance is 'more [the] effect than cause' of development. He makes the point that developing countries lack the resources to enforce good governance and such resources can only come from development itself.

In addition, Khan (2006: 1) notes that 'good governance' reforms are difficult to implement in any developing country. In his view, countries that did succeed in growing economically 'did not enjoy better market-enhancing governance conditions compared to the others'. He further claims that if some developing countries did well on both the development and governance fronts, they 'must have had some other governance capabilities that allowed them to achieve this'. He then suggests that such capabilities can be described as 'growth-enhancing governance' capabilities. For example, he has suggested that growth in some developing countries has depended not on the 'ex ante' achievement of stable property rights, but more likely on governance capabilities that could manage non-market asset transfers in ways that created incentives for productive investment. He points out that sustained growth requires the maintenance of political stability in a context,

> where patron-client politics is structural and difficult to change in the short run. Success or failure has not depended on the ability to achieve Weberian states at early stages of development, but has depended on governance capabilities that allowed states to manage political stability through patron-client politics at relatively low cost and without excessively disrupting productive investment and learning (Khan 2006: 1–2).

In Khan's (2006) view, such governance capabilities are different from the ones identified in the market-enhancing approach.

Booth (2015: 1) also argues along these lines that 'in some areas of development policy, deep-rooted assumptions are extremely hard to dislodge and [...] the importance of good governance for development is one such assumption'. According to Booth (2015: 1), 'if this means that a large set of worthy ideals – including transparency in public affairs, accountability of power-holders to citizens, ability of citizens to make demands, absence of corruption, freedom of enterprise, secure property rights and rule of law – are necessary conditions for development success, the answer is clearly no'. In his view, the history of human progress demonstrates quite clearly that good governance stems from economic progress and not the other way around.

THE AFRICAN UNION'S AGENDA 2063

The African Union is also of the view that good governance is important for growth and development. Its document *Agenda 2063 – The Africa We Want* (African Union

2015) highlights both ' "inclusive growth and sustainable development" and "good governance" as two of the continent's seven aspirations'.

For instance, Aspiration 1: A Prosperous Africa based on Inclusive Growth and Sustainable Development, states, inter alia, the following:

- We are determined to eradicate poverty in one generation and build shared prosperity through social and economic transformation of the continent;
- We aspire that by 2063, Africa shall be a prosperous continent, with the means and resources to drive its own development;
- By 2063, African countries will be amongst the best performers in global quality of life measures; and Africa's collective GDP will be proportionate to her share of the world's population and natural resource endowments (African Union 2015: 2–3).

With respect to governance, Agenda 2063 states the following:

Aspiration 3: An Africa of Good Governance, Democracy, Respect for Human Rights, Justice and the Rule of Law.

- Africa shall have a universal culture of good governance, democratic values, gender equality, respect for human rights, justice, and the rule of law;
- We aspire that by 2063, Africa will:
  1. Be a continent where democratic values, culture, practices, universal principles of human rights, gender equality, justice and the rule of law are entrenched.
  2. Have capable institutions and transformative leadership in place at all levels.
  3. Africa will be a continent where the institutions are at the service of its people. Citizens will actively participate in social, economic and political development and management. Competent, professional, rules-and merit-based public institutions will serve the continent and deliver effective and efficient services. Institutions at all levels of government will be developmental, democratic, and accountable (African Union 2015: 5–6).

GOVERNANCE AND SUSTAINABLE DEVELOPMENT

The concept of 'sustainable development' was derived partly from the recommendations of the 1987 Brundtland Report (World Commission on Environment and Development 1987), which defined the term to mean meeting the needs of the present generation without compromising the needs of future generations; partly from the Rio Declaration and other UN documents, and from work done by NGOs in the recent past (UNDP 2014a). Sustainable development seeks to enlarge the choices for all people in society, and makes the central purpose of development as creating an enabling environment in which all people can enjoy a long, healthy and creative life.

There are five aspects to sustainable human development: namely, empowerment, cooperation, equity, sustainability and security. The 1994 Human Development Report (HDR) defines SHD as follows: 'Sustainable human development is pro-people, pro-jobs and pro-nature. It brings human numbers into balance with the coping capacities of societies and the carrying capacity of nature [...] it also recognises that not much can be achieved without a dramatic improvement in the status of women and the opening of all opportunities to women' (UNDP 1994: 4).

According to the UNDP (2014a), there is a close and mutually reinforcing relationship between sound governance and sustainable human development. In this view, the linkages between SHD and governance can be seen through the contribution of human resource development. The aspects of human resource development that contribute most to SHD are health and nutrition, general education, vocational training, and managerial capability. In each of these areas, governance plays an important role.

Health and nutrition are seen to be essential to SHD because they have an immediate impact on people's productivity and long-term effects on increasing their ability to absorb new knowledge. Improvements in health and nutrition contribute to social harmony and well-being, as well as increase productivity by reducing worker absenteeism due to illness and lethargy, increase people's energy levels and stamina, and improve their mental processes. Economic and social benefits also accrue from the favourable impacts of better education, health and nutrition on the abilities of children and adults to learn and through prolonging the duration of their active participation in society (UNDP 2014b).

Human resource development also influences SHD through its positive impact on literacy, numeracy and skills. Primary and secondary education create access to opportunities and can increase labour productivity by increasing people's willingness and capacity to learn. Numeracy and literacy are essential for skills development, especially in technology-oriented activities. Vocational training contributes to SHD by enhancing workers' ability to make more productive use of capital and technology, and by better preparing them to work in specific occupations (UNDP 2014a).

In order to create a link between growth and human development, it is evident that countries must develop their human resources to enhance productivity. The

1996 HDR showed that there is no automatic link between growth and human development (UNDP 1996). The link between the two can be strong, weak, or unbalanced.

In countries within the first category (strong), both economic growth and human development have advanced rapidly, reinforcing each other through policy links. Resources generated by economic growth have financed human development and created employment while human development has contributed to economic growth. Among the most prominent examples in this category are the high-performing Asian countries – Hong Kong, Japan, Malaysia, South Korea and Singapore. In countries within the second category (weak), economic growth has been slow or negative and human development stagnant, one undermining the other. Without economic growth, resources to invest in human development are lacking, and with poor standards of health, education and nutrition, rapid or even moderate economic growth becomes very difficult to achieve. Most sub-Saharan African countries are in this category (see later). Development in the last category (unbalanced) of countries has been lopsided, with rapid economic growth but slow human development. Links have been weak in translating economic growth into human development (sub-Saharan African examples include Mozambique and Uganda). Development can also be lopsided, with rapid human development but slow or negative economic growth (e.g. Cuba – see Table 3.4). Although achieving human development despite slow growth is commendable, it is not sustainable in the long run and causes social tensions because of such imbalances as unemployment among the educated (UNDP 2014a).

IMPROVING GOVERNANCE

In practice, improving governance requires action in a wide range of areas, not all of which can be addressed at once, and not all can be the subject of a global consensus. The evidence drawn from the UNDP (2014a: 5–8) is summarised below. It is difficult to question any of these proposed actions – all are undoubtedly critical in terms of ensuring the presence of both appropriate institutions and processes for good governance.

Effective, responsive and accountable state institutions

State capacity, or the ability of states to formulate and implement policy across the whole of their territory, is an essential prerequisite for SHD. Many studies have demonstrated the importance of state capacity: for example, there is a causal link between the quality of public administration and economic growth. On the other hand, weak states are more prone to conflict and civil war. However, sustainable development also requires countries to be responsive to the needs and demands of its citizens.

Multi-stakeholders' engagement with institutions including parliaments, courts, auditors-general, ombudsmen, anti-corruption agencies, human rights commissions, civil society, media, and representatives of women's groups is required in order to help shape policy, ensure accountability and hold state institutions to account for their performance and the quality of services delivered.

Openness and transparency

Openness and transparency are essential to achieve sustainable development. There is evidence that informed citizens and the private sector are better able to engage in developing policy; they are better collaborators and partners with government on service delivery, and also better able to hold governments to account, leading to improved development outcomes.

Addressing corruption and curbing illicit financial flows

There is substantial evidence that corruption is a major hindrance to sustainable development, with a disproportionate impact on the poor and marginalised populations. Corruption is bad for health and education outcomes, equity, the rule of law, and foreign investment.

Conversely, there is evidence that anti-corruption and wider transparency and accountability policies are associated with improved development outcomes such as education, health and water management. Transparency International, for example, finds that good performance on anti-corruption initiatives and the rule of law is linked with higher youth literacy rates and lower maternal mortality rates.

Justice and the rule of law

The rule of law is critical for sustainable development. It has been shown that countries adhering to the rule of law have higher levels of growth and investment through the protection of property rights. In addition, this can promote equity, gender equality, and inclusion through, for example, the protection of legal identity and more equitable access to resources for both women and men.

Participation in decision-making

Participation is both a right, and a means to more sustainable development. When communities are actively engaged in their own development processes, project outcomes will be better targeted to local needs, and results will be more sustainable. Participation in policy development and the design of development interventions by communities and society at large, in any society or community, enhances trust between those who decide, those who implement the decisions, and the population at large.

Governance and management

Often there is a tendency to equate governance with management. Management usually refers to the planning, implementation and monitoring functions in order to achieve predefined results. Management encompasses processes, structures and arrangements that are designed to mobilise and transform the available physical, human and financial resources to achieve concrete outcomes. Management also refers to individuals or groups of people who are given the authority to achieve the desired results. Governance systems set the parameters under which management and administrative systems operate. Governance is about how power is distributed and shared, how policies are formulated, priorities set, and stakeholders made accountable. Table 3.2 summarises the difference between governance and management.

Table 3.2: Governance vs management

Governance	Management
• Set the norms, strategic vision and direction, and formulate high-level goals and policies • Oversee management and organisational performance to ensure that the organisation is working in the best interests of the public and, more specifically, the stakeholders who are served by the organisation's mission • Direct and oversee the management to ensure that the organisation is achieving the desired outcomes, and ensure that the organisation is acting prudently, ethically and legally	• Run the organisation in line with the broad goals and direction set by the governing body • Implement decisions within the context of the mission and strategic vision • Make operational decisions and policies, and keep the governance bodies informed and educated • Be responsive to requests for additional information

Source: UNDP 2014a

GOVERNANCE AND SUSTAINABLE HUMAN DEVELOPMENT

What does it mean to promote good governance for human development? Much discussion about the definition of good governance has centred on what makes institutions more effective and efficient, in order to achieve high levels of economic and social development.

The United Nations (UNDESA, UNDP, UNESCO 2012) identifies two key aspects of governance that are vital for human development. The first relates to institutions of governance, including public administration and public services connected, in particular, with the sound management of resources, delivery of and equitable access to public services, responsiveness to the views of citizens, and their participation in decisions that concern them. Strategies adopted to address these challenges include personnel management, transparency in public finance, a curb on corruption, citizen participation and enhanced accountability.

The second governance issue is concerned with concepts of democracy and the rule of law, including rights-based claims to equality before the law, judicial independence, participation in the conduct of public affairs, electoral integrity, political plurality, freedom of expression and media independence (UNDP 2014a). These claims include demands for gender equality and the inclusion of youth and marginalised groups. As discussed earlier, integral to effective implementation is an informed and empowered citizenry engaged in transparent and accountable governance processes.

The core tenet of human development, exemplified in Amartya Sen's (1999) work, is the understanding of development as a vehicle for enhancing human capabilities and opportunities, be they economic, social, or otherwise.

The Human Development Index (HDI) as a measure of human development is a somewhat crude, unweighted average of a nation's education and health status (measured respectively through mean years of schooling, and longevity), and income (GDP per capita), but is still widely used in the development discourse. The HDI, which replaced GDP per capita as the sole yardstick of development, has contributed to a growing acceptance of the fact that monetary measures are inadequate proxies of development. Because governance can act either to enhance or diminish human capabilities and opportunities, it has a strong link to human development.

INSTITUTIONS, DEVELOPMENT AND GOVERNANCE

In the recent past, scholars of development have emphasised the critical role of institutions in producing positive development outcomes. Two different strands of thinking on the issue can be identified in this regard.

First, new institutional economics (NIE) suggests that economic and social outcomes are largely determined by the 'rules of the game' of development. These rules can be seen as embedded at many levels in societies. Thus, for example, 'institutions can refer to shared normative expectations (such as enabling trust between people)' (Jayadev 2010: 2).

Institutions are also taken to mean the formal arrangements and property rights frameworks that exist in different societies. The quality of these institutions is argued to be more important to growth than other determinants such as natural endowments or openness to trade and finance. Inasmuch as human development is intimately intertwined with the process of economic growth, the quality of institutions therefore also determines human capability.

Second, while the above studies take the institutional environment as a given factor, another set of theories, most closely associated with theories of the developmental state (for example, Amsden 1989; Chang 2002) present evidence (primarily from East Asia) of the crucial role of active state institutions in producing developmental success. According to this viewpoint, institutions do indeed matter, but it is the robust public institutions reflecting 'good governance' which underpin the developmental state that are important in promoting human development. A good example of these effective public institutions is the public provisioning of collective goods such as education or health care which are critical to the expansion in capabilities experienced by those societies. Indeed, a central function of developmental states is to provide means whereby the poorest and most vulnerable can enhance and invest in their own capabilities.

INEQUALITY AND GOVERNANCE

The World Social Science Report (UNESCO and ISCC 2016) draws attention to, inter alia, the linkages between governance and inequality. Leach (2016: 186), for instance, points to the role of inclusive political and governance frameworks in reducing inequality:

> Changing the rules towards reduced inequalities is more likely to be feasible if those with an interest in such change are included in rule-setting processes. Such processes may include laws and policies such as quotas to bring women, indigenous people or other politically marginalised groups into formal political arenas. But while their significance for gender equality is great, rules and formal representation are insufficient. Promoting women's rights, and inclusion in politics and policymaking, also depends on informal institutions and norms.

At the same time, she notes that 'the quality of political and government institutions is vitally important. If they are perceived as incompetent, or beset by favouritism or corruption, there will be declining support for rule changes that alleviate inequalities – even among parts of a population that are politically included or ideologically in favour of such changes' (Leach 2016: 186).

Olukoshi (2016: 214) asserts that none of the global instruments (for example, as advanced by the World Bank) have addressed

> the structural roots of poverty and inequality in Africa; all have been based on the assumption that poverty and inequality can be tackled through technical and technocratic solutions. Bringing politics [and governance] back into the policy processes is a key priority if African countries are to be able to overcome the challenge of persistent poverty alongside growing inequality. A second priority, flowing from an acknowledgement of the central place of politics, will be the recovery of domestic policy space for building an integrated and holistic agenda of development that is able to reconcile economic policies with social vision and the active participation of an empowered citizenry.

Rothstein (2016: 245) draws attention to the relationship between corruption (a key element of governance) and inequality. First, he makes the point that

> it is important to consider the necessary amount and type of solidarity needed to produce public policies that enhance social and economic equality, and whether this solidarity can be politically manufactured. We take as our starting point the notion that the level of social solidarity in a society is not culturally determined. The Nordic countries are not more equal than, for example, the UK or the USA because there is something special about the Nordic culture. Instead, the unusually broad-based political support for the welfare state has been politically constructed 'from above' by the universal (or near universal) design of the policies concerned. The recent introduction of a more universal type of social policy reform in several Latin American countries in areas such as health care, pensions and education shows the existence of the same causal logic as the Nordic countries, as does the contingent support for the National Health Service in the UK and the social security system in the USA. In sum, it is the specific design of the institutions, not history or culture, that matters for the possibility of establishing sustainable policies that reduce inequality.

Rothstein (2016) also points to the fact that recent empirical research strongly supports Rawls' (1971) argument that individuals' perception of corruption or similar forms of malpractice in the public services influences their support for social solidarity. Using survey data for 29 European countries that includes questions about the fairness of public authorities (in the health sector and tax authorities), as well as questions about ideological leanings and policy preferences, Svallfors (2013) has shown the following: citizens who have a preference for more economic equality, but live in a country where they perceive that the quality of government institutions is low, will in the same survey indicate that they prefer lower taxes and lower social spending. However, the same 'ideological type' of respondents who happen to live in a European country where they believe that the authorities who implement policies are basically just and fair will answer that they are willing to pay higher taxes for more social spending. This result is supported in a study using aggregate data about welfare state spending and corruption in the public sector for Western liberal democracies (Rothstein 2011). The higher the quality of government, the more countries spend, controlled for variables that measure political mobilisation and electoral success by left-wing parties.

In summary, Rothstein's extensive work shows that citizens who live in a country where they perceive that corruption or other forms of unfairness in the public administration are common are likely to be less supportive of the idea that the state should take responsibility for policies for increased social justice, even if they support the goals of such policies ideologically. What can prevent this is high quality in the government institutions responsible for implementing social policies. Widespread notions of favouritism, lack of impartiality, corruption and incompetence will result in declining support for policies that alleviate inequality, even in the part of the electorate that is ideologically in favour of a society with more equality (Rothstein 2016: 246).

HUMAN DEVELOPMENT IN AFRICA

The lack of consensus on the role of governance in development articulated in the first part of this chapter throws up important policy questions for development in Africa, which is lagging behind the rest of the world in terms of 'development' however that term is defined.

It cannot be denied that African countries have made steady progress, with gains in education, health and living standards. However, the pace of progress in human development varies by country and sub-regions and is insufficient to reach the 2030

UN Agenda targets for sustainable development. Progress is hampered by several factors: inequality weakens the impact of growth on poverty reduction; weak structural transformation limits work opportunities; and limited advances in gender equality hamper skills and entrepreneurial development (African Development Bank, OECD, UNDP 2016). Ensuring human progress therefore remains a considerable challenge in most African countries.

Human development goes beyond the accumulation of wealth. It embodies the process of enlarging people's choices to live their lives in a way that is equitable, participatory, productive and sustainable. These choices are created by expanding human capabilities and functioning (UNDP 1996).

Human development in Africa, as measured using the UNDP's Human Development Index (which, as stated earlier, combines GDP per capita with education and health indicators), is improving, albeit from a low base. In spite of this progress, the level of human development on the continent remains low, particularly in comparison with other developing regions such as Latin America and Asia.

In 2014, 17 out of 52 countries achieved high or medium levels of SHD (African Development Bank, OECD, UNDP 2015); see Table 3.3. The remaining countries, all in the low SHD category (i.e. 35 out of 52 countries), presented a wide variation of scores. Niger scored lowest with a SHD score of 0.34, while Kenya ranked highest in this group with 0.54 (African Development Bank, OECD, UNDP 2015).

Table 3.3:   Categories of sustainable human development by country – Africa 2014

High human development (above 0.7)	Medium human development (between 0.55 and 0.7)	Low human development (below 0.55)
Algeria, Libya, Mauritius, Seychelles, Tunisia	Botswana, Cabo Verde, Congo, Egypt, Equatorial Guinea, Gabon, Ghana, Morocco, Namibia, South Africa, São Tomé and Principe, Zambia	Angola, Benin, Burkina Faso, Burundi, Cameroon, Central African Republic, Chad, Comoros, Côte d'Ivoire, Djibouti, DRC, Eritrea, Ethiopia, Gambia, Guinea, Guinea-Bissau, Kenya, Lesotho, Liberia, Madagascar, Malawi, Mali, Mauritania, Mozambique, Niger, Nigeria, Rwanda, Senegal, Sierra Leone, Sudan, Swaziland, Tanzania, Togo, Uganda, Zimbabwe

Sources: UNDP 2014b; African Development Bank, OECD, UNDP 2015

The *African Economic Outlook 2015* (African Development Bank, OECD, UNDP 2015) also shows that HDI values increased by 26 per cent from 1990 to 2013, making it the third fastest-growing region after East Asia (36 per cent) and South Asia (34 per cent). In comparison, SHD levels in the Arab States and Latin America for the same period were respectively 19 per cent and 18 per cent higher. These improvements in SHD in Africa are attributed to rapid economic growth based on increased resource flows from natural resource extraction, growth in agriculture and services, human capital development and improved governance (African Development Bank, OECD, UNDP 2015).

The level of SHD in Africa is also much lower than the world average. In sub-Saharan Africa, for example, the average level of SHD in 1990 was 0.40 compared to the world average of 0.60, representing a difference of 33 per cent. This level rose slightly to 0.50 in 2013 but still remained 28 per cent lower than the world average of 0.70 (UNDP 2014b). In general, progress in human development has resulted mainly from improvements in education and health, and from growth in income per capita. Countries that were further behind or began from lower initial conditions are now improving faster than those with higher initial levels of SHD (African Development Bank, OECD, UNDP 2015).

Table 3.4 shows the HDI rankings of a sample of countries including those categorised earlier as 'very high SHD', 'high SHD', 'medium SHD', and 'low SHD'. What is rather obvious from the data on schooling, life expectancy and income per capita is the huge discrepancy between those at the top of the SHD ranking and those at the bottom. In the very high and high SHD countries, it is evident that effective health and education systems, characterised by, inter alia, adequate financing and effective public institutions (i.e. good governance), have enabled high levels of economic growth over several decades and high income per capita.

For the sample of African countries (Table 3.4), in both the medium and low SHD categories, there is a significant discrepancy in schooling attainment and longevity compared to countries in the very high and high human development categories. This underdevelopment of the education and health sectors has clearly limited African countries' capacity for effective human resource development and hence their ability to generate and sustain high levels of equitable growth. In fact, African countries make up 35 out of the 44 countries in the low SHD category.

Growth with equity

Column 5 in Table 3.4 (GDP ranking minus HDI ranking) provides an interesting statistic. It shows the difference between a country's ranking on income (GDP or

Table 3.4:   HDI rankings 2014

HDI rank and country	Life expectancy at birth (years)	Mean years of schooling	GDP per capita (2011 $ PPP)	GDP ranking minus HDI ranking
Very high				
1 Norway	81.6	12.6	64 992	5
2 Australia	82.4	13.0	42 261	17
3 Switzerland	83.0	12.8	56 431	6
High				
50 Belarus	71.3	12.0	16 676	14
50 Russia	70.1	12.0	22 352	−1
52 Oman	76.8	8.0	34 858	−32
63 Mauritius	74.4	8.5	17 740	0
64 Seychelles	73.1	9.4	23 300	−19
67 Cuba	79.4	11.5	7 301	47
Medium				
106 Botswana	64.5	8.9	16 646	−41
110 Gabon	64.4	7.8	16 367	−42
116 South Africa	57.4	9.9	12 122	−29
126 Namibia	64.8	6.2	9 418	−21
138 Equatorial Guinea	57.6	5.5	21 056	−84
160 Ghana	61.4	7.0	3 852	−1
Low				
145 Kenya	61.6	6.3	2 762	9
152 Nigeria	52.8	5.9	5 341	−24
174 Ethiopia	64.1	2.4	1 428	2
180 Mozambique	55.1	3.2	1 123	1

Source: UNDP 2014b

GNI) per capita, and its position on the HDI ranking. First, there are a number of countries where there is a small or negligible difference between the two indicators (e.g. Norway, Switzerland, Russia, Mauritius, Ghana, Kenya, Ethiopia, Mozambique). Second, Cuba (and to a much lesser extent Australia) is an outlier because its SHD status is significantly higher than its economic status as reflected in GDP per capita. In other words, Cuba has invested significantly in its 'human capital' (education and health) but has failed to develop concomitantly appropriate economic policies to utilise this capital for high and sustained growth.

Third, there are a number of oil-producing countries (in Table 3.4, Oman, Equatorial Guinea, Gabon) and sub-Saharan African nations (Botswana, Namibia, Seychelles, South Africa, Nigeria) where the GDP per capita ranking far outstrips the HDI ranking. For example, Botswana ranks at 65 out of 187 countries on GDP per capita but only 106 on HDI, while South Africa's respective rankings on GDP per capita and HDI rankings are 87 and 116, and Equatorial Guinea's are 54 and 138 (calculated from UNDP 2014b). These discrepancies highlight the huge inequalities characterising these economies which is undoubtedly inhibiting their capacity for a) sustained economic growth, and b) equitable growth.

Finally, many sub-Saharan African countries (such as Kenya, Ethiopia, Mozambique, in Table 3.4) show small differences between their GDP per capita and their HDI ranking, implying low or moderate levels of inequality. This is indeed the case. So, although a country such as Tanzania (not shown in Table 3.4) may have a Gini coefficient for income of around 0.3, comparable to Norway's 0.25, there is a world of difference between the two countries in terms of living standards, GDP per capita, and, importantly in the context of this paper, their respective education and health status.

Education and health governance

Human development, as defined by the UNDP, is clearly one (albeit narrow) way of assessing 'development'. In the UNDP definition of 'human development', education and health are critical components. This final section of the chapter reflects briefly on the importance of governance in education and health for development without providing a comprehensive analysis of this particular topic.

Education governance

Education governance is not an abstract concept but something that affects the lives of parents, the school experience of children, and the efficiency and equity of education provision (UNESCO 2009). The consequences of bad governance are numerous and widespread, especially in developing countries. They include 'chronically under-financed schools, service providers and government agencies that are unresponsive to local needs and unaccountable to parents, large disparities in school access, participation and completion, and low levels of learning achievement' (UNESCO 2009).

UNESCO (2009) also draws attention to the lack of attention paid to the integration of education planning with broader poverty reduction and development strategies. The point is that sustained progress towards universal, high-quality education depends on the effective integration of education planning in wider poverty reduction and development strategies, 'primarily because poverty, poor nutrition and ill health are formidable barriers to success in education' (UNESCO 2009).

Lewis and Pettersson Gelander (2009: 4) stress that good governance in education systems promotes effective delivery of education services. In their view, important factors in this regard are 'appropriate *standards, incentives, informa-tion*, and *accountability*, which induce high *performance* from public providers (see information box). Sound provider performance in turn raises the level of education *outputs* (for example, school retention) and can contribute to improved *outcomes* (for example, student test scores).'

Moreover, good governance can discourage corruption, 'an *outgrowth* of poor governance, which directly affects performance of the education sector' (Lewis and Pettersson Gelander 2009: 5). The information box shows the 'enabling conditions' which are prerequisites for good governance in the education sector.

Good governance also requires effective incentives at all levels of the education system, and both benchmarks for and information on performance in order to induce and sustain desirable behaviour.

In education, poor governance results in inefficiency in service provision, and in some cases no service at all. Lack of standards, information, incentives, and account-ability can lead not only to poor provider performance but also to corruption. However, the line between poor governance and corruption is often blurred. Is poor service a function of corruption or simply of mismanagement? Improving governance and (thereby) discouraging corruption in education ultimately aims to

---

Governance and performance fundamentals in education

Standards are transparent and publicly known criteria or benchmarks used to assess and inform education policy, provision and performance.

Incentives are any financial or non-financial factors that motivate a specific type of behaviour or action, and can be positive or negative, i.e. encourage certain behaviours or deter them.

Information in the form of clear definitions of outputs and outcomes, combined with accurate data on performance and results collected at regular intervals, enables sanctions to be imposed when specified standards are not met.

Accountability refers to the act of holding public officials/service providers answerable for processes and outcomes, and imposing sanctions if specified outputs and outcomes are not delivered. Accountability requires that public servants have clear responsibilities and are held answerable in exercising those responsibilities.

Source: Lewis and Pettersson Gelander 2009: 4

---

increase the efficiency of education services so as to raise performance and, ultimately, improve student learning and labour productivity (Lewis and Pettersson Gelander 2009).

The key to good governance in education is that the public sector reaches an acceptable standard of performance. That performance entails basic functioning of the education system so that teachers are hired based on merit, administrators and teachers show up daily, adequate numbers of books are available, funds are budgeted and allocated transparently, incentives are set to promote good performance, and corruption is discouraged. Without these basic ingredients the broader education system objectives cannot be attained.

To improve governance, and subsequently the performance of education systems, it is critical to identify the weak points that contribute to poor performance and corruption. For example, pervasive teacher absenteeism in developing countries is a symptom of governance failure due to little or no accountability of teachers to employers or parents (Lewis and Pettersson Gelander 2009). Budget leakages, where public education funds fail to reach intended recipients, offer another sign of governance failure due to some combination of mismanagement, lack of incentives to track funds, weak information systems that thwart the ability to track funds, and absence of mechanisms that would hold officials to account (Lewis and Pettersson Gelander 2009).

Health governance

Health governance refers to policy agenda-setting processes, implementation and accountability within the health sector. It includes the management and administration of policies and resources in health, including processes for health systems strengthening.

Governance in the health sector refers to a wide range of functions carried out by governments/decision makers as they seek to achieve national health policy objectives that are conducive to universal health coverage. Governance is a political process that involves balancing competing influences and demands. It includes:

- Maintaining the strategic direction of policy development and implementation;
- Detecting and correcting undesirable trends and distortions;
- Articulating the case for health in national development;
- Regulating the behaviour of a wide range of actors – from financers of health care to healthcare providers; and
- Establishing transparent and effective accountability mechanisms (WHO 2016).

Beyond the formal health system, governance means collaborating with other sectors, including the private sector and civil society, to promote and maintain population health in a participatory and inclusive manner (WHO 2016). In countries that receive significant amounts of external development assistance, governance should also be concerned with managing these resources in ways that promote national leadership, contribute to the achievement of agreed policy goals, and strengthen national health systems. While the scope for exercising governance functions is greatest at the national level, it also covers the steering role of regional and local authorities.

The literature on health system governance mirrors the broader governance literature. A variety of definitions of health system governance can be found that draw on the broader concept of governance and principles and dimensions of good practice that have been developed for the health sector based on these definitions.

USAID, for example, has argued that health system governance is governance undertaken with the objective to protect and promote the health of the people. Governance involves '1) setting strategic direction and objectives; 2) making policies, laws, rules, regulations, or decisions, and raising and deploying resources to accomplish the strategic goals and objectives; and 3) overseeing and making sure that the strategic goals and objectives are accomplished' (WHO 2014).

WHO (2014) includes leadership in the concept of health system governance. Leadership and governance involves ensuring that a strategic policy framework exists and is combined with effective oversight, coalition-building, regulation, attention to system design and accountability. It requires overseeing and guiding the health system as a whole, not just the public system, in order to protect the public interest – broader than simply improving health status.

Consequences of poor governance in education and health in sub-Saharan Africa

It is well known that the education and health sectors in sub-Saharan Africa (SSA) are characterised by poor governance reflected in, inter alia, ineffective public institutions, inappropriate policies, ineffective policy implementation, and an unacceptably high level of wastage of scarce financial resources through both corruption and mismanagement.

In the education sector, poor governance on the continent has been the fundamental cause of inadequate inputs into the sector including insufficient funding, poor infrastructure, inadequate and often poorly qualified teaching stock, as well as poor teaching and learning materials. The consequence of poor governance is reflected in low outputs from the schooling and post-schooling sectors in terms of pass rates, and a high level of 'educational inefficiency' manifested in huge dropout and repetition rates. Finally, educational outcomes on the continent are on average the lowest in the world, reflected for instance, in exceptionally poor performance in international tests of mathematics, language, and science proficiency, and low levels of skills production, thus inhibiting the development and implementation of policies for a 'knowledge economy'.

In the health sector, SSA countries, on average, perform amongst the worst in the world on a range of indicators such as life expectancy, maternal mortality, infant mortality, and the incidence of tuberculosis, malaria, diarrhoea, and HIV and Aids. Poor governance in the health sector, again reflected in ineffective public institutions, inadequate funding, and inappropriate policy development and implementation, is a primary cause of the serious underdevelopment of this sector in SSA.

Finally, as illustrated earlier in the section on the HDI, the consequences of poor governance in the education and health sectors have far-reaching consequences for economic growth, and for human and broader sustainable development.

CONCLUSION

The notion that governance is key to development has dominated the literature not least because the most ardent proponents of this view have been the World Bank and the UNDP. However, as described in the first part of the chapter, the evidence is not conclusive. It may well be that both views – namely: a) governance is key to development; and b) growth and development lead to better governance – are relevant in the African context.

Africa has grown significantly in the twenty-first century. For example, between 2009 and 2013, some 30 countries achieved average annual growth rates in excess of 4 per cent, with 14 of these averaging more than 6 per cent (African Development Bank, OECD, UNDP 2015). Some of this growth has undoubtedly influenced the improvement in the African HDI. However, an important question to ask is why such high growth rates have not translated into more rapid development, and here the governance question appears to be relevant. For example, there is substantial evidence of collusion between African governments, local capital and multinational corporations to ensure that the fruits of growth benefit the few rather than the many. In other words, corruption, a key aspect of governance, has undoubtedly played a role in preventing more equitable patterns of development.

REFERENCES

African Development Bank, OECD, UNDP. 2015. *African Economic Outlook 2015*. Abidjan, Paris, New York.

African Development Bank, OECD, UNDP. 2016. *African Economic Outlook 2016: Sustainable Cities and Structural Transformation*, Chapter 3: Human Development in Africa; Chapter 4: Political and Economic Governance in Africa. Abidjan, Paris, New York.

African Union. 2015. *Agenda 2063 – The Africa We Want*. Addis Ababa: African Union Commission.

Amsden, A. 1989. *Asia's Next Giant: South Korea and Late Industrialization*. Oxford: Oxford University Press.

Asian Development Bank (ADB). 2013. *Asian Development Outlook 2013 Update: Governance and Public Service Delivery*. Manila: ADB.

Baland, J-M., Moene, K.O. & Robinson, J.A. 2009. *Governance and Development*. In: Rodrik, D. & Rosenzweig, M. (eds) *Handbook of Development Economics*. Amsterdam: North Holland Publishers.

Booth, D. 2015. Five myths about governance and development. *ODI*, 16 February. https://www.odi.org/comment/9274-five-myths-about-governance-and-development (accessed 2 August 2018).

Chang, H-J. 2002. *Kicking Away the Ladder – Development Strategy in Historical Perspective*. London: Anthem Press.

Jayadev, A. 2010. *Global Governance and Human Development: Promoting Democratic Accountability and Institutional Experimentation*. Human Development Research Paper, June. New York: UNDP.

Khan, M.H. 2006. *Governance and Development*. Paper presented at the Workshop on Governance and Development, Dhaka, November.

Leach, M. 2016. Towards equality: transformative pathways. An introduction to Part III. *World Social Science Report 2016*. Paris: UNESCO and ISCC.

Lewis, M. & Pettersson Gelander, G. 2009. *Governance in Education: Raising Performance*. Washington, DC: World Bank.

Olukoshi, A.O. 2011. *Democratic Governance and Accountability in Africa – In Search of a Workable Framework*. Uppsala: Nordiska Afrikainstitutet.

Olukoshi, A.O. 2016. Global Instruments for Tackling Inequality. *World Social Science Report 2016*. Paris: UNESCO and ISCC.

Rawls, J. 1971. *A Theory of Justice*. Oxford: Oxford University Press.

Rothstein, B. 2011. *The Quality of Government: Corruption, Social Trust and Inequality in a Comparative Perspective*. Chicago: University of Chicago Press.

Rothstein, B. 2015. The moral, economic and political logic of the Swedish welfare state. In: Pierre, J. (ed.) *The Oxford Handbook of Swedish Politics*: 69–86. Oxford: Oxford University Press.

Rothstein, B. 2016. Inequality and Corruption. *World Social Science Report 2016*. Paris: UNESCO & ISCC.

Sen, A. 1999. *Development as Freedom*. Oxford: Oxford University Press.

Sundaram, J.K. & Chowdhury, A. 2012. *Is Good Governance Good for Development?* New York: United Nations Publications.

Svallfors, S. 2013. Government quality, egalitarianism, and attitudes to taxes and social spending: a European comparison. *European Political Science Review* 5(3): 363–380.

UNDP. 1994. *1994 Human Development Report*. New York: UNDP.

UNDP. 1996. *1996 Human Development Report*. New York: UNDP.

UNDP. 2011. *2011 Human Development Report*. New York: UNDP.

UNDP. 2014a. *Governance for Sustainable Development – Integrating Governance in the Post-2015 Development Framework*. New York: UNDP.

UNDP. 2014b. *2014 Human Development Report*. New York: UNDP.

UNESCO. 2009. *Education for All: Global Monitoring Report 2009 – Overcoming Inequality, Why Governance Matters*. Paris: UNESCO.

UNESCO and ISCC. 2016. *World Social Science Report 2016*. Paris: UNESCO and ISCC.

United Nations (UNDESA, UNDP, UNESCO). 2012. *UN System Task Team on the Post-2015 UN Development Agenda: Thematic Think Piece*. New York: UN.

WHO. 2014. *Health Systems Governance for Universal Health Coverage: Action Plan*. Geneva: Department of Health Systems Governance and Financing.

WHO. 2016. Health Systems – Governance. http://www.who.int/healthsystems/topics/stewardship/en/ (accessed 3 June 2016).

World Commission on Environment and Development (WCED). 1987. *Our Common Future*. (Brundtland Report). Oxford: Oxford University Press.

4

South African Foreign Policy and Global Governance: Conflict from above and below

Patrick Bond

INTRODUCTION

Two meetings took place back-to-back in November 2016: both revealed the limitations of a favourite rhetorical technique deployed by South Africa's neo-liberal-nationalist politicians. Immediately after the first substantial challenge to President Jacob Zuma's power within the African National Congress (ANC), over his financing of the rural palace Nkandla from state funds and the number of corruption charges facing him, Zuma's connections to the infamous Gupta brothers (from India) were under the spotlight. His desired nuclear energy programme costing over R1 trillion would benefit the Guptas' Oakbay uranium company through an insider contract with the state electricity utility Eskom. Internet documents signed by Russia's state-owned Rosatom included a contract for construction and operation of the nuclear plants which Zuma had negotiated with Vladimir Putin two years earlier. Eskom's outgoing chief executive Brian Molefe had just arranged a $5 billion line of credit (from the China Development Bank) to pay for the first instalment on the nuclear project. As another relevant piece of context, six months earlier, there had been a right-wing putsch against Zuma's Brazilian ally Dilma Rousseff (who served from 2012 to 2016, having won re-election in 2015). This constitutional coup, numerous commentators believed, was arranged by Western powers to weaken the Brazil-Russia-India-China-South Africa (BRICS) network.

So it was that in November 2016, Zuma explained BRICS to ANC activists in the provincial city of Pietermaritzburg as: 'It is a small group but very powerful. [The West] did not like BRICS. China is going to be number one economy leader […Western countries] want to dismantle this BRICS. We have had seven votes of no confidence in South Africa. In Brazil, the president was removed' (Politicsweb 2016). In the second meeting in parliament the following week, during the president's Question Time, an opposition legislator asked Zuma: 'Which Western countries were you referring to? How did they plan on dismantling BRICS? And what will the effect of their actions be on our economic diplomacy with these Western countries over the next decade?' Zuma replied, according to the Hansard (2016), 'I've forgotten the names of these countries. [Laughter.] How can he think I'm going to remember here? He-he-he-he.'

Zuma (2017) reiterated this message in a mid-2017 speech to his party's policy conference, claiming 'the ANC is part of the global anti-imperialist movement. We are historically connected with the countries of the South and therefore South–South cooperation such as BRICS is primary for our movement.' A few weeks later, he announced to KwaZulu-Natal followers, 'I was poisoned and almost died just because South Africa joined BRICS under my leadership' (Matiwane 2017).

What can be learned from Zuma's paranoid talk-left narrative and walk-right moves? Simply, that the South African government persistently uses the global stage for theatrical posturing, while simultaneously lubricating relationships favourable to the prevailing power balance. Anti-imperialist rhetoric can be traced to the fight against the apartheid regime, but after 1994, the ANC regularly demonstrated its willingness to strengthen multilateral institutions and transnational corporations: Bretton Woods financiers and parallel private institutions; the United Nations Framework Convention on Climate Change (UNFCCC) and World Summit on Sustainable Development (WSSD); the World Trade Organisation (WTO) and related investment treaties; the New Partnership for Africa's Development (NEPAD) and African Union (AU); and businesses whose foreign direct invest-ment (FDI) was desperately sought, in spite of growing evidence of transfer pri-cing, false invoicing and other tax dodges costing the economy $20 billion annually (Global Financial Integrity 2015). By mid-2017, several major multinational corporations doing business with the Guptas or their close associates (including Zuma's son Duduzane) – Bell Pottinger, KPMG, McKinsey, two German software firms, as well as Transnet's Chinese train and crane suppliers – suffered unprece-dented humiliation and corporate self-delegitimisation (Bell Pottinger was even declared insolvent as a result).

Ultimately, this chapter makes the case that the interplay of Pretoria officials and Johannesburg business managers in global governance represents a dialectic, corresponding to sub-imperial practices disguised by anti-imperial political posturing. The counterfactual is also revealing: the leading case in challenging imperial power since the end of apartheid was the Treatment Action Campaign's (TAC) struggle to acquire free Aids medicines against the interests of global pharmaceutical capital and intellectual property rights. Ironically, this victory relied on the state and generic medicines industry in two of the BRICS members (India and Brazil). The TAC succeeded in spite of Pretoria's early-2000s Aids denialism under Thabo Mbeki's rule. In that respect, global influences from below – in the form of international solidarity activism – were necessary to overcome adverse national political power relations as well as multilateral pro-corporate biases. Subsequently, the US government's push to roll back these prerogatives was in full swing, with the new conservative leaders of India and Brazil more prone to Washington's techniques of persuasion, and Donald Trump cutting the US aid budget dramatically. Indeed, this case, like so many others in history, reflects the constant ebb and flow of power between imperialism from above and internationalism from below.

FROM ANC ANTI-IMPERIALISM TO ASSIMILATION 1994–99

With global power relations at their most adverse during the early 1990s, Nelson Mandela gazed upwards at Western power *not* as the anti-imperialist fighter who, in 1962, the US Central Intelligence Agency (CIA) had helped imprison for 27 years by alerting the police to block a road near Howick, KwaZulu-Natal. Instead, his 1990s role was to make peace with both local racists and world elites. Mandela's acceptability to both the National Party and imperialist powers during the transitional negotiations was confirmed by the time he was released in February 1990, and repeatedly rewarded during his presidency. Most importantly, Mandela conceded that international capital would be a central influence in the country's 1990s transition from racial to class apartheid, even if in retrospect it worsened the society's world-leading inequality, deindustrialised the economy, doubled the unemployment rate, and deeply damaged local and regional ecologies.

For, under rising pressure, Mandela and his aides made at least ten fateful decisions during the 1990s, namely:

- To repay $25 billion of inherited apartheid-era foreign debt (October 1993);

- To confirm the SA Reserve Bank's 'independence' in the interim constitution (November 1993);
- To borrow $850 million from the IMF with tough neo-liberal conditions (December 1993);
- To reappoint apartheid-era finance minister Derek Keys and SARB governor Chris Stals after firm IMF advice (May 1994);
- To join the General Agreement on Tariffs and Trade (later renamed the World Trade Organisation, WTO) on highly disadvantageous terms (August 1994) ;
- To lower primary corporate taxes from 56 per cent to today's 28 per cent, and maintain the most important of apartheid privileges for white people and corporations (1994–99);
- To privatise peripheral parts of the state and allow demutualisation of two huge insurance companies, Old Mutual and Sanlam (1995–99);
- To relax exchange controls (the 'Finrand') and, as a result of capital flight within a year, raise interest rates to historic levels (March 1995);
- To adopt the neo-liberal Growth, Employment and Redistribution (Gear) strategy and a variety of other neo-liberal economic, social and environmental policies (June 1996); and
- To grant permission to South Africa's largest companies to move their financial headquarters and primary stock market listings to London and New York (1999).

There were also extremely powerful domestic influences – for example, an informal network of the top businesspeople which met at the Oppenheimers' Johannesburg residence (Brenthurst, in Parktown) to review Mandela's major decisions (such as Trevor Manuel's 1996 appointment as the country's first black finance minister). Leading South Africans and their international allies continued to emphasise the primacy of constitutional property rights, neo-liberal economic policy and the need to suppress popular dissent.

Democratic South Africa also increasingly played a leadership role on the continent, notwithstanding occasional crises such as in Nigeria, where, in November 1995, Ken Saro-Wiwa and eight other Ogoni socio-environmental activists were executed by the Sani Abacha regime. Mandela's strong opposition to Abacha's brutality included a call for Nigeria's expulsion from the Organisation of African Unity (later the AU), but the backlash from other authoritarian presidents was sobering. (In early 1995, Deputy President Mbeki had taken a very different approach to diplomacy: he sought to appease Abacha by unilaterally cancelling a Johannesburg solidarity conference planned by Nigerian exiles led by Wole Soyinka.) Mbeki drew a tragic lesson from this incident: emphasis on protecting human rights was not a wise strategic approach within Africa, especially because that narrative had recently become a tool Washington increasingly deployed to justify so-called 'colour revolutions' for 'regime change'.

Another crucial international contradiction during this period involved partnerships with the ANC's state donors, leading to widespread accusations that foreign policy was up for sale. Mandela bestowed the 1997 Cape of Good Hope award on Indonesia's dictator Suharto after a $25 million donation to the ANC in 1994, just a few months before Suharto's overthrow in a popular uprising. For $20 million from the Taiwan government in 1993–94, Mandela continued to recognise Taipei – in violation of the UN's One China policy – but by 1997 was forced to do a U-turn. Another strange choice was the 1994 recognition of the Myanmar military junta as a legitimate government. There were also ill-considered arms sales authorised to countries which practised mass violence, including Colombia, Peru, Turkey and Algeria (and between 2000–2010, these were expanded to include rights-violators Sudan, Gabon, Djibouti, Ethiopia, Algeria, Egypt and the Central African Republic).

Just a year after South Africa led the UN campaign to ban landmines in 1997 (an important multilateral victory weakened dramatically when Washington refused to sign), Mandela's approval of $5 billion in European arms purchases – corvettes, submarines, light utility helicopters, lead-in fighter trainers and advanced light fighter aircraft – proved to be a devastating mistake, given the cost and systemic corruption involved. The French arms dealer Thales is being investigated again, and its alleged protector during the early 2000s, then deputy president Zuma, faces post-presidential prosecution on 783 cases of corruption.

But more generally, without an alternative to the Western neo-liberal power bloc, the overall balance of forces proved terribly hostile to Pretoria. The 1990s witnessed the West's dismissal of appeals for relief from unfair trade rules, debt and financial squeezes, speculative attacks on the currency, foreign investment strikes, and disputed patents on Aids medicines. Pretoria was generally pliant. As a result, international political power brokers showed increasing trust in Mandela, Mbeki, Manuel and trade minister Alec Erwin, giving them insider access to many elite forums. The UN Conference on Trade and Development (UNCTAD) summit was hosted in Midrand in 1996, for example, during which Erwin dissuaded the body from pursuing progressive economic advocacy, according to its chief economist Yilmaz Akyüz (author interview, Bond 2003).

Not long afterwards, the 1997–98 economic crisis roiled East Asia, Russia and Brazil as well as South Africa, demonstrating the necessity of resisting the Washington Consensus ideology. Yet given the strength of the neo-liberal lobby within the ANC by then, Pretoria put a higher priority on maintaining its role as a responsible member of the international community. In spite of repeated currency crashes – initially beginning after Mandela was rumoured to be ill in February 1996 – the SA Reserve Bank and finance ministry first cancelled the Finrand in March 1995 (thus liberalising all exchange controls on inflows and re-export of capital), and then in 1999 permitted international stock market relistings by most of the largest Johannesburg Stock Exchange (JSE) corporations: Anglo American Corporation, De Beers, Old Mutual, South African Breweries (SAB), Didata IT, Investec and Mondi.

It was here that the seeds of later economic destruction were sown, and that subsequent international financial pressures became most acute, as witnessed in a high, sustained current account deficit, thanks to relentless profit outflows. The resulting need to borrow much more hard currency to finance those outflows – both licit and illicit – ensured Pretoria would come under ever greater influence from the three international credit ratings agencies: Moody's, Fitch, and Standard & Poor's. Although this process only became evident around 2013 when 'junk' status was threatened (and then imposed in 2017), the rise of foreign debt and illicit financial flows (IFF) following exchange control relaxation were ultimately the most powerful determinants of South African fiscal policy from the early 2000s.

'GLOBAL APARTHEID' REFORM, COMMODITY SUPERCYCLE HUBRIS AND XENOPHOBIA 1999–2008

It was at the turn of the century that South African rhetoric ratcheted up fastest against world injustice. A bitter Mbeki introduced the term 'global apartheid' to South Africans in 2001 just after Germany won the hosting role for the 2006 Fédération Internationale de Football Association (FIFA) World Cup, allegedly as a result of bribery (Williams 2015). Ironically, when popular protests scuppered 1999 global leadership summits in Geneva (investment) and Seattle (trade), the first reaction by Mbeki's team was not to break global apartheid's chains, but to polish them. Manuel chaired the annual meetings of the World Bank and IMF in April 2000, just as South African educationalist Mamphela Ramphele was named the Bank's managing director in charge of poverty. Likewise, attempts to restore order at the WTO were partly led by Erwin, unsuccessfully, for by 2003, north–south and US–European conflicts at the Cancun WTO summit left the organisation paralysed for another dozen years. Other efforts to manage conflictual international processes were fumbled by Pretoria politicians, such as temporary presiding roles in the UN Security Council, UNCTAD, the British Commonwealth, the World Commission on Dams, and other important international and continental bodies. Simultaneously assuming Third World leadership, Pretoria also headed the Non-Aligned Movement, the AU and the Southern African Development Community.

Indeed, during a two-year stretch starting in September 2001, Mbeki and his colleagues hosted, led, or played instrumental roles at a dozen major international conferences or events (Bond 2003, 2006). But in retrospect, if attacking global apartheid was the objective, Mbeki's administration failed to capitalise on the opportunities. At the 2001 UN World Conference Against Racism in Durban, he colluded with the European Union to reject the demand of NGOs and African leaders for slavery/colonialism/apartheid reparations. The following month, NEPAD provided merely a homegrown version of the Washington Consensus, termed 'philosophically spot-on' by the US State Department's lead Africa official. A few days later at the 2001 Doha WTO summit, Erwin split the African delegation so as to prevent a repeat of the denial of consensus that had foiled the Seattle WTO summit in December 1999. At the 2002 Financing for Development summit in Mexico, Manuel was co-leader and legitimised ongoing IMF/World Bank strategies, including refusal to provide debt cancellation. Shortly afterwards, at the Johannesburg WSSD, Mbeki undermined UN democratic procedure and effectively facilitated the privatisation of nature. In 2003, after hosting a leg of US President George W. Bush's Africa trip in the midst of the illegal war against Iraq, Mbeki became the US 'point man' on Zimbabwe, in Bush's words. A few months later, at the failed 2003 Cancun WTO trade negotiations, Erwin was in the green rooms (as in Seattle four years earlier) during a mass walkout by African negotiators. At the Dubai IMF/World Bank meetings in 2003, with Manuel leading the Development Committee, there was again no Bretton Woods democratisation, no new debt relief and no 'post-Washington Consensus' policy reform (Bond 2003, 2006).

Throughout these events as well as the G8 and Davos World Economic Forum meetings, Mbeki departed with only rhetorical commitments, invariably to be violated in practice. Global elites continued to deflect or at best assimilate South Africa's challenges to global apartheid. Worse, no countervailing strategy was apparent in Pretoria until an invitation to join BRICS came from Beijing in 2010. Reflecting the adverse power relations, just prior to the 'Coalition of the Willing' invasion of Iraq in March 2003, Mandela declared that Bush, 'who cannot think properly, is now wanting to plunge the world into a holocaust. If there is a country which has committed unspeakable atrocities, it is the United States of America' (Associated Press 2004). Yet within weeks, three Iraq-bound US warships had docked and refuelled in Durban, and South Africa's state-owned weapons manufacturer, Denel, had sold $160 million worth of artillery propellants and 326 hand-held laser range-finders to the British army and 125 laser-guidance sights to the US Marines. Bush was warmly welcomed by Mbeki to Pretoria in July 2003, and by May 2004, Mandela had telephoned Bush in a cowed and conciliatory mood, for, as he put it, 'The United States is the most powerful state in the world and it is not good to remain in tension with the most powerful state' (Associated Press 2004).

After 2003, the pace slowed, with South African elites focusing more inwardly on their economic growth spurt and political power shifts during the 2002–11 'commodity supercycle' era. But vulnerabilities of global economic integration returned during the 2008–09 world recession, with South Africa's budget deficit rising to more than 6 per cent of GDP. Infrastructure spending, mostly related to the 2010 FIFA World Cup, helped the economy survive the world crash. Although China's vast Keynesian investment boom then raised global commodity prices in a last gasp for the extractive industries from 2009–11, the subsequent period was disastrous for an economy that had grown so reliant on mineral exports, resulting in the currency dropping from R6.3/$ in 2011, to a low of R17.9/$ in early 2016.

As a result, by mid-2016, South Africa's current account deficit had fallen to a critical level (–5 per cent of GDP) because of profit outflows. The other component, the trade deficit – that is, imports minus exports – is trivial in comparison, and indeed, in 2016–17 there were growing trade surpluses once mineral prices began to recover. Most disastrously for the macroeconomic balancing act, the net outflow of corporate dividends paid to owners of foreign capital was consistently more than $10 billion. Because repatriating profits must be done with hard currency, South Africa's external debt had, by mid-2018, soared to 50 per cent of GDP, topping $170 billion, from a level less than 16 per cent of GDP ($25 billion) in 1994.

Under the circumstances of a commodity supercycle growth boost prior to 2008, it may be surprising that no major global initiatives were taken from Pretoria aside from NEPAD – which soon faded in importance – and the follow-up African Peer Review Mechanism (APRM). The APRM was conceived so that African regimes would essentially review themselves with kid gloves, and, when civil society's own critique emerged, this was merely repressed (Bond 2009). The most notorious moment was Mbeki's dismissal of a December 2007 APRM report warning – 'xenophobia against other Africans is currently on the rise and must be nipped in the bud' – to which he replied that, this was 'simply not true' (SAPA 2007). In previous months, murders of shopkeepers (mainly Somali) occurred regularly in Western and Eastern Cape townships, and police brutality was notorious at the Lindela Repatriation Centre outsourced by the Department of Home Affairs. Then in May–June 2008, repeated xenophobic attacks over several weeks left at least 64 dead and at least 70 000 people displaced, mainly in the metropolitan areas of Johannesburg and Cape Town. Similar but lower-scale xenophobic upsurges were repeated in 2010 and 2015. The state's failure reflected, in part, a lack of structural analysis of tensions arising from the labour market, the housing market and the township retail market, as well as regional geopolitical pressures (especially against Zimbabweans and Congolese) (Amisi, Bond, Cele and Ngwane 2011).

FOIBLES OF CONTEMPORARY SUB-IMPERIAL POWER 2009–18

Ultimately, the most important feature of the anti-imperial/sub-imperial dialectic was Pretoria's maintenance of global neo-liberal corporate rule through multilateralism. When the consummate diplomat Mbeki was ousted from power in 2008, replaced by the much less sophisticated Zuma, South Africa enjoyed a brief respite from major world-event hosting responsibilities. Nevertheless, from 2009 to 2018 (the Zuma era), the three major events that advanced corporate-oriented multilateralism were: hosting FIFA World Cup leader Sepp Blatter's corrupt rule over international football in 2010; helping to forge a new, ineffectual global climate policy from 2009 to 2015 (especially as host to the UNFCCC in 2011); and providing the BRICS with an African 'deputy sheriff' ally starting in 2010. Considering each in turn, it appears that owing to the sub-imperial role Pretoria played in global governance, all three efforts backfired.

First, in 2010, the South African government (i.e. taxpayers) financed unprecedented FIFA World Cup profits by allowing the untaxed externalisation of $3.6 billion in revenue to FIFA headquarters in Zürich, Switzerland. The Mbeki-Zuma governments built (or rebuilt) ten stadiums across South Africa which mostly subsequently became 'white elephants'. In 2015, revelations from the US Federal Bureau of Investigation (FBI) confirmed that in order to win the hosting rights in 2004, a $10 million bribe had been paid to corrupt FIFA leaders by Mbeki's government.

Second, in 2011, the United Nations Conference of the Parties 17 (COP17) climate summit in Durban was, according to Washington's lead climate negotiator Todd Stern (2011), 'a significant achievement' for the US State Department. This was mainly because with Pretoria negotiators' help, Stern's delegation destroyed what he termed the 'firewall' between rich and poor countries (Stern 2011). Before that, the latter were not required to make emissions cuts in the earlier UN climate deals, especially the 2005 Kyoto Protocol. By 2015, Pretoria had joined the self-interested US, European Union and other BRICS regimes which together agreed the UNFCCC should *not* adopt binding emissions reduction commitments;

establish accountability mechanisms; incorporate military, maritime and air transport emissions; apply carbon taxation; dispense with (multiply-failing) carbon trading and offset gimmicks; respect historical 'polluter pays' responsibilities for the 'climate debt' covering 'loss and damage'; and compel fossil fuel owners to cease new exploration (and most current extraction) and simultaneously revalue their assets accordingly. The Paris Accord was, hence, labelled 'bullshit' by the world's leading climate scientist, James Hansen.

Third, in 2013, the BRICS heads of state summit was held in Durban, accompanied by prolific 'Gateway to Africa' claims about the importance to the guest countries and companies of having an African guide. Yet three days before the summit began, a firefight in the Central African Republic left more than a dozen South African troops dead (along with 800 local fighters), as they guarded Johannesburg businesses which operated thanks to tight relations between Pretoria and Bangui politicians (Bond 2016).

Two subsequent international mega-events hosted at the Sandton Convention Centre also revealed geopolitical relations. In mid-2015, the African Union's heads of state summit was dogged by controversy because of the presence of Sudanese president Omar al-Bashir, whom a South African court ruled should be arrested and deported for International Criminal Court (ICC) prosecution. Zuma blatantly ignored the ICC warrant, claiming his hosting responsibilities took precedence. In 2016, Zuma formally withdrew South Africa from the ICC, to the consternation of civil society, although the courts forced a reversal in early 2017. Zuma's camp made a compelling argument that the ICC was biased because, for example, it refused to prosecute the likes of former British prime minister Tony Blair – unequivocally an unrepentant war criminal (Chilcot, Freedman, Lyne and Prasher 2016) – yet the Pretoria government was perfectly happy to have Blair visit several times after the 2003 Iraq War and even sold Blair weapons for use in Iraq. Also in Sandton, in 2017, in a further example of Pretoria's blind eye to crimes committed by visiting dignitaries, Grace Mugabe – wife of Zimbabwean then president Robert Mugabe – allegedly attacked a young woman who was visiting Mugabe's son's Sandton hotel room, causing substantial facial injuries. Zuma provided Mugabe diplomatic immunity on apparently whimsical grounds (deemed unconstitutional a year later), allowing her to duck a police investigation and escape to Harare.

The second major event in Sandton in 2015 was the Forum for China–Africa Cooperation (FoCAC), which occurred just as China was radically reducing its purchases of African commodities, and as its dumping of steel led to the closure of South Africa's second-largest smelter (Evraz Highveld). Moreover, China's ubiquitous loans to African countries were beginning to come due, thus shutting down other hard currency outflows from countries, including oil exporters Nigeria and Angola. Embarrassing revelations were also emerging about the destructive local impacts of Chinese enterprises. In March 2016, for example, Mugabe implicated Chinese merchants in profits that went missing from Zimbabwe's Marange diamond fields (Mugabe claimed $15 billion in revenues were expected but only $2 billion materialised).

Other high-profile visits to South Africa included Bill Gates to deliver the Mandela Lecture in mid-2016 (Pheko 2016) and the World Economic Forum's mid-2017 Africa continental gathering in Durban. Taken together, this hosting profile suggests that South Africa remains the continent's most dynamic site for elite networking. In many of these cases – international football, climate policy and global economics – South Africa joins the BRICS as sub-imperial legitimators and facilitators of imperial interests, in spite of Zuma's claims to the contrary.

Three other major events in December 2015 strengthened the multilateral system at the expense of its periphery. The most obvious sub-imperial political stances taken by South African delegates occurred within the Paris climate summit (as noted above), but also in the WTO and IMF. In December 2015 in Nairobi, Pretoria and especially its BRICS allies helped craft a new WTO agreement that will end food sovereignty. The same month, the IMF's board was restructured so that four of the five sub-imperial BRICS countries won major increases in voting share (China 35 per cent, Brazil 23 per cent, India 11 per cent and Russia 8 per cent) while South Africa lost 21 per cent; Nigeria and Venezuela lost 41 per cent each, with most other African countries net losers.

Meanwhile, Pretoria's continent-wide power – both in economic and soft-diplomatic terms – was abused in many specific circumstances since the last countervailing example: Mandela's valiant but failed Nigerian intervention in 1995. So too have several high-earning South African corporations – MTN, mining houses, banks, retailers – super-exploited people and environments up-continent (Bond 2016). Although Mbeki, Zuma and Cyril Ramaphosa played decisive roles in various peace negotiations, the most substantial diplomatic victory they could claim on the African continent was the 2012 lobbying that allowed Zuma's ex-wife and former foreign minister Nkosazana Dlamini-Zuma to unseat Jean Ping as AU chair. Controversy surrounded this move, not only because the year before, Zuma had authorised a vote in the UN Security Council (UNSC) to allow a 'no-fly zone' in Libya enforced by the US and French air forces (against AU desires), resulting in Gaddafi's overthrow and ongoing regional destabilisation. Also, within the AU, other leading African governments (especially Nigeria, Egypt, Kenya and Algeria) had expected Pretoria to honour an informal pact that none of the major regional powers would take over leadership of the body.

The same controversy repeatedly emerged over Pretoria's claim to be the only African candidate sufficiently trustworthy (to the East and West) to seek a UNSC permanent seat, a claim Mugabe vetoed when he served as AU chairperson. He did so on grounds that at best, if it did materialise, that sole African seat would come without veto power and hence would be 'second-class' (an unacceptable compromise). Then, with Dlamini-Zuma serving as neither a popular nor effective AU chair, the pro-Zuma wing of the ANC lobbied hard for her to resign and stand against Ramaphosa in the December 2017 election for ANC president, a race she lost by a small margin.

Given such turmoil and resentment, it was already clear by 2012 that 'South Africa's foreign relations are becoming […] ineffective and the country is sliding down the scale of global competiveness and overall moral standing', in the words of government's National Development Plan (National Planning Commission 2012). Such standing declined due to incidents such as the 2016 al-Bashir affair, the Department of Home Affairs' repeated denial of visitor visas to the Dalai Lama (resulting from explicit Chinese pressure) starting in 2009, and Pretoria's votes at the UN Human Rights Commission against the victims of the Burmese military junta and homophobic Central African states' human rights violations (although the former stance was reversed in early 2019 and the latter in late 2016). The paucity of principled diplomats in the Department of International Relations and Cooperation (DIRCO) was exacerbated by a string of humiliating corruption allegations that stretched far and wide, including to the director general (Jerry Matjila), spokesperson (Clayson Monyela) and a chief director (Miriam Segabutla), and to high commissioners and ambassadors in the United States (Ebrahim Rasool), Britain (Obed Mlaba), Australia (Sbu Ndebele), the Netherlands (Vusi Bruce Koloane), Iran (Yusuf Saloojee), Uganda (Jon Qwelane) and Singapore (Hazel Francis Ngubeni). Only rarely did foreign minister Maite Nkoana-Mashabane take disciplinary action, and she was replaced in 2018 by Lindiwe Sisulu.

Managing sub-imperial relations is difficult when dubious politicians and officials understand the overall objective as personal or corporate rent-seeking rather than the ideals of human liberation. Occasionally, as in the cases above, the rot of corruption floats to the surface, and the scum conjoining the country's extreme consumerism and state–corporate patronage systems appears to suffocate any other values. The lack of any substantial prosecution of these men and women leaves South Africans embarrassed that US law enforcement agencies must step in when Pretoria cannot. (In another locally unpunished 2015 incident, Washington levied a $20 million fine against Hitachi for bribing the ANC on a $15 billion power plant contract.) The lack of accountability is also evident when, perhaps most spectacularly, PricewaterhouseCoopers (PWC 2018), which assessed corporate 'economic crime' on a biannual basis, from 2014 to 2018, gave the honour of world's most corrupt capitalist class to South Africa.

The structural conditions for this exceptional degeneracy come not only from the logic of capitalism, born in South Africa within colonialism and apartheid. There is also, finally, the malevolent influence of Western powers, which were apartheid's main allies for many decades notwithstanding their own citizens' growing anger, especially in the United States. To protect US corporate investment, to root out Islamic extremism and to keep control over rising African popular unrest (of the sort that in early 2011 overthrew the Mubarak regime in Egypt to such consternation and surprise at the US State Department), the Bush and Obama regimes dedicated an increasing amount of military support to these elites. Turse (2014) records the Pentagon's Africa Command (Africom) 'war fighting combatant command' in dozens of African countries, observing a still rather blunt division of labour at work between Washington and its deputy sheriff in Pretoria. Africom strategists explain why they train African militaries so aggressively, including the SANDF: 'We don't want to see our guys going in and getting whacked.' It was here that Zuma in August 2014 remarked:

> There had been a good relationship already between Africa and the US but this summit has reshaped it and has taken it to another level [...] We secured a buy-in from the US for Africa's peace and security initiatives [...] As President Obama said, the boots must be African (SAPA 2014).

Whether the same geopolitical agenda would remain intact after Barack Obama's replacement Donald Trump took office remained to be seen, but during most of 2017, Zuma avoided conflict. Both Zuma and Deputy President Ramaphosa were silent, for example, when in 2017 Trump banned citizens from four African countries – Chad, Libya, Somalia and Sudan – from even visiting the US.

CONCLUSION: SUB- AND ANTI- IN TENSION

The dialectic of vague anti-imperialist rhetoric and concrete sub-imperialist practice is rarely if ever discussed in polite academic circles, especially when it comes to the international relations and governance fields. Indeed, aside from myself, Dale McKinley (2004), Melanie Samson (2009) and Justin van der Merwe (2016), academics in South Africa have shied away from this conceptual apparatus, preferring instead mild-mannered notions of 'middle power' politics (for example, Schoeman 2000; Jordaan 2003; Alden and Schoeman 2016; Van der Westhuizen 2013; Monyae 2014); or 'hesitant hegemon' (Van Nieuwkerk 2014), a phrase more often applied (uncritically) to the US in the Middle East or Germany in Eastern Europe. Many analysts even consider the Pretoria regime to be a genuinely progressive force in world affairs, albeit with little or no reference made to the bulk of evidence to the contrary provided in the pages above (Landsberg 2007; Sidiropoulos 2014; Qobo and Dube 2015).

Yet this anti-/sub-imperialism dialectic should be second nature to critical intellectuals. After all, the interweaving of local and global corporate and state power takes extreme forms here, dating to the arrival of the Dutch East India Company settlers and their slaves in 1652. The influence of the global as articulated through local representatives remains obvious everywhere. In December 2015, financiers panicked when Zuma fired finance minister Nhlanhla Nene (claiming dishonestly that he was redeploying Nene to run the Johannesburg branch of the BRICS New Development Bank). They understood the ramifications of Desmond van Rooyen as Nene's replacement: 'state capture' and the Guptarisation of the Treasury. Within a few days, the local branch leaders of three major international financial institutions (Maria Ramos of Barclays-owned ABSA, Stephen Koseff of Investec, and Colin Coleman of Goldman Sachs), joined by the Chinese owners of Standard Bank, were capable of mobilising such persuasive power that Zuma was forced to replace Van Rooyen with Pravin Gordhan. Zuma complained bitterly about that pressure ever after. Over the next 18 months, the main banks and auditing firms cut off the Guptas' bank accounts and accounting services.

Another such decisive moment was the rapid response of the South African Police Service to London-based Lonmin's wildcat strike at its Marikana platinum mine in 2012 (Desai, Khanna, Hofmeyr, Kovel and Miller 2014). The key individual who ensured that the police force would meet worker protest with a 'more pointed response', according to emails he sent to minister of police Nathi Mthethwa a day before the Marikana massacre of 34 workers, was Ramaphosa, the 9 per cent local owner of Lonmin. At such moments of truth, in periods that can be considered crunch times when a great deal is at stake, the state–capital correlation is reaffirmed.

For Zuma, another global–local moment of truth came in September 2013, just prior to the 2014 elections, when the ANC suffered a dramatic fall in popular support as the rise of the leftist Economic Freedom Fighters (EFF) began in earnest (they took 6 per cent of that year's vote). The decision by Moody's to downgrade the South African National Roads Agency (Sanral) to junk status compelled Zuma's unpopular decision to legislate the Gauteng e-tolling system. This cost the ANC a large share of the province's vote eight months later and, by 2016, was still a factor when the ANC lost both the Johannesburg and Pretoria municipalities to an electoral coalition between the Democratic Alliance and EFF.

Resistance to corporate power sometimes generates countervailing trends of enormous importance. During the early 2000s, Aids medicines cost $10 000 per patient annually, due simply to the monopoly patent powers of foreign corporations. At the time, when the Treatment Action Campaign (TAC) demanded the medicines, Mbeki alleged the TAC was a stooge of transnational pharmaceutical corporations and the CIA. During a five-year period in which the ANC finally agreed to override Mbeki and authorise free antiretroviral treatment (ART), it was Mbeki's capacity to talk left so as to walk right that spread Aids-denialist confusion so far and wide in South Africa (Geffen 2010; Mbali 2013). But because of the TAC's campaigning, the global pressure against Mbeki had been relaxed already in 2001, when a patent exemption for essential medicines was fought for and won at the WTO summit in Doha. With that came a move to generic production, rollout of free treatment to nearly four million ART recipients, and a resulting rise in national life expectancy from 52 to 64 years from 2004 to 2018. This case fits a more general attempt at bottom-up internationalist solidarity, de-commodification and 'commoning' of resources. These processes characterised the new citizen movements' critique of the top-down internationalism of neo-liberalism and militarism.

A second inspiration for transcending imperial power comes from South Africa's anti-imperial/sub-imperial dialectic. The South African apartheid regime's 1970s–80s sub-imperialism was brutal (Seidman and Seidman 1977). Yet the anti-imperial forces in the liberation movements and their allies in the imperialist countries found that through public education and pressure, they had the ability to weaken the ties of international capital to apartheid by 1985. A breaking point was reached, and once white capital visited and seduced ANC leaders over the subsequent years, a new dialectical contradiction opened. Yet that particular strategy – later termed Boycott, Divestment and Sanctions – also gave hope for reversing adverse north–south power relations characteristic of multilateralism and the world economy during the neo-liberal era – for example, in relation to Israel's oppression of Palestinians and producers of fossil fuels, which, by the 2010s, were also subject to popular sanctions.

Ramaphosa's rule is likely to confirm both Western and BRICS' sources of the dialectic. Foreign direct investment was crashing across the world just as he took office (from 2016 to 2017, a 23 per cent decline globally, and 41 per cent in South Africa). South African trade suffered a longer-term fall (from 77 per cent of GDP in 2007 to 58 per cent in 2017). This 'de-globalisation' process may foil Ramaphosa's investment drive, even before considering Trump's new tariffs on steel, aluminium and auto exports to the US. There is no domestic political honeymoon either, as residual pro-Zuma characters cause more headaches, as worker militancy and community anger continue, and as painful budget cuts are demanded by the ratings agencies. No matter Ramaphosa's enormous talent, the longer-term vulnerabilities confirm the urgent need to break the global–local dialectic, perhaps to arrive at the next contradiction – between forces of capitalism and socialism.

REFERENCES

Alden, C. & Schoeman, M. 2016. Reconstructing South African identity through global summitry. *Global Summitry* 1(2): 187–204.

Amisi, B., Bond, P., Cele, N. & Ngwane, T. 2011. Xenophobia and civil society. *Politikon* 38(1): 59–83.

Associated Press. 2004. Mandela extends conciliatory hand to the US. *Washington Post,* 25 May.

Bond, P. 2003. *Against Global Apartheid.* London: Zed Books.

Bond, P. 2006. *Talk Left, Walk Right.* Pietermaritzburg: University of KwaZulu-Natal Press.

Bond, P. 2009. Removing Neocolonialism's APRM Mask: A Critique of the African Peer Review Mechanism. *Review of African Political Economy* 36(122): 595–603.

Bond, P. 2014. *Elite Transition: From Apartheid to Neoliberalism in South Africa.* London: Pluto Press.

Bond, P. 2016. BRICS Banking and the Debate over Sub-Imperialism. *Third World Quarterly* 37(4): 611–629.

Chilcot, J., Freedman, L., Lyne, R. & Prasher, U. 2016. *The Report of the Iraq Inquiry: Executive Summary.* Kingston upon Thames: Canbury Press.

Desai, R., Khanna, A., Hofmeyr, N., Kovel, J. & Miller, P. 2014. *Miners shot down* (DVD video). Johannesburg: Uhuru Films.

Geffen, N. 2010. *Debunking Delusions.* Johannesburg: Jacana Media.

Global Financial Integrity. 2015. Illicit Financial Flows from Developing Countries. Washington, DC, October. http://www.gfintegrity.org/report/illicit-financial-flows-from-developing-countries-2004-2013/ (accessed 15 July 2018).

Hansard. 2016. President Jacob Zuma's Oral Replies to Questions in the National Assembly. Cape Town, 23 November. https://pmg.org.za/hansard/23755/ (accessed 15 July 2018).

Jordaan, E. 2003. The concept of a middle power in international relations. *Politikon* 30(2): 165–181.

Landsberg, C. 2007. South Africa and the making of the African Union and NEPAD: Mbeki's 'progressive African agenda'. In: Adebajo, A., Adedeji, A. & Landsberg, C. (eds) *South Africa in Africa: The post-apartheid era.* Pietermaritzburg: University of KwaZulu-Natal Press.

Matiwane, Z. 2017. I was poisoned and almost died when SA joined Brics, says Zuma. *The Mercury,* 14 August. https://www.iol.co.za/news/special-features/zuma/i-was-poisoned-and-almost-died-when-sa-joined-brics-says-zuma-10782354 (accessed 15 July 2018).

Mbali, M. 2013. *South African Aids Activism and Global Health Politics.* London: Palgrave Macmillan.

McKinley, D. 2004. South African foreign policy towards Zimbabwe under Mbeki. *Review of African Political Economy* 31(100): 357–364.

Monyae, D. 2014. Learning to Lead: South Africa's Role in Africa – Lesotho, Zimbabwe, Burundi and the Democratic Republic of the Congo. Unpublished PhD thesis. Johannesburg: University of the Witwatersrand.

National Planning Commission. 2012. National Development Plan 2030. Pretoria: National Planning Commission.

Pheko, L. 2016. Mega-philanthropy: Charitable deeds or monopoly tyranny? *Pambazuka* 28: July. https://www.pambazuka.org/economics/mega-philanthropy-charitable-deeds-or-monopoly-tyranny (accessed 15 July 2018).

Politicsweb. 2016. I know who are the witches at work – Jacob Zuma. 19 November. http://www.politicsweb.co.za/news-and-analysis/i-know-who-are-the-witches-at-work-jacob-zuma (accessed 15 July 2018).

PricewaterhouseCoopers (PWC). 2018. Global Economic Crime Survey. Johannesburg. http://www.pwc.com/gx/en/services/advisory/consulting/forensics/economic-crime-survey.html (accessed 15 July 2018).

Qobo, M. & Dube, M. 2015. South Africa's foreign economic strategies in a changing global system. *South African Journal of International Affairs* 22(2): 145–164.

Samson, M. 2009. (Sub)imperial South Africa? Reframing the debate. *Review of African Political Economy* 36(119): 93–103.

SAPA. 2007. Mbeki critical of crime issues in APRM report. *Mail & Guardian*, 6 December. https://mg.co.za/article/2007-12-06-mbeki-critical-of-crime-issues-in-aprm-report (accessed 15 July 2018).

SAPA. 2014. Summit yields Agoa commitment. *IOL*, 7 August. http://www.iol.co.za/news/africa/summit-yields-agoa-commitment-1732265 (accessed 15 July 2018).

Schoeman, M. 2000. South Africa as an emerging middle power. *African Security Review* 9(3): 47–58.

Seidman, A. & Seidman, N. 1977. *South Africa and US Multinational Corporations*. Westport, CT: Lawrence Hill & Co.

Sidiropoulos, E. 2014. South Africa's Emerging Soft Power. *Current History* 113 (763): 197–202.

Stern, T. 2011. Durban wrap-up. United States State Department Email to Hillary Rodham Clinton. *WikiLeaks*, 31 December. https://wikileaks.org/clinton-emails/emailid/24887 (accessed 15 July 2018).

Turse, N. 2014. The US military has been 'At War' in Africa on the sly for years. *The Nation*, 14 April. https://www.thenation.com/article/us-military-has-been-war-africa-sly-years/ (accessed 15 July 2018).

Van der Merwe, J. 2016. Theorising emerging powers in Africa within the Western-led system of accumulation. In: Van der Merwe, J., Taylor, I. & Arkhangelskaya, A. (eds) *Emerging Powers in Africa: A New Wave in the Relationship?* London: Springer. http://link.springer.com/chapter/10.1007/978-3-319-40736-4_2 (accessed 15 July 2018).

Van der Westhuizen, J. 2013. Class compromise as middle power activism? Comparing Brazil and South Africa. *Government and Opposition* 48(1): 80–100.

Van Nieuwkerk, A. 2014. South Africa and the African peace and security architecture. *Journal of African Union Studies* 3(1): 37–60.

Williams, A. 2015. Report: Germany Paid Bribes to Host 2006 World Cup. *Handelsblatt*, 16 October. https://global.handelsblatt.com/companies/report-germany-paid-bribes-to-win-2006-world-cup-337653 (accessed 15 July 2018).

Zuma, J. 2017. Speech to the ANC. Reprinted in *Business Day*, 30 June. https://www.businesslive.co.za/bd/politics/2017-06-30-jacob-zumas-speech-to-the-anc--now-with-little-yellow-post-its/ (accessed 15 July 2018).

5

Governing Urban Food Systems: Lessons from Lusaka, Zambia

Caryn Abrahams

THE ESCALATING COST OF FOOD IN SOUTH AFRICA AND THE REST OF AFRICA

The cost of food is of great concern to governments – at national, provincial and local scales – to consumers, urban planners, development practitioners and producers, not only in the south but globally. In a 2017 report, The State of Food Security and Nutrition in the World, the Food and Agriculture Organization (FAO) asserts that globally, the escalating cost of food and the increasing control of food systems by powerful conglomerates are being further exacerbated by rising economic inequality and social discontent. The report says that

> [f]ood insecurity itself can become a trigger for violence and instability, particularly in contexts marked by pervasive inequalities and fragile institutions (FAO, IFAD, UNICEF, WFP and WHO 2017: 17).

Food insecurity, then, is not only a concern in regard to the cost of food, but has profound implications for political and societal stability.

In South Africa, Statistics South Africa (StatsSA) notes that food prices have soared since 2015, particularly of basic foodstuffs such as fresh fruit and vegetables, and grains and cereals, adversely affecting poor households (StatsSA 2016). The Gauteng provincial government has responded to rising food insecurity in the province by expanding its food assistance to indigent households. In his 2016 State of the Province Address (SOPA), Gauteng premier David Makhura indicated that the province had assisted over 227 000 residents through food banks in its various municipalities, and another almost 200 000 through food parcels and cooked meals at drop-in centres (South African Government 2016). He further acknowledged that the food security challenges facing the province lay not only in providing assistance to consumers, but also in supporting small farmers, agro-processing, urban agriculture and community gardens. Ordinary people, farmers and activists have initiated lobby efforts such as the Food Sovereignty Campaign, which seeks to engage the state, universities and big retail capital for more socially just solutions to increasing food security challenges faced by urban residents. As Makhura suggests, food insecurity is not just about the lack of food, but about the broader economic environment which produces inequalities. Yet the response did not essentially address systemic drivers of food poverty – of which the agribusiness and big retail capital are central. Instead, rather ironically, the address called for more socially just solutions to come from the very institutions to blame for food poverty. Despite the fact that Gauteng province has a food security plan (GDARD n.d.), there is no clear line of action in it to address the more systemic drivers of food poverty, or the way the province itself may be complicit in exacerbating food poverty.

In May 2016, a number of marches took place across South Africa to protest the high and increasing price of bread (Mogale 2016). These sentiments and the urgency they represent are not new, nor are they uniquely South African. In the aftermath of the 2008–9 global economic crisis, there has been a growing outcry about the cost of food by the urban poor and producers alike across the African continent, sparking a number of protests and also riots directed mainly at retailers (see Abrahams 2010).

Seen from a developmental perspective, the answer to the urban food crisis has tended to focus on urban agriculture as the panacea for urban food poverty (Abrahams 2011). Yet as Gareth Haysom and Jane Battersby-Lennard (2016) argue, seeing urban agriculture as a panacea assumes that the urban poor also have access to adequate land, inputs and knowledge. Instead, they urge governments to adopt a more systemic view of urban food insecurity which would make for strategic food security strategies, arguing that '[t]he state is largely unwilling to address the systemic drivers of food insecurity, which would entail regulating food companies and challenging the dominant development agenda' (Haysom and Battersby-Lennard 2016: 1).

Seen another way, outside a developmental perspective, as suggested by the last quote, the urban poor are also consumers, and food security (seen more expansively) not only requires developmental assistance from government, but also needs intervention in making food accessible to the urban poor – addressing in fact the systemic drivers of food insecurities. In 2013, the South African Department of Agriculture, Forestry and Fisheries (DAFF) with the Department of Social Development (DSD) published its National Policy on Food and Nutrition Security (NPFNS) (DSD and DAFF 2013). In it, there is recognition that food security is multifaceted and is not just a reflection of availability of food, and that tackling food security requires a coordinated approach between safety nets, production outputs, market interventions and agricultural assistance. It even goes so far as to acknowledge that 'household food security is threatened by globalisation, international trade regimes, climate change, and the poor storage and distribution of food' (DSD and DAFF 2013: 3). Yet despite recognition of 'trade regimes', the approach still considers the developmental aspects of food security as something discrete from domestic retail regimes. The notion of 'access to food', as seen in the document, does not implicate the range of actors in the food system that either encourage or inhibit opportunities for the (urban) poor to access food (see Frayne and Crush 2010), but rather focuses on technical and production-based aspects of an accessible agricultural system.

Furthermore, in trying to acknowledge a broader range of issues that affect food security, the NPFNS considers systemic thinking only so far as it means inclusion in value chains. This is, scholars argue, less than 'systemic' since the point of intervention is assumed to be at the level of agrifood chain, not policy oversight over the terms of inclusion. Agrifood scholars, speaking specifically to the urban context, suggest that 'if the evidence from other parts of the world is any guide, it is these agribusiness food chains, not small farmers, that are key to urban food security. The best that small farmers can hope for is some form of integration into these chains' (Frayne and Crush 2010: 7).

This argument complements a study about the role of supermarkets and other agribusiness firms in transforming the urban food landscape in Zambia, which argues that the state, and other non-state actors, have proven responsible for circumscribing the power of agribusiness food chains in significant ways by supporting alternative food retail markets and by instituting a measure of local sourcing (Abrahams 2010). However, recognising that access to food happens within a larger food system is not only about recognising the power of agribusiness and retail. Systemic thinking about the urban food system is essentially about recognising different players or agents within the urban political economy context, and the intersecting sets of rationalities, interests, imperatives and agendas which cumulatively shape the food system. This very act of expanding what the food system means helps us understand the governance challenges implicated in addressing urban food security.

This chapter examines the urban food supply system in Zambia and draws out important considerations for governance thinking outside the logics of the power of agribusiness capital. As a departure point, this chapter considers what governance means within discourses of agribusiness firms shaping food or value chains, and then retains key ideas about governance to think about the way the food system as a whole – including those firms – could be governed by food policy. The chapter offers considerations about governance thinking and concludes by making a case for an urban food policy in places, like Gauteng province, which has both food security and localised economic growth as mandates. The aim here is not to offer recommendations for content for such a policy, but to put forward ways of thinking about the form of such a governance policy (as social compact), and the intentionality (deliberative governance planning) that needs to inform it. It is hoped that the considerations in this chapter are useful to broader discourses on governance.

GOVERNING FOOD SYSTEMS

In the economic geography literature, governance of food systems is an integral part of discourse around global value chains, and the barriers to entry faced by producers to high-value markets driven by buyers and big retail. This body of work has shaped conceptions of more localised food chains, which looks at integrating farmers into markets, and has also focused on the power that retailers exert down the value chain, and across space (see Weatherspoon and Reardon 2003). While an important consideration, the conception of the value chain is significantly more nuanced – as seen in the global value chain literature. Peter Gibbon and Stefano Ponte (2005: 78), for instance, acknowledge the importance of agribusiness firms in shaping value chains right down to producers, in technical and transactional ways, in terms of quality and traceability. Although they do not specifically draw these out, they also acknowledge other forms of contractual subordination within value chains that have to do with access to social capital, or exploitative economic relationships between retailers and producers. From these forms of subordination and (often) exploitative transactions along the supply chain, we can conclude that exclusion rather than inclusion in high-value chains is one of the ways that agribusiness or *big food* retail controls food systems in very localised ways. Urban food systems, then, as a way of capturing the breadth of contractual relationships, allow us to see 'big food' fundamentally as creating other forms of economic and access exclusion, making the best hope for farmers, as an earlier quote suggested, a much more elusive endeavour.

If we expand Gibbon and Ponte's argument about governance over (global food) value chains by looking at other economic sociology studies, we are able to consider a wider range of actors or players in global production networks, which – as other scholars similarly note – 'shape the activities of firms in [the] particular locations' (Coe and Lee 2006: 66). In the studies which look at global electronics value chains and draw on a version of new institutional economics, scholars argue that non-firm institutions profoundly influence the way that lead firms embed in the local economy, and are themselves profoundly shaped by those particular contexts (Coe and Lee 2006; Coe, Dicken and Hess 2008; Bair 2008, 2009). This work, in sum, cautions the overly enthusiastic assumptions of neo-liberal retailers to deliver development gains. In practice, these large lead firms, together with non-firm actors and the state, can often govern production networks in profound ways. And if we add Gibbon and Ponte's argument about subordination and potentially exploitative oversight, then we must conclude that the outcomes for either producers, processors or consumers in those networks may not always be convivial. Seen in the food systems context, this work suggests that assuming that big food alone will administer the social goods envisaged in making food more accessible to the urban poor, is inadequate. Thus, even though economic networks or value chains are governed, the outcomes are typically more beneficial to buyers or big retail.

More recent work specifically on urban food governance in Africa seeks to describe the complexity of governance by outlining the 'range of governance actors with competing agendas' (Smit 2016: 84). In his comprehensive review of large bodies of work, Warren Smit finds that '[t]hese governance actors impact on urban food systems, and thus on urban food security, in a variety of ways', and asserts that while efforts have been made to develop urban food policies, for example, in Cape Town, South Africa (citing Haysom 2015), 'in general, the governance of urban food systems in African cities happens in an uncoordinated and unintegrated way' (Smit 2016: 82).

Smit details four forms of governance, the possible actors, and the typical infrastructural, political, economic and developmental concerns that may impinge on each. These are governance over urban and peri-urban agriculture; governance over distribution; governance over retail; and governance over safety/quality. Smit makes a useful distinction between these 'nodes' within the food system in order to review the actual and possible sets of governance actors and agendas. He also includes those influencing factors that may not necessarily or directly form part of food systems, such as, roads and infrastructure management, which inevitably come to have an effect on the food system's physical form. Yet he concedes that there remain gaps in our knowledge relating to the scale of cities (and city administrations), asserting that '[w]e need to better understand existing urban governance processes and the competing interests of urban governance actors in order to be able to collaboratively design interventions to improve urban food security in Africa' (Smit 2016: 84).

The Zambian example (described next), when one gazes within the urban food system, suggests a form of coordination or integration in governing the urban food supply system. This is not strung together haphazardly, but rather there appears to be a developmental rationality that runs through the food system, whether in promoting certain forms of interaction, or inhibiting other more exploitative forms of participation in these economic networks or value chains. This section does not review, in the same manner as Smit does, the range of possible and probable entities, agendas and structures that may influence the food system. Rather, it resonates with his concluding call to understanding existing city governance processes in order to design collaborative interventions. The view taken in this chapter is thus a consideration of a form of *deliberative governance*, 'coordinated' to an extent by the national farmers' union which represents both large- and small-format agribusiness, and lobbies the state on behalf of the formal agrifood system more generally. By deliberative governance, I mean forms of oversight, regulation and control over the outcomes of the food system that are intentionally directed to particular ends. This is in contrast to forms of governance that can be read as incidental, in that they happen to impact on the food system, but not intentionally in the aim of changing the outcome of that food system (Smit's [2016] version of infrastructures that shape food systems is a case in point).

The point is that the governance of food systems is happening anyway, by the breadth of actors and existing agendas within the food system as it plays out on the ground. The *intentionality of governance* is what is at issue here, functioning as tacit knowledge – not in terms of agricultural know-how but in terms of sets of rationalisations or governmentalities. There is indeed no integrated urban food policy that guides or regulates interactions within the food system per se, but this does not mean that the food system is ungoverned.

INTERSECTING GOVERNANCE: LUSAKA'S URBAN FOOD SYSTEM

In the Zambian case, my research shows intersecting sets of governance prerogatives that together shape the urban food system in its capital city, Lusaka. The research was conducted in 2007–2009, and included empirical findings from the poultry industry, and the fresh fruit and vegetable markets in the city. The governance considerations mentioned earlier informed the study, which was conducted using personal interviews, archival work and observation.

The urban food system encompasses a range of actors or players, which include the national farmers' union, agribusiness, supermarkets, wet markets (more commonly called informal markets), consumers, and city management. Each of these players has particular rationalities that inform the shape of their transactional relationships within the food chain. These rationalities may be developmental – providing affordable food for urban residents; economic – securing profit and market expansion; or localising – placing demands on big business to meet local demands. But these rationalities are also not discrete from particular players within the food system, or fundamentally at odds with other rationalities; they often present overlapping imperatives and shared interests.

In the case of the National Milling Corporation, a parastatal-turned-private-company acquired by the multinational Seaboard Kansas, the manner of sourcing maize for sale to consumers as the staple, and to poultry firms as feed, suggests that the local context profoundly shapes its business practice. Even though it is, in a sense, an agribusiness corporation, it sources from small-scale farmers at preferential rates, incentivising upgrades in the quality of product. This can be seen as a method of inclusion rather than the typically exclusive value chain practices of big food, which tends to centralise its supply from larger farms, able to absorb the quality requirements of these firms. The Zambian manager of National Milling asserts that this practice is not just logical since more than half the country's farmers are smallholders, but that it is also a commitment to developing the local economy. Similarly, a large poultry breeder (Ross Breeders) specifically argues that their business model is responsive not only to the local context in terms of sales (selling poultry to consumers and day-old chicks to producers), but also in terms of sourcing and growing capacity. Both these firms could grow much faster and engage in export. Instead, they have chosen the slower process of incremental growth while upskilling small producers in the area.

The case of the South African supermarket chain Shoprite, which entered Zambia in 1995, provides a similarly interesting insight. In Zambia, the chain has faced fierce criticism because of the way it uses notions of quality to exclude local producers from its value chain, thereby justifying its exploitative business practice (Miller 2008: 4). As a result, Shoprite faces extraordinary pressure from the Zambian government around its labour practices, and to source locally, which Kenny and Mather (2008) argue disciplines the power of the conglomerate. The supermarket chain, in turn, recognises this imperative. Yet its senior management in South Africa declared in an interview, 'We cannot just accept anything; it's like "we understand you are poor, but we've got a business to run"' (Interview: Head of Operations in Africa, Shoprite, Western Cape, 2007). Indeed, the supermarket has proven to hold significant power in the food chain, but its management admits that its image is at stake, and recalls (violent) riots outside Zambian stores about local sourcing.

The Zambian National Farmers' Union (ZNFU) comprises different (private) producer and processing associations – fresh produce, poultry, seed, fertiliser, animal feed, meat and dairy. The ZNFU frequently lodges collective lobbies against some of its own members (big agrifood business), supermarkets, and the government. In the first instance, it can make collective appeals to big food companies to provide training to small producers wishing to enter a formal supply chain; or lobby firms to double up their capacity to support other enterprises – for example, to agree to transport goods from outside the capital, which tends to be a big expense for small producers to bear. It also places pressure on supermarkets to source locally. It lobbies the state to provide electricity and water subsidies for agricultural producers on the peri-urban fringe of the city, and where a fair amount of food products are grown/reared. The ZNFU underscores the interconnectedness of the food system through its mediating role, and its dexterity in engaging the state in its decision-making about trade tariffs, export limits and price parities across years with variable rainfall. As noted already, the case of Zambia's urban food system suggests a reading of urban food systems elsewhere in Africa, where

> greater agency of local players in the changes that occur in the food systems is fostered by proactive domestic commitment to disciplining the dominance of supermarkets and other foreign food agro-processing firms, compelling them to adhere to local priorities of sourcing and procurement. Underlying this is the recognition of state openness to foreign investment, but there remains a need to balance this with a strong commitment to protecting and nurturing the domestic economy more generally (Abrahams 2010: 131).

The final case I wish to present here is that of the urban informal market in Lusaka. It is a thriving space where producers meet intermediaries and consumers, and where the bulk of locally produced fresh produce is sold and bought by urban residents. Although it faces some competition from the supermarket chains in Zambia, the market manager argues that 'we are not going anywhere' since the market caters to less affluent consumers, and has significantly upgraded its facilities in order to attract upwardly mobile residents who may have started shopping at the supermarket for symbolically aspirational reasons. The city management has pumped a large amount of money into the market – 'to modernise it', to upgrade its cold storage, retail spaces, and hygiene services (Interview: City Market Manager, Lusaka, July 2007) – and into supporting market trader associations. The Lusaka city management has also aligned the market upgrade with a large investment in public transport – the transport facility sits alongside the market, making it a logical hub for the movement of people, goods and wealth. The management also actively seeks the participation of urban consumers and informal traders in the planning processes. What we see in this case is increasing governance over the second (or informal) economy, which is often assumed to be ungoverned. As argued elsewhere,

> [i]nstitutional support for the informal food economy and traditional forms of retailing through processes of formalization and commercialization enhance its resiliency. These institutional interventions have implications for the future potential of the retail enterprise, as for the progressive development of informal market economies (Abrahams 2010: 133).

These cases give us a small sense of the ways in which different players in the food system shape it in interesting and often unexpected ways. In so doing, the firms, union, supermarket and market management constitute multiple sites of power. Governance can thus be seen as the tendency for institutions to further particular interests; to oversee and to promote/inhibit certain kinds of economic transaction; or to otherwise regulate the way economic interaction happens. Unlike the value chains governance model, what we see in this case is not simply 'who governs whom'; instead, we see intersecting modes of governance where actors in the food system circumscribe or bear up other actors' power in uneven ways. These are underpinned by particular (economic) developmental governmentalities.

There are no neat alignments of agendas with particular players or agents, since there are necessarily overlapping rationalities, as seen through the perspectives shared here. Thus institutions do not 'act' as a de-personified economic force in technical terms of high value, inclusion or exclusion. These are complex economic and developmental subjectivities, which, as I will show later, complicate the idea of what is the public versus private interest. We see also that different kinds of firms have similar sets of imperatives – upgrading supply chains or growing the local economy – since a growing consumer base benefits the local economy and local consumers, as well as big food retail.

Reading again from economic sociology, some of the institutions discussed here 'operationalise particular political and developmental priorities' (North 1991: 97) and offer a curious sense of mutuality that imbibes non-tangible factors that influence economic growth (see Granovetter 1982). More importantly, the mutuality seen in these cases has implications for the accessibility of food in the Zambian city. It suggests that urban residents' access to food is not simply divided on the basis of affluence, where some access food from higher-end outlets and less nutritious options are fobbed off on the urban poor (indeed, this may be because supermarkets have also expanded into smaller-format neighbourhood stores in areas outside the urban core). This shared sense of mutuality also comes to bear on facilitating markets for small producers, and lobbying the state for subsidies or incentives for the food system. Residents, in turn, are the beneficiaries of accessible, affordable and good-quality food, as a result of these almost deliberative forms of governance.

While this presents a somewhat romantic picture of the mutualities of deliberatively governing urban food systems, there remains a caution that the food system is not shaped only by those who participate in that food system – although not in the general sense that Smit shows. For instance, in an ongoing study between activists and academics in Philippi in the Western Cape, urban residential developers are seen to 'externally' shape the food system in quite damaging ways. This does not impinge on consumption access *within* the food chains themselves, as much as it has impacts on food security. The large lobby group opposed the seemingly approved development site which would encroach on the Philippi Horticultural Area (PHA). The group cited the surprising 'ease' with which environmental assessments were done and the failure of the mayor's office to include the evidence-based arguments made on behalf of the PHA on impacts on the water source and agricultural production of communities (see Future Cape Town 2016).

What the PHA case suggests for the governance of food systems is that not all forms of deliberative governance will be self-evidently beneficial for poor communities, as it may be in the Zambian case. In other words, even where there were deliberative processes of engagement with local communities, and mechanisms for gathering inputs from a wide range of governance actors, the outcome was not co-governed equitably. Instead, the mere recognition of the various governance actors did not translate into an egalitarian valuing of their agendas, demands or agency. Thus while the process was 'open' to state lobbying, the outcome of that governance process demonstrated that certain voices were heard more loudly than other voices, and developer capital interests were valued more highly than the communities who use that space and benefit from its protection. The key questions are what this means for governance of food systems, and what the purpose of governance thinking in this context is: What is the work of governance thinking? Why is it helpful to think in these terms?

GOVERNANCE THINKING

In answering such questions as 'what is the work of governance thinking?' or 'what does governance thinking achieve?', a first consideration is the idea of 'public interest'. Johan den Hertog (2010) reviews in detail the assumptions contained in regulatory policy (in general terms), as it pertains to public versus private interest. He asks a similar question of regulation policy – what does it do? He concludes, by looking at a range of public services and private technologies, that the governance task at hand is figuring out who the guarantors of such 'inclusive' sets of interests are. He argues that even regulatory agencies, which seek to formally and legislatively govern flows of services, commodities or knowledge, find themselves caught between conflicting interests (for example, developmental and economic), and having to trade certain interests off against other interests (Den Hertog 2010: 46). He argues that states cannot always claim to act in the public interest, and the state is often politically at odds with its own citizens. He also points to the unevenness in which parastatal-turned-private-firms play out their particular interests. These are never clearly either public interest or private interest. He also mentions hierarchies of power within 'the public' and those who advocate for public interest regulation. He further asks, given the above, who should take the lead in decision-making, assuming there was an open process of contestation. His discussion raises important questions for governance thinking. Is governance thinking in service of the public interest? And should governance be seen in this normative way, anyway?

Elizabeth Olson and Andrew Sayer (2009) make a case for normative political theory which seeks to identify what kinds of social organisation are conducive to the well-being of all, and preclude the many different kinds of oppression and avoidable suffering. '[It] concerns well-being and its preconditions, and difficult though these are to define, discover and create, they are not merely a product of collective wishful thinking' (Olson and Sayer 2009: 184–185). From this viewpoint, food governance thinking needs to find space within a broader policy framework so that it is positioned in a mandate that centres on the interests of the public.

The rest of this chapter, through a normative moral imagination lens, seeks to think through ways of achieving deliberative forms of governance – as a form of social compact – that will shape urban food systems in a manner that will ultimately benefit the urban poor. The discussion so far suggests that governance of a particular set of institutions – in this case, agrifood institutions – does not translate necessarily to equitable beneficial outcomes for all in that institution. The rest of the chapter considers governance thinking as framed normatively.

If we recall the meaning of governance as seen from an economic geography perspective, governing food systems may mean forms of subordination and over-sight of transactions in that food system, which may indeed be exclusionary and exploitative. Other chapters in this book discuss the idea of 'good governance' as a framework to thinking about transparent, fair outcomes within public manage-ment. Seen in a different way, just because food systems are governed does not necessarily mean they are governed well, or with benevolent intentions. Yet as some of the cases show, there are surprising mutualities that can be seen in the way firms govern their supply chains. The nature of capital accumulation in these firms asserts a form of governance that is logical in neo-liberal terms, but may be profoundly *not good*, in terms of the exploitative relationships within them, or the uneven power that different agents within a food system may have. As Haysom and Battersby-Lennard (2016) rightly argue, the issue at stake is the absence of concerted urban food strategies or policies in the global south more generally. But what, in the end, is the purpose of governance thinking if it is not also to guarantee a set of just or equitable outcomes for those within and affected by that (food) system?

If we see deliberative governance as a means to equitable agency within (food) systems, then governance thinking needs to go beyond mere recognition of the various factors/actors/agendas that come into play, and towards supporting the agency of residents/consumers/users in decision-making processes. It also needs to recognise the sets of interests represented by these various actors, and seek to discipline large agribusiness firms. It is a normative assumption of neo-liberal markets that retail or big food acts in ways that are simply procedural or technical. Instead, the forms of governance by big retail firms – subordination, oversight, and decision-making power – are also 'neo-liberally' rational. And, quite obviously, these forms of governance continue whether they are recognised or not. Thus food systems appear to be 'unintentionally' governed, but may hide sets of logics that are assumed to be 'just the way the market works', and thus outside public or political scrutiny.

Further, even if there are deliberative forms of governance that become part of urban policy, which would include consumers, communities of users, the state and private capital, there is no guarantee that the outcome will be equitable. Just because there are multiple voices that are recognised as being important to the food system, it does not automatically follow that these sets of agencies are valued equally. Deliberative governance towards equitable agency would mean that these sets of neo-liberal logics are not privileged, nor are the demands of urban consumers crowded out. Indeed, this raises further questions about certain everyday consumption demands seen as privileged, particularly those demands that come from affluent consumers. On one hand, not all consumers are poor; and on the other, those who are affluent typically have different sets of demands in a food system as compared to basic rights to food. Within discourses on food sovereignty, the escalating cost of basic foodstuffs serves as a quasi-subsidy for elitist expansion of food retail (see Patel 2009). The demands of affluent consumers, such as for organic or paleo food, fair trade or local sourcing, are more likely to find resonance with higher-end retailers who specifically cater to these demands. This, in sum, leaves the everyday demands of the poor, under the right to food, unmet. As a result, the only space for voicing these demands is through protests against food inflation of basic food, with the unsurprising anger that sometimes accompanies these protests – essentially from outside of the food system.

Food sovereignty is concerned with the rights of people to craft food policy in ways that meet their right to food. But as Raj Patel (2009) teases out, the right to food is often cast as a right to assert what food people can buy, rather than issues of access. He shows how the rights-based approach to food is often conflated with consumer rights to access markets. In this sense, food sovereignty for the urban poor is often cast as a contest between protesting high prices and demanding greater access. Patel (2009: 670) concludes that the food sovereignty challenge relies on 'radical egalitarianism', in which the urban poor's 'capacity to shape food policy can be exercised at all appropriate levels'.

In its official response to the South African government's National Policy on Food and Nutrition Security, the Food Sovereignty collective states, in a campaign declaration:

> We are not simply calling for technical solutions for households to access food as encapsulated in the governments' recently proposed National Food and Nutrition Security Policy and Implementation Plan. We reject the latter and instead are calling for the deep transformation of our food system by breaking the control of food corporations, repositioning the state to realise the Constitutional right to food as part of creating the conditions and space for the emergence of food sovereignty alternatives from below (Food Sovereignty Campaign 2015).

It is precisely the repositioning of state imaginaries that is at issue here. We can thus think of deliberative governance as a set of national imperatives for inclusion, where various governance actors are not recognised only in retrospect as having something to do with the (food) system, or as anonymised potential users or 'stakeholders', but are actively sought for their agency in the food system. The distinction I am making here is between seeing governance of food systems, as a backward-looking appraisal of the governance actors and agendas that are likely to have shaped the food system; and a forward-looking argument about deliberative or inclusive governance which considers the conditions for food sovereignty to emerge. The appraisal-of-governance view seeks to understand the factors that account for the current food system – even though, as Smit (2016) concludes, it is important to consider future collaborative design of food systems in view of existing city-level governance. The deliberative governance view seeks to insert an intentionality in policy terms into food systems which 1) constrains actors within food systems to function in ways that are just; 2) recognises, includes and allows the agencies of typically invisible actors such as communities or the urban poor to actually shape the food system; and 3) considers the existing forms of city-level governance as intrinsic to shaping the food system and, conversely, considers how the urban consumption imperatives shapes the form of city-level governance.

The first view of governance is positivist, while the second is normative. The first assumes that the food system is a set of unmalleable economic practices, logics and transactions within the food system. The second contends that the food system is malleable in that the logics that inform it should not be taken for granted – it could be influenced by different sets of rationalities. Food governance is a future-oriented view that would include an urban food policy and strategy of the kind Jane Battersby (2012) has argued for and has been involved in co-producing in the Western Cape (discussed later). This deliberative view of governance asserts that there are no preordained sets of outcomes within the food system – these outcomes are continuously attainable and place limits on erstwhile unfettered market logics and actions.

THE TASK AT HAND: TOWARDS URBAN FOOD STRATEGIES

Up to now, this chapter has discussed what governance thinking might entail: it encompasses a food systems view which makes sense of the contested forms of power within it; it is deliberative or intentional; it values the agencies of users, consumers and the urban poor; and it pays special attention to inclusion within the food system. An earlier section mentioned the importance of urban food policies which would be an outcome of future-oriented governance thinking.

As Battersby (2012) argues, an urban food policy would include a food security mandate and inform a range of choices within the food system, which directly influences city planning, economic growth, and ultimately also possibilities for the urban poor to access adequate food. Speaking to the need for an urban food strategy in Cape Town, she argues that:

> [t]he absence of a food security mandate for the city means that there is no food focus in spatial planning and economic development, which may lead to policies and by-laws that ultimately undermine urban food security. [… I]f the City had a food mandate and better understood the role that the informal food retail sector plays in the urban food system, more inclusive approaches would be taken to managing this sector (Battersby 2012: 20, 22).

Elsewhere, she argues that this mandate could in fact be included in urban planning policies, which exist already and have a broad urban mandate that encompasses issues of equality and the well-being of urban residents (Battersby 2018). Within this, she argues, is the potential for planners to do what they already have a mandate to do in an urban policy framework, while including a stronger knowledge of the food system more broadly – not just in terms of food provisioning per se, but also in terms of non-food planning decisions that have profound impacts on the kind of food system that is produced (Battersby 2018).

In addition to the content of future urban (food) policies, which may also include monitoring inflation and keeping big retail accountable to localised developmental concerns, what form could this policy take – ontologically speaking?

From the analysis in this chapter, we can conclude that an urban food policy would essentially be a forward-looking mandate for equitable and inclusive governance of food systems (with a flexible understanding of the contestations and mutualities that constitute the food system). While it would be state policy (at whatever tier of government), the (urban or local) state would not be the sole guarantor of such a mandate. Instead, an urban food policy would in essence be a form of social compact, with private and public sector accountability inscribed in it. An urban food policy or mandate would shape political discourse about what is in the public interest and what is in the private interest; seek to equitably manage the range of interests, demands and governmentalities that necessarily form part of urban food systems; and define procedures for adjudicating contestation. And finally, if we borrow from the economic geography literature, we recall that governing food systems also necessarily means modes of oversight and subordination. Thus, most importantly, an urban food policy should unapologetically be a normative document, which seeks to protect the rights to food of the poor, through subordination of the unfettered interests of capital, and oversight of potentially exploitative economic relationships within food systems. In the South African context, this process of including governance of food in the way I have outlined it in this chapter has implications both for the NPFNS and future city-region and provincial policies, and planning (as Battersby [2018] details). In addition to discrete areas of specific intervention, this chapter compels a rethinking of the ways that implicate the state's own choices about infrastructure planning, and oversight over the seemingly unfettered power of retail capital. Unless governance thinking at this level changes the choices of policy and planning intervention by the state, its programmatic interventions for agricultural support, or market access for small farmers, are not likely to have the kind of impact imagined by collectives and academic activists involved in food sovereignty movements.

ACKNOWLEDGEMENTS

The author is grateful for comments from the reviewers, and inputs by fellow panellists and participants at the Food and Nutrition Seminar: How Food and Nutrition Security is Understood and Measured, hosted by CLEAR-AA in November 2016 (Parktown, Johannesburg), where parts of this paper were presented.

REFERENCES

Abrahams, C. 2010. Transforming the region: Supermarkets and the local food economy. *African Affairs* 109(434): 115–134. https://doi.org/10.1093/afraf/adp068.

Abrahams, C. 2011. Supermarkets and urban value chains: Rethinking the developmental mandate. *Food Chain* 1(2): 206– 222. https://doi.org/10.3362/2046-1887.2011.018.

Bair, J. 2008. Analysing global economic organization: embedded networks and global chains compared. *Economy and Society* 37(3): 339–364.

Bair, J. 2009. Global commodity chains: Genealogy and review. In: Bair, J. (ed.) *Frontiers of Commodity Chain Research*: 1–34. Stanford, CA: Stanford University Press.

Battersby, J. 2012. Urban food security and the urban food policy gap. In: *Strategies to Overcome Poverty and Inequality*: 1–27. Cape Town: Carnegie, III 3–7 September. http://carnegie3.org.za/docs/papers/18_Battersby_Urban%20food%20security%20 and%20urban%20food%20policy%20gap.pdf (accessed 2 February 2019).

Battersby, J. 2018. Cities and urban food poverty in Africa. In: Bhan, G., Srinivas, S. & Watson, V. (eds) *The Routledge Companion to Planning in the Global South*. London: Routledge.

Coe, N.M., Dicken, P. & Hess, M. 2008. Global production networks: realizing the potential. *Journal of Economic Geography* 8(3): 271–295.

Coe, N.M. & Lee, Y.S. 2006. The strategic localization of transnational retailers: the case of Samsung-Tesco in South Korea. *Economic Geography* 82(1): 61–89.

Den Hertog, J. 2010. Review of Economic Theories of Regulation. Utrecht School of Economics Discussion Paper Series. Utrecht: Tjalling C. Koopmans Research Institute. http://www.uu.nl/sites/default/files/rebo_use_dp_2010_10-18.pdf (accessed 2 February 2019).

Department of Social Development (DSD) & Department of Agriculture, Forestry and Fisheries (DAFF). 2013. National Policy on Food and Nutrition Security. Pretoria: DSD & DAFF. http://www.nda.agric.za/docs/media/NATIONAL%20POLICYon%20food%20and%20nutriri003ion%20security.pdf (accessed 2 February 2019).

FAO, IFAD, UNICEF, WFP & WHO. 2017. The State of Food Security and Nutrition in the World 2017: Building resilience for peace and food security. Rome: FAO. http://www.fao.org/3/a-I7787e.pdf (accessed 2 February 2019).

Food Sovereignty Campaign (FSC). 2015. Declaration of South African Food Sovereignty Campaign. *Climate and Capitalism*, 5 March. http://climateandcapitalism.com/2015/03/05/declaration-south-african-food-sovereignty-campaign/ (accessed 2 February 2019).

Frayne, B. & Crush, J. 2010. *Pathways to Insecurity: Food Supply and Access in Southern African Cities*. Urban Food Security Series No. 3. Cape Town: African Food Security Urban Network (AFSUN). http://www.afsun.org/wp-content/uploads/2013/09/AFSUN_3.pdf (accessed 2 February 2019).

Future Cape Town. 2016. Why the Philippi Horticultural Area Matters: Securing Cape Town's Water, Food and Economic Security. *Our Future Cities*, 11 February. http://futurecapetown.com/2016/02/7-reasons-building-on-philippi-horticultural-area-makes-no-sense/#.V1JrgWZO-Rv (accessed 2 February 2019).

GDARD. n.d. Gauteng Department of Agriculture and Rural Development Strategic Plan 2010–2014. http://www.gauteng.gov.za/Document%20Library/Agriculture%20and%20Rural%20Development/AGRICULTURE%20APP.pdf (accessed 2 February 2019).

Gibbon, P. & Ponte, S. 2005. *Trading Down: Africa, Value Chains, and the Global Economy*. Philadelphia: Temple University Press.

Granovetter, M. 1982. The strength of weak ties: a network theory revisited. In: Marsden, P. & Linn, N. (eds) *Social Structure and Network Analysis*: 105–130. Beverly Hills, CA: Sage.

Haysom, G. 2015. Food and the City: Urban Scale Food System Governance. *Urban Forum* 26(3): 263–281. https://doi.org/10.1007/s12132-015-9255-7 (accessed 7 February 2019).

Haysom, G. & Battersby-Lennard, J. 2016. Why urban agriculture isn't a panacea for Africa's food crisis. *The Conversation,* 15 April. http://theconversation.com/why-urban-agriculture-isnt-a-panacea-for-africas-food-crisis-57680 (accessed 7 February 2019).

Kenny, B. & Mather, C. 2008. Milking the region? South African capital and Zambia's dairy industry. *At Issue eZine: Africa Files* 2: 1–8.

Miller, D. 2008. Food frontiers in Zambia: resistance and partnership in Shoprite's retail empire. *At Issue eZine: Africa Files* 3: 1–11.

Mogale, K. 2016. SAFSC Members march against high price of bread. *EWN News*, 13 May. Online edition. http://ewn.co.za/2016/05/13/Dozens-march-against-high-price-of-bread (accessed 7 February 2019).

North, D.C. 1991. Institutions. *Journal of Economic Perspectives* 5(1): 97–112.

Olson, E. & Sayer, A. 2009. Radical Geography and its Critical Standpoints: Embracing the Normative. *Antipode* 41(1): 180–198. http://doi.org/10.1111/j.1467-8330.2008.00661.x (accessed 7 February 2019).

Patel, R. 2009. Food Sovereignty. *The Journal of Peasant Studies* 36(3): 663–706. https://doi.org/10.1080/03066150903143079 (accessed 7 February 2019).

Smit, W. 2016. Urban Governance and Urban Food Systems in Africa: Examining the Linkages. *Cities* 58(1): 80–86. http://www.africancentreforcities.net/wp-content/uploads/2016/05/SMIT-Urban-governance-and-urban-food-systems-in-Africa.pdf (accessed 7 February 2019).

South African Government. 2016. State of the Province address delivered by Gauteng Premier, Honourable David Makhura at Saul Tsotetsi Sports Complex in Sebokeng Township, Sedibeng District Municipality, Gauteng, 22 February. http://www.gov.za/speeches/premier-david-makhura-gauteng-state-prov-state-province-address-2016-22-feb-2016-0000 (accessed 19 February 2019).

StatsSA. 2016. Taking Stock of Food Prices. Pretoria: Statistics South Africa. http://www.statssa.gov.za/?p=6421 (accessed 20 April 2018).

Todes, A. 2014. The Impact of Policy and Strategic Spatial Planning. In: Todes, A., Wray, C., Götz, G. & Harrison, P. (eds) *Changing Space, Changing City: Johannesburg after Apartheid*. Johannesburg: Wits University Press.

Weatherspoon, D. & Reardon, T. 2003. The rise of supermarkets in Africa: Implications for agrifood systems and the rural poor. *Development Policy Review* 21(3): 333–355.

6

African Crisis Leadership: A West African case study

Anthoni van Nieuwkerk and Bongiwe Ngcobo Mphahlele

'[…] crises are the unwanted by-product of complex systems'
(Boin, 't Hart, Stern and Sundelius 2005: 6)

INTRODUCTION

When a crisis violently disrupts a society's way of life, who reacts first? And how? In this chapter we use recent crisis management conceptual frameworks to explore the African dimensions. Do African decision makers and leaders approach crises differently from their counterparts elsewhere? Indeed, how do they make sense of a chaotic, even catastrophic situation, and act to preserve and protect what they can? Do they – and the institutions within which they operate – learn any lessons? We draw on the dynamics of the Ebola crisis that afflicted West Africa in 2014 and 2015 to explore the conceptual assumptions.

The patterns of response and early warning observed in our West African case study (Liberia, Guinea and Sierra Leone) lead us to conclude that weak governance is a challenge that goes beyond fragile health systems. In this chapter, we demonstrate the correlation between the spread of the disease and poor governance. We do this by pointing out how poor crisis management and weak institutions exacerbated the spread of Ebola.

The chapter concludes with an assessment of the value of crisis management models; points to areas in which it can be strengthened for use in settings where fragile states exist; and, finally, reflects on the underlying reasons for weaknesses, absences and failures in such states.

ORIENTATION

A crisis is a sudden and unexpected event that threatens an established way of life. Crises tend to disrupt people's understanding of the world around them, therefore testing the resilience of a group or society, and often exposing the shortcomings of its leaders and public institutions. Another way to understand crisis is to think of it as 'breakdowns of familiar symbolic frameworks that legitimate the pre-existing sociopolitical order' (Boin, McConnell and 't Hart 2008: 3). Anti-imperialists tend to view these 'breakdowns' as problems of capital accumulation – when a system's reproduction cannot be self-corrected using the internal logic of the system (Cox 1987: 269). It may very well be that external intervention is required, an aspect we will examine below. From the perspective of the complexity paradigm, crisis is understood as escalatory processes that undermine a social system's capacity to cope with disturbances. The agents of disturbance may come from anywhere, but the cause of the crisis lies in the inability of the system to deal with the disturbance through established or routine processes. Indeed, the causes typically remain unnoticed – or key policymakers fail to notice them. In the process leading up to a crisis, seemingly innocent factors combine and transform into disruptive forces that come to represent an undeniable threat to the system.

Crisis leadership denotes a set of actions undertaken by a leader to bring about immediate change in people's behaviour and beliefs, as well as to achieve needed outcomes (Alkharabsheh, Ahmad and Kharabsheh 2013). In a crisis situation, a leader provides stability, reassurance, confidence and a sense of control (Alkharabsheh *et al.* 2013). However, Vera and Crossan (2004) suggest that no one leadership style is appropriate for all situations. In fact, not much research is available on how leaders effectively respond to a crisis (Hadley, Pittinsky, Sommer and Zhu 2011), and so we cannot easily identify the 'ideal type' of leader to manage a crisis, whether they be a 'transactional' or a 'transformative' leader.

In sum, we can view disaster management as an intervention phase (response) in the political management of crisis.

Conceptual approach to political crisis management

Our interest lies with the strategic rather than managerial dimensions of crisis management. Relevant literature (Boin *et al.* 2005) suggests crises make and break political careers, shake bureaucratic pecking orders and shape organisational destinies. Crises fix the spotlight on those who govern. As Boin *et al.* (2005: ix) note,

> [m]any experienced policymakers understand this catalytic momentum in crises. They may talk about national unity and the need for consensus in the face of a shared predicament, but this reflects only part of their reasoning. Their other calculus, less visible to the public, concerns contested issues: dilemmas of responsibility and accountability, of avoiding blame and claiming credit.

Clearly then, crisis management is in part a political process. Public leaders must manage a crisis in the interests of society, and in so doing demonstrate the interplay of power, conflict and legitimacy. In the discussion that follows we will examine the performance of African leaders when faced with a significant crisis.

Based on the assumption that public leaders understand that they have a responsibility to help safeguard society from the adverse consequences of a crisis, the research team comprising Boin, 't Hart, Stern and Sundelius developed a model for understanding and interpreting the political role of public leaders in crisis management (Boin *et al.* 2005). According to Boin *et al.*, crisis leadership involves five critical tasks: sense making, decision-making, meaning making, terminating, and learning. We summarise each task below (adapted from Boin *et al.* 2005: 10–15).

Sense making

Although there might be exceptions, most crises do not arrive with a big bang: they are the product of escalation. Policymakers must recognise from vague, ambivalent, and contradictory signals that something out of the ordinary is developing. The critical nature of these developments is not self-evident; policymakers have to 'make sense' of them.

In fact, the systems approach suggests we think of crises as subjectively construed threats. As Boin *et al.* (2005) point out, before we can speak of a crisis, a considerable number of players must agree that a crisis exists and must be dealt with urgently. This 'consensus-building' among key decision makers is also known as constructing a 'definition of the situation', and is currently being studied intensively as its dynamics are not always fully understood. There are several barriers to crisis recognition including significant organisational and psychological factors (Kaarbo 2015).

In sum, leaders must appreciate the threat and decide what the crisis is about. Leaders have to determine how threatening the events are, to what or to whom, what their operational and strategic parameters are, and how the situation will develop over time.

Decision-making

Crises leave governments and public agencies with pressing issues to be addressed. These can be of many kinds. The needs and problems triggered by the onset of a crisis may be so great that the scarce resources available will have to be prioritised. In addition, time to think and respond is limited. Crises force governments and leaders to confront issues they do not face on a daily basis, such as deployment of the military, the use of lethal force, or the restriction of civil liberties.

An effective response also requires interagency and intergovernmental coordination. Getting public bureaucracies to adapt to crisis management is a daunting if not impossible task in itself. There is good reason for this: routine business answers to values such as fairness, legality and efficiency. The management of crisis requires flexibility, improvisation, redundancy, and the breaking of rules. Coordination, however, remains critical to prevent miscommunication, overlap and conflicts between role players. And the question of who is in charge typically arouses great passion.

The experience from the literature is that leaders have to contend with how difficult it is to retain control over the course of events. When we reflect on leaders and their crisis teams, group dynamics become important. As a rule, crisis decision-making takes place in some type of small-group setting in which political and bureaucratic leaders interact and reach some sort of collective decision – whether by unanimity or by majority rule. These crisis teams become the critical nodes of what are often vast and highly complex multi-organisational and intergovernmental networks that come into being in response to crises. Small groups have virtue in crisis decision-making, but they can just as easily become a liability: false cohesion, excessive cordiality and conformity, and the bunker syndrome leading to group-think.

It would be wrong to assume that crisis teams are always in control and able to make clear decisions. Often, a key decision is not made by an individual leader or team but emerges from a network of interaction among key players. Even then, several forms of non-decision-making takes place: decisions that are not taken, decisions not to decide, decisions not to act, strategic evasion of choice opportunities (Boin *et al.* 2005).

Crisis teams work well when their members communicate and share, display trust, and are clear on who leads and who advises.

Meaning making

A crisis generates a strong demand from citizens to know what is going on, and to determine what they can do to protect their interests. Authorities cannot always provide correct information immediately. They struggle with the amount of raw data (for example, reports, rumours, images, social media comments) that quickly amass when something extraordinary happens. Turning them into a coherent picture of the situation is a major challenge in itself. Getting it out to the public in the form of accurate, clear, and actionable information requires a major communication effort.

In a crisis, leaders are expected to reduce uncertainty and provide an authoritative account of what is going on, why it is happening, and what needs to be done. When they have made sense of the events, have arrived at some sort of situational appraisal and made strategic policy choices, leaders must get others to accept their definition of the situation. They must impute 'meaning' to the unfolding crisis in such a way that their efforts to manage it are enhanced. If they do not, or cannot, their decisions will not be understood or respected. In fact, if other actors in the crisis (political opponents, mass media, other interested parties) succeed in dominating the meaning-making process, the ability of incumbent leaders to decide and manoeuvre is severely constrained. Indeed, the effectiveness of governmental crisis communication efforts depends on the degree of preparedness, the degree of coordination and ongoing information, and the degree of professionalisation.

In sum, leadership credibility enhances the quality of the crisis response and increases the chances of political survival in the post-crisis phase.

Terminating

Governments cannot stay in crisis mode forever. A sense of normalcy will have to return sooner or later. This is a critical leadership task.

Crisis termination is twofold: It is about shifting back from emergency to routine. This requires some form of downsizing of crisis operations. At the strategic level, it also requires rendering account for what has happened and gaining acceptance for this account.

Political accountability is a key institutional practice in the crisis termination stage. The most important stakeholders in crisis-driven accountability processes and reviews include the media, bureaucracies, legislators, ad hoc commissions, and citizens, victims, survivors and interest groups.

The burden of proof in accountability discussions lies with leaders: they need to show who is responsible for the occurrence or escalation of a crisis. These debates can easily degenerate into 'blame games', with a focus on finding culprits rather than discursive reflection about the full range of causes and consequences.

In sum, crisis termination depends on the way leaders deal with these accountability processes.

Learning

A final strategic leadership task in crisis management is political and organisational lesson drawing. The crisis experience offers a reservoir of potential lessons for contingency planning and training for future crises.

However, the political reality is different. Can governments and leaders learn from a crisis experience? The literature alerts us to the wide variety of constraints that operate on both individual and organisational learning capacity (Fiol and Lyles 1985; Turner 1976). Some argue that there is no such thing as 'crisis-induced learning' (Boin *et al.* 2005: 119).

Crises become part of collective memory. To depict a crisis as a failure would force people to rethink the assumptions on which policies and systems rest. Other role players might seize on the lessons to advocate reforms that incumbent leaders reject. To maintain position, leaders will have to achieve a dominant influence on the feedback stream that crises generate.

None of these inhibiting complexities seem to dent the belief that crisis presents opportunities – to clean up, start anew, or undergo structural reform. Crisis response, lesson drawing, and reform activities are often at odds with one another.

Application: The African dimension

Our search for literature on crisis leadership by African scholars, on African cases specifically, produced meagre results. As discussed earlier, there is interesting literature on disaster management – also from a South African perspective – but little on crisis leadership. On the theme of military responses to crisis, it is worth noting the lively academic debate on successful and failed peacemaking, peacekeeping, and peace-building efforts – usually under the rubric of the African Peace and Security Architecture (APSA) – as well as the critical appreciation of the role of outsiders in peace operations (Engel and Porto 2013; Charbonneau 2015). On non-military crisis responses, we have seen some literature on the management of natural disasters or crises, including those relating to food or water (Cromwell and Chintedza 2005; Haile 2005), or, more recently, the Zika virus (Muula 2016).

Given that we have little African data to go on in terms of shaping a model of crisis leadership to complement or contrast with Boin *et al.*'s (2005) five-task model of crisis management, we thought it valuable to put the model to an initial test. In the process, we hope to be able to deduce a number of lessons that speak to relevance and appropriateness.

To undertake this task we have identified a large range of crises in Africa. The list is quite lengthy and covers socio-economic and political as well as natural events. The pool of cases for consideration includes acts of terror in Kenya and Nigeria, state collapse in Somalia, genocide in Rwanda, the Ebola virus disease (EVD) in West Africa, energy and water crises in South Africa, xenophobia in South Africa, sexual violence in the Great Lakes region, civil war in Burundi, and economic meltdown in Zimbabwe.

In the event, we identified a case that was manageable in terms of data availability, collection and interpretation: the Ebola epidemic in West Africa. We start by describing the nature of the crisis: a timeline, the antecedents and triggers, and its closure. We then turn to an identification of the leaders and their responses according to the five-task model of Boin *et al.* (2005). Each task as described earlier is applied in a manner that allows us to probe the leadership response.

The conclusion offers new understandings of crisis management in the African context and in particular the role of leaders. Despite the single-case analysis, we view this chapter as an exploratory essay that might lead to a more substantial exploration.

EBOLA IN WEST AFRICA

The 2014 outbreak of Ebola in West Africa epitomises a crisis management emergency. The global community, ill-prepared, was taken by surprise by the rapid spread of the epidemic. Local and global health governance structures appeared wholly inadequate.

In addition, the international commitment to bolster pandemic preparedness and response capacity in poor countries was tardy, and global support for strengthening health systems was and remains weak (Nkwanga 2015; Robinson and Pfeiffer 2015).

The Ebola virus causes an acute, serious illness with a high fatality rate. Its symptons include fever and vomiting, accompanied by bleeding; it is highly infectious and transmitted by contact with body fluids, handled objects and fruit bats. The Ebola virus disease first appeared in 1976 in two simultaneous outbreaks, one in Nzara, Sudan, and the other in Yambuku, Democratic Republic of Congo. The latter occurred in a village near the Ebola River, from which the disease takes its name. The more recent outbreak in West Africa (officially declared in March 2014) is the largest and most complex Ebola outbreak since the virus was first identified in 1976.

The epidemic started in the Guekedou region of Guinea and became a sub-regional health problem whose complexity has since undermined the very basis for development in West Africa. According to the World Health Organization (WHO), the first known infection was an 18-month-old boy who died on 26 December 2013 in Meliandou, a remote village located in Guekedou, at a short distance from the Sierra Leone and Liberia borders, known as the Parrot's Beak (a conflict zone).

On 15 February 2014, the virus reached the capital, Conakry, through an infected member of the same child's extended family. Between January and March 2014, the epidemic spread to other areas of Guinea's southern region – particularly Kissidougou and Macenta. However, the status of epidemic was only confirmed on 21 March 2014. In the beginning, the WHO reported 29 deaths in 49 cases in Guinea. Two days later, these numbers were revised to 59 deaths per 86 cases. Liberia recorded its first case in the Foya district (Lofa county) on 30 March 2014, and by 2 April 2014, the virus had been transmitted to people in the capital, Monrovia. In Sierra Leone, the official declaration of the epidemic occurred on 28 May 2014. While the human casualties were minimal, neither Senegal nor Mali were spared. The virus travelled as far south as Lagos, Port Harcourt and Enugu in Nigeria. Victims were also counted in Spain, Italy, Germany and the USA.

As of 11 February 2015, there were 22 859 EVD cases – Guinea (3044), Liberia (8881) and Sierra Leone (10 934) – and a total of 9162 deaths. The deceased included 488 out of a total of 830 infected health workers.

Political and socio-economic context of Guinea

Characterised by poor governance, political instability, a weak economy, corruption and minimal infrastructure, Guinea is one of the poorest countries in Africa. While the country has not experienced civil war like its neighbours such as Liberia, Côte d'Ivoire and Sierra Leone, it has failed to contain political conflicts, piracy, transnational drug trafficking, and ethnic tensions. Guinea gained independence from France in 1958, followed by years of authoritarian rule: the second president, Lansana Conté, came to power through a military coup in 1984 and held power until his death in 2008. President Alpha Condé then took over after winning Guinea's first democratic elections in 2010. Although Condé has pushed through reforms of Guinea's legislature and economy, he has been criticised for the country's lack of democratic progress and high level of corruption (Arieff 2014).

Guinea's economy is strained, with a very low standard of living as a result of political instability, inept macroeconomic management, labour unrest, limited infrastructure, and corruption. Guinea boasts abundant natural resources such as aluminium ore, uranium, gold, diamonds and hydroelectricity. In fact, it has been reported that 30 per cent of Guinea's GDP come from natural resources. Even though the country's economy shows promising growth potential, poor living conditions are still prevalent (Arieff 2014).

Political and socio-economic context of Liberia

The Republic of Liberia on the West African coast shares borders with Guinea, Sierra Leone and Côte d'Ivoire. Founded in 1847, with its current republican constitution dating to 1986, the country has a population of 3.9 million people. Liberia, like other sub-Saharan African countries, is experiencing increasing HIV/Aids infections and deaths. Poverty, poor access to clean water and health care remain challenges. The country experienced a devastating civil war which ended in 1997, claiming more than 200 000 lives. This left the country's economy in ruins and poor control of weapons by government.

Despite these challenges, Liberia's economy has since improved with its GDP growing from 6.9 per cent in 2010 to 7.7 per cent in 2011 (International Development Law Organisation 2010). Liberia became the first African country to be led by a woman when President Ellen Johnson Sirleaf took office in 2006, committing to fight corruption. She was succeeded by George Weah, a former professional football player, who was elected president in 2018.

Political and socio-economic context of Sierra Leone

Sierra Leone, on the south-west coast of West Africa, has a population of 6 million, 70 per cent of whom are Muslim. The country boasts mineral resources such as diamonds, titanium and bauxite which contribute significantly to the economy. Other commodities include agricultural produce, coffee, cocoa and fish, which are produced for export. Despite its natural wealth, Sierra Leone remains devastatingly poor due to poor governance, corruption and self-enrichment by leaders.

Diamonds, for example, a key part of the economic base, have become a curse instead of a blessing because of the endemic corruption of leaders and officials. The country is faced with further socio-economic challenges such as a ruined infrastructure, weak medical systems, low literacy and unavailability of basic services such as water and electricity, all of which have retarded development (Lancaster 2007).

While Sierra Leone has had democratic presidents since 1967, they have not been able to build the sound governance that promotes accountability and rule of law. A brutal civil war broke out in Sierra Leone in 1991 which claimed 50 000 lives over the next 11 years, and sent thousands of refugees into Guinea and Liberia. Many cases of rape, mutilation, torture, looting and the press-ganging of child soldiers were reported. Muammar Gaddafi (Libya), Blaise Compaoré (Burkina Faso) and Charles Taylor (Liberia) were counted among those who contributed to this war by training and providing fighters, and funds. When the war was finally defused in 2002 with the assistance of United Nations peacekeepers and a Nigerian-led West African military force, the country was devastated, with medical and education systems destroyed and most communities displaced (Lancaster 2007).

KEY ACTORS IN THE EBOLA CRISIS

Lack of crisis management experience within the West African region was a key contributor to the delayed response to the Ebola epidemic. This was accompanied by a host of related challenges including over-centralised governance with deficient accountability systems, poor infrastructure, weak health systems, geography and culture.

In response to the outbreak of the epidemic, a multi-partner response effort or mission was established between the governments of Sierra Leone, Guinea and Liberia on the one hand; and the United Nations (UN), World Health Organization (WHO), European Union (EU), World Bank (WB) and African Development Bank (ADB) on the other, whose joint mandate was to put together recovery strategies for the three countries and tackle the virus through medical response. These key role players in the crisis are briefly discussed next.

National governments (Sierra Leone, Guinea and Liberia)

According to the WHO, the Liberian government, guided by President Ellen Johnson Sirleaf, played a critical role in fighting and overcoming Ebola in the country (WHO 2015a). Although response to the outbreak was slow to begin with, over time it was treated with a sense of urgency by Liberian government departments, with the president at the centre of decision-making. The role of the Presidential Advisory Committee was critical in the response to the crisis, as well as the mobilisation of community members in different parts of Liberia. The rapid response model and containment of Ebola strategy was later also applied in Sierra Leone and Guinea (WHO 2015a).

Community leaders

Community leaders were highly involved in the fight against Ebola, particularly in Liberia, where community members were mobilised through awareness and participation. Leaders encouraged the involvement of volunteers, especially in remote rural areas where health systems were far from the affected people.

International and regional partners

The US Centers for Disease Control and Prevention (CDC) and WHO emerged as key international players who actively responded to the Ebola outbreak in West Africa. Both organisations built incident management systems that served as focal points for international assistance. Their technical support ranged from capacity building, infrastructure, health systems, public mobilisation, contact tracing, epidemic containment, and awareness. This played a major role in halting the disease in Sierra Leone, Guinea and Liberia.

The African Union (AU) maintained its role as a regional coordinator, calling for intervention and assistance from regional organisations and governments, international organisations and institutions, and international civil society. Other organisations, such as the West African Health Organization (WAHO) and the Economic Community of West African States (ECOWAS), played a critical supporting role in the African sub-region.

ASSESSING THE IMPACT

The Ebola epidemic has threatened the social fabric that holds West African societies together. Even more disturbing is the ability of the EVD to push people into further poverty, thus making them more vulnerable. The incidence of poverty is approximately 50 per cent in Guinea, 31 per cent in Sierra Leone, and 64 per cent in Liberia (UNDG-WCA 2015).

Table 6.1:   Economic cost of the epidemic

Country	Low scenario	Actual GDP loss (in millions)	High scenario	Actual GDP loss (in millions)
Guinea	4.9%	$184	9.6%	$315
Liberia	13.7%	$188	18.7%	$245
Sierra Leone	6.0%	$219	8.0%	7.1% (N/A in $)

Source: UNDG-WCA 2015

The cost of the epidemic in terms of GDP is very high. In the medium term, the gains in the economic growth of the past decades seem to have been reversed. Looking at the 'low scenario' projection in Table 6.1, the loss of GDP for the whole region will be about US$3.6 billion – approximately 1.2% of the region's GDP (UNDG-WCA 2015). This is a substantial economic loss for a region that is struggling to catch up with other sub-regions, particularly when it comes to translating past growth into better living conditions for its populations.

Application of the Boin model

In this section we apply the five-task model to the response of West African leaders who faced the outbreak of the Ebola epidemic (Appendix A shows our operationalisation of the model).

Sense making

How did leaders understand the threat? Empirical evidence shows that leaders in the countries affected and infected by Ebola did not understand the threat and hence were not proactive: 'Porous, populous borders linking three states and the fact that Ebola was unknown in the region and easily confused with other pathologies contributed to silent expansion' (International Crisis Group 2015: 8).

Unpreparedness in terms of functioning disaster management systems, health systems, and a lack of capacity and skills have been identified as the areas of weakness that resulted in the failure to contain the disease and prevent further infection since the first case was reported in late December 2013 (see timeline in Figure 6.1). For instance, in Guinea, where the outbreak had started, the government was unable to identify and combat the disease because of the unavailability of laboratories, forcing authorities to have blood samples taken to France while EVD continued to spread

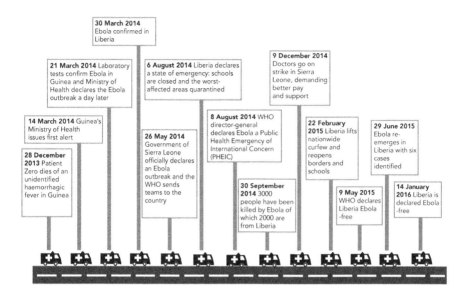

Figure 6.1: The Ebola crisis in West Africa: Timeline

Source: Authors

unattended. This inability of the leaders and government to identify the threat and treat the first case as an emergency undoubtedly contributed to the unprecedented Ebola crisis in West Africa. One study reported that even when WHO declared the Ebola outbreak on 23 March 2014, both the Guinea and Sierra Leone governments continued to downplay the crisis (DuBois, Wake, Sturridge and Bennett 2015). Guinea's government completely failed to identify the disease as a serious threat: the first case was reported in December 2013, but Guinea's Ministry of Health was only able to raise the alert of an unidentified disease on 14 March 2014 (Thomas, Ma'ani and Frankuchen 2014).

The Liberian response was quite different: both the Liberian government and citizens were galvinised into action by the impact of the disease in Monrovia. As soon as the first cases were reported in the capital, President Johnson Sirleaf declared a state of emergency and sounded the alarm for international assistance in August 2014 (DuBois *et al.* 2015: 22).

How did leaders understand what was happening? In Guinea, where the EVD originated, government was not aware of the nature of the disease until reports came from France. The government also did not understand what was happening and why until further research by WHO was conducted to produce information about EVD. However, when the disease broke out in Liberia, the government was able to act with promptness because information was now available. As a result, the Liberian government understood the severity of the threat and treated it with urgency.

Did leaders understand what needed to be done? Even though the governments of the three countries – Guinea, Liberia and Sierra Leone – set up structures to combat the EVD, their response was noticeably slow, resulting in exacerbating the spread of the disease. To this end, the UNDP noted in their report that 'the failure of key international actors to raise the alarm and the failure of national and international actors to respond quickly enough in the early phase of the outbreak contributed to a "criminally late" response and failure to control the outbreak before it spiralled out of control' (UNDP 2015: 6).

One could argue that the failure to identify the disease in Guinea contributed to sluggish action because the governments could not determine what needed to be done at that point. The failure to recognise an unfolding crisis was critical especially when the first cases were reported in December 2013 and in March 2014 – together with the number of unreported cases flowing from Sierra Leone to Guinea and Liberia.

There are numerous theories to explain the delayed response to the first wave of the Ebola outbreak, and why the beginning of the second wave was missed. Prominent suggestions include health sensitisation messages that led to the intentional hiding of cases; overconfidence about ability to contain the threat, which meant that not enough people were on the ground or those present left too quickly; and 'poor flow of information', complicated by poor cross-border coordination (International Crisis Group 2015: 8–9).

Decision-making and response coordination

Who led decision-making? In Sierra Leone, the president and government ministers led operations, setting up response strategies and committees. For instance, President Koroma designed and administered a National Ebola Response Committee (NERC) led by the Ministry of Defence, and also set up an Emergency Operations Centre headed by the Ministry of Health.

In the case of Liberia, President Johnson Sirleaf stepped up to lead her country in the fight against Ebola. Unlike the two other countries, the Liberian health and social welfare ministries had a pre-existing task force that was reactivated when the first Ebola diagnoses were made in March 2014. When Ebola escalated in Liberia, President Johnson Sirleaf declared a state of emergency in August 2014 and called for international assistance. The Liberian government formed structures with organisations such as WHO and CDC to absorb as much support and advice from their experience as possible.

Guinea was not as hard hit as the other two countries and the situation could have been managed. Yet EVD persisted because a lack of capacity and resources meant that it was not fully eliminated. Following the first cases as reported in December 2013, President Alpha Condé declared a state of emergency. Operations were coordinated by the Ministry of Health (DuBois *et al.* 2015: 20).

Were resources mobilised and allocated? Poor health systems, lack of infrastructure, shortages of human resources and health supplies before the Ebola outbreak magnified the impact of the disease in Guinea, Liberia and Sierra Leone.

According to DuBois *et al.* (2015: 45), 'systemic weaknesses in these countries' health systems and services – including insufficient funding, an inadequate workforce, poor infrastructure, shortages of medicines and supplies, and weak health information and disease surveillance systems – all contributed to the spread of Ebola and undermined efforts to respond.' To this must be added the debilitating role of multilateral agencies as 'resource-rich' sources of support, which initially seemed more concerned with downplaying the crisis.

The absence of sufficiently qualified health workers in most rural areas contributed to the EVD containment failure. Even basic services such as running water and electricity were limited. Poor linkages between the peripheral and central levels of government broke down mobilisation of resources, especially to the rural areas of Liberia. Moreover, government health expenditure was low compared to other expenditures, resulting in poor mobilisation of resources needed to respond to the EVD outbreak. DuBois *et al.* (2015: 15) reported that in Sierra Leone, '[b]y October 2014 it was clear that there is not enough logistical capacity within the Ministry of Health and Sanitation to manage the response'.

Were responses coordinated? The three West African countries were not prepared for the crisis and were hard hit, particularly Liberia, where addressing EVD was an additional burden to already constrained national institutions. Government employees in Liberia described the initial response to stopping the spread of the virus as 'constrained and uncoordinated' (Thomas *et al.* 2014: 3).

Initially, there was no proper coordination in the three countries and decision-making was delayed. However, the president of Liberia later created an Emergency Operations Centre charged with coordination and decision-making. With this centre running, the government was able to create a central line of command to ensure efficient flow of communication. Coordination also improved in both Guinea and Sierra Leone after government's establishment of coordination committees. Evidently, the lack of coordination in the beginning exacerbated the spread of EVD due to gaps in response. Coordination of international response was carried out by the UN, together with WHO and CDC in all three countries.

Meaning making

To what extent did leaders develop a coherent picture of the situation? According to analysis by the International Crisis Group (2015), misinformation – including inaccurate mortality data – was constant in the early stages. Even as Guinea's health ministry declared the outbreak on 22 March 2014, followed shortly by ECOWAS ministers calling Ebola 'a serious threat to regional security', its potential impact was underestimated. Porous borders linking three states, and the fact that Ebola was unknown in the region (or at least not identified) and easily confused with other pathologies, contributed to the silent expansion of misinformation, which was constant in the early stages. There was an assumption for several months that despite their geographic spread, cases were declining in Guinea and Liberia. The assessment that there were no confirmed cases in Sierra Leone can now be seen as a particular failure.

By the time the first case was confirmed (at the end of May 2014), the situation was unmanageable. What was seen as a 'hidden outbreak' had recrossed borders and reignited the outbreak in neighbouring countries. It was the unreported cases in Sierra Leone that eventually led to the massive numbers throughout the region. That country's officials have acknowledged that warnings were not disseminated widely enough, and 'the damage from the disease could have been mitigated with early information' (International Crisis Group 2015: 8). It appears that information during this key period was actively being hidden. That officials were downplaying the impact by only reporting confirmed laboratory cases was apparent early on, but the underreporting skewed perceptions and meant resources mobilised to fight the epidemic were initially limited (International Crisis Group 2015: 8).

Did other stakeholders develop a coherent picture of the situation? It was not only regional governments that prevaricated during the first half of 2014. The WHO downplayed warnings that the epidemic was out of control from the outset; as late as 19 May 2014, Ebola was only briefly mentioned at the annual World Health Assembly. Until mid-year, only limited information was shared between countries, and both the domestic and international priority was not to spread panic among populations – and especially investors.

To what extent and how was information shared with the public and other stakeholders? Learning lessons from the beginning, Liberia was able to successfully control the Ebola outbreak because they relied throughout on a localised approach.

Local community engagement teams increased outreach and handled issues by going to households door-to-door. And since each of the teams was managed within the communities themselves, they had the freedom to design responses they knew would be effective in their particular context. While the national government laid out the initial framework for containing and eliminating Ebola, it fell to local communities to actually implement these strategies. For example, to execute the national government's sterilisation goal, local communities placed hand-washing kiosks in markets, stores and schools, and stressed the importance of frequent use. To carry out the government's goal to increase disease awareness, communities improved education on the spread of Ebola and the measures taken to combat its impact (WHO 2015b).

Terminating

How did leaders and governments shift back from emergency to routine mode? After the three countries in West Africa were declared Ebola-free in June 2015, recovery and rebuilding commenced (DuBois *et al.* 2015). Ebola had not only taken human lives, but it also crippled the economy, people's trust, development and health systems of Guinea, Liberia and Sierra Leone. Poor governance and broken health systems were the main emerging issues during the Ebola crisis. At the end of the crisis, the government of Sierra Leone developed a recovery strategy to use as a framework to ensure prompt recovery of economic activities and provision of basic services in the country (Government of Sierra Leone 2015: 32). The strategy puts increased emphasis on restoring socio-economic activities and accelerates economic growth.

Similarly, the Liberian strategy focused on strengthening health systems and rebuilding socio-economic activities. Further, Liberia prioritised mitigation of consequences in affected households through cash transfers, and also worked on reopening health facilities and schools to enable affected communities to adjust to their normal routine.

How was political accountability undertaken? Reports indicate that the three states initially failed to provide legitimate information about EVD and misinformed citizens of the truth about the disease, particularly about effects of the disease and mortality data. According to The Africa Report (2015) there was an acute lack of information flow in Sierra Leone during the early stages of Ebola, to the extent that this prevented mitigation of the disease in its early stages. Further, in Guinea officials also hid information because they did not want to scare away international airlines and mining companies. The Ebola outbreak also exacerbated citizen distrust of state authority as a result of initial response activities, where the military were dispatched to instil order in Liberia. The president of Liberia later acknowledged that this decision was rushed (DuBois *et al.* 2015). Reports indicate that government's response was a typically militarised one, where affected areas were subject to forced stay-at-home days and blockades. The Liberian government also deployed soldiers to conduct door-to-door searches to identify infected people. This process triggered a backlash of violence from frustrated citizens who could not go out to get food and, with no information, were engulfed by fear. The government also failed to provide food, clean water and adequate medication for people in quarantined areas.

The road to recovery requires that these three states become more transparent and account for Ebola donations and funding, and also build confidence in government institutions such as health systems which was absent in the initial phase of the outbreak (The Africa Report 2015).

Learning

Have leaders been able to learn lessons? The presidents of the three countries have indicated that even though the Ebola outbreak was a devastating crisis for their countries, it provided an opportunity to strengthen health systems, build human resource capacity in health institutions, tighten their borders, and build trust with the citizens.

In one instance, the president of Liberia acknowledged that using soldiers and police to quarantine entire neighbourhoods 'created more tension in society', and she later amended this error by involving more community members in the process. Further, Liberia became more transparent and provided legitimate information on the scale of the EVD. Liberia thus stood out among the three countries in its learning from mistakes, showing relative transparency in acknowledging the disaster's scale and in its requests for international help (International Crisis Group 2015: 11).

Has institutional learning taken place? Reports indicate that weak and poor health systems were the root cause of the problem (Roache, Gostin, Hougendobler and Friedman 2014). This saw the three countries failing to provide for the basic health needs of affected citizens.

The crisis has exposed the unpreparedness of Guinea, Liberia and Sierra Leone for the complexities of the EVD outbreak. Sierra Leone failed to identify and distinguish EVD from other diseases; appropriate laboratories in the three countries were not available, and neither were isolation units and a system of contact tracing.

The government of Sierra Leone has indicated in their recovery strategy that strengthening of health systems will be a top priority as they begin the rebuilding process. Health systems in Guinea had challenges long before the EVD outbreak mainly due to lack of financial resources and of qualified medical personnel. Moreover, the country was already experiencing infrastructure decay and non-functioning communication systems which were needed to link and especially reach isolated rural areas (UNDP 2015). The militarised response has also demonstrated weakness in the governance of the countries, especially Liberia, where the country had already endured ongoing governance challenges due to instabilities caused by the civil war.

What was the outcome of 'lessons learnt'? All three affected countries have indicated that the strengthening of health systems, rebuilding the trust of citizens, renewing infrastructure, building capacity and communication networks, and tightening the porous borders have been prioritised.

Following the first EVD case on 28 December 2013 in Guinea, the first national alerts noted isolated cases in multiple places. The limited capacity of the health systems in the three countries made it difficult to identify this as a possible EVD outbreak, particularly as the countries had never before seen the disease. In addition, they had no laboratory capacity to confirm the disease quickly: ill patients had to be sent to the capital for diagnosis, which led to further delays in the confirmation of cases and facilitated the spread of the virus to capital cities. This raises the question of whether the spread of the epidemic would have been avoidable at all through any kind of government agency.

Reflecting the poor implementation of International Health Regulations (IHR), systems for early warning and response were inadequate, lacked the necessary accountability and links with, or support from, national disaster management mechanisms, and were not prepared to scale up an appropriate response to this type and scale of epidemic.

OVERALL CONCLUSIONS

In this chapter, we applied the logic of the crisis decision-making model as developed by Boin *et al.* (2005) to determine its usefulness in the African setting. We developed a sense of governance capacity and crisis response by examining the Ebola outbreak in West Africa in 2014. We conclude that the logic of Boin *et al.*'s crisis management model has value, particularly in its description of how public leaders engage in sense making, decision-making, meaning making, terminating and learning, as they work through a crisis and its aftermath. In many ways, the model is applicable to the African setting.

Beyond the application of the crisis management model, how can one explain any government's failure to provide information, detect Ebola in its infancy stage, develop an urgent response, and put containment strategies in place? Who had the power and resources to identify the Ebola crisis and act? Why are those resources, which determine if an outbreak is serious, not available in the postcolony, but instead largely located within CDC and to an extent WHO?

Two themes emerged throughout our research that seem to have explanatory value. First, Guinea, Sierra Leone and Liberia are marked by extreme levels of post-independence fragility. Socio-economic and political instability follows when robust governance architecture is absent, compounded by the deliberate creation of economic and cultural dependence on neocolonial powers (Rodney 1973). This is true for the countries in our case study, where poverty and underdevelopment, in concert with violent contestation for access to resources, including political power, became the hallmark of their post-independence profile. The second theme follows closely from the first. Our systematic coverage of responses to the Ebola crisis shows how decision makers in government and the non-state sector were unable to detect the nature of the Ebola crisis and respond timeously and adequately. This is a consequence of the absence of a governing structure for the management of large and transnational challenges and crises. In addition, decision makers seemingly did not have the management training, exposure and resources at their disposal to effectively deal with the deadly disease. This apparent weak skills base – a consequence of dysfunctional governance and continuing dependence on former colonial powers – explains to a large measure why the crisis unfolded over a period of time. It has to be noted that the international community intervened once it became apparent that the deadly virus might spread beyond African borders and the African continent, into Europe and North America.

REFERENCES

Alkharabsheh, A., Ahmad, Z.A. & Kharabsheh, A. 2013. Characteristics of crisis and decision making styles: the mediating role of leadership styles. *Procedia – Social and Behavioral Sciences* 129: 282–288.

Arieff, A. 2014. Guinea: In Brief. *Congressional Research Service*: 1–11. https://fas.org/sgp/crs/row/R40703.pdf (accessed 28 June 2018).

Boin, A., McConnell, A. & 't Hart, P. 2008. *Governing after Crisis: The Politics of Investigation, Accountability and Learning.* Cambridge: Cambridge University Press.

Boin, A., 't Hart, P., Stern, E. & Sundelius, B. 2005. *The Politics of Crisis Management: Public Leadership under Pressure.* Cambridge: Cambridge University Press.

Centers for Disease Control & Prevention (CDC). 2015. *2014–2016 Ebola Outbreak in West Africa: CDC Role.* https//www.cdc.gov/vfh/ebola (accessed 27 January 2016).

Charbonneau, B. 2015. The politics of peacekeeping interventions in Africa. *International Peacekeeping* 22: 275–282.

Cox, R. 1987. *Power, Production and World Order: Social Forces in the Making of History, Vol. 1.* New York: Columbia University Press.

Cromwell, E. & Chintedza, A. 2005. Neo-patrimonialism and Policy Processes: Lessons from the Southern African Food Crisis. *IDS Bulletin* 36(2): 103–108.

DuBois, M. & Wake, C. with Sturridge, S. & Bennett, C. 2015. *The Ebola Response in West Africa: Exposing the politics and culture of international aid.* Humanitarian Policy Group (HPG) Working Paper. London: ODI. https//www.odi.org/sites/org.odi.uk/ files (accessed 9 February 2016).

Engel, U. & Porto, J. (eds) 2013. *Towards an African Peace and Security Regime.* Farnham, VT: Ashgate.

Fiol, M. & Lyles, M. 1985. *Organisational learning.* Faculty Working Paper No. 1110. College of Commerce and Business Administration. University of Illinois at Urbana-Champaign.

Government of Sierra Leone. 2015. Hadley, C., Pittinsky, T., Sommer, A. & Zhu, W. 2011. Measuring the efficacy of leaders to assess information and make decisions in a crisis: the C-LEAD scale. *The Leadership Quarterly* 22(4): 633–648.

Haile, M. 2005. Weather patterns, food security, and humanitarian response in sub-Saharan Africa. *Philosophical Transactions of the Royal Society: Biological Sciences* 360(1463): 2169–2182.

International Crisis Group. 2015. *The Politics Behind the Ebola Crisis.* https//www.crisisgroup. org/files (accessed 1 February 2016).

International Development Law Organisation. 2010. *Liberia Country Report.* http://www. youthpolicy.org/library/wp-content/uploads/library/2010_Liberia_Country_Report_ Eng.pdf (accessed 28 June 2018).

Kaarbo, J. 2015. A Foreign Policy Analysis Perspective on the Domestic Politics Turn in IR Theory. *International Studies Review* 17(2): 189–216.

Lancaster, C. 2007. 'We Fall Down and Get Up': State Failure, Democracy and Development in Sierra Leone: 1–9. London: Centre for Global Development. https://www.cgdev.org/ sites/default/files/14314_file_Lancaster_Sierra_Leone.pdf (accessed 28 June 2018).

Muula, A. 2016. Why Africa can't afford to have an outbreak of the Zika virus. *The Conversation,* 10 February. https://theconversation.com/why-africa-cant-afford-to-have-an-outbreak-of-the-zika-virus-53738 (accessed 28 June 2018).

National Ebola Recovery Strategy for Sierra Leone. 2015. https//www.ebolaresponse.un.org/ sites/default/files/Sierra_Leone_recovery_strategy_en.pdf (accessed 1 February 2016).

Nkwanga, W. 2015. The Ebola crisis in West Africa and the enduring legacy of the Structural Adjustment Policies. *Africa at LSE,* 26 January. http://blogs.lse.ac.uk/ africaatlse/2015/01/26/the-ebola-crisis-in-west-africa-and-the-enduring-legacy-of-the-structural-adjustment-policies/ (accessed 28 June 2018).

O'Sullivan, T., Kuziemsky, C., Toal-Sullivan, D. & Corneil, W. 2013. Unraveling the complexities of disaster management: a framework for critical social infrastructure to promote population health and resilience. *Social Science and Medicine* 93: 238–246. doi: 10.1016/j.socscimed.2012.07.040 (accessed 28 June 2018).

Pelling, M. & Wisner, B. 2009. *Disaster risk reduction: Cases from urban Africa.* London: Earthscan.

Roache, S., Gostin, L., Hougendobler, D. & Friedman, E. 2014. *Lessons from the West African Ebola Epidemic: Towards a Legacy of Strong Heath Systems.* O'Neill Institute Briefing Paper

Number 10, 10 February. https//www.law.georgetown.edu/oneillinstiute/resources (accessed 9 February 2016).

Robinson, J. & Pfeiffer, J. 2015. The IMF's role in the Ebola outbreak. *The Bretton Woods Observer*, 2 February. http://www.brettonwoodsproject.org/2015/02/imfs-role-ebola-outbreak/ (accessed 28 June 2018).

Rodney, W. 1973. *How Europe Underdeveloped Africa*. London: Bogle-L'Ouverture Publications; Dar es Salaam: Tanzanian Publishing House.

The Africa Report. 2015. Liberia Country Profile 2015: Virus devastates the economy. 23 November. http://www.theafricareport.com/West/liberia-country-profile-virus-devastates-the-economy.html (accessed 28 June 2018).

Thomas, A., Ma'ani, R. & Fankuchen, A. 2014. All hands on deck: The next generation of Liberia's leaders on building innovation and responsiveness into government. In: Dalberg Global Development Advisors *From Response to Recovery in the Ebola Crisis: Revitalising Health Systems and Economies*: 1–22. http://docplayer.net/35847490-Revitalizing-health-systems-and-economies.html#show_full_text (accessed 28 June 2018).

Turner, B.A. 1976. The organizational and interorganizational development of disasters. *Administrative Science Quarterly* 21(3): 378–397.

United Nations Development Group – Western and Central Africa (UNDG-WCA). 2015. *Socio-economic Impact of Ebola Virus Disease in West African Countries: A call for national and regional containment, recovery and prevention*. https//www.africa.undp. org/content (accessed 27 January 2016).

United Nations Development Programme. 2015. *Recovering from the Ebola crisis*. Summary report. https//www.ilo.org/wcmsp5/groups (accessed 1 February 2016).

Vera, D. & Crossan, M. 2004. Strategic leadership and organisational learning. *The Academy of Management Review* 29(2): 222–240.

WHO. 2015a. Accelerating WHO Emergency Response to Ebola Outbreak in Liberia. https// apps.who.int/ebola/ebola situation report (accessed 16 January 2016).

WHO. 2015b. The Ebola Outbreak in Liberia is Over. https//apps.who.int/ebola/ebola situation report (accessed 15 January 2016).

APPENDIX A

MODEL OF CRISIS LEADERSHIP: OPERATIONAL QUESTIONS

1. **Sense making**: Leaders must appreciate the threat and decide what the crisis is about.
   - Do leaders understand the threat? How?
   - Do they understand why it is happening? How?
   - Do they understand what needs to be done? How?
   - Do they have a sense of how the situation will develop over time?

2. **Decision-making**: The needs and problems triggered by the onset of crisis may be so great that the scarce resources available will have to be prioritised.
   - Who leads? Who decides this?
   - Are resources mobilised and allocated?
   - Are responses coordinated?

3. **Meaning making**: In a crisis, leaders are expected to reduce uncertainty and provide an authoritative account of what is going on, why it is happening, and what needs to be done.
   - To what extent did leaders develop a coherent picture of the situation?
   - Did other stakeholders do this?
   - To what extent and how did leaders share this with the public and other stakeholders?
   - Did other stakeholders do this?

4. **Terminating**: A sense of normalcy will have to return sooner or later. This is a critical leadership task.
   - How did leaders and governments shift back from emergency to routine mode?
   - How was political accountability undertaken?

5. **Learning**: A final strategic leadership task in crisis management is political and organisational lesson drawing. The crisis experience offers a reservoir of potential lessons for contingency planning and training for future crises.
   - Have leaders been able to learn lessons? How?
   - Has institutional learning taken place? Where and how?
   - What was the outcome of 'lessons learnt' – repair, reform, or none?

Public Policymaking through Adversarial Network Governance in South Africa

Susan Booysen

INTRODUCTION AND CONCEPTUAL POSITIONING

This chapter assesses complex forms of public policymaking in South Africa. It utilises three case studies that show how opposition formations took charge of controversial policy issues and prevented government from making or implementing its preferred policies, fast-forwarding policy implementation or, alternately, pushing government into making policy that it had not envisaged. The study covers three specific policy cases in the period 2011 to 2018: opposition to legislation that impacts freedom of speech; subverting the implementation of e-tolling; and the fast-forwarding of free access to post-secondary education that was linked to the #FeesMustFall protest against financial and cultural exclusion in South African universities.

The analysis uses the phrase 'opposition network policymaking' to denote the cumulative actions through which civil society – along with select opposition parties and some governing party structures and state institutions – used primarily legal process and civil society mobilisation to subdue, delay or defeat undesired policy actions of government and the African National Congress (ANC) as the predominant governing party; or, in some cases, to elevate policy action in ways government had not planned. To the extent that the pressures of these networks imposed new, de facto but enduring public policy regimes in specific policy areas, the analysis uses the notion of adversarial network governance. The notion involves collaboration in the sense of the begrudging confluence of pro- and anti-forces, pushing original 'policy decisions' to become non-decisions (which are recognised as de facto policy decisions). Alternatively, it involved cooperation by pushing government into policy decisions that are stronger than the original government intentions had been. These forms of collaboration prevail in particular policy areas, rather than across government.

'Network governance' is conceptualised in the conventional (not adversarial) sense as describing a particular mode of organisation that contrasts with hierarchies (see Klijn and Skelcher 2007: 589). It comprises a patterned relationship between state and society which links public and private or citizen sector agencies into a set of relationships. The term 'networks' denotes a relatively stable, tightly knit group of relationships, with greater insulation from other institutions that may be known as policy communities (Hajer and Wagenaar 2003). These relationships are conventionally cooperative, constituting communities of interest. In the words of Tanya Börzel (1998: 254), '[t]hese actors share common interests with regard to policy and exchange resources to pursue these shared interests, acknowledging that cooperation is the best way to achieve common goals'. The interdependent participant actors may exchange resources (matter, information, energy) to pursue policy through cooperation; these non-hierarchical associations result in relations of 'aggregate complexity', in the words of Steven Manson (2001: 409). As these definitions suggest, the *conventional picture* concerning networks and network governance is one of considerable coherence, cooperation and consensus.

The current analysis extends network governance to also cover *contrariness or adversity amidst interdependence* as the foundation for networks in public policymaking. These de facto governance networks are held together through contest and policy compromises to which government does not agree. It also does not concern merely a case of building successful and adversarial civil society coalitions: in holding government and its (selected) undesired policies at bay, these networks of opposition are interdependent with government and share government power. They forge begrudging albeit de facto co-governance arrangements on the specific policy issues.

In the three case studies, the ANC mostly took exception to and worked at undermining or occasionally co-opting the opposition networks, portraying them as, for example, counter-democratic and in denial of the right of the majority to govern. This is in line with the liberal approach, which argues, in the words of Elena Bessusi

(2006: 10), that 'policy networks are seen to undermine democracy, because they limit the power of […] elected governments'. This type of adversity was reflected in a former South African president's words (Zuma 2016), himself a frequent network target, on the opposition networks' strategy to use the court system to help oppose unwanted policies:

> Democracy and the democratic expression of the will of the majority must be protected by all citizens. There should be no spurious attempts to circumvent the legitimate exercise of people's power. Emerging tendencies to engage in low-intensity 'law-fare' are attempts to divert the legitimate demo cratic outcomes. These actions fly in the face of the fundamental majority party that has won an election […] (Zuma 2016).

The three cases in this study are chosen for their illustration of policy contest and complex, often adversarial, public policymaking in South Africa. Such network governance in the country demonstrated its power in the virtual defeat of the Gauteng automated e-toll system (albeit with ongoing legal and political challenges up to at least early 2019); the continuous 'inbox' status of the Protection of State Information Bill (Posib) – by early 2019 still awaiting the South African president's signature that would turn it into law; and the rapid escalation and extension of government policy to get improved access to and transformation of higher education, in particular for the poor.

There are multiple other cases of adversarial network governance in South Africa that are not detailed in this study. They include de facto networks challenging and obstructing poorly considered aspects of the implementation of the national health insurance (NHI) process; contestation around the Draft Firearms Control Amendment Bill of 2015; postponement of pension scheme reforms after objections from the Congress of South African Trade Unions (Cosatu); and the struggle against South Africa's nuclear deal, an energy policy option that had flourished under the rule of former president Zuma.

'ADVERSARIAL NETWORK GOVERNANCE' – LINKING THEORY AND APPLICATION

Oppositional-adversarial network governance – an extension of the 'new opposition framework' (Booysen 2015) – is the theoretical framework that is advanced for the current study. The new opposition framework dealt with the new and powerful networks comprising civil society, selected state institutions and opposition parties that had started taking central positions in policy contestation, and consequent de facto policymaking in South Africa. It is focused on the high impact of these *oppositional networks* on public policy. Recognising that the oppositional networks in fact help deliver de facto public policy and governance, at the same time as being oppositional, the current contribution assesses and theorises these networks through the lens of *adversarial network governance*.

Conventionally, network governance finds substance in relations of cooperation and consensus between a variety of civil society organisations and government. The cooperative nature of these relationships is evident from the work by Catherine Lyall and Joyce Tait (2005), who stress that policy network governance, an interactive phenomenon, helps contemporary governments to assert joined-up policies to deal with new orders of complexity, where no single actor owns all the knowledge and resources to solve social problems unilaterally. Cooperation and collaboration supersede more traditional and hierarchical demarcations of power. It is acknowledged in such cooperative policymaking endeavours that networks work best when the internal dynamics include the recognition of mutual dependency and cooperation in the exercise of authority (Colgan 2015). Adversarial network governance, in contrast, centres on reluctant, even hostile coexistence of policy actors to enact policy holding patterns, disruption of official policy positions, or policy acceleration. Interdependence prevails in that, given the contestation, the original policy notions are in effect amended – for as long as the adversarial action remains manifest or latent (but with the potential to be reactivated with relative ease). Cooperation is manifested through begrudging ceding of space to the adversarialists – because they command strong popular support and moral-popular gravitas, and government actors cannot outlaw the institutions, organisations or individuals involved. The emphasis is on the begrudging nature of the cooperation and interdependence, along with the network-outcome-equivalent of non-decisions: non-implementation through adversarial mobilisation.

The current study is located in the governance school (German model) of policy networking, although cooperation is substituted for adversarial relations of interdependence. The governance school argues that network operations are an alternative form of governance to that of the hierarchy of the state and market. Policy networks hence offer a model to analyse non-hierarchical forms of policymaking interactions between public and private actors (Rhodes and Marsh 1992; Börzel 1998; Rhodes 2006). Networks in policy context typically link a range of actors who 'share common interests with regard to policy and exchange resources to pursue these shared interests, acknowledging that cooperation is the best way to achieve common goals' (Börzel 1998: 76). Network relationships are generally regarded as constituting relatively stable, non-hierarchical and interdependent (Hazlehurst 2001: 10) policy institutions (formal or informal), and the participants can be seen as constituting a policy community. The interdependence, writes Laurence O'Toole (1997: 45–52), is due to network members' inability to achieve their policy goals on their own.

This converges with Elinor Ostrom's work in which she demonstrates that agencies develop cooperative networks for delivering on public goods, driven by a set of agreed social rules and norms that make people cooperate (see Poteete and Ostrom 2010; also Ostrom 2005). Eva Sørensen and Jacob Torfing (2005: 2) use networks in the context of 'negotiated government' where public–private partnerships, strategic alliances, dialogue groups, consultative committees and inter-organisational networks flourish due to the failures of both state and market regulation.

The central thrust is that networks arise from the recognition that policy will be advanced through *cooperation* with the state, where 'the state' comprises agencies that cohere as the central drivers in the policy process. In contrast, the current study focuses on opposition policy networks that jointly contest government policy actions, on occasion cooperate with selected government institutions, and then, as multi-actor oppositional networks, constitute an adversarial governance network. In this network, the government actors that had been pursuing a certain course of policy action are forced into non-implementation of that position. This network's policy positions come to constitute the de facto government policy position of the day, because government lacked the power to enforce its policy will against that of the oppositional component of the network. Stalemate situations define many of these networks – government cannot proceed and implement effectively its formal policy position.

Specifically, civil society organisations in networks of influence have secured de facto policy change through enforcing non-adoption of new policy and hence delivered the maintenance of the status quo. The groundwork for non-decisions as de facto policymaking is elaborated in Steven Lukes' (1993: 50–58; building on, for example, Bachrach and Baratz 1962) conceptualisations of political power in public policymaking. These theoretical points of view anchor the argument that, besides policy change, civil society networks (sometimes in cooperation with selected state and party political forces) also obstruct effective implementation of adopted legislative measures, or gain policy acceleration, change and implementation through networks.

In the focal areas of this study, government was pushed through civil society alliances, which often drew on selected state institutions, to abort, amend or accelerate implementation of existing policy. To illustrate this, the largely adversarial #FeesMustFall (#FMF) actions (at the height of this struggle in October 2015) forced government to extend hitherto long-term envisaged measures to implement free (or freer) post-secondary education, pushed universities to end exploitative outsourcing of service workers, and solve urgently outstanding work of racial transformation. Government had been reluctant, unwilling or complacent – until the network took effect. The actions penetrated government operations, and became fused with the internal workings of government. The network presence compelled the president in another of the case studies, Posib, to delay signing controversial information control measures into law. On e-tolls these actions compelled national government bodies, along with the Gauteng provincial government, to concede gradually (and yet not explicitly) that e-tolls had become a political no-go territory.

The chapter now presents the research findings on each of three case studies, extracting the trends of adversarial network governance, based on two phases of network operations: first, the new opposition networks mobilised and then exercised influence; and second, when they became operational and successful in their influence, they constituted adversarial network governance in relation to the formal institutions and processes of government. The cases indicate how, through adversarial engagement and reluctant settlement between non-state and state actors, policy effects materialised.

THREE CASES OF ADVERSARIAL NETWORK GOVERNANCE[1]

The research demonstrates that networks of policymaking and governance often work effectively to change governance – not because of internally consensual relationships (except for convergence between the opposition agencies), but because mobilised oppositional networks act to disrupt, obstruct or legally challenge government policy positions, and government becomes compelled to cooperate or succumb. The oppositional policy actors hence forge adversarial forms of governance.

The anti-e-tolling, anti-Posib and anti-financial-exclusion-of-students networks in South Africa show how it was possible, albeit with sacrifices (and in the face of the ongoing threat of state legal sanction, co-option, etc.), to take on a government that was determined to use all available legal and legitimate state means against those who challenged its governance (for illustration of opposition to e-tolls, see Duvenage with Serrao 2015; Duvenage 2012). In cases such as the student revolt, clashes alternated cyclically with settlement and co-option, new student actors and formations dominating, new battles erupting (see Booysen 2016) – and unstable adversarial governance networks becoming the norm.

Civil society movements, as well as organised components of civil society, non-government organisations (NGOs), along occasionally with opposition political parties, were the key driving forces in adversarial network governance (see Table 7.1). The networks included but mostly did not depend on opposition political parties. The Democratic Alliance (DA) had supported the anti-tolling campaign, amongst others financially, in order to prolong the anti-tolling alliance's legal challenges. Although #FMF shunned party political approaches generally, the Economic Freedom Fighters (EFF), Black First Land First (BLF) and other Black Consciousness organisations were ideologically and strategically close to #FMF. Many of the #FMF leading figures were in the ANC-aligned Progressive Youth Alliance (PYA: comprising the ANC Youth League; the South African Students Congress or Sasco; the Congress of South

Table 7.1:   Comparison of actors in adversarial governance networks – roles in relation to policy issue

	Supporting the anti-government policy position	Vacillating/Dual roles/ Roles varying over time	Opposing network intervention
Posib	15+ NGOs and NGO alliances Opposition parties (DA, Cope) Individual ANC MPs Constitutional Court SA Council of Churches	ANC and ANC factions fear being targeted themselves	Parliamentary committee NCOP Security agencies Tripartite Alliance
E-tolls	Outa, multiple NGOs & interest groups, including Justice Project of SA Opposition Parties (DA, EFF)	Cosatu Taxi associations High Court Gauteng ANC, national ANC Gauteng government	Department of Transport Parliament Sanral ANC
#FMF	Fallist students in multiple hashtag identities Outsourced workers Select academic staff Opposition parties (EFF, BLF)	SRCs, PYA, ANC Department of Higher Education President Vice-chancellors/USAf, university councils, top management NSFAS	Reactionary student formations Criminal or 'hired activists' or instigators Security forces – state and private

Source: Author's analysis and synthesis of trends, as detailed in the text

Note: Acronyms in this table are explained in the text

African Students or Cosas; and the Young Communist League or YCL) and some-times cooperated with the ANC mother body (Booysen 2016). The PYA stood out as predominant in the period of peak #FMF influence. The NGO sector, trade unions and trade union collectives (or, on occasion, informal groupings of academic staff in support of students, or journalists and the media in support of access to informa-tion) assumed major roles in all three case studies.

The emphasis in the rest of the chapter is on how the networks were constituted, what we learn about the complex relations between the actors, and how they affected policymaking and governance.

Protection of State Information Bill

The Protection of State Information Bill (Posib) – also known as the Secrecy Bill, or the Media Bill (see Rawoot 2011) – was intended to replace in the main the *ancien régime*'s Protection of Information Act (No. 84 of 1982). In general, the Bill deals with the classification and protection of state information. It provides for the regula-tion of access to state information and introduces punitive measures for those who publish classified state information. However necessary it was to replace legislation that had apartheid roots, the Bill's road to adoption was obstacle-ridden, given a new zeitgeist of heightened distrust of state, government and, in particular, political leadership. Objections to the Bill concerned provisions that undermine the right of access to information, as well as the rights of whistle-blowers and the media.

Section 32 of the Constitution of the Republic of South Africa, 1996 (No. 108 of 1996), provides that every citizen has the right of access to any information held by the state. Provisions of the Promotion of Access to Information Act (PAIA) (No. 2 of 2000), which stood in the context of heightened ANC and government sensitivity to media exposés, help shed light on the problems with Posib. The PAIA specifies the procedures for access to information and the reasons why a request for infor-mation may be refused. It also strikes a 'balance between the right to governmental transparency and the need to protect important countervailing interests', such as national security, defence, economic interests and the criminal justice system (Harris 2013). The government's goal was to get new legislation that would super-sede the PAIA (see Sosibo 2012; amaBhungane 2015).

Legislative trajectory and policy implications

Posib's legislative trajectory shows that the original 2008 version (the 'Kasrils Bill' in the time of Ronnie Kasrils as minister of intelligence) had provided for declassifica-tion of apartheid-era records and for records maturing at 20 years. The Bill lapsed with the onset of the 2009 South African elections and the altered political climate of Zuma's 2009 rise to state power (see Smuts 2011). Post-election, the ANC government revived the initiative. Concerns notwithstanding, the National Assembly passed the new Bill, Posib, in November 2011. Two months later, with evidence of widespread public resistance, the National Council of Provinces (NCOP; parliament's second house) ad hoc committee hearings commenced, and went on a national public participation road show. Public participation is enshrined in the 1996 Constitution (see the Constitution's sections 59, 72, 118, for example). The consultation process, however, was flawed and partisan. Opposition party, the Inkatha Freedom Party (IFP), called for the hearings to be suspended due to the events being used to mobilise ANC supporters and suppress opposition voices (Underhill and Donnelly 2011).

The democratic pretences of the policy process were also undermined when in 2012 state security officials intervened in parliamentary processes and appeared before the NCOP ad hoc committee (the Department of State Security had already been allowed repeatedly to make inputs into the parliamentary process). The security contingent rejected all changes proposed by MPs, including ANC MPs. A few months later, the NCOP passed amendments and, in April 2013, the National Assembly approved the Bill. Six months later, President Zuma invoked his powers under Section 79 of the Constitution, referring the Bill back to the National Assembly. Zuma cited technical problems in sections 42 and 45 (a cross-reference and punctuation error, respectively), which had rendered meaningless a safeguard on state powers to classify information. In October 2013, the National Assembly adopted the revised Posib and again sent it to the president for his assent. Opposition parties argued that the Bill remained open to a Constitutional Court challenge.

The 2012–13 political climate counter-indicated the ANC proceeding with Posib. The events of the ANC's centenary, the ANC's contested Mangaung elections (amid mounting resistance to his leadership, Zuma won a second term as ANC president), the then pending 2014 election campaign, the death of former president Nelson Mandela in 2013, and the Nkandla exposés as examples of corruption charges against Zuma, all suppressed the ANC's appetite for more controversy. In the run-up to this hiatus there had been ongoing calls for Posib's withdrawal and new action to ensure that the 1982 legislation would be updated, without the Posib errors and associated suspicions of party political expediency. Some wondered whether the 2015 scandal around the leaked spy cables – *The Guardian* and *Al Jazeera* had obtained dossiers, files and cables from the world's top spy agencies to and from South Africa – would trigger a sign-off on Posib (Smith 2015). From 2015 to 2017, however, there were several statements that suggested equally that the ANC government might take the plunge and formalise Posib.

At one stage, the then state security minister asserted that he was at an advanced stage of drafting regulations for the Bill's implementation (Makinana 2015). By May 2017, the Bill was still in the presidential inbox, no presidential speech referred to it, and the political climate was turning towards presidential succession and the associated reluctance to proceed with controversial legislation again. Constitutional expert Pierre de Vos (2018) at the time pointed out that South African presidents are obligated to act, although they are limited in their options. They 'can only refer those parts of the Bill first to the [National Assembly] and then to the Constitutional Court, but only if they truly have reservations about the constitutionality of these sections'. Permanent inaction, De Vos (2018) argued, would mean that the president (even if the incumbent has changed in the course of the process) arrogates powers that he does not have. Such arguments notwithstanding, successor South African president Cyril Ramaphosa (in the period 2018–19) was not moved to sign the Bill into law.

The network's critiques of the Bill

Specifically, the opposition policy network's critiques of the Bill (see Bhardwaj 2013) concerned the stiff penalties, including jail terms, for leaking documents. The need for a public interest defence also dominated the debate. Such a defence would exempt individuals from prosecution should they be in possession of classified documents that reveal state ineptitude or corruption. The narrow public interest defence that was incorporated into Posib protected disclosures in the public interest where such disclosures reveal outright criminal conduct. Disclosing suspect tendering practices, improper appointments and flawed policy decisions – manifestly in the public interest – would not qualify for such protection.

Further problems were that Posib's espionage offences, which criminalised the unlawful receipt of state information, could be used to punish researchers, activists, whistle-blowers and journalists who disclose classified information, even if this was in the public interest. Posib proposed that such actions would carry a severe prison sentence. The proponents argued that the need for a public interest defence is eclipsed since such information will no longer be classified. The remaining problems centred on the extension and protection of state power against citizens and agencies that might reveal abuses of power.

Posib policy action network: For and against

A formidable anti-Posib network coalesced over time, changing in focus and composition as the campaign to counter the proposed legislation unfolded. At the height of mobilisation, it comprised civil society advocacy organisations, local and international; the Right2Know campaign (a coalition at the time of approximately 400 civil society organisations and community groups); Cosatu, and specifically the South African Democratic Teachers Union (Sadtu) within Cosatu; Corruption Watch; the Media Institute of Southern Africa; South Africa National Editors' Forum, Nelson Mandela Foundation; Committee for the Protection of Journalists; Human Rights Watch; Human Rights Commission; Helen Suzman Foundation; veteran struggle lawyer George Bizos; and many others. Several opposition parties were involved. From within the state the then public protector (a Chapter 9 state institution supporting constitutional democracy) opposed Posib. The NCOP 2012 ad hoc committee received approximately 260 submissions, 41 of which were from organisations or concerned citizen groups.

Major anti-Posib protest actions included a September 2011 march on parliament, prompting the ANC to remove the Bill from the parliamentary programme and make it available for further public consultation (in 2012, the Alternative Information Development Centre was removed from the NCOP ad hoc committee for linking the legislation to intra-ANC developments; see Molete 2012). The ANC sent a top-level delegation to the Press Freedom Commission, arguing for the reining in of the press through Posib, and for setting up a media tribunal that would have the power to deregister or jail errant journalists. Media veteran Joe Latakgomo (2012: 11) remarked: 'It is the stick with which the government wants to beat the media into submission, and having done so allow the pillaging of our resources to flourish even as voters go hungry, are homeless, jobless […].' In March 2012, opposition parties in parliament threatened to lodge a Constitutional Court challenge if the ANC failed to amend Posib. Eleven opposition parties – including the DA, Cope (Congress of the People) and the ACDP (African Christian Democratic Party) – joined forces for a protest rally in Khayelitsha, Cape Town. ANC MPs Ben Turok and Gloria Borman refused to vote in favour of the Bill. The ANC parliamentary caucus laid a complaint, but an intervention by the ANC's Pallo Jordan averted an ANC disciplinary hearing.

For a while, political parties and the media moderated publication of presidential and other leader scandals. However, the exposés of then president Zuma's dubious actions and associations, such as his abuse of public funds for 'security' upgrades at his Nkandla private homestead, personalised state capture in association with the Gupta business dynasty, and involvement in South Africa's costly arms and potential nuclear deals, again escalated in 2015–17. Government first toyed with taking the plunge on Posib, but then retreated: the president had become an inappropriate person to sign off on the legislation. In an attack that illustrated the power of the opposition network, the Tripartite Alliance objected that civil society, NGOs and opposition parties were combining forces to defeat the ANC in ways that were not possible via the ballot box. This was the same sentiment as expressed by President Zuma in 2016, and in 2017 by Zumaists when a division of the High Court ordered the president to reveal his reasons for his March–April cabinet reshuffle (interestingly, the latter action to let the president retain powers to appoint cabinets without revealing reasons has continued under the presidency of Cyril Ramaphosa).

Factional differences in the ANC also helped halt Posib. ANC National Executive Committee (NEC) members were angered by being asked to endorse Posib without having discussed it (Malefane 2011). They feared factional manipulation of the Bill and factions spying on one another. In 2015, then president Zuma had appeared to gain ground. Narratives such as 'enemies that are out to get us', 'vigilance is required to protect the victories over apartheid and colonialism', and 'opposition parties align with white monopoly capital to undermine the gains of our liberation' were used to try to create a bulwark to prompt clampdowns. However, the turning of the tide especially from December 2015 (the time of another ill-fated cabinet reshuffle to promote close associates) onward, against former President Zuma and his use and abuse of state power, reinforced the network's critiques and confirmed the 'non-Posib policy'. As President Ramaphosa assumed government power in February 2018, Posib remained dormant. The oppositional network had faded by then, but the governance impact of the network's actions – stopping and in effect subverting Posib – remained in place.

Gauteng e-tolling

The attempted regulation of payment for Gauteng e-tolls veered between legislation, thwarted implementation, policy reviews, a commission of enquiry, amendments to the system, court action to enforce payment, the ANC calculating political costs, and protest – including civil disobedience (see Outa 2014, 2018). The resistance process indicated a complex interplay of civil society (both organised and informally constituted), and government (pro and anti) in making, amending and obstructing (and thus making de facto) public policy. The campaign amounted to what was arguably the largest thwarting (by a few million citizens) of public policy implementation, and the most formidable constitution of de facto policy-specific network governance, that democratic South Africa had ever experienced.

Resistance to the e-tolling project

The Gauteng Freeway Improvement Project's (GFIP) gantries on major sections of the N1, N3, N12 and R21 freeways around Johannesburg leveraged new forms of mass protest in direct challenges to government. Non-implementation of the policy followed.

E-tolling touched the pockets of all Gauteng residents, directly or indirectly, across all classes, and also affected business. There were fears of extension into the Western and Eastern Cape provinces, but some of these fears were removed through the Constitutional Court's dismissal of a South African National Roads Agency Limited (Sanral) case in 2017. By mid-2014, estimates were that only about one-third of freeway users paid their e-tolls. By early 2017, estimates were that roughly 18 per cent of Gauteng motorists using these freeways were paying, despite pro-payment advertising campaigns and attempts to escalate sanctions for non-payment, such as Sanral moving for default judgments against toll boycotters (see, for example, Duvenage 2015; Mzekandaba 2016). Sanral's pro-payment campaign escalated in 2017. Yet, during the 2017–18 period, Sanral reached no more than 25 per cent compliance, spending more money on collecting than it managed to collect (Outa 2018: 16).

The company, Electronic Toll Collection (ETC), collected e-toll fees on behalf of Sanral. ETC is a consortium comprising South African company TMT Services and Supplies (TMT) and Austrian traffic company Kapsch. Resistance to e-tolls was driven by the pricing (even if substantially reduced, in several tranches), by suspicions of corruption, by resentment of a foreign company benefiting substantially, and eventually by the increasingly ingrained culture of non-payment. Several companies connected to the ANC and Cosatu were suspected of benefiting from the e-tolls contract and its multiple subcontracts. Cosatu's investment arm, Kopano Ke Matla, was revealed to own shares in Raubex, a construction company that won a tender to build one of the freeways that were being tolled to pay for construction (Rossouw and Ndlangisa 2012). Amid a lack of transparency, no singular financial benefit relationship for the ANC could be proven.

Anti-tolling network and government actions

The anti-e-tolling network was the most formidable adversarial-to-government alliance yet to emerge in post-1994 politics. (It could be matched if one adds up cumulative service delivery protests and non-payment for electricity, with mobilisation mostly at working- and sub-working-class levels.) The movement became part of a governance network in that it dictated (even if consistently challenged by government) the de facto policy on e-tolling: in its adversarial role it forged a 'policy' of non-payment for the use of the major freeways. It showed how ideologically diverse and multi-class actors converged to oppose, block and undermine unwanted policy – and deliver an adversarial form of governance.

Gauteng citizens' mobilisation was due largely to the work of the Opposition to Urban Tolling Alliance (Outa) – later renamed the Organisation Undoing Tax Abuse (still Outa) – and the anti-tolling networks that formed the resistance. Significant supporters of the project also included the Justice Project South Africa (JPSA) and Cosatu (besides also having a financial stake in the operation). Further network actors were, in different capacities, the courts and the DA (for example, through the party's funding of R1 million for Outa to continue its anti-e-toll legal challenges). The South African Communist Party (2012) urged cabinet to take note of mass opposition to the system and instruct Sanral to abandon it. The QuadPara Association of South Africa was on board. Church bodies, including the South African Council of Churches (arguing the impact of e-tolling on the poor), swelled the ranks of the alliance. The EFF in its 2014 election campaign threatened to physically remove the gantries, describing e-tolls as robbery of people who already cannot cope with the high cost of living. The Road Freight Association and the National Taxi Alliance were occasional participants, the latter because many of its taxis had not been issued with operating licences, making them liable for billing. Taxis generally had secured exemption in the pre-election time of early 2014, as millions of financially burdened working-class citizens use taxi transport daily in Gauteng (and the ANC feared that their voting allegiance might shift away from the party).

The most powerful 'member' of the anti-tolling alliance was the freeway-using citizenry (specifically, private rather than commercial road users), the bulk of whom continued to defy the system despite growing obstacles. Government tried continuously to lure the freeway users into compliance, using both stick and carrot. In May 2015 it announced a government compromise position: the stick was that unpaid fees would be attached to the renewal of motor vehicle licences; the carrot was overall lower fees, a lower cap on total monthly fees, exemption of public transport and discounts for arrears. In late 2015 government initiated legislation that would make it a points-demerit penalty-bearing traffic offence not to pay e-tolls. Yet the boycott continued. In the wake of the Gauteng ANC's defeat in core metropolitan municipalities in local election 2016, Gauteng premier David Makhura denounced e-tolling (Mzekandaba 2017). The minister of transport announced in mid-2017 that government, again, was set to review Gauteng's e-toll policy. The National Roads Amendment Bill was to propose that future e-toll routes be paired with alternatives that are comparable in distance, of good quality and suitable for increased usage. It was also proposed that municipalities and provinces get a bigger say in the decision to introduce tolled roads and that public consultation will be meaningful. In July 2018 the Gauteng ANC, again, denounced e-tolls Gauteng, adopting a resolution to scrap e-tolls and relieve the financial burden on motorists and commuters. Reminiscent of the Gauteng ANC's 2014 intervention, Panyaza Lesufi (2018) referred to the ANC's 'firm decision to ensure that e-tolls are terminated and terminated permanently'. He added that an ANC team was to 'go to national and speak to those that will assist us [to] realise this particular decision'. By 2019, there was little progress in resolving the stalemate. While the premier told citizens that President Cyril Ramaphosa had assured him that e-tolls were receiving urgent presidential attention, Sanral, the Department of Transport and the Gauteng City Region Observatory worked to legitimise a payment regime (see Sanral 2019).

Although it was illegal not to pay, Sanral at first and up to March 2016 refrained from pushing legal action against offenders. Outa and others had pledged legal support for anyone being formally charged. It initiated a collective 'defence umbrella'. Sanral won default cases, but by mid-2018 the e-toll GFIP test cases aimed at individuals and companies were still tentative. Outa was still challenging the e-tolls simultaneously in a renewed Constitutional Court bid. Government handed Sanral further bail-outs while it tried to close legal loopholes and enforce payment (despite possible policy change). Sanral nevertheless failed to improve its e-toll debt collection, despite its Less60 discount dispensation and issuing of many thousands of summonses. E-toll debt to Sanral escalated to around R14 billion by 2017–18, while the debt for construction and accrued interest owed by Sanral amounted to R67 billion by 2018.

Staggered and halting policy implementation

For a long period, Sanral had vacillated in implementing Gauteng e-tolls. It stalled through protracted legal challenges by organised civil society, especially from Outa. Implementation was supposed to have commenced in February 2012; it eventually followed in December 2013. The year 2012 brought mobilisation and Outa court challenges. National government tried to compromise through an annual budget provision for it to cover 25 per cent of the cost of the GFIP, enabling Sanral to drop the e-toll fees. Protest grew, irrespective. Cosatu's resistance to e-tolling went nationwide. Outa filed a founding affidavit in the North Gauteng High Court, seeking an interim interdict which was granted pending a full judicial review. The Treasury filed an application to appeal the interdict in the Constitutional Court. In September that year, the court set aside the temporary interdict, thus enabling Sanral to proceed with implementation. The year ended with High Court hearings and a judgment that overruled Outa. The Gauteng e-toll process also revealed some of the schisms in the Tripartite Alliance, besides those between the ANC's national and provincial (Gauteng in this instance) units. In addition, it challenged Sanral to be more transparent in the details of funding mechanisms. In the Western Cape province, the DA took court action to force Sanral to reveal its planned tolling rates on some provincial roads. The details were only revealed later, when the Supreme Court of Appeal in Bloemfontein set aside a Western Cape High Court ruling that had ordered the particulars to remain secret.

Back in 2013, Outa received leave to appeal. By mid-year Sanral handed over contract documents to the DA, including the hitherto secret ETC files. The Supreme Court heard Outa's appeal in September 2013. In the interim, then president Zuma signed the Transport Laws and Related Matters Amendment Bill into law, effecting further legislation to regulate implementation. The DA challenged the legality of the Bill, arguing that it should have been handled as a law that affects provinces, and been routed via the NCOP. The Supreme Court of Appeal ruled against Outa. An additional line of division was the national ANC and government against the Gauteng ANC and provincial government. The tolls were implemented, but as Gauteng voters showed their discontent and the anti-ANC vote grew in both the 2014 provincial and the 2016 local elections (with fragility again in the 2019 provincial elections), government attempted further compromises.

Before the ANC reached the point of its 2018 conference resolution condemning e-tolls, the years 2014–2018 had brought multiple complications, with vacillating voices from within the ANC and government strengthening the opposition network. The High Court dismissed the DA's challenge to the implementation legislation. ANC secretary general at the time Gwede Mantashe told Gauteng motorists to stop whining and pay (*SA Breaking News* 2014), calling e-toll opposition misplaced and emotional. Gauteng's transport MEC noted that moves were afoot to scrap e-tolls as means to fund freeway improvement. Premier Makhura announced an advisory panel to review the impact of e-tolls. Sanral blamed Makhura for its partly failed bond option issue (Sanral relied on bond options to help raise operational capital). October 2014 saw the ANC Gauteng conference resolve to oppose the application of e-tolls *in its current form*, at that stage leaving the door open to a fuel levy. A national Department of Transport spokesperson reminded these provincial actors that it is the function of the national minister of transport, and not the ANC (nor the Gauteng ANC), to change policy. The Gauteng ANC also presented its proposals to the advisory panel and Paul Mashatile (2014) stressed the need to compromise: '[…] National government won't be there if they do not have the people to support them.' The Gauteng review panel was pressured to comply with national policy, and the ANC continued vacillating between compromised implementation and promising citizen-voters to do away with the tolls. Mashatile (2015) attacked opposition party calls for an e-toll referendum, arguing that the people had already spoken through inputs into the review process. By 2017, Makhura (see Mzekandaba 2017) said the e-tolls were a mistake. Soon afterwards, the national ministry promised a substantive policy review which would comply with consultation requirements and viable alternative routes.

The ANC's (including the Gauteng ANC) vacillating role in and out of the complex and adversarial anti-e-tolling network was one of the main factors contributing to the relative success of the network. The Gauteng ANC at first was prepared to rise in mild opposition to e-tolls, then succumbed to the dictates of central government and top ANC structures. In 2016–19, the ANC government, through its agency Sanral, came to the point of closing the legal loophole to strangle the network and force citizens to pay, while simultaneously in 2018 it was promising to abandon the tolls, and in 2019 suggesting that it was working on a solution.

#FeesMustFall

The #FeesMustFall (#FMF) case of adversarial policymaking represented a similar governance phenomenon, yet also diverged from the preceding two cases. The first two case studies concerned stalling and thwarting the implementation of government policy initiatives that had failed to gain legitimacy. The #FMF policy initiative was both a new policy challenge, pushing government out of a comfort zone of incremental policymaking and long-established budgetary parameters, and about getting the government to implement existing policy commitments to free higher education for the poor. It simultaneously pushed government and universities to realise institutional transformation that had been envisaged when the 1994 post-apartheid order took root. Many in the movement demanded outright free post-secondary education for all.

The #FMF movement was rooted in the youth generation's anger with persistent racial inequality and the coloniality of universities' institutional cultures and curricula. Young people in South Africa, and in particular the student youth, suffer a triple jeopardy 25 years into democracy: despite many layers of transformation, large numbers grew up in poverty and, suffered school education that prepared them poorly for a life of employment or higher education. Once those who gained access to higher education arrived at these institutions, they found themselves frequently culturally alienated and/or financially excluded. The students' grievances and experiences of this intersectionality resonated with a broad youth community. Vice-chancellors asked themselves how it happened that despite their ongoing attention to the exact matter of the revolt it actually materialised (see Badat 2016). At least some of the answers lie in insufficient prioritisation of transformative policies at the university front, and in policy neglect and assumptions of youth patience at the national front.

In this policy gap a powerful and diverse network of student organisations and social media groups (with many iterations along gender, language, political, geographic and cultural lines), and a broad social movement, designated the #FeesMustFall movement, took hold. As in the previous two case studies, they formed adversarial policy–governance networks with the formal university and state institutions. In contrast, the government was more willing to cooperate, co-opt, concede and comply.

For example, the opposition side of the network challenged and subdued top government and governing party figures – ranging from the (former) president of South Africa and the minister of higher education to the secretary general of the ANC, and university figureheads. The ANC retreated strategically, compromised with the students on state-sponsored education for the poor, required the National Treasury and universities to fund, inter alia, zero per cent fee increases for 2016 and a capped 8 per cent for 2017, followed by full funding for poor students (through bursaries rather than loans) to be delivered through the National Student Financial Aid Scheme (NSFAS). The latter was introduced by then president Zuma on the eve of his exit from the ANC presidency in December 2017. By mid-2018 (and continuing beyond), NSFAS was under severe strain.

The ANC's position in the #FMF policy network was affected by the fact that organisationally and as government it had accumulated a litany of policy documents and legislative initiatives that held out the promise of transformed institutions and cultures of learning, along with the right to education for all. The ANC's abundance of pre-revolt statements and policies included the 1955 Freedom Charter's call that 'the doors of learning and of culture shall be opened!' and the ANC's continuous elevation of the charter as its guiding document. Undertakings in the 1993 Reconstruction and Development Programme (RDP) to attend to the needs of access to and finance for higher education did not go far enough. Many of the ANC's own key documents offered ambiguous commitments and vague policy suggestions. For example, the 2009 ANC election manifesto stated that 'the ANC has always stood for' the 'right to access health, education'. It then simply mentions the national financial aid scheme that 'is helping to improve participation of the poor in higher education' and that 'much needs to be done to improve the quality of health care and education'. The 2014 manifesto referred to higher education and student access in elusive terms: '[…] we will intensify efforts to support the needs of poor students, including (and through) adequate student funding […]'. The manifesto boasted that student enrolment at higher education level had increased from 49 per cent in 1995 to approximately 66 per cent in 2010. More than 1.4 million students, it stated, had benefited from NSFAS

(ANC 2014: 37). By 2015 the ANC's National General Council political report had emphasised school education primarily, stating that there will be 'work towards a free and compulsory education for all children'. The ANC's 2015 National General Council, a few months prior to the start of the revolt, reported that 'higher education has implemented its plans and programmes despite the shortage of skills and resources' (2015: 19).

On government side, the 1997 Department of Education's White Paper (also *Government Gazette* No. 18207) promised a programme for higher education transformation. At first it was seen as visionary, but subsequently it was questioned (HESA 2009). The 2008 report by the Ministerial Committee on Transformation and Social Cohesion and the Elimination of Discrimination in Public Higher Education Institutions (also known as the Soudien Report 2008) identified pervasive discrimination and evidence that South Africa's universities were not geared to inclusion of African students. In a later report, Soudien *et al.* for the Department of Higher Education and Training (2012) found further that free higher education for the poor is possible and affordable in South Africa (Soudien 2014). However, the report became stuck in bureaucratic and political quicksand. The 2012 National Development Plan (NDP) 39 recommends that government.

> provide all students who qualify for the National Student Financial Aid Scheme with access to full funding through loans and bursaries to cover the costs of tuition, books, accommodation and other living expenses. Students who do not qualify should have access to bank loans, backed by state sureties. Both the National Student Financial Aid Scheme and bank loans should be recovered through arrangements with the South African Revenue Service (National Planning Commission 2012: 71).

The NDP also recognised the need to advance black academics.

The #FMF student network found fertile ground to anchor their demands – demands that had been recognised by the ANC, the ANC government and its commissions of inquiry. The policy initiatives recognised the need to assist poor students with funding to gain access, and provide all students with a postcolonial study environment. The specifics of funding to sustain students through all university costs, and the lag in the transformation of colonial and racist or racially oriented institutional cultures and decision-making styles, however, did not feature adequately. Besides the declarations of neglect of the higher education sector, there are multiple fiscal indications that government had been guilty of sectoral neglect (see Butler-Adams 2015: 1).

Hostile exchanges ruled between the #FMF network actors, on the one hand, and the ANC, ANC government, and various university managements, on the other hand. Given the insufficient outcomes of previous policy decisions, the liberation-history credibility of the ANC and government did not leverage moderation of student demands at first. Later in the process, some of the bonds between the ANC and parts of the student body would again emerge sporadically. The ANC had also been nurturing nationalism in public discourse (see Booysen 2015: chapter 4). Emphasis on the bigger enemy of racism and colonialism helped veil government delivery deficits. The ANC could also not dismiss the students when their revolt focused on the untransformed racial character of South African universities. In fact, once the phase of revolt-insurrection had been averted, the students' 'campaign' reinforced the ANC narrative.

Power dynamics of the #FeesMustFall network

The predominant #FeesMustFall (#FMF) network comprised the hashtag Fallist community. Over time, it included #FeesMustFall, and several derivatives and variations of Fallism, including #RhodesMustFall, with #RhodesSoWhite, #OpenStellenbosch, #TransformWits, #NationalShutdown, #OutsourcingMustFall, #FeesWillFall, #FeesMustFall, #ANCMustFall and #FeesHaveFallen. Socio-economically the students had multiple additional social media networks formed around poverty, exclusion, inequality, intersectionality and gender derivatives.

Ideological and party political diversity – along with the national solidarity asserted in the earlier phases of the uprising – characterised the student network. The network at the time shunned many of the efforts by party politicians to insert their parties in the revolt. Nevertheless, the EFF's campaigns through its Student Command structures were central to the uprising, and the ANC retained a central role in the network's deliberations. This was due to both its governing party status and pre-existing party political bonds.

The network had a series of power moments that impacted on governance in South Africa. The week of 18–22 October 2015 brought evidence of substantial student social movement power over government. Within a peak period of roughly ten days, government and university policies were changed or amplified, as politicians were humbled and humiliated (yet often tolerated and listened to by some of the same protesters out of the public eye). As students mobilised nationally and then converged on both parliament and the Union Buildings, they dictated terms of settlement to the politically embarrassed government. In the course of Thursday, 22 October 2015 (on the eve of the march on the Union Buildings and negotiations between student leaders and the then president), the ANC produced a series of media statements (ANC 22 October 2015) that revealed how the ANC realised it had to produce specific and immediate concessions, or risk losing control of the revolt.

The ANC recovered, largely by dividing the national network on lines of ANC loyalty. It deflected pressures by appointing the Commission of Inquiry into Higher Education and Training (the Fees Commission 2016). Students maintained high levels of pressure through 2016–17 while awaiting the report. The president had received the report in August 2017, but stalled on releasing it. Flare-ups continued, sparked by dissatisfaction with fees, accommodation, and student debt. Private and state security forces became core network members as the state and university managements suppressed the 2016–17 on-campus revolt. The National Education Crisis Forum, a platform or network of civil society constituted largely to find solutions in the education sector, convened the Higher Education National Convention in 2017 but postponed it indefinitely after disruption by fractious student factions. Universities South Africa (USAf), a vice-chancellors' forum, formed a tight core of the network and worked to maintain coherence in how universities were responding to the diverse student network. Workers and campus-specific worker unions helped maintain the pressure on university management, while monitoring closely universities' progress on insourcing of essential services – one of the major gains of the #FMF network.

In an apparently seamless network link, former president Zuma conceded wide-ranging free access to students in what came across as a poisoned chalice handover to his successor as ANC president, Cyril Ramaphosa, in December 2017 (see Pather 2017). Amidst growing student pressures on him directly, Zuma in effect also severed the preceding network. He put huge pressures on the National Treasury and NSFAS to find funds not previously budgeted for, and in due course brought the entire NSFAS system to baulk under administrative pressures. As students expanded their demands for better-quality accommodation and services in 2019, the minister of finance positioned subsidised higher education and training for the poor as a flagship intervention. Over the medium term, government would be spending R111.2 billion 'to ensure that 2.8 million deserving students from poor and working class families obtain their qualifications' (Mboweni 2019). These strains on the relatively well-functioning network for fast-tracked and enhanced policymaking had potentially severe impacts on future national-level fiscal planning and policy development.

Table 7.2: Comparison of governance through three policy networks

	Problems	Interventions	Network governance arrangements
Posib	Limited consultation; security interventions; government fears freedom of information, media and whistle-blowers; permanent inbox of the president; ANC fears of factional hijacking	Legal challenges; forced additional consultation; leverage through high public profile and specialist high-profile network with credibility	Network thwarting implementation; de facto policy is status quo ante; stalemate arrangement with network power is boosted by legal system
E-tolls	Unpopular measure; expensive project with overtaxation; suspicions of corruption; culture of 'lawlessness'; electoral fate of ANC; divisions in ANC	Court challenges; legislative tightening; highly organised civil society civil disobedience; network remains mobilised; ANC refuses referendum; Sanral wins default cases	Network fends off effective implementation; legal options for network exhausted; Outa awaiting final legal tests; civil disobedience continues to counter closing of legal noose by government; ANC's fear of electoral costs recurs
#FMF	Low political will to implement existing policy; problems recognised but little effective action on the issues of sub-transformation and student exclusions; NSFAS grinds into action and higher education consumes a huge proportion of national resources	Mass action that accelerates policy implementation, holding government to account; ANC calls in political loyalties (PYA, etc.) and divides the network; NSFAS improved; incremental university transformation; high security force presence; Fees Commission unfolds; student network remains mobilised	Network of student organisations accelerates implementation; concessions grow amidst ANC narratives of radical economic transformation; approximate holding pattern of university management and government power being held in check by #FMF; NSFAS offers hope but flounders; students continuously ready to restart protest

Source: Synthesis of author's analysis, as detailed in the text

Note: Acronyms in this table are explained in the text

CONCLUSION: ANC COMPROMISES AND ADVERSARIAL GOVERNANCE PREVAILS

The three case studies of network policymaking and de facto governance show in diverse ways the power of adversarial governance networks (see Table 7.2). At first, and in remarkable acts of mobilisation to counter government power, the networks claimed territory, and either stopped the government in its policy tracks, or propelled it forward into rapid policy augmentation and implementation. Next, government retreated and compromised, exercising constrained power in the respective policy areas, or it stepped up policy delivery and burdened fragile networks.

In all three cases, the ANC government continued exercising final state power. However, its weaknesses showed up: it was forced to adopt policy positions that had been constituted adversarially through the policy networks. The de facto policy that was being implemented was not of government's own planning, making or choosing. Through measures such as civil disobedience, social media and physical mobilisation, and legal recourse, the networks forced policy compromises or policy elevation. Government compromised, as in the case of post-#FMF policy adaptations of late 2015, when faced with the choice of conceding from a position of power or being embarrassed in power. In wars of attrition with the Posib and e-tolls networks, the ANC government persisted in not recognising formally that its Posib and e-toll policies were ineffectual, and that new, network-driven policy–governance positions had taken hold. Network power – constituted adversarially because new, applied policy positions prevailed that were not of government choice – took over when government had no choice but to succumb to the new de facto positions that were derived on the basis of adversarial interdependence.

On Posib, government was in a stalemate because it could not be seen to be clamping down on information flows; this would be construed as covering up wrongdoing (corruption, mismanagement, etc.) in government. Factions in the ANC feared exploitation by opponents. In the prevailing political climate, and with ANC presidential and NEC leadership changes looming at the time, it would have entailed great political risk to proceed and formalise adoption of Posib. This political cycle was repeating itself and by 2019, in the wake of intra-ANC and government leadership change away from the political order that had initiated Posib, the 'time of Posib' had passed and a form of legal-constitutional retraction appeared inevitable. The adversarial policy influence and governance network had come full circle.

On e-tolls, the Outa-driven campaign exhausted most legal options short of reconsidering the regulatory framework, but retained a compelling civil disobedience edge. Meanwhile, the ANC national government persisted in condoning the tightening of the legal noose. The ANC itself was, however, a key network accelerator. As the main governing party, it had the power to push for enforcement. Yet politically and in terms of electoral costs it could not afford to. The ANC in Gauteng practised double-speak in an effort not to alienate voters in the 2019 provincial elections. The ANC government owed the public accountability and it dared not move more explicitly against public sentiment. The adversarial network was enforcing ANC compliance with non-implementation of the e-toll policy.

On #FeesMustFall, the ANC as party and government rushed to compromise on policy action. Many of its own supporters in the revolt's heyday of 2015 – also core voices in the rising new generation of voters – were campaigning against it publicly, refusing insufficient offers by ANC leaders, and they had the power to ignite the institutions of higher learning. The network of 2015–2017 protesters was situated in powerful intellectual centres, had mastered mobilisation through social media, and could mobilise for both agreed policy positions and more radical demands. Many of them projected themselves as 'the children of the ANC' and the outsourced workers as 'our mothers and fathers', inserting an additional layer of opposition-versus-consent that would direct the future policy trajectory of the network. The network, however, became vulnerable, not only due to changing movement leadership and political parties overreaching into the student domain, but also because the intra-government and ANC network partners became misaligned in relation to the rest of the network. The network's policy impact, however, persisted and remained compelling. Despite the problems, the push for further policy implementation did not abate.

This wall of largely effective and policy-specific network opposition and governance thrived on methods ranging from civil disobedience to violent community and student protests, actions that included community justice, occupation, looting and arson, threatening widespread destabilisation and withdrawal of electoral support, or maintaining stalemate non-implementation ultimatums that the government dared not breach. The protesters and practitioners of civil disobedience forced government to amend its policy positions; de facto implementation of the adversarially derived policy positions became ingrained. In the process, new and combative forms of governance were forged, which may become a model for policy action in the period where a weakening ANC retains power generally, but often lacks the ability to exercise power on specific policy issues.

NOTE

[1] The first two of the three case studies used in this chapter draw on – but extend beyond – fieldwork that was done for the chapter, 'ANC in the cauldron of protest' in Booysen 2015.

REFERENCES

African National Congress (ANC). 2009. Working Together We Can Do More. Election Manifesto. Johannesburg.

African National Congress (ANC). 2014. Together We Move South Africa Forward. Election Manifesto. Johannesburg.

African National Congress (ANC). 2015a. *Mid-term review: State of organisation, 2012–2015.* National General Council. Johannesburg.

African National Congress (ANC). 2015b. Series of email broadcasts to author: Statement of the ANC on policing of student protests (10:47); Statement on the NEC meeting with the Progressive Youth Alliance (14:26); Statement of the ANC on ongoing student protests against fee increments (10:16). 22 October.

amaBhungane. 2015. Submission on the Draft Cybercrimes and Cybersecurity Bill to the Department of Justice. 30 November. http://www.r2k.org.za/wp-content/uploads/151130_amaBhungane-DOJ_CC-Bill-submission.pdf (accessed 2 March 2016).

Bachrach, P. & Baratz, M.S. 1962. The Two Faces of Power. *American Political Science Review* 56(4): 947–952.

Badat, S. 2016. Deciphering the Meanings, and Explaining the South African Higher Education Student Protests of 2015–16. Seminar paper and discussion. Johannesburg: WISER, University of the Witwatersrand.

Bessusi, E. 2006. *Policy Networks: Conceptual Developments and their European Applications.* Paper 102, Working Paper Series. Centre for Advanced Spatial Analysis. London: University College London.

Bhardwaj, V. 2013. Concourt: Likely Next Step for Secrecy Bill. *Mail & Guardian,* 23 October. http://mg.co.za/article/2013-10-23-concourt-likely-next-step-for-secrecy-law (accessed 1 June 2014).

Booysen, S. (ed.) 2015. *Dominance and Decline: The ANC in the Time of Zuma.* Johannesburg: Wits University Press.

Booysen, S. 2015. ANC in the cauldron of protest. In: Booysen, S. (ed.) *Dominance and Decline: The ANC in the Time of Zuma*: 263–276. Johannesburg: Wits University Press.

Booysen, S. 2016. Revolt, uprising, protest – Changing governance in South Africa. In: Booysen, S. (ed.) *#FeesMustFall – Student Revolt, Decolonisation and Governance in South Africa*: 22–52. Johannesburg: Wits University Press.

Börzel, T. 1998. Organizing Babylon – on the Different Conceptions of Policy Networks. *Public Administration* 76(2): 253–273.

Butler-Adams, J. 2015. Is the Decline and Fall of South African Universities Looming? *South African Journal of Science* 111(11/12): 1–2. doi: http://dx.doi.org/10.17159/sajs.2015/a013 (accessed 3 January 2016).

Colgan, D. 2015. The Role of Government and Civil Society in Ensuring Access to Social Justice for Children. Unpublished PhD thesis. Johannesburg: University of the Witwatersrand.

Commission of Inquiry into Higher Education and Training (The Fees Commission). 2016. http://www.justice.gov.za/commissions/FeesHET/docs.html (accessed 8 March 2017).

Department of Higher Education and Training (DHET). 2012. Report of the Working Group on Fee Free University Education for the Poor in South Africa. October. http://www.citizen.co.za/842977/breaking-free-education-report-released-read-full-report/ (accessed 12 January 2016).

De Vos, P. 2018. Why the Failure of Presidents Zuma and Ramaphosa to Deal with the Secrecy Bill is Constitutionally Delinquent. *Constitutionally Speaking,* 18 July. https://constitutionallyspeaking.co.za/why-the-failure-of-presidents-zuma-and-ramaphosa-to-deal-with-the-secrecy-bill-is-constitutionally-delinquent/ (accessed 7 August 2018).

Du Toit, P. 2018. NSFAS chair Sizwe Nxasana resigns after 'extreme strain' on the payments system. *News24*, 9 August.

Duvenage, W. 2012. Interview with Charl du Plessis: Avis man had appetite for battle. *City Press*, 5 May: 9.

Duvenage, W. 2015. Interview on SABC-SAFM, 22 May.

Duvenage, W. with Serrao, A. 2015. *The E-Toll Saga: A Journey from CEO to Civil Activist.* Johannesburg: Pan Macmillan.

Hajer, M. & Wagenaar, H. (eds) 2003. *Deliberative Policy Analysis: Understanding Governance in the Network Society.* Cambridge: Cambridge University Press.

Harris, V. 2013. What is Still Wrong with the Protection of State Information Bill? Research and Archive of the Nelson Mandela Centre of Memory. 10 October. http://www.nelsonmandela.org/news/entry/what-is-still-wrong-with-the-protection-of-state-information-bill (accessed 4 October 2014).

Hazlehurst, D. 2001. Networks and Policy Making: From Theory to Practice in Australian Social Policy. Australian National University. Discussion Paper No. 83.

Higher Education South Africa (HESA). 2009. HESA Statement to the Higher Education Summit. https://www.cput.ac.za/storage/services/transformation/he_summit_prof_pityana.pdf (accessed 12 March 2016).

Klijn, E-H. & Skelcher, C. 2007. Democracy and Governance Networks: Compatible or not? *Public Administration* 85(3): 587–608.

Latakgomo, J. 2012. A Stick to Beat the Media into Submission. *Sowetan*, 10 February: 11.

Lesufi, P. 2018. Interview on Talk Radio 702. *The Karima Brown Show*, 12 July.

Lukes, S. 1993. Three distinctive views of power compared. In: Hill, M. (ed.) *The Policy Process: A Reader*: 50–59. New York: Harvester/Wheatsheaf.

Lyall, C. & Tait, J. 2005. *New Modes of Governance: Developing an Integrated Policy Approach to Science, Technology, Risk and the Environment.* Burlington, VT: Ashgate/Routledge.

Makinana, A. 2015. Secrecy Bill creeps closer. *City Press*, 10 May: 8.

Malefane, M. 2011. ANC Revolt Blocked Secrecy Bill. *Sunday Times*, 29 September: 2.

Manson, S.M. 2001. Simplifying Complexity: A Review of Complexity Theory. *Geoforum* 32: 405–441.

Mashatile, P. 2014. Interview with Sakina Kamwendo. *Forum@8,* SABC-SAFM. 8 October.

Mashatile, P. 2015. E-tolls train has already left the station. *IOL*, 25 March. http://www.iol.co.za/the-star/e-tolls-train-has-already-left-the-station-1.1837021#.VRVAJOEQvq0 (accessed 27 March 2015).

Mboweni, T. 2019. Budget speech. Parliament of South Africa, Cape Town, 20 February. https://www.gov.za/speeches/budget_vote (accessed 21 February 2019).

Molete, M. 2012. MPs Defend Secrecy Bill Expulsion. *Sunday Times*, 1 April: 4.

Mzekandaba, S. 2016. Outa Dismisses 'Hollow' E-toll Threats. *ITWeb Business*, 5 December. http://www.itweb.co.za/index.php?option=com_content&view=article&id=158079:Outa-dismisses-hollow-e-toll-threats&catid=69 (accessed 7 May 2017).

Mzekandaba, S. 2017. No love for e-tolls. *ITWeb Business*, 21 February. http://www.itweb.co.za/index.php?option=com_content&view=article&id=159569:No-love-for-e-tolls&catid=69 (accessed 7 May 2017).

National Planning Commission. 2012. National Development Plan 2030: Our future – make it work. https://www.gov.za/sites/default/files/gcis_document/201409/ndp-2030-our-future-make-it-workr.pdf (accessed 1 February 2019).

Organisation Undoing Tax Abuse (Outa). 2014. The Court Case. 20 October. http://www.outa.co.za/site/the-court-case/ (accessed 10 October 2014).

Organisation Undoing Tax Abuse (Outa). 2018. Gauteng Freeway Improvement Project's e-tolls: A story of failure. Report. Johannesburg. 13 July.

Ostrom, E. 2005. *Understanding Institutional Diversity*. Princeton, NJ: Princeton University Press.

O'Toole, L.J. 1997. Treating networks seriously: Practical and research-based agendas in public administration. *Public Administration Review* 57(1): 45–52.

Pather, R. 2017. Zuma offers 'grants not loans' plan. *Mail & Guardian,* 16 December.

Poteete, A.R. & Ostrom, E. 2010.*Working Together: Collective action, the commons, and multiple methods in practice.* Princeton: Princeton University Press.

Rawoot, I. 2011. Stories that wouldn't have been told. *Mail & Guardian,* 9–15 September: 4.

Rhodes, R.A.W. 2006. Policy Networks. In: Goodin, R.E., Moran, M. & Rein, M. (eds) *The Oxford Handbook of Public Policy*: 425–447. New York: Oxford University Press.

Rhodes, R.A.W. & Marsh, D. 1992. New directions in the study of policy networks. *European Journal of Political Research* 21(1–2):181–205.

Rossouw, M. & Ndlangisa, S. 2012. Tolls: Cosatu Cashed In. *City Press*, 1 April: 2.

SA Breaking News. 2014. ANC Lost Support over E-tolls – OUTA. 12 May. http://www.sabreakingnews.co.za/2014/05/12/anc-lost-sup (accessed 13 January 2016).

Sanral. 2019. *Hello Gauteng*. Newspaper insert, 3 March.

Smith, D. 2015. South Africa scrambles to deal with fallout from leaked spy cables. *The Guardian,* 24 February. http://www.theguardian.com/world/2015/feb/24/south-africa-scrambles-to-deal-with-fallout-from-leaked-spy-cables (accessed 4 March 2015).

Smuts, D. 2011. The Sinister Heart of the Secrecy Bill Laid Bare. *Sunday Times Review*, 18 September: 5.

Sørensen, E. & Torfing, J. 2005. Introduction: Governance Network Research: Towards a Second Generation. In: Sørenson, E. & Torfing, J. (eds) *Theories of Democratic Network Governance*: 1–21. London: Palgrave Macmillan.

Sosibo, K. 2012. MP's input on Secrecy Bill spurned. *Mail & Guardian*, 8–14 June: 8.

Soudien, C. 2014. Inclusion, innovation and excellence: Higher education in South Africa and its role in social development: Part 2: HELTASA 2012 Special Section. *South African Journal of Higher Education* 28(3): 907–922.

Soudien, C., Michaels, W., Mthembi-Mahanyele, S., Nkomo, M., Nkateko, G., Seepe, S., Shisana, O. & Villa-Vicencio, C. 2008. Report of the Ministerial Committee on Transformation and Social Cohesion and the Elimination of Discrimination in Public Higher Education Institutions. Pretoria: Department of Education.

South African Communist Party (SACP). 2012. Ban labour brokers! Stop e-toll highway robbery! Pamphlet.

Underhill, G. & Donnelly, L. 2011. NEC Members Deny Prompting Halt of Secrecy Bill. *Mail & Guardian*, 23–29 September: 8–9.

Zuma, J. 2016. Statement of the National Executive Committee on the occasion of the 104th Anniversary of the African National Congress. Rustenburg, 8 January.

PART II

SECTORS AND LOCATIONS

8

Governance versus Government: As reflected in water management

Mike Muller

INTRODUCTION: WATER, GOVERNMENT AND GOVERNANCE

Since water flows through all aspects of a society's life, and all human activities depend on it in one way or another, it is a useful medium through which to consider how collective decisions are made about issues of common interest, such as the governance of natural resource use. The overarching objective of the management of water has been defined succinctly as the achievement of water security: 'the reliable availability of an acceptable quantity and quality of water for health, livelihoods and production, coupled with an acceptable level of water-related risks' (Grey and Sadoff 2007).

The objective is easy to state but its realisation is more difficult. One critical question is: who is responsible for the achievement of water security? For some aspects of water, this is relatively easy to define – for instance, the supply of safe water for domestic purposes to a large town is usually the job of that town's local government. But responsibility for other functions is more difficult to pin down – for instance, who apportions water from a small river in a heavily populated rural area where many farmers want to take more water than the river can provide?

Governments, particularly in poorer developing countries, seldom have the means to administer natural resources at this level of detail. And while agreements may be reached between local people on water sharing, how can these be prevented from breaking down if there is a shortage? If a dam could store water to increase and assure the farmers' supplies, who should authorise, build and pay for its construction?

Who gets priority if there is also a factory and a town that need supplies? Who controls water quality and decides how much waste may be dumped into rivers by industries and municipalities, and under what conditions? How is the extraction of underground water regulated to ensure that wells do not run dry? And who decides how much effort – and sacrifice – should be devoted to environmental protection, since this invariably means restraining the use of the resource?

To successfully undertake the wide range of activities necessary to achieve water security, complex information has to be collated, alternative solutions need to be developed and analysed, and many different interests have to be reconciled. These are matters that require agreements about the approach to be taken within the communities concerned and the wider society. That approach must then be operationalised and enforced with rules to guide decisions and actions through more or less formal organisations; in other words, governance arrangements are needed.

A further complication is one of scale. Because water flows within its own natural 'infrastructure', whose boundaries are invariably different to those of political and administrative jurisdictions, it is often difficult to determine which institution should have authority, responsibility and accountability for what activities. When rivers cross national boundaries, must issues of allocation, management and development of the resource be resolved at interstate level as a matter of foreign relations?

South Africa provides many examples of how these challenges of water management and its governance may be addressed. But, first, the sectoral efforts need to be placed in their broader context.

GOVERNMENT AND GOVERNANCE

If water and its management are complex, the same can be said about the concept of governance. This review starts by discarding the Washington Consensus, donor-aid definition of 'good governance' (which effectively meant that countries would implement the policies they were told to). The concept of 'governance' then becomes useful because practical challenges – such as collectively managing water to achieve water security – highlight the limits to the reach of conventionally defined *governments*.

Simply stating that governance 'has too many meanings to be useful' (Rhodes [1996] suggested that there were at least six) is not particularly helpful. Equally, Fukuyama's definition (Fukuyama 2013: 3) of '[…] governance as a government's ability to make and enforce rules, and to deliver services, regardless of whether that government is democratic or not', does not take us forward in relation to many of the complex local issues that have to be addressed.

Rhodes' advice was to 'rescue' the confused and contested concept simply 'by stipulating one meaning' (Rhodes 1996: 660). But Fukuyama's later reflection (Fukuyama 2016: 100) is more helpful, when he points out:

> The two apparently opposed meanings of governance – on the one hand, governing without government, and on the other, traditional state-based public administration – are in fact linked.

The focus on the role of non-state actors was, he suggested, driven by the 'perceived failures of traditional public administration to "deliver the goods"'. In this, he is not very far from Rhodes, who decided that, for his purpose, 'governance refers to governing with and through networks' (Rhodes 2007: 1246). To this end, he defines a 'core executive' and 'decentralised, steered networks'. As it happens, while his purpose was the study of British government and public administration, his conceptual structure was not too distant from the vision of Elinor Ostrom, who, around the same time, was explaining how the use of 'common pool' natural resources such as water could effectively be governed. Specifically, she suggested that we need to conceptualise a series of 'nested' or 'polycentric' institutions (Ostrom 2009b).

Water management can thus provide a useful medium through which to understand some interpretations of the concept of governance and the challenges it presents. If formal government is not able by itself to make and enforce all the decisions needed to ensure the effective functioning of society in a complex world, it must at least enable a framework within which non-state actors – businesses, trade unions or simply people who use water – can act to meet their needs. So, for the purposes of this chapter, the 'governance' considered is the structured interaction between a central government authority and decentralised groups (or networks) of other agencies and non-state actors that have a direct interest in the use of water and its management.

WATER GOVERNANCE IN HISTORY

The other introductory perspective that is helpful is a historical one. In the deep past, one radical solution to the complexities of water governance was simply to organise the life of communities around it. And this has occurred in different ways in different places and times.

Water has long been associated with government, and historians continue to argue about the role of water and its management in the very establishment of states and systems of government and governance. The classical example is Wittfogel's analysis suggesting that great 'hydraulic civilisations' in India, China and Central America emerged through their control of water infrastructures (Wittfogel 1955). More recently, it has been suggested that California is a 'hydraulic state', the product of a similar process (Worster 1982).

At a more local level, the evolution of one of Europe's earliest forms of local government is attributed to the need for formalised cooperation in small communities to manage the challenges of reclaiming and living along the unstable coastline of the Netherlands at the beginning of the second millennium. Even today, the Dutch refer to 'poldering' to describe the system of consultation and consensus building that guides public decision-making (OECD 2014).

The measure of the success or failure of these approaches to water management has often been to consider the success or failure of the society itself. So there is a substantial literature which suggests that civilisations like the Maya in Central America and the Khmer in South East Asia collapsed when, due to internal conflicts or external environmental change, they were no longer able to sustain their water security (Diamond 2005).

Meanwhile, other societies have flourished despite their water management challenges. California's thriving economy is founded on a complex hydraulic system that brings water from far-off mountains in the north to the near-deserts of Los Angeles in the south. Arguably, its expensively constructed water security enabled the growth of the economy, which in turn provided the resources to continue to support its water management! Evidence of this is that the value of its agricultural production was sustained over the four years of the worst drought in its history, even as cities struggled to find enough water to meet their basic needs. Perversely, this 'success' is built on what many believe to be a dysfunctional governance system (Reisner 1993). If nothing else, this is evidence that the very nature of water resources and how they can sustainably be used is poorly understood, which makes it difficult to pursue a substantive discussion of their governance.

SUSTAINABLE USE AND MANAGEMENT OF WATER AS A 'COMMON POOL RESOURCE'

Because water is a natural resource, there are understandable concerns about the long-term 'sustainability' of its use. However, because it is a renewable resource replenished in nature on a seasonal if often irregular and unpredictable basis, the reasons for this concern and the nature of the desired sustainability are often poorly articulated.

At a very local level, water and its management provided Elinor Ostrom with many examples of cooperation in the use of a 'common pool resource' (Ostrom 1990), which she used to demonstrate that Hardin's prediction of an inevitable 'tragedy of the commons' (Hardin 1968) was unduly pessimistic. In small communities at least, the resource was generally not overused to the point where irreconcilable conflicts or damage occurred. She found that increased demands on water resources often led to cooperative action rather than to conflict. Her insights into these outcomes, synthesised in her seminal collection *Governing the Commons: The Evolution of Institutions for Collective Action* (1990), saw her become the first woman to win the Nobel Prize for economics in 2009.

At the other extreme, water has become a focus of concern in global environmental policy: the twenty-first century challenges of establishing a social and economic order that is environmentally sustainable. Indeed, the history of water policy over the past four decades illustrates not just efforts to impose a global water management regime on individual nation states (Conca 2006), but also to achieve this through a system of deliberative governance that goes well beyond governments (Dryzek 2013), and back into Ostrom's small communities.

The active promotion of a global governance regime for water can be considered to have begun at the Stockholm Environment Conference in 1972, which sought to place environmental issues on the global agenda. It continued when Gro Harlem Brundtland, in her 1987 report to the United Nations (UN) General Assembly, made the link between environment and development (World Commission on Environment and Development 1987). However, water resources were not initially a priority in these discussions, but regarded as a local rather than global matter, aside from those cases where rivers inconveniently flowed across national boundaries. So although the UN held its first (and to date only) conference to address water issues in Mar del Plata in 1977 (United Nations 1977), the 1980s was considered a 'lost decade' for water resource matters (Scheumann and Klaphake 2001), aside from the mobilisation of a practical programme to increase access to water supply and sanitation services.

This changed in the 1990s with the 1992 Rio Earth Summit on Sustainable Development (at which some important global agreements emerged, including the

UN Framework Convention on Climate Change and the Biodiversity Convention). The development and use of water resources was discussed at a preparatory meeting in Dublin and, while many of the Dublin recommendations were rejected, a whole chapter of the Rio Action Plan 'Agenda 21' was devoted to water issues, which were now placed on the global environmental governance agenda.[1]

Many of the contentious issues at the Rio meeting had their roots in the economic domain. In the 1980s, heavily indebted developing countries had become enmeshed by structural adjustment and were told that they should comply with the prescriptions of the Washington Consensus. Following the Rio Earth Summit in 1992, these prescriptions were extended to the way in which their water was governed (Muller 2013a). Specifically, it was to be treated as an 'economic good' and the costs of its provision to be recovered in full from its users; in general, the role of government was to be reduced and private provision preferred to public.

While these provisions were rejected in Rio, it was inevitable that developing countries would still be pressurised to adopt reforms through development aid processes. Prior to and separate from Washington Consensus pressures, a development aid orthodoxy had evolved that promoted participatory approaches as crucial to development. At one level, these were just practical responses to challenges of sustaining various kinds of services after external interventions. So in the water sector, the challenge was to ensure that someone in a village took responsibility for maintaining a handpump once the government team had supplied and installed it.

While the initial emphasis was simply to ensure the sustainability of water services, the other driver was a desire to tackle structural causes of poverty and underdevelopment by ensuring that poor people had greater agency: 'Participation is the process whereby such people seek to have some influence and to gain access to the resources which would help them sustain and improve their living standards' (Oakley 1991). Other commentators specifically linked this to the evolving role of non-governmental organisations (NGOs) and civil society more broadly in new forms of governance, reflecting Rhodes' understanding of the term: 'NGOs can play an important role as interlocutors and facilitators of public consultations, catalyse public debate, and contribute to improving governance' (Clark 1995: 598). This approach was then linked to generic concepts of subsidiarity (see Neef 2009). In the water sector, this approach gave rise to recommendations that water resources should be managed by special-purpose, stakeholder-driven institutions.

The net result of the focus on sustainable development has thus been that since the 1990s, developing countries have been under significant external pressure to adopt a specific set of approaches to water governance.

SOUTH AFRICA REFLECTS GLOBAL PROCESSES

South Africa's democracy was achieved at the same time as these global developments. As a result, South Africa not only reflects the global discourse of the time in its water management reforms, but it has subsequently provided an empirical context through which many of the global prescriptions about water governance can be assessed.

So it is that the 1996 Constitution has provided a case study of the governance implications of federal approaches and subsidiarity for water management (Muller 2014b). Beyond that, the implementation of the Constitution's Bill of Rights has informed debates about rights-based approaches to water governance. South Africa's introduction of free basic water supplies upset the advocates of treating water primarily as an economic good. While 'free basic water' pleased those who believed that governance should be based on human rights considerations, in practice the benefits of the policy may have been undermined by too great a focus on human rights at the expense of other, more traditional, dimensions of governance (Muller 2008).

At the institutional level, the failure to establish the water resource management institutions proposed in the 1998 National Water Act (NWA) reflects the generic challenge of balancing the interests of strong and weak participants in the stakeholder-driven governance future envisaged by some environmentalists (Faysse 2006). Similar conclusions may be drawn about approaches to the management of shared rivers.

More generally, the South African experience also illustrates the weakness of the links between the empirical and the theoretical, which puts in question the usefulness of many of the academic debates about water governance.

GOVERNANCE OF WATER SERVICES – THE PRIMARY CONCERN OF MOST SOUTH AFRICANS

In 1994, the priority for the majority of South Africans was access to water services, the reliable supply of safe water, and sanitation. This has continued and protests about poor service provision, often related to water and sanitation, have become a dominant feature of local politics.

This raises broad questions about how public services, particularly those that fall in the municipal domain, are governed under the 1996 Constitution. One outcome of the constitutional negotiations is that responsibility for these lies primarily at the municipal level (s.156). So how are municipal activities in service provision governed; what is the responsibility of national government; and, more specifically, how is the performance of other spheres of government guided by from a 'rights' perspective?

Nominal commitments to stakeholder governance (African National Congress [ANC] 1994) through participatory planning processes have generally been unsuccessful; the resulting plans have either reflected community desires for extensive interventions unrelated to available financial resources, or programmes defined by officials or their consultants after formalistic consultation. During the first decade of democracy, it was, however, notable that service provision was dramatically expanded.

Current concerns are more about the quality and sustainability of the services provided; in 2019, it was acknowledged that municipalities have failed to sustain reliable services to as many as 35 per cent of the population nominally served by infrastructure. While there have often been calls for national government intervention to resolve these matters, its ability to do so is severely constrained. It has the 'legislative and executive authority' for regulating the effective performance of local government (which it can do, for instance, by setting standards and monitoring performance). But first responsibility to intervene when a local government fails to perform satisfactorily lies with the relevant provincial authority (s.139); only if provincial intervention fails does national government have the power to intervene directly (s.100). So while the national government's Water Services Act (No. 108 of 1997) sets out a range of duties for local government which are elaborated in more detail in regulations on service standards and water pricing, these are often simply ignored.

Even where the behaviour of local government contravenes national legislation – for example, controls on water pollution – national government is often constrained by constitutional provisions on cooperative government which require it to 'exhaust all other remedies' before it approaches a court to resolve a dispute (s.41). While there is an obvious administrative logic to this arrangement, its political impact is unfortunate. The structure of the ANC, currently the ruling party in eight out of nine provinces, gives local branches the power to determine provincial leadership. As a consequence, provincial governments are often unwilling to act against poorly performing (or corrupt) local administrations on which they depend for their own survival (Muller 2014b).

In this respect, the global policy consensus that governance of water service matters is best delegated to the lowest possible level (ICWE 1992) is flawed. In theoretical terms, it fails to take cognisance of Ostrom's more nuanced approach which recognises that local arrangements will only be successful if 'nested' within larger frameworks that can provide direction and oversight – and have the powers to intervene when things go wrong. The experience of South Africa, specifically the experience of the weaker municipalities where the poorest South Africans live, would seem to bear that out.

Human rights and water governance – more for some, less for others?

One response to the crisis of service provision in poorer communities has been a recourse to the Constitution's Bill of Rights on environment, housing, health, and – specifically – water (sections 24, 26, 27). The 'rights-based' approach has given expression to the notion that governance must involve more than simply government and its direct agencies. There has been significant involvement of civic groups and NGOs in campaigns to demand faster progress towards the 'progressive realisation' of the 'right to water' (see Mehta 2006), albeit with limited attention to its longer-term sustainability.

However, the promotion of these 'social rights' is difficult and contentious. This was demonstrated when a group of residents from the Johannesburg suburb of Phiri went to court about water: specifically, they wanted more 'free basic water'; they opposed the use of prepaid water meters; and they objected to services being restricted for non-payment if they used more than the free basic supply provided by the municipality (Muller 2008). They were led in this campaign by the Anti-Privatisation Forum (APF). Described as 'a left-wing social movement alliance comprising affiliated community-based organisations, activists and movements, the latter group including the Soweto Electricity Crisis Committee (SECC)' (Dugard 2010: 87), the APF had been formed to oppose the City's commercialisation and corporatisation agenda. The campaign was supported by legal rights NGOs such as the Centre for Applied Legal Studies as well as other organisations such as the Freedom of Expression Institute.

Although lower courts supported the residents, the Constitutional Court disagreed, emphasising that 'government has the authority to decide how to provide essential services, as long as the mechanism it selects is lawful, reasonable and not unfairly discriminatory'. It decided that, because national government had explained in detail why it had set the minimum standards of 6000 litres of free water per household per month, and Johannesburg Water had carefully reviewed its approach to the implementation of that policy, it would be incorrect for the courts to seek to take on government's policymaking role. Only '[…] if the process followed by government is flawed or the information gathered is obviously inadequate or incomplete' could the courts intervene (Constitutional Court 2009).

One reason that a minimum standard was set for the whole country (DWAF 2001) was to achieve some equity in access to water. If available funds were used to provide additional amounts in some areas, there would be fewer resources available for others. Subsidies for free basic services are calculated and provided by the National Treasury as part of local government's 'equitable share of revenue'; if these funds are used by a municipality to provide higher levels of service, there will not be sufficient available to provide basic services for all the citizens of that area. There is already evidence that this is occurring.

While the Constitutional Court's judgment supported the government's approach, arguments during the court case strengthened the belief of many people that they were entitled to more free water. This has undermined water provision more generally across the country. High levels of access to water services, over 93 per cent, were achieved in the 15 years since 1994 (as measured by the provision of water supply infrastructure). However, the current trend is for actual access to working services to decline.

One problem is that in many parts of South Africa, there is no control on the use of water by people lucky enough to have access to it. An obvious result is that in large systems, people at the start of the pipeline use as much water as they want, while people at the end of the line often get nothing at all. As a consequence, it has been estimated that as many as 5 million people, 10 per cent of South Africa's population, have water supply infrastructure that often does not provide water (StatsSA 2016). This may be one product of campaigns that encourage people to demand rights and entitlements without reference to the associated responsibilities.

A further impact of campaigns has been on the provision of 'free basic water'. Because of the widespread demands for an increase in the amount provided free of charge, some municipalities have stopped providing a basic amount free of charge and, instead, introduced means testing to reduce the number of households eligible for the free service. Since such administrative systems often exclude those who qualify and create opportunities for corruption, the result has been that many eligible households no longer receive free basic water. Because people outside Johannesburg who had no safe water supplies at all were not part of the court action, many of these issues were not raised. One characterisation of the action could thus be that the 'have somethings' were campaigning for more for themselves, potentially at the expense of the 'have nothings'.

These outcomes illustrate a key challenge for participatory mechanisms. To the extent that governance is a process whereby rules may be set informally, by a group of stakeholders rather than imposed formally by an authority such as a government, the 'rights activists' may have been successful. However, from a governance perspective, this institutional framework allows local protest to achieve better conditions for some households but at the expense of many others. While the formal rules, as set by the Constitutional Court, moderated this, it can be argued that the net effect of the campaign had the opposite effect: it legitimated informal rules that encouraged communities to resist attempts to achieve equitable use of the limited resources available.

GOVERNANCE OF WATER AS A NATURAL RESOURCE – ECONOMIC ISSUES

The simple politics of interest groups and their mediation by the formal and informal mechanisms of democracy are well illustrated by the governance challenges of water supply services. The governance of water as a natural resource raises even more complex issues. Unlike piped water supply or other utility services such as electricity, water is derived from the natural hydrological cycle that renews the water over periods of days in the atmosphere, weeks in rivers, or centuries in the case of deep underground water (Shiklomanov and Rodda 2003). So there is no formal 'provider' who can set conditions on its use.

Some commentators have suggested that many water resource management problems could be resolved by using market mechanisms – in other words, 'putting a price on water'. But these rarely pass the test of practicality, even at local levels (Dellapenna 2000). Because water is used for many different purposes, a balance has to be struck between the needs and interests of many different users. Some users actually consume water – notably farmers, but so do power stations which use water for cooling. Other 'users' want water to be left in rivers – these include producers of hydroelectricity but also recreational users and environmentalists who seek to protect the aquatic ecosystems. Many users take water and return it to the rivers after use, but often in a highly polluted state – these include most domestic, commercial and industrial users. All water users want to be able to access water during droughts, and communities near large rivers want protection from floods.

Each of these users values water in a different way. For some, reliability of supply is critically important; for others, the quality of the water is the primary concern. It is difficult to determine an agreed value for environmental protection: hydropower producers do not want to pay for water that simply passes through their turbines but do seek compensation if they are required to reduce power production to manage water flows for flood protection. So the principal flaw of market approaches is that many of the diverse uses of water are not 'commensurable' – they cannot effectively be valued on a common scale (WEF 2014). The allocation of water between environmental protection, navigation, cooling power stations and irrigating farmers' fields cannot be made using financial measures but will require trade-offs and, invariably, be the result of a political process.

The notion that water 'rights' should be property that can be traded has often provoked objections because it is seen to threaten to make water unaffordable for poor people, while it raises concerns about the resource being monopolised by powerful financial interests. South Africa is no exception to these trends, and recently policy positions have been adopted that would see even seasonal trading between farmers banned (DWA 2014). This ignores the substantial societal benefits that such trading offers, not least achieving the most productive use of water during times of drought, as has recently been demonstrated in both Australia and California (Muller 2013b). The discomfort that this raises shows that policy initiatives in this area must convince political constituencies that a natural resource in the public domain is not going to be captured for private interests.

SCALE, SCOPE AND STRUCTURE OF INSTITUTIONS FOR WATER RESOURCE GOVERNANCE

The formal institutional framework for water development and management necessarily reflects the intended approach to water governance. Specifically, it has to address the scope of water management functions to be attended to, the scale at which they will be carried out, and the structure that will be put in place to undertake the work.

These issues were expressly addressed in South Africa's 1998 National Water Act (No. 36 of 1998) (NWA), with extensive inputs from international experts as well as local stakeholders. It widely is recognised to be a state-of-the-art, modern instrument which applies best practice to many of the difficult issues that such legislation has to address. An important feature of the Act is that it is drafted as an enabling, rather than prescriptive, instrument. It is also adaptive, allowing for changes in water use permits as the social, economic and environmental context changes. As a consequence, the degree to which different elements have been used provides an indication of the attractiveness and challenges of the new approaches.

In particular, it provides for different approaches and scales for different functions. Aside from the provision of local government water services, which are covered by separate legislation (Water Services Act [No. 107 of 1997]), the smallest scale addressed is that of single-sector irrigation use.

Irrigation and its institutions

The most 'local' direct users of water resources are irrigation farmers. Their ability to use water often depends on cooperation to develop, operate and maintain the collective storage and transmission infrastructure needed to capture and store water, and bring it to where it can be used. In many countries it has been found that groups who use water for the same purpose – such as irrigation – can often agree about the management and allocation of water between themselves. They can be encouraged to work cooperatively if empowered to do so by government author-ities, particularly if the recourse is to have their disputes resolved by such outside parties. Key to this cooperation is an evolved set of rules of behaviour, the know-ledge that each party knows what the other is doing, and the existence of formal or informal sanctions for breaking the rules.

In South Africa, there were historically two types of collective institution – inde-pendent irrigation boards, and government-controlled irrigation schemes. One key difference was that irrigation boards were self-managed by the farmers whereas the 'schemes' were run by government-appointed managers. However, the lines between these had become increasingly blurred over time, since the irrigation boards also received substantial subsidies for their infrastructure. In government-controlled water schemes, even operating costs were often subsidised, not least because staffing levels, duties and conditions of employment were determined through national public service negotiations and were often considerably higher than in self-managed schemes.

The 1996 water policy aimed to transform all these institutions into 'water user associations' (WUAs) which would take responsibility for operation and mainten-ance, and eventually for investment in their expansion; the 1998 NWA provided a framework within which this should be done. The Act recognised that WUAs 'are in effect cooperative associations of individual water users who wish to under-take water-related activities for their mutual benefit' (National Water Act [No. 36 of 1998]). However, since almost all commercial farmers were white, reflecting the country's divided history, WUAs were directed to achieve a degree of racial and gender representativity in their governance structures by appointing aspirant farmers, farmworkers or representatives from local municipalities. This created challenges since such stakeholders had a direct interest not in the running of the schemes but in changing how they operated.

While there have been a handful of cases in which new WUAs took proactive initiatives to promote and support the inclusion of new farmers in their schemes (for example, in the Blyde, Impala and Koekedouw Water User Associations), this has been the exception rather than the rule. However, since the primary barriers to transformation have generally been land and agricultural policy and its patchy implementation, the existing structures have continued to function. Since the WUAs have limited financial resources and do not offer much scope for patronage appointments, there has been limited political interference in their operations.

It is significant that at a commercial level this has been relatively successful, if only as measured by the continued growth in irrigation-based agricultural production. However, in some of the larger government schemes, the objective of greater self-sufficiency in relation to operation and maintenance of large schemes has not been achieved, and farmers continue to seek public finance to support major rehabilitation and maintenance work (NAMC/SWPN 2015).

Catchment management agencies

While stakeholder governance can work in the case of WUAs, these conditions do not apply as easily when there are new claims on the resource by outside parties – for instance, if a mine or a town wants to use water currently used by farmers. For these cases, external rules are needed that provide protection for existing users while specifying how, and under what conditions, new users can enter and existing uses be modified. This requires an overarching regulator to act as intermediary between potentially conflicting parties, classically a role for government. The NWA provides for this situation in terms of the rules on water allocation (which allow for water to be reallocated in a structured way over medium- to long-term periods (5–40 years). However, this has proved too administratively complex for the Department of Water Affairs (DWA) to implement except in small pilot areas. The Act also provided for catchment management agencies (CMAs) to be established, empowered to develop catchment management strategies that would cover many of these issues. The powers to administer the allocation process can also be delegated to them.

However, in the South African context, with much water use (in terms of total volumes) still serving mines, industry and large commercial farmers, it has been difficult to structure a governing board that could satisfactorily address the issues. One concern has been that the governance of the CMAs would be 'captured' by powerful existing water users and that it would not be possible to achieve equitable outcomes. From the other side, there has been the fear that a radical board might demand changes that would undermine existing economic activities. This situation is not unique to water, nor to South Africa. Rhodes (2013: 3) described the process by which his version of network governance proceeds as follows:

> Behaviour in policy networks is game-like, grounded in trust and regulated by rules of the game negotiated and agreed by network participants. Variations in the distribution of resources and in the bargaining skills of

actors explain both the differences in outcomes in a network and variations between networks. These actors are interdependent and policy emerges from the interactions between them. Such networks have a significant degree of autonomy from government.

It is the recognition that the outcomes from network-type governance in a CMA will depend on 'the resources and bargaining skills of actors' that explains much of the reluctance to press ahead with the establishment of the CMAs.

Interim informal arrangements

Despite the lack of progress on the establishment of formal CMAs, there is considerable evidence of effective informal water resource governance to address critical issues. Perhaps the most important and best known are the management arrangements for the Vaal River system on which much of the country's economy depends.

In the absence of a formal CMA, stakeholders are involved through less formal mechanisms such as strategy committees which are advisory and have no formal decision-making powers. The committees involve not only large industrial users that have a direct interest in supply assurance but also a range of civil society representatives, notably environmental groups concerned about water quality issues (Muller, Hollingworth and Mdluli 2011). Although municipalities are supplied by a bulk water utility (Rand Water), they are often included in consultation processes, which helps to ensure that environmental interests are balanced against more prosaic concerns about tariffs and reliability. There are also representatives of agriculture, other water utilities, and national departments and provincial government.

In addition, because the system is so complex, its operation needs to be modelled annually to determine whether supplies are adequate for the coming season, and whether more expensive sources (such as pumped transfer supplies) may be required. This modelling exercise is open to observation by all major users who can thus assure themselves about the reliability of their supplies. The system also enables the quality implications of different scenarios to be tested to determine whether different configurations of water releases are needed to maintain quality objectives. This is arguably an example of network governance in action.

River basin organisations and shared rivers – balancing water and political boundaries

One thrust of environmental governance generally has been to promote the management of natural resources within environmental rather than administrative or political boundaries. In that respect, South Africa's CMAs are a compromise. While their boundaries reflect those of river basins, they are divided into areas of economic and social activity rather than entire rivers. In the original configuration, the Orange River catchment was divided into five separate management areas, while in other areas a number of rivers are consolidated under the management of a single CMA.

This was in line with the recognition that water management affects many sectors of social and economic activity and needs to be undertaken in collaboration with them. Internationally, some authors have answered the question: 'Why does water management practice generally not use the basin approach?' with the simple statement: 'Because creating agreements and institutions is a costly practice, and so the focus is on real-world problems' (Giordano and Shah 2014). It has been specifically recognised in the case of South Africa that water may best be managed in its 'problemsheds' rather than 'watersheds' (Herrfahrdt-Pähle 2014).

In support of this process, an overarching National Water Resource Strategy sets out the extent to which each CMA can allocate water and also sets quality limits and environmental flows for different river reaches. This hybrid arrangement is consistent with the Ostrom concept of self-management within a larger framework of rules.

Governance in shared rivers

Although this 'problemshed' arrangement is widespread in developed countries (Mollinga, Meinzen-Dick and Merrey 2007), it does not meet the objectives of the promotors of environment-focused governance, particularly when it comes to rivers shared between countries. The governance of such rivers has attracted a great deal of academic interest, sometimes disproportionate to the materiality of the issues, for two reasons. First, at a global level, there are a few shared river systems where there are significant tensions. Principal amongst these are the Nile, where Egypt is at odds with upstream countries; the Jordan, whose water Israel has fought to control; the Tigris and Euphrates, which rise in Turkey and cross a zone of intense conflict in Syria and Iraq; and the Indus and the Ganges, where India regularly finds itself at loggerheads with its neighbours Pakistan and Bangladesh.

The tensions in these river basins – which encompass huge populations – have coloured ideas about how shared resources should be managed and encouraged the notion that there should be a global approach to shared water management. Taking advantage of these sensitivities, environmental advocates have sought to establish global regimes for the management of shared rivers (Conca 2006). The Southern African Development Community's (SADC) first technical protocol on shared rivers was developed in 1995 as part of a process to finalise and promote a

UN Convention on Transboundary Water Courses (McCaffery 2001). This in turn was part of a concerted effort to establish a new international governance regime for water resources.

As a consequence, southern Africa has been in the forefront of shared river management advocacy. Through SADC, foreign donors actively encouraged the formation of specialised river basin organisations (RBOs) to take water management decisions. The reality is that such RBOs play only a marginal role. It has long been recognised that natural resource governance is unlikely to be successfully undertaken within environmental boundaries when all the related social and economic decisions are taken within different political and administrative geographies.[2]

This is demonstrated in southern Africa (Muller, Chikozho and Hollingworth 2015) by the fact that most major developments on shared rivers have been undertaken by a national government (Zambian irrigation and hydropower projects on the Kafue tributary of the Zambezi, for example; or the lower Usutu Irrigation Project in Swaziland on a tributary of the Pongola). In other cases, there have been partnerships between riparian countries with a direct interest in a specific development (Zimbabwe and Zambia through the Zambia Revenue Authority (ZRA) on Kariba power development; Malawi and Tanzania on the Songwe River development, both in the basin of the Zambezi River; as well as the Lesotho Highlands Water Project between South Africa and Lesotho on the Orange-Senqu). The Cahora Bassa project on the Zambezi in Mozambique is an intermediate case, developed as a national project but serving, initially, to provide power to South Africa, which lies completely outside the river basin.

For these projects, the relationships between countries have generally been conducted through bilateral or multilateral commissions: when cooperation was required, collaborative arrangements were made or special-purpose vehicles established. Despite this evidence of the success of bilateral cooperation, external governments have actively promoted the establishment of RBOs on the Orange, Limpopo, Zambezi and Okavango rivers. Meanwhile, active cooperation on operations and development has continued to be undertaken on a bilateral basis through organisations such as the ZRA and the Lesotho–South Africa Joint Water Commission, and by a joint committee between the Tanzania and Malawi governments for the Songwe River project in the Zambezi river basin.

At the interface – governing the impact of water services on the environment

A final challenge for South Africa's water governance has been to manage the interface between the provision of water services, particularly sanitation, and water resource management. At issue is the need to ensure that municipalities, which have the constitutional responsibility to manage waste water and its disposal, do so in accordance with the law. Over the past decade, they have systematically failed to do this, as has been documented in the DWA's own monitoring reports (DWA 2010); indeed, the results have been so poor that government has been reluctant to publish the results of subsequent surveys, although they have a legal obligation to do so. For many municipalities, particularly smaller municipalities in poorer communities, it is clear that the protection of the aquatic environment is a low priority. This is hardly surprising since, in such communities, priorities within the water sector are, first, to achieve an affordable and reliable supply of safe domestic water; then, to have acceptable forms of sanitation in the household, with a strong preference for flush toilets connected to waterborne sewerage. Since the latter is still largely unaffordable (both in terms of the amount of water required and the infrastructure needed to remove the waste water), the treatment of the waste water collected is a low priority. As a consequence, little is spent on building and operating sewage works and rivers are polluted.

In the absence of formal catchment management agencies, empowered to monitor and intervene to maintain water quality, the default position is that the national government department has to undertake this function. It finds itself constrained by the Constitution, limiting its ability to intervene in the operations of the municipality, and by legislation, since the Intergovernmental Regulations Framework Act (No. 13 of 2005) explicitly states that '[a]ll organs of state must make every reasonable effort [...] to settle intergovernmental disputes without resorting to judicial proceedings'.

DISCUSSION AND CONCLUSION

This review of the governance of different dimensions of water, as a service and a natural resource, supports the value of a conceptual approach that considers governance as a framework of interaction between a core institution and related networks or stakeholders. This conclusion is reinforced by the South African and southern African examples.

One of the factors that constrains the adoption of more open and accommodating governance arrangements is the disparity in access to information and the quality of the information available. In the field of water services in South Africa, an example of the theoretical/empirical disconnect is the focus on private sector provision. There is extensive literature about the privatisation of water supply services in South Africa (over 1600 references on Google Scholar). Although legislation enables private participation, there is little evidence that this has been a significant feature of water governance; there have been only six privatisation contracts since 1994, affecting just 1 per cent of the population.

Similarly, in the field of water resources, an extensive literature about the 'water crisis' is often poorly informed about the basic challenges. An often-cited example is the statement that. 'South Africa already uses 98 per cent of its water'. A primary source for this is a report stating

> South Africa has allocated around 98 per cent of the national water resource at a high assurance of supply […] [F]or purposes of the argument being presented here, South Africa simply has no more surplus water and all future economic development (and thus social well-being) will be constrained by this one fundamental fact that few have as yet grasped (Turton 2008).

The factual situation is that South Africa was using 98 per cent of the water that had been captured, stored and managed, and was reliably available at a high degree of assurance (DWAF 2002); this is less than 35 per cent of the total 'mean annual runoff', the average flow of rivers in the country. There is thus still scope for more water to be made available by building more infrastructure. The absence of these insights might be explained by the fact that the author of the quoted report is a political scientist by training and former intelligence agent by profession. Yet, although he has achieved some notoriety amongst practitioners for other serious technical misstatements, the message of imminent scarcity has persisted. A minister of Water Affairs was still citing it five years later, stating that 'the situation currently in South Africa is that we have 98 per cent of the water in the country being considered "fully allocated", this means that my child and your child that is being born tomorrow has two per cent of water for use going into the future' (Molewa 2013).

In the same speech, the minister repeated another fundamental error, stating that 'South Africa buys some of its water from Lesotho'. Yet, in terms of the bilateral treaty between South Africa and Lesotho governing the Lesotho Highlands Water Project, it is clear that the water transferred from Lesotho to South Africa is South Africa's; it would normally flow south-west, down the Orange River into South Africa near Aliwal North. The agreement with Lesotho is to divert it so that it flows north into South Africa's Vaal River instead. The treaty between the countries simply shares the savings achieved by not having to pump the water from the point where it enters South Africa (Treaty Article 12.2)! But the minister is not to blame.

Even US Professor Aaron Wolf, a world expert who maintains the world's most comprehensive database on shared rivers, makes the same mistake. His 'fact sheet' states simply that 'South Africa buys water from Lesotho and finances diversion' (Wolf and Newton 2007).

If the 'experts' and authorities have so little understanding of the real challenges, it is clearly going to be difficult for either politicians or a wider public to engage in meaningful debate about them. Since effective governance requires informed participants, these complexities will necessarily impact on approaches to water governance. The recent travails of the City of Cape Town provide an eloquent example of this.[3]

Indeed, characterised as it is by a population with diverse priorities and capabilities, an economy of extremes of wealth and poverty, and constrained by a difficult natural resource base, South Africa provides many examples of the challenges of implementing the more active and participatory approaches inherent in a focus on broad *governance* rather than narrow *government*. Three principal challenges can be identified:

1. The complexity of the issues involved and the limited ability of many of the stakeholders to mobilise the technical resources required for effective engagement;
2. The extreme diversity of interests and power and resource differentials between stakeholders; and
3. The engagement required with a wide range of other polities and technical sectors.

Failure to recognise these challenges has led external agencies, driven by a desire to strengthen environmental governance, to promote single-sector management arrangements in southern Africa's shared river basins. These well-intentioned efforts have, however, often marginalised the new sectoral institutions from key political, administrative and economic actors who operate within different, usually national, boundaries. Decisions are, as is increasingly recognised, taken in 'problemsheds', not watersheds.

Similar considerations apply at the more local level. The focus on watershed governance has proved to be problematic even at national level. So it is that the establishment of CMAs prescribed by South Africa's NWA has stalled for almost two decades because politicians were not convinced that stakeholder management arrangements could be configured to ensure equitable outcomes rather than continued capture of benefits by powerful interests.

These challenges arise even amongst sectorally homogeneous groups of water users such as irrigation farmers or users of municipal services. The disparities of interest between, for instance, large-scale commercial farmers and putative smaller-scale new entrants make cooperation difficult; similar challenges arise between the interests of commercial users of water services, established suburban residents and residents of low-income areas. This all suggests that South Africa's water sector will, for the medium term at least, continue to see relatively strong centralisation of functions in government and its agencies, and limited devolution of functions.

To the extent that there are no irreconcilable differences between actual and potential water users at a local level, it would be a matter of good administrative practice to allow local parties to manage their own affairs – provided they do so within the country's overall policy framework, respecting basic constitutional principles, for instance. The recourse will usually be that, in the event of a stale-mate, government will be called upon to adjudicate – or at least to set up a frame-work within which adjudication can occur. In other jurisdictions, it has been demonstrated that the threat of government intervention may often be a strong incentive to local parties to reach an agreement.

For South Africa, the interim challenge is to develop the capabilities of different groups of stakeholders to enable, in the longer term, more effective and equitable participation in the governance of a resource that is too complex and unpredictable to be governed and managed primarily by politicians and bureaucracies.

This evolutionary process would be consistent with Fukuyama's (2016) for-mulation of governance as an effective interface between government and other, non-government actors. It would also fit Rhodes' (2013: 3) formulation of 'steered networks', 'the sets of formal institutional and informal linkages between govern-mental and other societal actors structured around shared, if endlessly negotiated, beliefs and interests in public policymaking and implementation'.

From all of this, what emerges is Ostrom's vision of the governance of common pool resources taking place with the participation of a variety of institutions and actors, acting at a range of scales, in what she termed 'nested polycentric govern-ance'. The one point on which most of the authors agree is that these processes are messy and complex. As Ostrom concluded in her Nobel Prize lecture in 2009,

> To explain the world of interactions and outcomes occurring at multiple levels, we also have to be willing to deal with complexity instead of rejecting it. [...] When the world we are trying to explain and improve [...] is not well described by a simple model, we must continue to improve our frameworks and theories so as to be able to understand complexity and not simply reject it (2009a).

NOTES

[1]   The recommendations of the International Conference on Water and the Environment (ICWE) in Dublin (1992) that were later rejected in Rio (1992) were those calling for water to be treated as an economic good; for it to be managed within watershed boundaries by institutions with stakeholder participation; and for the global water agenda to be taken forward by global stakeholder organisations outside the formal multilateral system.

[2]   As early as the 1930s, American geographers had considered what would be the appropriate boundaries for natural resource management. They generally found that river basins were not good units (see Meyer and Foster 2000; and full discussion in Muller, Chikozho and Hollingworth 2015).

[3]   Subsequent to the completion of this chapter, the City of Cape Town provided an example of the challenges of network governance as political heads from three spheres of government blamed one another for failure to take adequate measures to mitigate a catastrophic drought. The influence of environmental NGOs, which had strongly and consistently advocated the conservation-oriented approach that failed to address the city's needs, further illustrated the difficulty of attributing accountability in network governance (Muller 2018).

REFERENCES

African National Congress (ANC). 1994. *Reconstruction and Development Programme*. Johannesburg: Umanyano Publishers.

Clark, J. 1995. The state, popular participation, and the voluntary sector. *World Development* 23(4): 593–601.

Conca, K. 2006. *Governing Water*. Cambridge, MA: MIT Press.

Constitutional Court of South Africa. 2009. *Mazibuko and Others v City of Johannesburg and Others*. Case CCT 39/09, ZACC 28.

Dellapenna, J.W. 2000. The Importance of Getting Names Right: The Myth of Markets for Water. *William & Mary Environmental Law and Policy Review* 25(2): 317. http://scholarship.law.wm.edu/wmelpr/vol25/iss2/4 (accessed 16 August 2018).

Diamond, J. 2005. *Collapse: How Societies Choose to Fail or Survive*. New York: Viking.

Dryzek, J.S. 2013. *The Politics of the Earth* (3rd edn). Oxford: Oxford University Press.

Dugard, J. 2010. Civic action and legal mobilisation: The Phiri water meters case. (Draft chapter 4.) https://www.researchgate.net/profile/Jackie_Dugard/publication/265104232_CIVIC_ ACTION_AND_LEGAL_MOBILISATION_THE_PHIRI_WATER_METERS_CASE/ links/56b0888308ae9ea7c3b00fd9/CIVIC-ACTION-AND-LEGAL-MOBILISATION-THE-PHIRI-WATER-METERS-CASE.pdf (accessed March 2019).

DWA. 2010. Green drop report V.1. South African waste water quality management performance. Pretoria: Department of Water Affairs.

DWA. 2014. National Water Policy Review (NWPR) – Approved Water Policy Positions. Pretoria: Department of Water Affairs.

DWAF. 2001. Regulations relating to compulsory national standards and measures to conserve water. Regulation Gazette No. 7079 Vol. 432 No. 22355: Pretoria.

DWAF. 2002. National Water Resource Strategy. Pretoria: Department of Water Affairs and Forestry.

Faysse, N. 2006. Troubles on the way: An analysis of the challenges faced by multi-stakeholder platforms. *Natural Resources Forum* 30(3): 219–229.

Fukuyama, F. 2013. *What is Governance?* CGD Working Paper 314. Washington, DC: Center for Global Development.

Fukuyama, F. 2016. Governance: What Do We Know, and How Do We Know It? *Annual Review of Political Science* 19: 89–105.

Giordano, M. & Shah, T. 2014. From IWRM back to integrated water resources management. *International Journal of Water Resources Development* 30(3): 364–376.

Grey, D. & Sadoff, C.W. 2007. Sink or swim? Water security for growth and development. *Water Policy* 9(6): 545–571.

Hardin, G. 1968. The Tragedy of the Commons. *Science* 162(3859): 1243–1248.

Herrfahrdt-Pähle, E. 2014. Applying the concept of fit to water governance reforms in South Africa. *Ecology and Society* 19(1): 25.

ICWE. 1992. The Dublin statement and report of the conference. International Conference on Water and the Environment: Development Issues for the 21st Century. Dublin, 26–31 January.

McCaffrey, S. 2001. The contribution of the UN convention on the law of non-navigational uses of international watercourses. *International Journal of Global Environmental Issues* 1(3–4): 250–263.

Mehta, L. 2006. Do human rights make a difference to poor and vulnerable people? Accountability for the right to water in South Africa. In: Newell, P. & Wheeler, J. (eds) *Rights, Resources and the Politics of Accountability.* London: Zed Books.

Meyer, W.B. & Foster, C.H.W. 2000. New Deal Regionalism. Discussion Paper E-2000-02. Kennedy School of Government, Harvard University.

Molewa, E. 2013. Media briefing by Minister of Water and Environmental Affairs, Ms Edna Molewa, on Water Policy and Fracking in the Karoo, 3 September. https://pmg.org.za/briefing/19053/ (accessed 16 August 2018).

Mollinga, P.P., Meinzen-Dick, R.S. & Merrey, D.J. 2007. Politics, plurality and problemsheds: A strategic approach for reform of agricultural water resources management. *Development Policy Review* 25(6): 699–719.

Muller, M. 2008. Free basic water – a sustainable instrument for a sustainable future in South Africa. *Environment and Urbanization* 20(1): 67–87.

Muller, M. 2013a. The regulation of network infrastructure beyond the Washington Consensus. *Development Southern Africa* 30(4–5): 674–686. doi: 10.1080/0376835X.2013.830558.

Muller, M. 2013b. The dangers of divergent dialogues about drought, *Business Day*, 10 September.

Muller, M. 2014a. Allocating power and functions in a federal design: the experience of South Africa. In: Garrick, D., Anderson, G., Connell, D. & Pittock, J. (eds) *Federal Rivers: Water Management in Multi-Layered Political Systems*: 179–194. Cheltenham, UK: Edward Elgar Publishing.

Muller, M. 2014b. Constitutional Crisis – For the taps to flow, government needs to end the sunset clause on local autonomy. *City Press* Voices, 2 February: 30.

Muller, M. 2018. Developmental states, the role of experts and Cape Town's water crisis. *New Agenda: South African Journal of Social and Economic Policy* 69: 13–19.

Muller, M., Chikozho, C. & Hollingworth, B. 2015. Water and regional integration, final report, Project No. K5/2252. Pretoria: Water Research Commission.

Muller, M., Hollingworth, B. & Mdluli, M. 2011. Prospects and processes for the establishment of stakeholder-initiated catchment management agencies, final report, WRC Project K5-1972. Pretoria: Water Research Commission.

NAMC/SWPN. 2015. Funding and Investment Plan for the Vaalharts/Taung Irrigation Scheme Revitalisation Project. Prepared for National Agricultural Marketing Council/ Strategic Water Partners Network. Johannesburg.

Neef, A. 2009. Transforming rural water governance: Towards deliberative and polycentric models? *Water Alternatives* 2(1): 53–60.

Oakley, P. 1991. *Projects with people: The practice of participation in rural development.* Geneva: International Labour Organization.

OECD. 2014. Water Governance in the Netherlands: Fit for the Future? OECD Studies on Water. Paris: OECD Publishing.

Ostrom, E. 1990. *Governing the Commons: The Evolution of Institutions for Collective Action.* Cambridge: Cambridge University Press.

Ostrom, E. 2009a. Beyond Markets and States: Polycentric Governance of Complex Economic Systems. Nobel Prize lecture, 8 December. https://www.nobelprize.org/ uploads/2018/06/ostrom_lecture.pdf (accessed March 2019).

Ostrom, E. 2009b. Design Principles of Robust Property Rights Institutions: What Have We Learned? In: Ingram, G.K. & Hong,Y-H. (eds) *Property Rights and Land Policies.* Cambridge, MA: Lincoln Institute of Land Policy.

Reisner, M. 1993. *Cadillac Desert: The American West and its Disappearing Water.* New York: Penguin.

Rhodes, R.A.W. 1996. The new governance: governing without government. *Political Studies* 44(4): 652–667.

Rhodes, R.A.W. 2007. Understanding governance: Ten years on. *Organization Studies* 28(8): 1243–1264.

Rhodes, R.A.W. 2013. How to manage your policy network. Workshop paper for Commonwealth Secretariat, London, 7–8 February. https://www.researchgate.net/profile/R_A_W_Rhodes/ publication/289750649_HOW_TO_MANAGE_YOUR_POLICY_NETWORK_1/ links/56926eae08ae0f920dcd65eb/HOW-TO-MANAGE-YOUR-POLICY-NETWORK-1. pdf (accessed March 2019).

Scheumann, W. & Klaphake, A. 2001. *Freshwater resources and transboundary rivers on the international agenda: From UNCED to RIO+10.* Bonn: Bundesministeriums fur Wirtschaftliche Zusammenarbeit und Entwicklung.

Shiklomanov, I.A. & Rodda, J.C. (eds) 2003. *Water Resources at the Beginning of the Twenty-first Century.* Cambridge: Cambridge University Press.

StatsSA. 2016. GHS Series Report Volume VIII: Water and Sanitation, in-depth analysis of the General Household Survey 2002–2015 and Community Survey 2016 data. Pretoria: Statistics South Africa.

Turton, A. 2008. Three Strategic Water Quality Challenges that Decision Makers Need to Know About and How the CSIR Should Respond. Keynote Address: A Clean South Africa, (prepared for but not presented at) CSIR Conference Science Real and Relevant, Pretoria, 18 November.

United Nations (UN). 1977. Report of the United Nations Water Conference. New York: UN. http://www.ircwash.org/sites/default/files/71UN77-161.6.pdf (accessed May 2016).

Wittfogel. K.A. 1955. Developmental aspects of hydraulic states. In: Steward, J.H., Adams, R.M., Collier, D., Palerm, A., Wittfogel, K.A. & Beals, R.L. (eds) *Irrigation Civilizations: A Comparative Study.* Social Science Monographs No. 1. Washington, DC: Pan-American Union.

Wolf, A.T. & Newton, J.T. 2007. Case Study Transboundary Dispute Resolution: the Lesotho Highlands Water Project. Institute for Water and Watersheds. Oregon State University.

World Commission on Environment and Development. 1987. *Our Common Future* (Brundtland Report). Oxford: UN/Oxford University Press.

World Economic Forum (WEF). 2014. Water Security: Towards a Values-based Approach. Global Agenda Council on Water Security. Switzerland: World Economic Forum.

Worster, D. 1982. Hydraulic Society in California: An Ecological Interpretation. *Agricultural History* 56(3): 503–515.

9

Broken Corporate Governance: South Africa's municipal state-owned entities and agencies

William Gumede

INTRODUCTION

Municipalities in South Africa are increasingly making use of state-owned municipal entities and agencies to deliver public services. This follows global trends in which city and municipal public sectors, facing intense pressure to deliver economic and social development, with increasingly limited resources, yet perceived as shackled by bureaucratic constraints, decreasing income and lacking entrepreneurial nous, increasingly use alternative service delivery (ASD) methods (Stumm 1997; Jessop 2003; Wilkins 2003).

In 1994, the ANC government set about transforming the apartheid-era public service from a racially exclusive entity in terms of staff, public service delivery and ethos, to one that is developmental, efficient, democratic, and racially inclusive in both delivery and make-up (Fraser-Moleketi and Saloojee 2008; Gumede 2015). While transforming, the public service had also, at national, provincial and municipal level, to dramatically increase the quantity and quality of service delivery, as well as reduce historical public service delivery backlogs.

However, it soon became clear that at municipal level, massive capacity constraints, limited financial and human resources, and ongoing institutional weaknesses hamstrung public service delivery. ANC government policymakers started looking at alternative ways of delivering public service efficiently, cheaply and quickly, beyond the weak municipalities (Stacey 1997; SACP 1999; Khumalo, Ntlokonkulu and Rapoo 2003; Gumede 2005).

From 1996 onwards, the ANC government at municipal level increasingly used state-owned entities and agencies, run along business lines yet still owned by municipalities, either by restructuring existing ones or creating new ones, to deliver public services. The irony is that by 2016, many of these entities were so inefficient, corrupt and poorly managed that new Democratic Alliance (DA) Johannesburg mayor Herman Mashaba threatened, in the case of the Johannesburg city-owned entities, to close them down, and incorporate the staff back into the city's public service (Mashaba 2016). This chapter will look at the reasons for the broken governance of South Africa's municipal-owned entities.

THE DIVERSE LANDSCAPE OF MUNICIPAL ENTITIES AND AGENCIES

Municipal entities are essentially ring-fenced businesses (IoDSA 2010) which have a mandate to deliver a specific public service, can operate autonomously from the municipality, and ideally would have fewer bureaucratic constraints to innovate and improve performance (Peters 2012: 255). Most municipal entities concentrate on local social and economic development, tourism, social housing, and the provision of water, power and cleaning services.

When South Africa became a democracy in 1994, it inherited a number of municipal entities from the old white city councils and from the Bantustans, homelands and self-governing 'states'. These entities were either merged with similar others, or incorporated into provincial and national state-owned enterprises (SOEs) or into the new democratic municipalities.

In the post-1994 era, a number of new municipal entities and agencies have also been formed. According to the National Treasury (2011), as at 30 June 2010, there were 63 municipal entities and agencies. Most of the municipal entities were in Gauteng (26), 15 of these under the jurisdiction of the City of Johannesburg. The Eastern Cape has 11 and KwaZulu-Natal has nine. Northern Cape and Mpumalanga have none, and the remainder are spread across the other provinces.

The Auditor-General usually assigns municipal entities into four types: the *first* group are service utilities, such as Pikitup and the Johannesburg Social Housing Company. The Local Government: Municipal Systems Act (No. 32 of 2000), Section 82(2)(a), provides for the setting up of service utilities through a by-law of the municipality. The municipality exercises ownership. The governance of service utilities is similar to that of their national SOE equivalents.

The *second* group are municipal entities which are specifically incorporated to run along private sector lines, such as City Power, Johannesburg Development Agency, and the Overstrand Local Economic Development Agency in the Western Cape. Entities that have been corporatised, meaning they have been restructured to run like private companies, can raise finance from the financial markets, using their revenue streams and assets, and can pay dividends to the municipality, the shareholder (Khumalo *et al.* 2003).

The *third* group are section 21 companies, such as the Johannesburg Tourism Company, Johannesburg Road Agency, or the Blue Crane Development Agency in the Eastern Cape. These are public companies that are not for profit, but resemble the business structure of for-profit companies. They cannot have multiple owners, are entirely dependent on funding from the municipality and cannot give a dividend to the municipality. They have the advantage of not being subjected to public sector procurement requirements (Ashira Consulting 2003). This structure has often been used when funding comes from a donor.

The *fourth* group comprises entities incorporated as trusts, such as the Rustenburg Water Services Trust, which manages services on behalf of the municipality. Trusts are regulated by the Trust Property Control Act (No. 57 of 1988). Trusts have more flexibility to opt out of aspects of the standardised financial and compliance control measures applicable to the public sector. This automatically makes municipal oversight over them more difficult (Ashira Consulting 2003).

In 2012, the Financial and Fiscal Commission (FFC) concluded that although municipal entities were set up because they were deemed better than, say, municipalities or government departments to improve public service delivery, very few of them have delivered in the areas in which they are operating – social housing, water and waste management, and economic development. Many have also failed to become sustainable organisations (Auditor-General 2010, 2011, 2012b, 2013a, 2014, 2015). According to government's own reports, assessments and surveys, a significant reason for the failure of many municipal entities is governance-related (Auditor-General 2010, 2011, 2012, 2013, 2015).

Not only do many municipal entities not deliver effective services, but if they do, the quality of those services is often poor. Struggling municipal entities are regularly bailed out financially by municipalities, in the process taking away scarce resources from poor communities. Municipal entities which are incorporated to run as private companies and which can raise funding from financial markets also add to the sovereign country risks of South Africa – if they are not prudently managed. Almost all of the diagnostic assessments of the poor performance of municipal entities point to poor governance as a central reason for their failure.

METHODOLOGICAL APPROACH

This chapter examines the governance of municipal public entities or municipal SOEs in South Africa. Public entities are non-departmental institutions that have increased in number and have been delegated increasingly greater responsibility for service provision in the country. The chapter uses the definitions of governance at entity level based on those of the Organisation for Economic Cooperation and Development Principles of Corporate Governance (OECD 2015); the United Kingdom Committee on the Financial Aspects of Corporate Governance (Cadbury Committee; Cadbury 1992); and the South African King III Code of Governance Principles (King III 2009). All broadly argue that governance in public entities is 'the system' by which entities are 'directed', 'controlled', and held accountable, and by which the efficient use and stewardship of their resources for the greatest public value is judged.

Despite the growth of 'agencification', there remains a dearth of research on the governance of municipal entities. This chapter aggregates the results of a number of government-commissioned reports and surveys dealing with the governance, efficiency and performance of municipal entities, over the period 2009 to 2014. It specifically looks at the annual Auditor-General Local Government Audit Outcomes reports. It further interrogates reports from the National Treasury, the Department of Cooperative Governance and Traditional Affairs (CoGTA), and the South African Local Government Association (SALGA).

Furthermore, it also looks at key government-wide assessments of governance, effectiveness and the performance of local government and municipal entities, including the reviews of the performance of the state, done by the South African Presidency, National Treasury, Department of Public Service and Administration, FFC, and other relevant government surveys, reports and studies. It takes an overview of the slew of legislation, regulations and rules governing municipal entities.

Finally, the chapter will analyse whether inadequacies in the legislation, regulations and rules are to blame for municipal entity and agency failures; or whether the roots of the problems may lie elsewhere, and if so, where. Broadly, the chapter argues that poor governance in municipal administration is mirrored in how municipal entities function.

Trends in the literature on the governance of municipal entities

Establishing municipal entities and agencies to deliver public services has become increasingly popular not only in South Africa, but in developed and developing countries throughout the world (Ford and Zussman 1997; Good and Carin 2003; Wilkins 2003; Schick 2002). The establishment of such entities is usually part of broader reforms to overcome state 'failure', like initiatives to decentralise government, and bringing in the private sector in an effort to boost efficiency, accountability and performance (Stumm 1997; Polidano 1999; Jessop 2003; Wilkins 2003; Gumede 2015).

The typical municipal entity 'has a single or relatively narrow purpose, and each has substantial operating independence' (Schick 2002: 8). The rationale behind these municipal entities is that unlike municipalities and, provincial and national departments, they are 'specialised', and have 'significant operating independence' and more operational flexibility (Peters 2012: 255). Theoretically, this allows them 'to bypass many of the challenges that their bureaucratic counterparts experience', thus providing the potential to 'innovate and improve performance' (Peters 2012: 255).

Some researchers have criticised the use of alternative public service delivery models which ring-fence municipal entities from the rest of the state, arguing these are technical solutions, and that the real problems that lead to state failure are often political (Paquet 1997; Fyfe 2004). Proponents of this view argue that if successful, stand-alone municipal-owned entities may become enclaves of efficiency while the rest of the public sector continues to be wasteful, ineffective and corrupt. In such cases, systemic public service failures continue – and governments may not tackle them with the necessary resolve because the municipal-owned entities are apparently 'delivering'.

Researchers have identified a number of potential governance risks that often undermine the effectiveness of municipal entities in both developed and developing countries (Ford and Zussman 1997; Schick 2002; Wilkins 2003; Laking 2005). Many countries lack effective laws, regulations and oversight structures to hold municipal-owned entities accountable for delivering on their public service obligations, such as providing reliable public services at reasonable prices and ensuring equitable access of services (Fyfe 2004: 641).

In some cases, the rationale for the municipal entity has not been significantly thought through (Laking 2005). The 'precise functions and services' (IoDSA 2010:

4) the entity would provide are often not thoroughly interrogated. In many cases, municipal entities fail because there is not a 'sound rationale for the establishment of the entity' (IoDSA 2010: 4).

Many municipal entities are formed or used to sidestep corruption in local government, with the argument that because the entity is ring-fenced from the rest of the public sector, corruption will be reduced. However, unless there is better oversight from elected representatives, the public and the media; there is adequate regulation, which is enforced; and the corrupt 'culture' of the public service is not imported to the municipal entity, corruption will flourish in the municipal entity (Gumede 2015).

Established municipal entities in many countries often lack adequate governance legislation, rules and systems – and if present, lack the capacity to, firstly, monitor that entities are compliant and, secondly, hold entities accountable (Peters 2012: 257; see also Laking 2005). There is often a failure to adequately monitor the performance of entities – and hold them to account for their performance (Schick 2002; Laking 2005; Peters 2012: 257).

Key local government legislation applicable to municipal entities

The core legislation for municipal entities is the Local Government: Municipal Systems Act (No. 32 of 2000) which sets out the framework for the administration of the municipal entity. The Municipal Systems Act (Section 78) sets out the issues a municipality must consider when deciding what *form* – public–private partnerships, privatised, state-owned entity, or some other alternative delivery arrangements – to take.

According to the Municipal Systems Act (2000), municipal entities could be established along three lines: private companies, service utilities, or multi-jurisdictional service utilities. In alternative delivery arrangements, the state must still have effective control in that it can appoint or remove the majority of the board and have the majority voting rights.

The Local Government: Municipal Finance Management Act (No. 56 of 2004) (MFMA) oversees the fiscal and financial affairs of municipalities. The MFMA also urges municipalities to consider the impact on employment and their assets – whether it would be value for money, and whether it would affordable – to establish a municipal entity to deliver services.

The MFMA aims to strengthen accountability by separating political and management roles, bringing in service delivery performance measurements, and strengthening reporting and disclosure requirements (National Treasury 2011:

74). The MFMA takes precedence over any other legislation, including the New Companies Act (No. 17 of 2008), with the exception of the Constitution itself.

In municipal entities, the municipality is the shareholder and plays an oversight role over the entity. The Municipal Systems Act states that the parent municipality must ensure 'the municipality is managed responsibly and transparently, and meets its statutory, contractual and other obligations' (Section 93A(a)(ii)).

The MFMA says a mayor 'may monitor the operational functions of the entity, but may not interfere in the performance of these functions' (Section 56(2)). It also states that councillors may not interfere in the financial affairs or in the responsibilities of the board of a municipal entity (Section 103).

The MFMA also pushes for transparency in information provided by municipal entities in order for stakeholders to hold them better accountable. The MFMA (Section 127(5)(a)(i)) requires that a municipal entity must make their annual report public. However, very few municipal entities do so (Peters 2012: 263).

On paper, the MFMA clearly defines the roles, duties and responsibilities of the different governance players in municipalities. If genuinely implemented, it also provides elected representatives with seemingly sufficient enforcement tools to hold municipal entities accountable.

The new Companies Act and municipal entity governance

Many municipal entities are registered companies, assigned as state-owned companies (SOCs) in terms of the Companies Act (No. 17 of 2008). Municipal entities which are companies are regulated by the Companies Act. The majority of the provisions of the Act which apply to a public company will apply to an SOE or municipal entity, which is incorporated as a company, unless specifically exempted by the minister.

Furthermore, if there is a conflict between provisions in the Companies Act and the Municipal Systems Act, the Municipal Systems Act prevails (Municipal Systems Act: Section 86c). If there is a conflict between provisions in the Companies Act and the MFMA, the MFMA prevails (Section 3(2) of the MFMA). This is a major flaw in the governance structure.

The Companies Act entrusts the boards of companies to play an oversight role in the entity. The Companies Act (Section 76) sets the fiduciary duties for individual board members, whereas the Municipal Systems Act (Section 93H) only does so for the board collectively, specifically only focusing on financial management.

According to the Companies Act, a director, prescribed officer, or a member of a board committee may be held liable for indiscretions including any loss suffered by the company; for a breach of fiduciary duty; or for acquiescing to the company carrying on business in 'insolvent circumstances'. The board (Section 71) may remove a director who it has determined is ineligible, disqualified, incapacitated, negligent, or guilty of dereliction of duty. Again, the key governance aspects of the Companies Act highlighted here, if adhered to, will greatly improve the effectiveness of municipal SOEs.

Role of the board of directors in the governance of municipal SOEs

The MFMA and the Municipal Systems Act govern the role of boards of the municipal entities. The Municipal Systems Act stipulates that the board of directors and CEO of municipal entities must be given the powers to manage the entity. The MFMA states that the accounting officer of a municipal entity is the CEO.

The Municipal Systems Act (Section 93J(1)) gives the power to the board to appoint the CEO. However, in reality, the CEO of municipal entities is more often than not appointed by the parent municipality. And in many cases such appointments are made on political or patronage reasons, rather than competency.

The Municipal Systems Act has provisions against interference by the parent municipality in the responsibilities of the directors and CEO of the municipal entity. The Municipal Systems Act does not have strong provisions on the duties of directors of municipal entities (Municipal Systems Act: Section 93H). In municipal entities that are private companies, the Companies Act sets out clear duties for directors. However, the problem is that the provisions of the MFMA override that of the Companies Act – leaving a corporate governance weakness in the oversight of municipal entities.

The Municipal Systems Act states that Councillors' Code of Conduct applies to directors of municipal entities also (Municipal Systems Act: Section 93L and Schedule 1). The Councillors' Code of Conduct is not very onerous compared to the fiduciary duties of directors in the Companies Act. The lack of strong fiduciary duties of municipal entities' directors means they can essentially escape accountability for mismanagement, waste and corruption.

The Municipal Systems Act (Section 93E) provides for a director appointment process that must look at expertise, advertise vacancies widely, and make publicly available the details of the nominees. In spite of this, however, patronage appointments to municipal entity boards are widespread.

The Municipal Systems Act gives the power to remove a director to the 'parent municipality of a municipal entity' (Municipal Systems Act: Section 93G). The reasons for the removal of a director are poor performance, inability to perform, whether through ill health or other reasons, and inappropriate conduct, whether convicted of criminal acts or contravening laws or codes related to the conduct of a director. However, in reality, individuals who have contravened these rules, if they are politically connected, are often appointed as directors; or if already directors, are often protected.

The MFMA (Section 121(4)(d)) requires the municipal entity in its annual report to include an assessment by the accounting officer (CEO) of the entity's performance, measured against the service delivery agreement between the entity and the parent municipality.

Combined, the MFMA, Municipal Systems Act and Companies Act overall not only clearly set out the governance roles, duties and responsibilities of boards, they also give municipal entity boards sufficient power to ensure these entities are managed accountably. However, the political will to implement them is often absent (IoDSA 2010; Auditor-General 2012; Gordhan 2012b).

Governance role of the parent municipality

The Municipal Systems Act obliges the parent municipality to see to it that the municipal entity is 'managed responsibly and transparently, and meets its statutory, contractual and other obligations' (Municipal Systems Act, Section 93A(a)(ii)). The MFMA also stipulates that the board must give monthly financial reports to the parent municipality (Section 87(11)). Furthermore, the CEO of the municipal entity must provide the parent municipality with a mid-year budget and performance assessment of the entity (MFMA: Section 88(1)(b)), both of which need to be made public (MFMA: Section 88(2)).

According to the MFMA, the parent municipality or the mayor cannot run the operations of the municipal entity (Section 56(2) of the MFMA). Municipal councillors can also not get involved in the operations of the municipal entity (MFMA: Section 103). Neither can the parent municipality, mayor or councillors take over the responsibilities of the municipal entity board. The parent municipality could delegate a representative to the municipal entity board meetings (Municipal Systems Act: Section 93D(1)(a); Section 93D(3)(a)). However, such a representative must be 'non-participating' when it comes to the decision-making of the board (Municipal Systems Act: Section 93D(1)(a)).

The Municipal Systems Act and MFMA do give the parent municipality the power to close down the entity if its performance is unsatisfactory, if it experiences persistent financial problems, or if the municipality has terminated its service agreement with the entity (Municipal Systems Act: Section 93B; MFMA: Section 85(5)(d)).

The Municipal Public Accounts Committee (MPAC) plays a financial oversight role in the municipal entity on behalf of the council. The Auditor-General has been very emphatic that MPACs must ensure far greater oversight than is currently the case in many municipalities, over the performance of the municipality and the municipal entity in terms of the priorities and objectives set out in the municipality's Integrated Development Plan (IDP) (Auditor-General 2011).

The MFMA stipulates that the audit committee is an independent advisory body in municipalities and entities (Section 166). In some cases, according to the MFMA, municipalities may have a single audit committee for the municipality and municipal entities in their jurisdiction. The audit committee reports on the financial position of the entity, the key risks the municipal entity faces, the effectiveness of the internal controls and the areas of non-compliance (Sections 165 and 166). Again, the governance role, duties and responsibilities of the parent municipality in ensuring proper governance at the municipal entity are clearly enunciated by the different laws, rules and frameworks governing municipal entities.

2009 King III Code of Governance Principles for South Africa

The *Report on Governance for South Africa 2009* and the *Code of Governance Principles for South Africa 2009*, collectively known as King III, contains a corporate governance code of principles and practices on a non-legislated basis. Principles are drafted on the understanding that, if they are adhered to, any entity (including SOEs) would have practised good governance. King III is specifically aligned to functional responsibilities within public sector structures.

The King III report emphasises that boards should be at the centre of corporate governance (King III 2009: 1.1 and 1.6). It says the shareholders are responsible for the composition of the board. The board should appoint the CEO (King III 2009: Principle 1.6) and should elect the chairperson, who should be an independent non-executive director.

King III (2009) has wider reporting requirements, in that it encompasses the principles of 'sustainability' and 'corporate citizenship', as part of a greater emphasis on more integrated reporting. In King III (2009) therefore, the emphasis is not only on the interests of the shareholders but on a more inclusive (or enlightened) stakeholder approach. In the public sector, this means that municipal entities cannot only focus on pleasing the shareholder (the government), but must report much more widely on whether the interests of the broader public, consumers and the environment have been served. It recommends an annual integrated report that focuses on the impact of the organisation in the economic, environmental and social spheres.

King III states that boards should ensure entities have effective risk-based internal audits and internal financial controls (King III 2009: 1.10–1.11). King III recommends the governance of risk through formal risk management processes.

Although the King III principles are non-statutory, adhering to them would mean that municipal entities are practising good corporate governance, and this would dramatically cut down on the incidence of mismanagement, corruption and inefficiency currently plaguing these entities.

SYSTEMIC GOVERNANCE FAILURES IN MUNICIPAL SOEs

In many cases, public service delivery has not significantly improved under municipal entities – ironically, the very reason for creating them (Carrim 2009; CoGTA 2010; Gumede 2011; IoDSA 2010b; Gordhan 2012; Masego 2016; Moody's 2016; Nkashe 2016). The National Treasury, CoGTA and the Institute of Directors in Southern Africa (IoDSA) have consistently pointed out blurred accountability responsibilities between municipal councils and municipal entity boards; complex multiple governance laws, regulations and codes; and instances of milking municipal entities for patronage rather than to deliver services as some of the key reasons for governance failures at entities.

Municipal entities are often not necessarily more responsive to residents' concerns either. This is in contradiction to the rationale for the creation of municipal entities in the first place: because they would be more efficient and responsive than a municipality in delivering the public services directly.

In many cases, the systemic governance failures in municipalities, national government departments and national SOEs are also seen in municipal SOEs (Carrim 2009; CoGTA 2010; IoDSA 2010; Gumede 2011b; Gordhan 2012; Masego 2016; Moody's 2016; Nkashe 2016). The internal operational inefficiencies, patronage appointments and corruption plaguing the wider public sector also appear to have infested the organisational culture of many municipal entities (Momoniat 2002; Parliament of South Africa 2002; IoDSA 2010; Gumede 2011, 2015). Furthermore, the corrosive political culture of city and branch structures of the ANC, where factions battle over leadership positions, and where holders of positions in the local party catapult into positions of power in municipalities and municipal SOEs, is also spilling into municipal councils controlled by the ANC and municipal entities (ANC 2005, 2012; IoDSA 2010; Gumede 2011).

The Auditor-General (2011, 2012a, 2013a, 2013b, 2014, and 2015) lists non-compliance with laws and regulations; supply change management transgressions;

unauthorised, irregular, fruitless and wasteful expenditure; and corruption as some of the key failures of municipal entities. Internal controls in many municipalities and municipal entities are often lacking.

The Auditor-General, in his General Report on Audit Outcomes for Local Government 2009–2010, reported that 75 per cent of municipal entities struggled with compliance. In the 2010–2011 financial year, the Auditor-General reported that 88 per cent of municipal entities had problems meeting compliance. In the 2010–2011 financial year, only four municipal entities achieved clean audits.

In the 2012–2013 financial year, only eight municipal entities, representing 9 per cent of the municipal entities, achieved clean audits – that is, unqualified audits with no findings (Auditor-General 2014). The Johannesburg Social Housing Company and the Johannesburg Fresh Produce Market were exceptions in securing clean audits during the period. About 90 per cent of municipalities and municipal entities audited during the 2012–13 financial year had negative findings on compliance with laws and regulations, many of them related to supply management failures. Irregular spending occurred in 83 per cent of auditees, mainly because of 'lack of basic controls and inadequate implementation of appropriate consequences where there has been poor performance or transgressions' (Auditor-General 2014: 3).

In the 2012–13 financial year, no municipal entity in the Eastern Cape, Free State, Limpopo and North West provinces received a clean audit (Auditor-General 2014). The Auditor-General also stated that transgressions often emanated because 'a number of rules and regulations that apply to financial management and reporting matters were not observed as required in specific legislation' (Auditor-General 2014: 2).

In the 2013–14 financial year, only 40 out of the 278 municipalities and 18 out of 57 municipal entities achieved clean audits. In the 2013–14 financial year, 14 per cent of the municipalities and 32 per cent of the municipal entities achieved clean audits (Auditor-General 2014: 7).

In the 2013–14 financial year, the number of municipalities and entities with supply chain management irregularities increased from 278 (87 per cent) in the financial year before, to 290 (90 per cent). Furthermore, 68 per cent of municipal-ities and 42 per cent of municipal entities had negative findings on compliance with supply chain management legislation (Auditor-General 2015: 7). Non-compliance with supply chain management (SCM) legislation was the cause of 98 per cent of the irregular expenditure that occurred in municipalities and municipal entities during the 2013–14 financial year (Auditor-General 2015: 9).

In the 2013–14 financial year, of the 335 audited municipalities (including 57 municipal entities), 264 incurred R11.4 billion in irregular expenditure. Municipal entities in municipalities that received clean audits were often also more likely to be better managed and get clean audits. For example, in the 2013–14 financial year, one-third of KwaZulu-Natal municipalities scored clean audits.

It emerged that municipalities and municipal entities depended heavily on consultants. In the total budget, R315 billion for all municipalities, R3.1 billion was spent on consultants in the 2013–14 financial year. The heavy use of consultants clearly did not yield the desired results: in the 2013–14 financial year, there were weaknesses at 184 of the 293 audited municipalities and municipal SOEs which used consultants.

Officials in many municipalities and municipal entities lack even minimum competencies, especially in financial management. According to former Auditor-General Terence Nombembe (2012: 1), '[w]e are seeing the impact of the lack of skills, the slow response of leadership to owning key controls, as well as the absence of managing poor performance and the risks that municipalities continue to face.' The Auditor-General's 2010–11 report also said that 37 per cent of municipal entities are not sustainable (Auditor-General 2011).

The Auditor-General has decried the 'low level of action' against wrongdoers and the 'lack of consequences for transgressions', and called for 'leaders and officials who deliberately or negligently ignore their duties and contravene legislation' to be 'decisively dealt with' (Auditor-General 2012b: 2). Nevertheless, the municipal entities in the municipalities that achieved clean audits were also often better governed. Countrywide, there are a number of exceptionally well-run municipal entities, such as the Durban Marine Theme Park and the Johannesburg Social Housing Company. In fact, the poor governance of most municipal entities mirrors that of the local government sphere itself – in other words, they are often not efficiency-, results- or performance-driven.

How politicisation undermines governance in local government and municipal entities

A key priority to improve the governance of South Africa's municipalities and, by implication, municipal entities is to depoliticise the sphere, to create a firewall between party political governance and municipal governance. Key positions in municipal government and politics provide access to lucrative government contracts and tenders and the power to appoint staff. Contests in ANC branches over leadership positions are increasingly becoming acrimonious affairs, as prominent positions in branches often offer a route into local government (ANC 2005).

Former ANC deputy president Kgalema Motlanthe, in his 2005 ANC organisational report to the ANC's national general council, said that many of the municipal governance problems have much to do with the 'preoccupation on the part of [ANC] public representatives with securing access to and control over public resources' (ANC 2005: point 27).

In 1998, the ANC adopted a comprehensive Cadre Policy and Deployment Strategy and established a national deployment committee following recommendations by the ANC's 1997 national conference, and later followed this with setting up provincial and local deployment committees. Deployment committees were set up as ANC party structures that would operate parallel to those of the spheres of government (ANC 1998).

The ANC's various deployment committees – national, provincial and local – play a role in nominating individuals to boards and management of SOEs and municipal entities (ANC 1998). It is expected that executive authorities/shareholder departments/ministers under which a state-owned entity falls will consult with the ANC's deployment committee when they recruit individuals for positions on boards and executive management of SOEs (ANC 1998).

Politically elected representatives often intervene in the operations of municipal entities (Momoniat 2002; Gumede, Mosoetsa, Monyae, Wilschutt and Van Meelis 2010; ANC 2005, 2012; Mashaba 2016). In some cases, a senior party leader is 'deployed' to a role in the municipal entity. Juniors to the 'deployee' may have senior positions in the municipal council. Although they are senior in the municipal governance structure, they are junior to the party deployee in the entity, and therefore have to defer to their party senior, undermining the governance hierarchy of reporting and accountability (Gumede *et al.* 2010; ANC 2005, 2012; Kanyane 2012; Mantashe 2013).

The South African Local Government Association (SALGA) has warned that this deployment phenomenon 'needs to be reviewed' because it undermines governance at municipal governments and entities (SALGA 2012). The former deputy minister of cooperative governance and traditional affairs, Yunus Carrim (2009), has also warned about deploying 'senior ANC officials, regardless of their managerial and technical skills', as board members and executives to municipal SOEs.

The one real danger is that the deployment strategy may undermine South Africa's formal constitutional lines of accountability and governance arrangements – and introduce an informal parallel and competing governance and accountability system, including at local level. Clearly, such politically motivated appointments of board members and CEOs of municipal SOEs may lead led to the appointment of members to boards and executives without the appropriate skills to perform their jobs adequately – leading to inefficiencies and governance failures at SOEs and municipal entities.

Some politically appointed SOE and municipal entity executives and board members may see their roles as accountable to their political sponsors rather than the interests of the municipal entity SOEs – the opposite of what good corporate governance demands (Kanyane 2012).

The Auditor-General regularly deplores slow responses by political leadership at local government level to deal with corruption, incompetence and waste (Auditor-General 2010: 79). Appointing the right, competent and honest candidates as executives, board members and staff to municipal entities hinges strongly on the necessary political will.

CONCLUSION AND RECOMMENDATIONS

In broad terms, South Africa has a plethora of very effective laws, governance codes and regulations to guide municipal entities. Even if there are weaknesses, genuinely implementing the current governance regime, without any other interventions, without any changes, will improve the governance of municipal entities.

Nevertheless, there is a strong case to be made for adopting an approach where, in instances in which the Companies Act has the 'more onerous requirement' in relation to other legislation, compliance with the Companies Act should be the preferred application (IoDSA 2009: 2).

In the final analysis, municipalities must enforce laws, governance codes and regulations governing municipal entities. Municipalities will have to provide better strategic guidance to municipal entities, without political interference or micromanaging. Municipalities will have to strike a balance in their providing strategic guidance in giving ' "arm's-length" operational freedom and to have them operationally accountable' (Mountford 2009: 25).

Many municipal entities appear to be established without a clear rationale, mission or strategic framework. It would be essential for municipalities to do regular reviews to measure the operational effectiveness of municipal entities, their development impact, and whether they still need to exist in the form they presently do. This can be done every five years.

Municipal entities must become more transparent, and make their operational and financial information more widely accessible. They should make their annual reports publicly available. Municipal-owned entities are also supposed to have service delivery agreements (SDA) which set out their delivery obligations. However, in most cases, municipalities do not hold entities accountable according to whether they have met their SDA goals. In fact, municipal-owned entity managers often receive huge annual bonuses even though the entity is loss-making and has not met its SDA targets. Municipalities must hold municipal entities accountable for their SDA outputs.

Lack of human capital is clearly a weakness for many municipal entities. It is often very difficult to secure competent staff for municipal entities with the 'right mix of public and private sector experience and know-how' (Mountford 2009: 24). Political appointees without the appropriate skills exacerbate capacity constraints. Cadre deployment to municipal entities should be abolished. Merit-based appointments are crucial to improve the performance of municipal entities.

The danger of stand-alone entities is that democratic control over them is often the first thing to fall by the wayside. When Johannesburg City Power was established as a ring-fenced municipal entity, there was a requirement that the entity set up a User Forum – including customers, civil watchdogs and community groups – envisaged to provide additional oversight in the entity (City Power 2001).

Establishing genuine User Forums and Customer Charters which involve users, civil society and stakeholders may help a great deal to monitor whether entities fulfil their contractual and social obligations, and to hold them accountable. In the end, even if the current weaknesses in the governance system of municipal entities are strengthened, if the political will to implement the governance system is lacking, compliance will remain uneven.

The type of governance of local ANC structures which corresponds with local government structures where the party is in government, is also often mirrored in the corresponding municipal government structures. This means that unless the ANC local party structures are reasonably 'clean' or cleaned up, the governance of municipalities the party manages will also suffer. This applies equally to opposition parties in charge of municipalities.

Unless the governance of parent municipalities is improved, it will be very difficult to raise the performance of municipal entities. The governance of the ANC – or at least political parties in charge of parent municipalities – will have to be drastically improved in order to boost the performance of municipal entities under their jurisdiction. The ANC has already lost a number of city councils in the 2016 local government elections. Increased political competition may put pressure on incumbents in municipalities to improve the management of councils – or face being voted out. Opposition parties, civil society, community groups, consumers and the media must be steadfast in holding municipal entities and agencies far more accountable.

REFERENCES

ANC. 1998. ANC Cadre Policy and Deployment Strategy. Johannesburg.

ANC. 2005. Organisational Report by the ANC Secretary General Kgalema Motlanthe. Johannesburg: ANC National General Council.

ANC. 2012. Report of the ANC National Executive Committee Task Team on Candidate List Irregularities, chaired by Nkosazana Dlamini-Zuma. Johannesburg.

ANC. 2015. Annual Report 2015: Key Development Results Annual Progress Report. Johannesburg.

Ashira Consulting. 2003. Treatment of Municipal Entities in the Municipal Finance Management Bill. Memorandum Commissioned by the National Treasury and the Department of Provincial and Local Government, Cape Town, 15 January.

Auditor-General. 2010. Consolidated General Report on the Local Government Audit Outcomes 2009/2010. Pretoria.

Auditor-General. 2011. General Report on the Local Government Audit Outcomes for 2010/2011. Pretoria.

Auditor-General. 2012a. General Report on the Local Government Audit Outcomes for 2011/2012. Pretoria.

Auditor-General. 2012b. Press Statement. Pretoria, 26 July.

Auditor-General. 2013a. Consolidated General Report on the Local Government Audit Outcomes – Audit Committees and Internal Audit Units 2011/2012. Pretoria.

Auditor-General. 2013b.General Report on the Local Government Audit Outcomes for 2012/2013. Pretoria.

Auditor-General. 2014. General Report on the Local Government Audit Outcomes for 2013/2014. Pretoria.

Auditor-General. 2015. General Report on the Local Government Audit Outcomes for 2014/2015. Pretoria.

Cadbury, A. 1992. The Committee on the Financial Aspects of Corporate Governance (Cadbury Committee). London: London Stock Exchange.

Carrim, Y. 2009. Addressing the Financial Challenges in Municipalities in the Context of a Review of the Local Government Model: Keynote address of the Deputy Minister of Cooperative Governance and Traditional Affairs, Institute of Municipal Finance Officers Annual Conference, Johannesburg, 6 October.

City Power. 2001. Service Delivery Agreement – City of Johannesburg. Johannesburg.

Department of Cooperative Governance and Traditional Affairs (CoGTA). 2010. State of Local Government 2009 Report. Pretoria.

Department of Municipal and Local Government. 2003. Municipal Systems Amendment Bill: Briefing to the Select Committee. Joint meeting of the Provincial and Local Government and Finance Portfolio Committees, National Assembly. Cape Town, 19 August.

Department of Provincial and Local Government. 1998. White Paper on Local Government. Pretoria.

Department of Provincial and Local Government. 2004. White Paper on Municipal Service Partnerships. Pretoria.

Department of Provincial and Local Government. 2005. Guidelines for the Implementation of the National Indigent Policy by Municipalities. Pretoria.

Department of Public Service Administration. 1995. White Paper on the Transformation of the Public Service. Pretoria.

Ford, R. & Zussman, D. (eds) 1997. *Alternative Service Delivery: Sharing Governance in Canada*. Toronto: KPMG Centre for Government Foundation and Institute of Public Administration of Canada (IPAC).

Fraser-Moleketi, G. & Saloojee, A. 2008. South Africa's Public Service: Evolution and Future Perspective. Address to the New World, New Society, New Administration Conference. Quebec City, Canada, 3 June.

Fyfe, T. 2004. Alternative service delivery – responding to global pressure. *International Review of Administrative Sciences* 70: 637–644.

Good, D.A. & Carin, B. 2003. Alternative Service Delivery. Paper prepared by Canadian team as part of CEPRA project on Sector and Regional Specifics of Reformation of Budgetary Institutions. www.aucc.ca/_pdf/english/programs/cepra/ASDPaper.pdf (accessed 2 March 2019).

Gordhan, P. 2012a. National Treasury Budget Vote Speech by Minister of Finance. Cape Town, 12 February.

Gordhan, P. 2012b. Press statement on Auditor-General's report on municipalities. Minister of Finance, Pretoria, 23 July.

Gordhan, P. 2015. Minister of Cooperative Governance and Traditional Affairs responding to the Auditor-General's Report on the Local Government Audit Outcomes for 2013/2014. Cape Town, 1 June.

Gordhan, P. 2016. Minister of Finance – Budget Speech to National Assembly. Cape Town, 24 February.

Gumede, W. 2005. *Thabo Mbeki and the Battle for the Soul of the ANC*. Cape Town: Struik Random House.

Gumede, W. 2009. Delivering the Democratic Developmental State in South Africa. In: Munslow, A. & McLennan, B. (eds) *The Politics of Service Delivery*: 43–103. Johannesburg: Wits University Press.

Gumede, W. 2011. Building Effective Institutions: Driving Change through Institutional Innovation. In: *South African Development Report 2011: Prospects for South Africa's Future*: 303–338. Midrand: Development Bank of Southern Africa.

Gumede, W. 2015. Administrative Culture of the South African Public Service: A Finity of Transformation. *Journal of Public Administration* 50: 589–599.

Gumede, W., Mosoetsa, S., Monyae, D., Wilschutt, A. & Van Meelis, T. 2010. Background Paper on the Causes of Local Government Public Service Delivery Protests. Development Bank of Southern Africa. Midrand: DBSA.

Hirsch, A. 2005. *Season of Hope: Economic Reform from Mandela to Mbeki*. Pietermaritzburg: University of KwaZulu-Natal Press.

Hlongwane, S. 2012. Auditor-General's report on municipalities: Cloudy, with remote chance of improvement. *Daily Maverick,* 23 July.

Institute for Democratic Alternatives in South Africa. 2011. Local Government Citizens' Satisfaction Survey. Pretoria: Local Government Unit, Institute for Democracy in South Africa.

Institute of Directors in Southern Africa (IoDSA). 2009. *State-Owned Companies: Companies Act, PFMA and King III in Perspective.* Public Sector Working Group: Position Paper 1. Johannesburg.

Institute of Directors in Southern Africa (IoDSA). 2010. Municipal Entities: Governance Challenges. Public Sector Working Group, IoDSA, DBSA and PwC. Discussion Paper 1. Johannesburg.

Jessop, B. 1997. The Entrepreneurial City: Re-imaging Localities, Re-designing Economic Governance, or Restructuring Capital? In: Jewson, N. & MacGregor, S. (eds) *Realising Cities: New Spatial Divisions and Social Transformation*: 28–41. London: Routledge.

Kanyane, M. 2012. Seminar Address, Human Sciences Research Council (HSRC). Pretoria, 12 July.

Khumalo, G., Ntlokonkulu, L. & Rapoo, T. 2003. *Alternative service delivery arrangements at municipal level in South Africa: Assessing the impact of electricity service delivery and customer satisfaction in Johannesburg*. Research Report 100. Johannesburg: Centre for Policy Studies.

King III. 2009. *Report on Governance for South Africa* and *Code of Governance Principles for South Africa*. Johannesburg: Institute of Directors in Southern Africa.

Laking, R. 2005. Agencies: Their Benefits and Risks. *OECD Journal on Budgeting* 4(4): 7–25.

MacDonald, D.A. & Pape, J. 2002. *Cost Recovery and the Crisis of Service Delivery in South Africa*. Pretoria: HSRC.

Mantashe, G. 2013. ANC General Secretary Address to the ANC's 101st Anniversary. Richmond, 9 January.

Masego, P. 2016. Joburg mulls absorbing municipal entities. *Business Day*, 8 November. https://www.businesslive.co.za/bd/national/2016-11-08-joburg-mulls-absorbing-municipal-entities/ (accessed 3 March 2019).

Mashaba, H. 2016. City of Johannesburg Mayor Herman Mashaba Speech. City of Johannesburg Mayoral Lekgotla, Johannesburg, 5 November.

Moody's Investor Services. 2016. Government of South Africa – Baa2 Negative: Annual Credit Analysis, Johannesburg, 9 December.

Momoniat, I. 2002. Presentation of the Deputy Director-General of Intergovernmental Relations of the National Treasury to the Finance and Provincial and Local Government Portfolio Committees Working Group. Finance Standing Committee, National Assembly, Cape Town, 19 November.

Mountford, D. 2009. Organising for local development: the role of local development agencies. Paris: Organisation for Economic Coordination and Development (OECD).

National Planning Commission. 2011. National Development Plan: Vision 2030. Pretoria: National Planning Commission.

National Treasury. 2011. Local Government Budgets and Expenditure Review. Pretoria: National Treasury.

Nkashe, M. 2016. Presentation of the Chief Director for Anti-corruption of the Department of Cooperative Governance and Traditional Affairs. Parliamentary Portfolio Committee on Cooperative Governance and Traditional Affairs, National Assembly. Cape Town.

Nombembe, T. 2012. Statement by Auditor-General on local government audit results. Pretoria, July 23.

Organisation for Economic Cooperation and Development (OECD). 2015. *OECD Guidelines on Corporate Governance of State-Owned Enterprises, 2015 Edition*. Paris: OECD.

Paquet, G. 1997. Alternative Service Delivery: Transcending the practices of governance. In: Ford, R. & Zussman, D. (eds) *Alternative Service Delivery: Sharing Governance in Canada*: 31–58. Toronto: KPMG Centre for Government Foundation and Institute of Public Administration of Canada (IPAC).

Parliament of South Africa. 2002. Transcript of the Entities in Municipal Finance Bill Discussion. Finance Standing Committee. National Assembly, Cape Town, 19 November.

Parliament of South Africa. 2015. Statement by the Select Committee on Appropriations on National Treasury's decision to withhold equitable share to municipalities. National Assembly, Cape Town.

Peters, S. 2012. Alternative Service Delivery Arrangements: The Case of Municipal Agencies. Chapter 8 in *FFC: Technical Report – Submission for the 2013/2014 Division of Revenue*: 255–270. Midrand: Finance and Fiscal Commission.

Polidano, C. 1999. *The new public management in developing countries*. Institute for Development Policy and Management. Working Paper. Manchester: IDPM.

PricewaterhouseCoopers (PwC). 2009. King's Counsel: King III – A Municipal Perspective – At a Glance. Corporate Governance Series. Johannesburg.

Public Sector Audit Committee Forum (PSACF). 2012. Principles for the audit committee's role in performance management. Discussion Paper. Johannesburg.

Public Sector Audit Committee Forum (PSACF). 2013. The Relationship between the Audit Committee and Council (Local Government) . Public Sector Audit Committee Forum. Discussion Paper. Johannesburg.

Republic of South Africa. 1996. Constitution of the Republic of South Africa, 1996 (Act No. 108 of 1996). Pretoria.

Republic of South Africa. 1996. Growth, Employment and Redistribution (Gear) – A Macroeconomic Strategy. Pretoria.

Republic of South Africa. 1998. White Paper on Local Government. Pretoria.

Republic of South Africa. 2000. Local Government: Municipal Systems Act (No. 32 of 2000). Pretoria.

Republic of South Africa. 2004. Local Government: Municipal Finance Management (Act No. 56 of 2004). Pretoria.

Schick, A. 2002. *Agencies in Search of Principles*. OECD Global Forum on Governance Paper. Paris: OECD.

South African Communist Party (SACP). 1999. Public–Private Partnerships: The Challenges for Local Government. Discussion Document. SACP Strategy Conference, Johannesburg, 3–5 September.

South African Local Government Association (SALGA). 2012. The State of Municipal Audit Committees. Municipal Finance National Working Committee. Discussion Document. Johannesburg.

Stacey, S. 1997. *New capacities for old? Prospects for public–private partnerships in service delivery in South Africa, Angola and Mozambique*. CPS Governance Series Research Report 61. Johannesburg: Centre for Policy Studies.

Stumm, T.J. 1997. Comparing alternative service delivery modes: Municipal enterprises require special consideration. *Journal of Urban Affairs* 19: 275–289.

Wilkins, J.K. 2003. Conceptual and Practical Considerations in Alternative Service Delivery. *International Review of Administrative Sciences* 69: 173–189.

10

Law and Governance: Has the South African judiciary overstepped its oversight mandate?

Chelete Monyane

INTRODUCTION

One of the distinguishing features of South Africa's Constitution is its stance on the inclusion of socio-economic rights as justiciable on the same basis as political and civil rights (De Vos 2009b). The South African Constitution is further strengthened by judicial independence and the rule of law. Its transformative nature is founded on the 'doctrine of separation of powers' that divides the power between the legislature, judiciary and the executive (De Vos 2009b). The judiciary keeps its counterparts within their constitutional mandate through judicial oversight (Dube 2016). This chapter begins by evaluating the doctrine of the separation of powers, emphasising the origin or historical development of the doctrine. Exploring the concept of judicial oversight, the chapter goes on to review Constitutional Court jurispendence. Further, the chapter discusses whether the judiciary has surpassed the legislature in providing oversight and, thereby, overstepped its oversight mandate and tried to impose judicial supremacy.

The Constitutional Court is the apex court in South Africa on constitutional matters (De Vos 2011), with powers to exercise its exclusive jurisdiction. The court's powers can be used to appeal jurisdiction in matters that raise an arguable constitutional point of law that may be deemed of public importance. The Supreme Court of Appeal (SCA) is the highest court on matters that are not of a constitutional nature. The SCA has some sweeping jurisdiction in constitutional matters, limited by the fact that all constitutional matters are under the exclusive jurisdiction of the Constitutional Court. The High Courts are not final courts but they have similar jurisdiction to the SCA (De Vos 2011). Section 165(2) of the Constitution outlines that courts are subject only to the Constitution and the law, which they are meant to apply impartially and without fear, favour or prejudice. Section 165(4) of the Constitution (1996) requires that the organs of the state, through legislative and other measures, must protect the courts to ensure their independence, impartiality, dignity, and effectiveness.

Recently, the South African judiciary has faced extraordinary challenges as the result of the rulings that courts have made against the legislature and the executive. Political attacks on the judiciary have also intensified (Klug 2010a). Madlingozi (2008) argues that the judiciary has been perceived as impeding the realisation of common social and political goals. The courts have further become an avenue for determining the political disputes of the day (Dube 2016), and 'lawfare' has also entered the political lexicon. For instance, there were two successful challenges to the presidential appointment of the National Director of Public Prosecutions (NDPP). The first case succeeded on the basis that former president Zuma failed to consider the information that his choice suffered from a lack of integrity, and provided dishonest evidence to a court and to a commission of enquiry (*Democratic Alliance v. President of the Republic of South Africa and Others* 2013 (1) SA 248 (CC)).

In another case, the judiciary ordered President Zuma to give reasons for firing minister of finance Pravin Gordhan and deputy minister of finance Mcebisi Jonas from cabinet; the firings led to South Africa being downgraded to junk status on 3 March 2017 (ICAB 2018). The order against the president was a landmark judgment since it challenged the dismissal of ministers who are meant to serve at the behest of the president. In yet another case, the Eastern Cape provincial government was ordered to develop a comprehensive programme to upgrade rural roads; failing to do so would mean that private companies were authorised to upgrade roads and claim from the government (ICAB 2018).

Some African National Congress (ANC) leaders have been calling for a 'review' of the Constitutional Court to limit its powers due to concerns about the judiciary's perceived disregard for the principle of 'doctrine of separation of powers' (Radebe 2012: 11). The ANC has further called for the transformation of the 'collective mindset of the judiciary', arguing that it must be brought into consonance with the vision and aspirations of the millions who participated in the struggle to liberate the country from apartheid (ANC 2005). As result of the ongoing criticism from key political quarters, the judiciary is anxious of its institutional position (Klug 2010b), presumably the reason that Chief Justice Mogoeng requested an urgent meeting with President Zuma in 2015 (*The Citizen* 2015).

DOCTRINE OF SEPARATION OF POWERS

Philosopher John Locke (1632–1704) was instrumental in advocating for the 'doctrine of the separation of powers'. In his *Second Treatise of Government* (1689), he states that 'it may be too great a temptation for the humane frailty, apt to grasp at powers, for the same persons who have the power of making laws, to have also in their hands the power to execute them, whereby they may exempt themselves from the law, both in its making and execution to their own private advantage' (Ratnapala 1993: 203). De Vos (2011) and Dube (2016) relate that in eighteenth-century France, Montesquieu reasoned that when the powers to make, interpret and enforce law are vested in one person or entity, there is bound to be abuse of personal liberties as the ruler would make tyrannical laws and execute them arbitrarily. Jowett (1882) arges that Montesquieu's writings speak to and align with those of Plato, the ancient philosopher who argued that the over-concentration of power in the hands of one person leads to 'wantonness of excess'. According to Lord Mustill in *R v. Home Secretary*, the doctrine of separation of powers in England was defined as

> [...] a feature of the peculiarly British conception [...] that Parliament, the executive and the courts have each their distinct and largely exclusive domain. Parliament has a legally unchallengeable right to make whatever laws it thinks right. The executive carries on the administration of the country in accordance with the powers conferred on it by law. The courts interpret the laws, and see that they are obeyed.

The doctrine of separation of powers is one of the pillars of constitutional democracy, and is characterised by the equality of the legislative, executive and judicial organs of state (*Glenister v. President of RSA* 2009 1 SA 298 (CC); De Vos 2011; Dube 2016). The doctrine denotes the institutional and functional independence of the three branches of government from one another (Roux 2013). South Africa derives several constitutional and democratic benefits from the doctrine in that it promotes respect for the rule of law, balances public power, gives the government legitimacy, and contributes to economic development and social stability (Klug 2010b). The institutional and functional independence of various organs of the state was eloquently put in *South African Association of Personal Injury Lawyers v. Heath 2001 5 BCLR 77*, in which the Constitutional Court stated:

> [...] parliament and the provincial legislatures make the laws but do not implement them. The national and provincial executives prepare and initiate laws to be placed before the legislatures, implement the laws thus made, but have no law-making power other than that vested in them by the legislatures. Although parliament has a wide power to delegate legislative authority to the executive, there are limits to that power. Under our Constitution, it is the duty of the courts to ensure that the limits to the exercise of public power are not transgressed.

This court ruling shows that state organs ought to exercise functions conferred upon them by the law, in accordance with the law. They may not usurp the functions of each other and may not delegate their plenary powers. The delegation of powers can only be acceptable where there is legitimate reason to believe that it would facilitate effective running of government operations without upsetting the separation of powers (Dube 2016). In the matter *Executive Council Western Cape Legislature v. President of Republic of South Africa*, the court held that the legislature may delegate powers to the executive to make subordinate legislation to facilitate effective promulgation of regulations. The delegation of power ensures that the government has enough power to govern while preventing an accumulation of absolute power in the hands of one person or organ of state (*De Lange v. Smuts NO and Others* 1998 7 BCLR 779 (CC)).

Gubbay (2009) indicates that the doctrine of separation of powers is a prerequisite for the independence of the judiciary as this is important for the rule of law and the attainment of justice. Siyo and Mubangizi (2015) assert that judicial independence is one of the cornerstones of democracy. Strasberg-Cohen (2005: 11) argues that judicial independence means that the 'judge [must be able to] adjudicate freely, without outside influence, pressure, or incentives, without fear, without bias [and only] subject to the law'. Judges must exercise judicial independence while discharging their professional discretion, sense of justice and conscience. It seems that the stanchions of law pass seamlessly from colony to postcolony in an unbreakable thread. That contestation ensues should not come as a suprise.

Cumaraswamy (2002) is of the view that the doctrine of separation of powers underpins democracy. Mhodi (2013) concurs and submits that the doctrine of separation of powers is a basic requirement for constitutionalism. The doctrine provides a form of checks and balances between the various organs of government, where the principal aim of a separation of powers is to limit the excessive concentration of power and promote accountability (Okpaluba 2003). The most conspicuous issue is the absence of judicial power to review executive decision-making. It is clear that judicial review constitutes neither an executive nor a judicial function. It is a simple check on the exercise of executive and legislative power. It is thus a power exercised by the judiciary to safeguard constitutional compliance and not to exercise the power of another authority (Mojapelo 2013).

Corder (2009) argues that the 'doctrine of separation of powers' is not expressly provided for in the text of the Constitution of South Africa, which has resulted in a battle of power between the judiciary and executive emanating from the perception that the judiciary is overstepping its mandate. Roux (2013: 23) cautions that courts need to be careful in their approach to judicial review to avoid upsetting the balance of institutional comity:

> For a constitutional court like the South African one, working in a relatively well developed legal culture that favours firm textual bases for democratic rights and in a political context marked by an ever-present threat of populist attacks on the Constitution, the role it plays in democratic consolidation must necessarily be quite cautious. In particular, courts in this situation need continually to strike an optimal balance between the risk to their independence posed by a failure to protect the democratic system from dominant-party attack and the risk to their independence posed by over-zealous, legally unsupported enforcement of democratic rights. Measured against that standard, the CCSA's [Constitutional Court of South Africa] recent record, though not without flaws, is generally to be admired.

An important aspect here is that the judiciary risks overstepping its mandate (or being seen to do so), thereby losing its legitimacy (Roux 2013), especially in the South African political context. It is therefore worth pondering how the Constitutional Court may exercise its constitutional mandate sustainably, while maintaining the institutional comity between the judiciary and its counterparts, particularly in the light of harsh criticism from the executive. Mendes (2010) observes that while exercising their oversight role, courts are likely to become political targets, particularly where there is political resistance to their decisions.

WHAT IS JUDICIAL OVERSIGHT?

De Vos (2011) argues that judicial interference in government matters has largely been influenced by the lack of executive efficiency and appropriateness in doing its job. In the United Kingdom, the notion of judicial interference in both the legislative and executive actions is classified as 'judicial activism'. In India, this form of interference is known as 'judicial overreach'. Judicial interference occurs when the judiciary actively engages with laws and oversight functions, which can be problematic in cases where the state loses its case in the courts. When the state is victorious, the political elites or state organs often give resounding praise to the judiciary. Citizens may be confounded by the distance between a legal test and contending perceptions.

In *Dictionary of Law,* Collin (2004: 12) defines judicial oversight as 'the power and competence of the courts to assess and set aside legislation and executive actions for their unconstitutionality'. Thus, judicial oversight is a core component of transformative constitutionalism, intertwined with the 'doctrine of separation of powers' (Dube 2016: 45; *Glenister v. President of RSA* 2009 1 SA 287 (CC): 28). The Constitution gives a greater role to the judiciary to protect individual rights against legislative and executive encroachment. South Africa's Constitution has numerous provisions which empower the judiciary to serve as the guardian and trustee of the constitutional values and principles in the Bill of Rights. The judiciary fulfils this mandate through judicial oversight (De Vos and Friedman 2014).

Judicial oversight continues to present numerous challenges for the courts and the constitutional order as a whole in South Africa. The wide powers of review bestowed on the judiciary by the Constitution have presented conceptual and practical problems, especially in the relationship between constitutional democracy, separation of powers, and judicial review. An important aspect of the Constitution is that the judiciary has the final say on the meaning of constitutional provisions, and the constitutionality of legislative and executive action (Dube 2016; De Vos and Friedman 2014; *Economic Freedom Fighters v. Speaker of the National Assembly* 2016 3 SA 580 (CC)). Only the courts can decide the nature, extent and applicability of the doctrine of separation of powers. There is no existing constitutional mechanism that can prevent the judiciary from overstepping its jurisdiction. Therefore, it is up to the courts to determine the limits of their power by striking a balance between the doctrine of separation of powers and the constitutional accountability of the legislature and the executive (Dube 2016).

The judicial branch of government is the institutional mechanism with which the Constitution ring-fences the limits for legislative and executive conduct. It ensures that the state does not roll back its promises to protect individual rights, particularly those of minorities and marginalised groups. As the guardian and trustee of the Constitution, the judiciary has a duty to ensure that all conduct involving the exercise of public power promotes the spirit, purport and object of the Bill of Rights (Klassen 2015). Judicial oversight is the vehicle through which the courts confine the legislative and executive branches of government to their constitutional powers (De Vos and Friedman 2014).

Judicial oversight is also useful in providing the meaning and effectiveness to constitutional supremacy (De Vos and Friedman 2014). In addition, Section 2 of the Constitution provides that the obligations imposed by the Constitution must be enforced. Section 172(1)(a) of the Constitution gives superior courts the power to declare invalid any conduct or act inconsistent with the Constitution. Section 165(5) of the Constitution further binds all state organs and all persons, public or private, to court orders and decisions (Constitution of South Africa 1996; Klassen 2015). It gives the judiciary the authority to investigate and redress constitutional violations. The courts can declare what an organ of state should have done in specific circumstances and prescribe what it must do to mitigate an offending act. This mitigates ongoing violations and prevents future ones from occurring (Van Vuuren 2005).

Judicial oversight places the legislature, executive officials, and government departments under the scrutiny of the courts, which can determine whether they have acted within or outside their powers. It also prevents the legislature, executive and government departments from undermining democratic principles and the Bill of Rights (*Doctors for Life International v. Speaker of the National Assembly,* 2006 4 SA 416 (CC)). Judicial oversight provides constitutional protection and individual rights by allowing for the review of legislation to ensure that laws are constitutionally compliant (Klassen 2015). Judicial oversight involves enforcing executive accountability to make certain that executive decisions are lawful, reasonable, proportional, and procedurally fair (Constitution of South Africa 1996: Section 33). It is easy to see how the sanguine statement of legal rules and principles rubs up against the sense of elected legitimacy enjoyed by politicians.

Chidyausiku (2010) argues that judicial oversight enables the courts to force the legislative and executive organs of the state to abide by the Constitution, its values and principles, by declaring invalid all acts which go against democratic values and principles. Hence there is a close nexus between separation of powers, democracy, and judicial oversight. De Vos (2009a) submits that the courts must act within their constitutional powers to preserve the legitimacy of the legal system and their decisions. Political actors counter that the court has no legitimate mandate equivalent to that granted by elections.

Pius Langa (2006) indicates that judicial oversight is based on the need to review legislative and executive action. Judicial oversight aims to ensure that accountability, the rule of law, and human rights are safeguarded. Langa (2006) further argues that there is an entrenched relationship between judicial oversight and the separation of powers. He notes that the over-concentration of power in one individual or organ of state could be solved by dividing state power. He concludes that the protection of individual rights and liberties as proposed in the separation of the powers of government into executive, lawmaking and judicial functions remains the best way to ensure government abides by the rule of law and is accountable to citizens.

Has the South African legislature been surpassed by the judiciary?

According to the Constitution of South Africa 1996, the National Assembly has a duty to oversee the executive authority in discharging its responsibilities. It has a responsibility 'to represent the people and to ensure government by the people under the Constitution. It does this by choosing the president, by providing a national forum for public consideration of issues, by passing legislation, and by scrutinising and overseeing executive action' (Constitution of the Republic of South Africa 1996: Section 74).

Parliament further has the constitutional duty to implement measures to ensure that the executive is accountable to it (Section 55(2)(a) of the Constitution of South Africa), and must ensure legislation is implemented (Section 55(2)(b(i) of the Constitution of South Africa 1996). In addition, the Rules of the National Assembly give members of parliament (MPs) a chance to hold the executive accountable using question-and-answer sessions. According to the cluster rotation system, Rule 109 of the Rules of the National Assembly discusses the issue of questions for cabinet ministers. The deputy president is also obligated to answer questions every fortnight (Rule 110 of the Rules of the National Assembly 1999), while the president must appear at least once per term (Rule 111 of Rules of the National Assembly 1999).

As ever, the rules of the game are written on the assumption that players in the game will abide by those rules. When those rules are grafted directly onto a developing country emerging from centuries of violent colonial occupation and racist minority government, the rules will inevitably be challenged. The test is not whether they are challenged or not, not whether the resistance to change is absolute, but what space exists between past and present to develop better rules that reflect local needs.

Parliament provides a form of checks and balances on the executive and the judiciary through appointment and dismissal. Members of the National Assembly elect the president (Section 42(3) of the Constitution of South Africa 1996). If the president and cabinet do not undertake their constitutional obligations in one or more respects, the National Assembly can pass a motion of no confidence; this may result in the situation where the president and cabinet are forced to resign (Section 102 of the Constitution of South Africa 1996). The president must reconstitute the cabinet if the National Assembly passes a vote of no confidence in the cabinet (excluding the president) (Siyo and Mubangizi 2015).

The checks and balances exercised by the legislature over the judiciary are ineffective (Dube 2016: 40). The only form of oversight that the legislature exercises over the judiciary is through appointment of judges. Parliament and the executive have the collective responsibility to appoint and dismiss judicial officers (Langa 2006). Section 180 of the Constitution gives parliament the authority to keep judicial officers in check by enacting legislation that specifically deals with judicial misconduct and complaints against judges. Section 177(b) of the Constitution regulates the dismissal of judges. It provides that the National Assembly may, by a vote of a two-thirds majority, adopt a resolution for the removal of a judge who the Judicial Service Commission has found to suffer from an incapacity, gross incompetence, or gross misconduct. Section 14(4) of the Judicial Service Commission Act (No. 20 of 2008) elaborates gross judicial misconduct as conduct that it is 'unbecoming of the holding of judicial office, including any conduct that is prejudicial to the independence, impartiality, dignity, accessibility, efficiency or effectiveness of the courts'. It is this weakness of formal checks that has led to the judiciary being perceived as becoming too powerful or exceeding its powers.

Parliament has been confronted with a host of problems which have affected its ability to provide meaningful oversight. Malapane (2015) argues that resolutions made by Public Accounts Committees (PACs) are not implemented, and in most cases no action is taken to address issues raised by the PACs. It has become more complex for the PACs to provide effective oversight due to political interference. Continuous monitoring and the submission of annual reports to parliament is absent and/or deliberately or unintentionally delayed (Malapane 2015). While parliamentary committees are meant to provide oversight of particular government departments, in practice they operate on a limited budget, and MPs and support staff are not adequately trained (and when training is offered, some do not get the opportunity to attend) (Rapoo 2004).

Problems of institutional support result as the committees are unable to perform their functional responsibilities optimally. The quality and accuracy of reports presented to the committees has been concerning, with some reports being found to be unreliable. Resolution-tracking mechanisms are not functional, so parliament has not been effective in tracking resolutions.

The rooted political culture and ethos of the majority party, the ANC, continues to encourage solidarity rather than critical engagement or public debate. No ANC MP has critically questioned a member of cabinet in parliament. The nature of the parliamentary form of government in South Africa has resulted in the development of protective relationships between parliament's majority and the executive. The ANC has continuously used its majority to shelve critical engagement. The situation has been worsened by increasing political competition, partisanship, and power relations between the executive and parliament, resulting in the reluctance of the executive to cooperate (Malapane 2015).

Parliament operates in an environment characterised by a high level of political party influence. The electoral model of proportional representation gives more power and influence to political parties than their representatives. The power of political parties over MPs has had a negative impact on the notion of oversight as party loyalty moves to the fore, and representatives are continually faced with the need to balance their legally mandated responsibility with their partisan affiliation (and their political future). It is owing to this partisanship that political parties such as the Economic Freedom Fighters and the Democratic Alliance have regularly approached the judiciary to intervene on issues of oversight (Malapane 2015). In the context of weak legislative oversight, legislative authority has been subjected to constant reviews by the judiciary.

Has the South African judiciary overstepped its oversight mandate?

The judiciary has been accused of activism and overstepping its mandate under the pretext of 'constitutional scrutiny' (Democratic Governance and Rights Unit [DGRU] 2014: 21). Allegations have been rife that judges are driven and influenced by their personal opinions on public policy and are on the lookout for any constitutional violations (Roux 2013). Furthermore, it has been alleged that the judiciary is manipulated by external elements that seek to undermine democratic processes in South Africa (Mokone 2012; Roux 2013). The Constitution of South Africa 1996 was intended to transform South Africa from an era of impunity and abuse of human rights to a constitutional democracy (*Glenister v. President of RSA* 2009 1 SA 287 (CC): 28). It regulates the exercise of public power by constraining the political arms of government through the doctrine of separation of powers. Judicial review is the constitutional mechanism through which the courts constrain the legislative and executive organs of state to their constitutional powers (Roux 2013).

The most prominent issue has been the judiciary's perceived disregard for the principle of the doctrine of separation of powers (Dube 2016; Roux 2013). The doctrine has also featured consistently in Constitutional Court cases. An important observation was made in the case of *South African Association of Personal Injury Lawyers v. Heath* 2001 5 BCLR 77 (CC), which compared the constitutional dispensations of South Africa, the United States of America, and Australia. It was indicated that 'in all three countries [...] there is a clear though not absolute separation between the legislature and the executive on the one hand, and the courts on the other'. The South African Constitutional Court held that the doctrine of separation of powers does not always have to be strictly applied (Mojapelo 2013). Mojapelo (2013) further argues that in any constitutional dispensation, the doctrine of separation of powers is not fixed or rigid, and that South Africa's judiciary has made dedicated efforts to develop a home-based (though not explicitly postcolonial) model of the doctrine of separation of powers, as envisioned in the Constitution.

The judiciary's protective mandate over the Constitution stands far above the democratic doctrine of separation of powers, and even goes beyond the system of checks and balances (Dube 2016). According to Michelman (2008: 12), 'no part of South African law can be allowed to remain outside the Constitution or beyond the Constitution's gaze'. This suggests that judicial oversight is vital for constitutional democracy, and that the judiciary must do everything in its power to intervene where there is reason to believe that there is not compliance with the Constitution. It does not matter if it encroaches into the domains of the legislature and the executive (Dube 2016).

The Constitutional Court has also interpreted its mandate in the following manner, as cited in *De Lange v. Smuts NO and Others* 1998 7 BCLR 779 (CC):

> [...] in our constitutional democracy, the courts are the ultimate guardians of the Constitution. They not only have the right to intervene in order to prevent the violation of the Constitution, they also have the duty to do so. It is in the performance of this role that courts are more likely to confront the question of whether to venture into the domain of other branches of government and the extent of such intervention [...] But even in these circumstances, courts must observe the limits of their powers.

In the enforcement of rights, courts depend on Section 38 of the Constitution, which provides that they 'may grant appropriate relief' (Constitution of South Africa 1996). Section 172(1) of the Constitution further stipulates that such relief may include a declaration of invalidity of 'any order that is not just and equitable'. The driving mechanism that guides the judiciary is Section 8 of the Constitution which provides that the judiciary may develop common law (where legislation does not give effect to a right), or may rely on the limitations clause to limit a right. The interpretation clause is important in guiding the judiciary, which 'must promote the spirit, purport and object of the Bill of Rights' (Constitution of South Africa 1996: Section 39(2)). This means that the remedy must be effective in preventing, correcting, and reversing constitutional violations (see *Steenkamp v. Provincial Tender Board, Eastern Cape* 2007 3 SA 1210 (CC): 29).

Other remedies include reading from a statute and declaration of rights (interdicts and damages) (Dube 2016). In most cases, the courts handle each case on its own merits. Hence the remedies that the courts may grant in safeguarding the Bill of Rights are 'open-ended and contextually flexible' (Currie and De Waal 2015: 12). The judiciary of course *ought* not to use their power of review to supervise the legislative and executive arms of government (De Vos 2011).

The failures of the South African government have further created a useful field for judicial intervention – although future, stable and law-abiding governments may find their room for manoeuvre has been limited by these past failures. In 2013, the Constitutional Court ruled that the allocation of the contract in the Department of Social Development for providing social grants was not lawful. The court oversaw the entire process from the review of failed tenders and played an oversight role in the payment of social grants. Significantly, in *Black Sash Trust v. Minister of Social Development & Others* (*Freedom Under Law NPC Intervening*) 2017 (3) SA 335 (CC), the court acknowledged that it was pushing beyond its limits and entering the domain of executive powers. It was now actively involved in matters of policy implementation. Once done, this cannot be walked back: precedent has been set.

The association between the judiciary and executive was aptly described by De Vos (2011: 45):

> The executive, as elected officials, has the sole discretion to decide policies for the Government. This challenge is perhaps articulated clearly by Justice VR Krishna Iyer of India who observed that: 'Legality is the court's province to pronounce upon, but canons of political propriety and democratic dharma are polemic issues on which judicial silence is the golden rule.'

This shows that the judiciary has no authority to approve or reject government policy. Policy can only come to the judicial organ when it is reflected in legislation or some other legal instrument (DGRU 2014). When so reflected, it must comply with the Bill of Rights and other constitutional imperatives. In cases where the government policy is involved in litigation, the duty of the courts does not go beyond determining whether there is compliance with the Constitution (Dube 2016). Courts are not supposed to manipulate the interpretation process to give the Constitution any meaning which they desire, lest they be considered activist (*State v. Zuma* 1995 1 SACR 568 (CC)).

De Vos (2011) indicates that before a court entertains a matter, there must be satisfaction that, constitutionally, it has the jurisdiction to act. It needs to ascertain if it is the appropriate forum to decide the dispute (Ginsburg and Garoupa 2011). This is where the question of the doctrine of separation of powers comes in.

CONSTITUTIONAL COURT JURISPRUDENCE: AN ACTIVIST COURT?

Constitutional Court jurisprudence is instructive in terms of judicial oversight and how the judiciary has played an activist role on matters of policy and oversight. In the matter *Minister of Health v. Treatment Action Campaign (TAC)* 2002 5 SA 721 (CC), the court forced the executive to develop a policy for providing antiretroviral treatment to poor South Africans. In this case, the executive had adopted a hard-line stance on the subject by refusing to provide antiretroviral treatment to those suffering from HIV and Aids. The executive insisted that those who were HIV-positive should strengthen their immune systems with, inter alia, garlic, beetroot and the African potato (De Vos 2009b). Critics indicated that that this was an irrational and cruel response to a people whose very existence was endangered by the virus. While there was no comprehensive research on this stance, Dube (2016) argues that hundreds of thousands of deaths could have been avoided if the government had promptly shifted its policy.

The Constitutional Court decision to order the executive to provide antiretroviral treatment to infected persons was a positive step towards fulfilling socioeconomic rights and respect for the dignity of patients (De Vos 2009b; Dube 2016). The judiciary overlooked the technical aspects of the provision of such treatment with respect to the budgetary allocation that comes with such a large-scale exercise. As such, the judiciary arguably overstepped its mandate by ordering the executive function without due regard for the financial implications of the decision. The development and implementation of national policy is the prerogative of the president and cabinet (Section 85(2)(b) of the Constitution of South Africa 1996; Dube 2016). An activist court saw things differently.

In *De Lange v. Smuts NO and Others*, the court held that a member of the executive may not be given the power to commit an uncooperative witness to prison.

This is because the courts have the power to send someone to prison; this was seen as a judicial function and not an executive one. In *South African Association of Personal Injury Lawyers v. Heath,* the court found that a judicial officer may not be appointed as the head of a criminal investigation unit, because the power to investigate and prosecute crimes is an executive function and not a judicial function. In *State v. Dodo* 2001 3 SA 382 (CC), the court held that the legislature may regulate a minimum sentence for a specific crime, but it cannot determine the sentence that should be imposed in a case because the power to impose a sentence on the offender is a judicial function and not an executive function. In *Executive Council Western Cape Legislature v. President of Republic of South Africa* 1995 (10) BCLR 1289, the court held that the legislative organ of the state cannot delegate unlimited lawmaking powers to the executive, but it can delegate subordinate lawmaking powers. In this instance, the court confirmed that lawmaking falls within the scope of the legislature and it was designed to be non-delegatable (Mojapelo 2013: 39). This case shows how the judiciary has often reviewed legislative decisions; in some instances, it did not directly interfere on issues of policy in government.

Moseneke (2015) argues that the judiciary has not overstepped its constitutional mandate. He observes that any decision that the judiciary makes in any constitutional dispensation can be met with hostility or cause uproar – but that should not be equated with overreach. Section 34 of the Constitution entrenches the right of everyone to approach the courts and have their grievances resolved impartially (Constitution of South Africa 1996). Moseneke (2015: 7) states that 'courts safeguard public interest and help to preserve and deepen the democratic project [in South Africa]'. Further, Moseneke (2015) argues that the Constitution requires that government respect and promote the rights of everyone as contained in the Bill of Rights. Thus, in situations where government policy on issues of oversight is inconsistent with the Constitution, the judiciary ought to intervene to ensure that the government fulfils its constitutional obligation.

Moseneke (2015) asserts that the judiciary has created a fair, trial-driven criminal justice jurispendence. He notes that the judiciary, in a series of notable cases, has refused to tolerate inequality and discrimination. Dube (2016) also states that the judiciary promotes respect for diversity and substantive equality through effective oversight, and that judicial oversight has provided adequate protection for children, migrants, people with disabilities, and refugees. Both Dube (2016) and Moseneke (2015) argue that access to socio-economic rights for the poor in South Africa has been fast-tracked through judicial oversight. The judiciary has ensured that there is access to proper health care and reminded the executive of its duty to provide access to housing. The tension between different branches of state are a sign of thoughtfulness, not concern: the tension is, in effect, governance in action.

The theory of transformative constitutionalism states that there should be an ongoing and insistent engagement to fundamentally generate large-scale societal change through the non-violent political process guided by the law (Pieterse 2010; Roux 2009). Janson and Van Leeve (2015: 141) indicate that

> transformative constitutionalism envisages a meaningful improvement in the material conditions of people's lives together with real change in legal culture. The content and implementation of transformative constitution-alism, therefore, cannot be considered in the abstract, but must be informed by actual socio-economic conditions.

Klare (1998) argues that in the interpretation of theory of transformative constitu-tionalism and application of the law, courts must keep in mind the transformation of the lives of all South Africans within the framework of human rights and other con-stitutional imperatives. Moseneke (2012a) argues that the judiciary ought to make rulings based on the need to transform the material conditions of people's lives and resolve divergent disputes, provided they can be resolved by application of the law.

In the matter between *New National Party of South Africa v. Government of RSA* 1999 3 SA 191 (CC), the court noted that the regulation of elections is the preroga-tive of parliament, and that it would be unsuitable for the courts to prescribe to the legislature on how to regulate elections. In *United Democratic Movement (UDM) v. President of the RSA and Others* 2002 (11) BCLR 1213 (CC), the court refused to invalidate floor-crossing, thereby enabling the National Assembly to regulate its own affairs without judicial interference. In the matter between *Minister of Home Affairs v. Fourie* 2006 1 SA 524, the court chose to defer to the legislature to prom-ulgate as statute, rather than read provisions into the Marriage Act (No. 25 of 1961). These cases demonstrate the importance of institutional competence and demo-cratic considerations in judicial review. They highlight the crucial role played by the judiciary in enforcing separation of powers through judicial review as a measure of checks and balances. The cases demonstrate that the Constitutional Court places the need to protect individual rights above the desirability of a strict adherence to the doctrine of separation of powers. The cases show that the courts have become active actors around executive and legislative issues.

The judicial branch of government is the institutional construct with which the Constitution ring-fences the limits for legislative and executive conduct. It ensures that the state does not roll back on its promise to protect individual rights, particularly those of minorities and marginalised groups (*State v. Makwanyane* 1995 3 SA 391 (CC): 88). Considering the supremacy of the Constitution provided for in Section 2, it has a mandate to set aside all law or conduct which is in violation of the Constitution. As the guardian and trustee of the Constitution, it has a duty to ensure that all conduct involving the exercise of public power promotes the spirit, purport, and object of the Bill of Rights (Klassen 2015).

The crux of the argument against judicial review is that it lacks democratic legitimacy. Contrary to the legislature and the executive, the judiciary does not derive its mandate from the people through the ballot, but directly from the Constitution (Klassen 2015). A narrow view of the situation reveals that judicial oversight interferes with democracy because it substitutes a few judges' decisions for the majority will.

The Economic Freedom Fighters (EEF), United Democratic Movement (UDM), Congress of the People (Cope) and Democratic Alliance (DA) brought an application against the National Assembly and Speaker Baleka Mbete. The basis of the application was that the speaker and National Assembly failed to act after the Constitutional Court ruled in their favour in the Nkandla judgment. The court indicated that President Zuma had not protected, defended, and upheld the Constitution, and had violated his constitutional oath of office. The judgment stated that the way in which parliament handled the Nkandla Report violated the constitutional duty of the National Assembly to oversee the actions of the executive. The court ordered parliament to create rules that will regulate the removal of the president in terms of Section 89 of the Constitution. The National Assembly's failure to determine whether the president had breached Section 89 of the Constitution was declared to be inconsistent with Section 42 of the Constitution (*Economic Freedom Fighters and Others v. Speaker of the National Assembly and Others* 2017 ZACC 47; 2018 (3) BCLR 259 (CC)).

In the Nkandla case, the Constitutional Court granted a supervisory order compelling the National Treasury, an integral part of the executive, to determine the reasonable amount that ex-president Zuma was to pay back to the state for non-security upgrades to his private home. It further gave an instruction that the National Treasury report to it in 60 days (*Economic Freedom Fighters and Others v. Speaker of the National Assembly and Others*). Although the Nkandla decision was hailed as a victory for the people against corrupt elements within the executive, Ngobeni (2016: 1) argues that the court exceeded its mandate. He asserts that the court had no legal authority to order an inquiry into aspects relating to the president's security because such matters are not justiciable. Ngobeni (2016: 1) further argues that the court did not heed the provisions of Section 198 of the Constitution, which grants the National Assembly 'a superior constitutionally-derived and exclusive authority' to determine security features at the president's residence. Ngobeni does not define 'national security' and fails to provide an instructive point on whether the courts are 'constitutionally-permitted to test claims of national security' in circumstances where it is *prima facie* evident that public funds have been abused for personal gain (Dube 2016). There is also a perception that the judiciary is assertive only when it can garner and exploit overwhelming public support (Davis and Le Roux 2009). For instance, the Constitutional Court took advantage of the public outcry that was generated by the Nkandla controversy to castigate the executive for spending more than R250 million on upgrading President Zuma's private residence when many South Africans cannot afford the basics of life (Dube 2016).

A critical evaluation of the jurispendence of the Consitutional Court shows that there are no instruments deployed to correct any possible mistakes in judicial adjudication. In addition, the Constitution does not give any form of recourse for the legislative and executive organs of government with any avenues to hold the judiciary to account for any wrongful decisions. On the contrary, the available obligation is on everybody and organs of the state to abide by court decisions, irrespective of whether their reasoning is defective. Only the courts can decide the appropriate boundaries of judicial authority, as evident from the wide jurisdiction of the Constitutional Court, which has made the judiciary more powerful than its counterparts (Dube 2016).

South African courts have regularly made decisions with a direct political impact. This means that they do not give full recognition to the doctrine of separation of powers. The courts have adjudicated over the disputes between political parties and their members, the National Assembly and its members, and between the National Assembly and political parties. This has been caused by the wide jurisdiction of the courts, their powers of review and the abstract nature of constitutional issues which arise in certain matters. It is compounded by the behaviour of other branches of state, and the willingness (in multiple quarters) to resolve political or administrative disputes in court.

Transformative constitutionalism in South Africa gives the judiciary and the Constitutional Court enormous powers which has resulted in judicial supremacy. The courts in South Africa constantly use judicial oversight to intervene in matters of policy. They downplay the doctrine of separation of powers by intruding into legislative and executive domains (Pieterse 2010).

CONCLUSION

The South African parliament as an oversight body is well placed and is vested with the powers to ensure that accountability and accessibility to socio-economic rights are met within available resources (Malapane 2015). The judiciary is barred through the doctrine of separation of powers and constitutional provisions from encroaching on the executive and legislative domains of governance. However, court judgments have been instructive about policy and forcing the executive to account. In *National Coalition for Gay and Lesbian Equality v. Minister of Justice* 1999 1 SA 6 (CC), the necessity of the courts to exercise respect was highlighted so as not to trespass 'onto that part of the legislative field which has been reserved by the Constitution, and for good reason, to the Legislature'. This means that there is a need to exercise judicial restraint and judges have to confine their role to the interpretation of legislation. The judiciary has overstepped the boundaries of its authority by failing to exercise constitutional deference and judicial restraint.

Constitutional Court jurispendence has demonstrated the wide-ranging influence on how the judiciary has acted beyond its domains. This was evident in the landmark Grootboom (*Grootboom v. Government of the Republic of South Africa* 2000 SA 46(CC)) and TAC (*Minister of Health v. Treatment Action Campaign* 2002 (5) SA 721 (CC)) cases, as well as in the case of *Economic Freedom Fighters and Others v. Speaker of the National Assembly and Others*, where the legislature was ordered to make appropriate rules that will regulate the removal of the president in terms of Section 89 of the Constitution.

The legislature has been weak in asserting its control to undertake effective oversight over the executive. Recent evidence to the contrary – such as suddenly active portfolio committees, or the newly energised ministers under President Ramaphosa – suggests this may be changing. However, precedents have now been established. Whether this weakness is a result of a shortage of resources and an entrenched political culture that encourages solidarity rather than critical engagement in the ruling ANC, is open to debate. Such incidences have become fertile grounds for judicial interference as a theory of transformative constitutionalism that 'envisages a meaningful improvement in the material conditions of people's lives together with real change in legal culture' (Janson and Van Leeve 2015: 141). While the judiciary has no legal authority to order an inquiry into the domains of oversight and governance as the doctrine of separation of powers outlines, the judiciary has continued to provide guidance on a host of policy issues and on access to socio-economic rights.

Moseneke (2012b) concludes that as articulated in the doctrine of separation of powers, other state organs are not immune from the judicial interference. The judiciary must ensure that all other branches of government execute their mandate within the domains of the Constitution. This injunction is influenced by the fact that the Constitution remains the blueprint of South Africa's transformative project to ensure access to civil, political and socio-economic rights.

REFERENCES

African National Congress (ANC). 2005. Statement of the National Executive Committee on the occasion of the 93rd Anniversary of the ANC. http://www.anc.org.za/content/statement-national-executive-committee-occasion-93th-anniversary-anc (accessed 30 May 2018).

Chidyausiku, G. 2010. Modern challenges to the independence of the judiciary. Conference and AGM of the Southern African Chief Justices' Forum. Johannesburg, 13–14 August. www.venice.coe.int/SACJF/2010_08_RSA_Johannesburg/Zimbabwe.pdf (accessed 30 May 2018).

Collin, P.H. 2004. *Dictionary of Law* (4th edn). London: Bloomsbury Publishing.

Corder, H. 2009. Principled calm amidst a shameless storm: Testing the limits of the judicial regulation of legislative and executive power. *Constitutional Court Review* 2(1): 239–267.

Cumaraswamy, D.P. 2002. Justice is not a cloistered virtue: Are judicial criticisms inter se permissible? *INSAF Journal of the Malaysian Bar* 31(4): 32–42.

Currie, I. & De Waal, J. 2015. *The Bill of Rights Handbook.* Cape Town: Juta.

Davis, D. & Le Roux, M. 2009. *Precedent and Possibility: The (ab)use of law in South Africa.* Cape Town: Juta.

Democratic Governance and Rights Unit (DGRU). 2014. Has the South African Constitutional Court overreached? A study of the court's application of the separation of powers doctrine between 2009 and 2013. University of Cape Town: DGRU. http://www.dgru.uct.ac.za/news/has-south-african-constitutional-court-overreached-study-court%E2%80%99s-application-separation-powers (accessed 4 June 2018).

De Vos, P. 2009a. Between judicial activism and judicial restraint. *Constitutionally Speaking,* 20 January. http://constitutionallyspeaking.co.za/between-judicial-activism-and-judicial-restraint. (accessed 25 May 2018).

De Vos, P. 2009b. Between moral authority and formalism: *Nyathi v Member of Executive Council for Department of Health, Gauteng. Constitutional Court Review* 2: 409–427.

De Vos, P. 2011. Zuma speaks at the access to justice conference. *Constitutionally Speaking,* 8 July. http://constitutionallyspeaking.co.za/president-zumas-keynote-address-to-access-to-justice-conference (accessed 25 May 2018).

De Vos, P. & Friedman, W. (eds) 2014. *South African Constitutional Law in Context.* Cape Town: Oxford University Press.

Dube, F. 2016. Judicial Oversight and the Constitution: Is the South African Judiciary Overstepping its Jurisdiction? Unpublished LLM dissertation. Mafikeng: University of North West (UNW).

Ginsburg, T. & Garoupa, N. 2011. Building Reputation in Constitutional Courts: Political and Judicial Audiences. *Arizona Journal of International and Comparative Law* 28: 540–568.

Gubbay, R. 2009. The rot started many years ago: The progressive erosion of the rule of law in independent Zimbabwe. www.barcouncil.org.uk/media/100365/rule_of_law_lecture_agubbay_091209.pdf (accessed 10 June 2018).

Janson, B. & Van Leeve, Y. 2015. Transformative Constitutionalism – Guiding Light or Empty Slogan? In: Bishop, M. & Price, A. (eds) *A Transformative Justice: Essays in Honour of Pius Langa*: 141–143. Cape Town: Juta.

Jowett, B. 1982. *Laws III: The Dialogues of Plato*. Oxford: Oxford University Press.

Klare, K. 1998. Legal Culture and Transformative Constitutionalism. *South African Journal on Human Rights* 1: 146–157.

Klassen, A. 2015. Public litigation and the concept of 'deference' in judicial review. *Potchefstroom Electronic Law Journal* (PELJ) 161: 1901–1929.

Klug, H. 2010a. Finding the Constitutional Court's place in South Africa's democracy: The interaction of principle and institutional pragmatism in the court's decision-making. *Constitutional Court Review* 3: 1–32.

Klug, H. 2010b. *The Constitution of South Africa: A Contextual Analysis*. London: Bloomsbury Publishing.

Langa, P. 2006. The Separation of Powers in the South African Constitution. *South African Journal on Human Rights* 99: 8–22.

Madlingozi, T. 2008.The Constitutional Court, court watchers and the commons: a reply to Professor Michelman on constitutional dialogue, 'interpretive charity' and the citizenry as sangomas. *Constitutional Court Review* 1: 63–75.

Malapane, T. 2015. Effective Oversight in the South African Legislative Sector: A Demand for Accountability. *Journal of Public Administration* 4: 863–872.

Mendes, C. 2010. Fighting for their place: constitutional courts as political actors: A reply to Heinz Klug. *Constitutional Court Review* 3: 33–43.

Mhodi, P.T. 2013. The Constitutional Experience of Zimbabwe: Some Basic Fundamental Tenets of Constitutionalism which the New Constitution Should Embody. Unpublished LLM dissertation. Durban: University of KwaZulu-Natal (UKZN).

Michelman, I. 2008. Constitutional Supremacy and Appellate Jurisdiction in South Africa. In: Woolman, S. & Bishop, M. (eds) *Constitutional Conversations*. Pretoria: Pretoria University Law Press.

Mojapelo, P. 2013. The Doctrine of Separation of Powers (a South African Perspective). *Advocate Forum* 12: 37–39.

Mokone, T. 2012. Ramatlodi flays the judiciary. http://www.timeslive.co.za/th etim-es/2012/06/07/ramatlodi-flays-the-judiciary (accessed 25 May 2018).

Moseneke, D. 2012a. Courage and principle: Reflections on the 30th anniversary of the assassination of Ruth First. http://www. constitutionalcourtreview.co.za/wpcontent/uploads/2015/08/Courage-of Principle.pdf (accessed 25 May 2018).

Moseneke, D. 2012b. Striking a balance between the will of the people and the supremacy of the Constitution. *South African Law Journal* 3: 9–22.

Moseneke, D. 2015. Separation of powers: Have the courts crossed the line? GroundUp, 24 July. https://www.groundup.org.za/article/separation-powers-have-courts-crossed-line_3152/ (accessed 25 May 2018).

Ngobeni, P. 2016. Concourt erred on Nkandla ruling. *Sunday Independent*, 10 April. http://www.iol.co.za/ruling https://iol.co.za/sundayindependent/concourt-erred-on-nkandla-ruling-2007309 (accessed 25 May 2018).

Okpaluba, C. 2003. Justiciability, constitutional adjudication and the political question in a nascent democracy: South Africa (Part 1). *Public Law* 17: 331–348.

Pieterse, M. 2010. What do we mean when we talk about transformative constitutionalism? *SA Public Law* 20(1): 155.

Radebe, J. 2012. Media statement by Minister Radebe about Constitutional Court 'Review'. https://constitutionallyspeaking.co.za/media-statement-by-minister-radebe-about-con court-review/ (accessed 25 May 2018).

Rapoo, T. 2004. Rating the Effectiveness of Legislative Oversight Methods & Techniques at Provincial Level. The Views of Senior Public Service Officials. Pretoria: HSRC.

Ratnapala, S. 1993. John Locke's doctrine of the separation of powers: A re-evaluation. *American Journal of Jurisprudence* 38: 189–220.

Roux, T. 2009. Principle and pragmatism on the Constitutional Court of South Africa. *International Journal of Constitutional Law* 7: 106–138.

Roux, T. 2013. *The Politics of Principle: The First South African Constitutional Court, 1995–2005.* Cambridge: Cambridge University Press.

Siyo, L. & Mubangizi, J. 2015. The independence of South African judges: A constitutional and legislative perspective. *PELJ* 18: 817–846.

Strasberg-Cohen, T. 2005. Judicial Independence and the Supervision of Judges' Conduct: Reflection on the Purpose of the Ombudsman for Complaints against Judges Law of 2002. *Mishpatim v Asakim. Law and Business* 21: 1–26.

The Citizen. 2015. Zuma in high-level meeting with SA's top judges. 27 August. http://citizen. co.za/655996/zuma-in-high-level-meeting-with-sas-top-judges (accessed 11 June 2018).

Van Vuuren, H. 2005. *Democracy, Corruption and Conflict Management.* Johannesburg: Centre for Development and Enterprise (CDE).

CASES

Black Sash Trust v. Minister of Social Development & Others (Freedom Under Law NPC Intervening) 2017 (3) SA 335 (CC).

De Lange v. Smuts NO and Others 1998 7 BCLR 779 (CC).

Democratic Alliance v. President of the Republic of South Africa and Others 2013 (1) SA 248 (CC).

Doctors for Life International v. Speaker of the National Assembly 2006 4 SA 416 (CC).

Economic Freedom Fighters and Others v. Speaker of the National Assembly and Others 2017 ZACC 47; 2018 (3) BCLR 259 (CC).

EFF v. Speaker of the National Assembly 2015 JDR 1593 (WCC).

EFF v. Speaker of the National Assembly 2016 3 SA 580 (CC).

Executive Council Western Cape Legislature v. President of Republic of South Africa 1995 (10) BCLR 1289.

Glenister v. President of RSA 2009 1 SA 287 (CC).

Grootboom v. Government of the Republic of South Africa 2000 SA 46 (CC).

Minister of Health v. Treatment Action Campaign (TAC) 2002 (5) SA 721 (CC).

Minister of Home Affairs v. Fourie 2006 1 SA 524 (CC).

National Coalition for Gay and Lesbian Equality v. Minister of Justice 1999 1 SA 6 (CC).

New National Party of South Africa v. Government of RSA 1999 3 SA 191 (CC).

R v. Home Secretary, Ex parte Fire Brigades Union 1995.

S v. Dodo 2001 3 SA 382 (CC).

S v. Makwanyane 1995 3 SA 391 (CC).

S v. Zuma 1995 1 SACR 568 (CC).

South African Association of Personal Injury Lawyers v. Heath 2001 5 BCLR 77 (CC).

Steenkamp v. Provincial Tender Board, Eastern Cape 2007 3 SA 1210 (CC).
United Democratic Movement (UDM) v. President of the Republic of South Africa and Others 2002 (11) BCLR 1213 (CC).

STATUTES

Constitution of the Republic of South Africa, 1996 (No. 108 of 1996).
Judicial Services Commission Act (No. 20 of 2008).
Marriage Act (No. 25 of 1961).
Rules of the National Assembly 1999 (9th edn. 2016).

REPORTS

International Council of Advocates and Barristers (ICAB). 2018. Report of the World Bar Conference 2018. 30 March, Stellenbosch.
Public Protector. 2013/14. Secure in Comfort: A Report of the Public Protector. Report No. 25 of 2013/14.
Report by the Minister of Police to Parliament on security upgrades at the Nkandla private residence of the President, 25 March 2015. http://www.gov.za/sites/www.gov.za/files/speech_docs/REPORT%20BY%20THE%20MINISTER%20OF%20POLICE%20TO%20PARLIAMENT%20ON%20SECURITY%20UPGRADES%20AT%20THE%20NKANDLA%20PRIVATE%20RESIDENCE%20OF%20THE%20PRESIDENT.pdf (accessed 11 June 2018).

11

Factoring in the 'Real World':[1] Governance of public higher education in South Africa[2]

Kirti Menon and Jody Cedras

WHAT IS 'GOVERNANCE' IN HIGHER EDUCATION?

Few are those who maintain the view that 'the university' remains a legitimately isolated institution, run by the few to address the governance preferences of still fewer. By contrast, and in recognition of the ways in which contemporary universities are embedded in the social, political and ethical realities of their communities, academic governance in higher education (HE) is better understood in the context of organisational theory. From this vantage point, questions are raised as to how decisions are made in and for public universities in South Africa. What is the nature of power, persuasion and legislative influence between and among the different participants? Three models of governance are presented: the bureaucratic model, the collegial model, and the political model, in order to understand more effectively the governance of public HE in South Africa at present. Governance is essentially about decision-making: What issue is to be decided? Who is or should be involved in the decision? When and how should involvement happen? Where or at what level should such involvement happen? It will be argued that the system or sector of higher education has always remained a space where government or the state has intervened constantly. This is true for both pre- and post-apartheid South Africa.

THREE MODELS OF GOVERNANCE IN HIGHER EDUCATION

Bureaucratic model

In his groundbreaking work on bureaucratic theory, Max Weber (1947) described an organisation as a system of hierarchical roles and formal chains of command acting in unison towards realising a set of defined goals. Core to this theory is the linear and vertical relationship among decision makers informed by role and rank in the organisation, and the formalisation of rules and policies followed by organisational players. The complexity and costliness associated with higher education institutions make the bureaucratic approach attractive in its ability to insert control over public higher education. The leverage provided by the rule-based approach to governance, as characterised by the bureaucratic model, has the potential to offer institutional stability and certainty for both the HE sector and institutions. However, as Riley and Baldridge (1977) have argued, the bureaucratic model tends to focus more on formal power and the hierarchical structures that define it at the expense of informal power relations that often exist in organisations and that, crucially, change over time depending on the issue or policy at stake. The #FeesMustFall[3] movement illustrates informal power relations and their impact on the governance of HE. Students at the HE institutions captured and responded to a key ideological issue because of government's inaction – perceived or otherwise – in making free education a reality.[4] In this context, it is key to note that the ruling party's resolutions on the matter indicated that education should be free, albeit introducing this in a progressive way, starting with the poorest first, before addressing the middle classes.[5] However, the slow pace of implementation has, for whatever reasons, caught up with government. Among those at the forefront of the #FeesMustFall movement, some were from the ranks of the middle class: the so-called missing middle, which government has been unable to assist as this category of student is 'too rich' to qualify for student financial aid through the National Student Financial Aid Scheme (NSFAS), and yet 'too poor' to afford university fees (DHET 2011b). Also evident is that in the bureaucratic model, the state is preoccupied with policy formulation rather than policy execution. Overall, the model has a tendency to minimise the role of multiple interest groups and the multilayered political struggles that exist among the different groups. The weakness of the bureaucratic model is reflected in the state's approach to the sector which has, until recently, taken little cognisance of the differentiation in the system. Recent steps by the state to adopt the principle of differentiation in its dealings with the constituent universities means that it is in the early stages of accounting for the distinct and different sociopolitical and economic conditions under which each of the universities has been established and functions. Thus, critics like Jonathan Jansen (2001) and Nico Cloete (2012) have identified four key areas that feature in South African policymaking:

1. The drive to achieve the entire suite of objectives and goals with limited capacity and fiscal constraints;
2. The impact of macroeconomic conditions on government's ability to spend and on individual achievement based on graduate employment;
3. Imported policy ideas with insufficient contextualisation; and
4. Excessive policy production with unreasonable demands placed on institutions (Menon 2014: 43–44).

Finally, it would be negligent not to appreciate the economic impact on universities and the response of a bureaucratic model of governance. The consistent decrease in subsidy income has 'pushed' universities to consider income from other sources, and resulted in a phenomenon known as the commodification or commercialisation of public higher education. This development has led to competing interests between the public interest (the traditional function of the public university) and commercial interests (the profit motive). Given the rule-based nature of the bureaucratic model, university councils would have to balance, in a delicate way, the interests that would emerge as a result of commercialisation and the public good functions of a university.

Collegial model

This model was first introduced by Millett (1962), and promotes the notion of a community governing by consensus. Millett (1962) argues that applying hierarchical principles to the university environment fails to account for the decision-making pluralism that exists in the higher education landscape. He further states that the focus on hierarchy means that undue emphasis is placed on the role that absolute authority has in relationships in the context of the formal power structures and the system of superior and subordinate relationships purported by the bureaucratic model. By way of contrast, and central to the collegial model, are the values shared by the university community which may be expressed in different ways depending on the individual institutional contexts (Austin 1994). While the pursuit of harmony is a treasured value, embodied in the collegial model, the fact is that decision-making remains the consequence of authority. The collegial model is unable to account for the primacy of the state in certain issues relevant to the governance of public higher education and the necessity for accountability in respect of these decisions.

Political model

In this model, governance is characterised as a political process, and universities are part of a political system (Baldridge 1971). In this system, as in any other, competing interest groups participate in a fluid decision-making process depending on the nature of the specific issue facing the constituency at a particular time. Policy formulation is a key focal point, and creating and adopting policy is directly related to the institutional mission and is reflected in the various operational decisions emanating from the body of policy. Decision-making within the university, and that outside of it which affects the university, usually follows prescribed systems of review and consultation with various persons or/and entities depending on the nature of the decision to be made. Involving different interest groups by virtue of their role and expertise gives legitimacy or credibility to the concept of shared governance as developed by Mortimer and McConnell (1978). Decision-making in a shared governance context is undertaken through the exercise of influence rather than that derived from formal positions. The paradox is that the notion of shared governance involves accepting the authoritative rights that certain constituencies have based on their expertise and/or formal position. Environmental factors, including the resourcing of universities and the state's efforts to ensure greater accountability on the part of universities, have impacted substantially on how university governance takes place. Given that the state is increasingly concerned with how diminishing and precious resources should be spent, the need to balance this against society's expectations means an increased emphasis on outcomes from those investments.

From this brief discussion of the models, it is clear that elements of all three remain present in the institutions and their governance forms in South Africa. At different times in our history, one or two models have emerged as dominant with variances across the institutional landscape influenced by the political history of both institution and country, and are reflected in these systems. An additional impact on the governance of HE derived from the twentieth-century trend to call for greater alignment of the purpose and functions of the university with the social and economic imperatives of the country. The 'steering' role of the state and its agencies[6] is present in the early post-apartheid policy discussion documents (NCHE 1996). The term 'steering' is often conflated with governance and management of institutions. Policy documents like the Education White Paper 3: A Programme for the Transformation of Higher Education (DoE 1997a) and the National Plan for Higher Education (NPHE) (DoE 2001) assert that higher education is a public good and that, in line with public interest, government resourcing will be made available to institutions. In this vein, government sets broad policy goals and is required to ensure that resourcing is adequate and congruent with achievement of the goals. As public institutions, the institutions are expected to deliver on these goals. However, amendments to the Higher Education Act (No. 101 of 1997) (which accorded the minister of education powers to establish, close or merge institutions, determine funding allocations to institutions, declare the seat of an institution and in some instances be advised of loans or overdrafts of institutions) were met with rumblings that this expansionary role was tantamount to interference. The concept of steering in higher education was clearly flagged in early policy documents (DoE 1997b; DoE 2001), with funding, quality and planning being identified as the three steering mechanisms.

In terms of government's role of actively steering the higher education sector, it is salient to refer to Osborne and Gaebler (1992: 32), who state, 'after all, those who steer the boat have far more power over its direction than those who row it'. This assertion broadly refers to the concept of steering by governments and is not specific to the South African context. Part of the New Public Management (NPM) focus, and its infusion into the discourse of a strong focus on delivery and account-ability, was the need for government to clearly delineate goals and objectives and work with partners in the system to achieve delivery.

As a result, the NPM paradigm shifted government's control function to a steering role, with the main levers being planning, funding and quality assurance. While these steering levers may appear to be stand-alone, they are integrated and interdependent, as the indicators suggest. The indicators of the control function reside in activities such as enrolment planning; institutions' approved Programmes and Qualifications Mixes (PQMs); research funding (through, for example, accredited journals and the work of the National Research Foundation [NRF]); infrastructure funding; quality assurance mechanisms such as accreditation of programmes and qualifications; institutional audits; national reviews and registra-tion of qualifications and part-qualifications; student funding; minimum admission requirements; the size and constitution of councils; criteria for institutional statutes; and so forth. From a brief survey of these, it appears that several straddle more than one of the indicators (such as planning and funding; or planning and quality assurance; or quality assurance and funding). It is argued that these mechanisms form the core of the government controls of the public higher education system. The rationale presented for higher education interventions ranges from poor gov-ernance, administration and management of institutions, to financial instability or

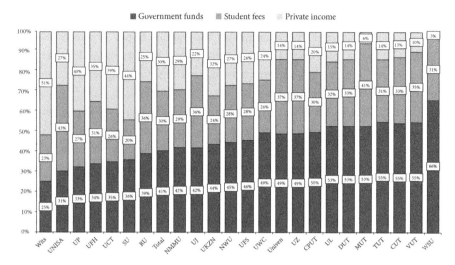

Figure 11.1: Proportion of income sources for universities in 2010

Source: DHET (2013: 146)

corruption, the need for reimagining the mission and vision of institutions, and a range of what can be termed accountability or transformation demands. One view that could be posited is that the interventions are a rational response to specific sets of problems. For example, the rationale underpinning mergers was to achieve new identities for institutions and efficiency in the system and to reduce dupli-cation, amongst other goals (DoE 2001). The jury is still out as to whether or not the mergers and restructuring impinged on other policy agendas like widening of access, redress for historically disadvantaged institutions and broader transform-ation imperatives of the system.[7]

It is also clear that the events of 2015 and 2016 may precipitate major transform-ation in the system-wide governance approach. The argument posed for increased intervention by the state is evident in two critical aspects directly linked to the stu-dent protests that began in 2015. The first of these is that the state has a clear interest in controlling university-determined student fees, perceived as spiralling upward, and unarguably exceeding the inflation rate year on year (Makoni 2014). According to the Ministerial Committee for the Review of the Funding of Universities, 'between 2000 and 2010, state funding per full-time equivalent (FTE) enrolled student fell by 1.1% annually, in real terms. (DHET 2011a). During the same period, perhaps as a response to declining state funding, 'tuition fees per FTE student increased by 2.5% annually, in real terms' (DHET 2014: 7). It is clear that no mechanisms through which universities could calibrate tuition fees with the income level of existing and potential students are in place, and thus fee increases and the impact of this could not take cognisance of the effect on the students' ability to pay. The second argument is that the increase of state funding to the public institutions needed to enable the realisation of 'free education' warrants tighter control and higher levels of state control over the institutions themselves.

Figure 11.1 shows the trends in state support and the increased dependence of universities on tuition fees and alternate sources of income. For the year 2010, it can be seen that the reliance of universities on tuition fees and other income outweighs the proportion of government funds in most institutions.

It is argued that the increasing intrusion of the state into the management of universities has been enabled by the numerous amendments to the Higher Education Act (No. 101 of 1997) made between 1994 and 2016. In response, public institutions have chafed at measures characterised as control over what have been deemed 'university spaces' of institutional autonomy. A brief overview of the major changes indicates that many areas of the universities' functioning have been affected. The more significant of these changes are in financial management brought about by the introduction of the Regulations for Reporting by Public Higher Education Institutions (DHET 2014) and the prescripts of the Higher Education Act, which are designed to control and ensure fiscal accountability of institutions. Enrolment planning too has been implemented, and made even more challenging by the intractable tension of the goal of widening access and controlling numbers in the institutions. The promulgation of statutes addressing university governance arrangements within the universities, setting out the requirements for membership of the governance structures, has determined participation in the governance structures of the institutions. Academic programme accreditation and approval processes impact on the universities' ability to develop and implement new offerings. The pressure to produce research affects both funding and staff workload and reward. Finally, the state controls infrastructure expenditure, a key factor given the continuous pressure on facilities brought about by substantially increased student numbers. Thus, while analysts point to an increase in the interventions by the state, Hall, Symes and Luescher (2002) describe the varying degrees of autonomy experienced by universities in the pre-1994 period. The state was arguably intrusive with the politics of apartheid framing the organisation and governance of the higher education sector. A case could be made that the intrusive nature of the state in current-day governance of the higher education system is palpable, although the extent to which it erodes institutional autonomy is yet to be seen.

South Africa has a very rich political context of citizen activism. This was provided more traction when parliament adopted the Constitution in 1996, setting the country on the path towards constitutional democracy. The policymaking process has been formalised through public participation processes as part of affording broader society a voice in governance processes. Universities are part of the social fabric of South Africa and as such are subject to the precepts of the country's Constitution, including that of shared governance. Having broad representativity on its councils may well assist universities to counterbalance any intrusive tendencies that an 'overzealous' state may have. It could be argued that the 'political model' will be the norm in the post-#FeesMustFall period given the enormous interest and scrutiny of universities.

ACCOUNTABILITY AND OVERSIGHT

The system of government in South Africa comprises three spheres – namely, national, provincial and local. Higher education is a national competence. While departments such as the Department of Higher Education and Training (DHET), and public entities such as the Council on Higher Education (CHE), are often the primary intermediary between government and institutions, it is parliament that establishes the parameters of the interactions through the budget it approves, the legislation it enacts and the responsibilities of entities receiving public funding that it approves. Parliament also retains its oversight over public entities including the CHE, the National Student Financial Aid Scheme (NSFAS) and the South African Qualifications Authority (SAQA), all of which are engaged in activities of national interest that directly impact on the workings of a university. There is a natural assumption that the government line department (DHET), through representation on the governing structures and, quarterly and annual reports, manages oversight and accountability.

There is no question that higher education is central to the development of a nation's culture and economy. In addition, national government contributes billions of rands each year towards research, student access, and infrastructural developments such as student housing. The #FeesMustFall movement and the demand for free education together with the decolonisation of university campuses from imperialist symbols caught the attention of many members of parliament and other players in the state. The movement has raised questions about the political nature of the governance of higher education institutions. The events since October 2015 have necessitated a reimagining of our institutions, specifically in relation to the role, purpose and governance of universities in a decolonised and post-apartheid context. The sense is that '[m]any of the dominant' cultures of governance and leadership 'simply morphed into the new era, with its essential features, symbols and practices left more or less unbroken' (Universities South Africa 2015: 7). Parliamentary interest sometimes results in legislative changes affecting higher education, but more often manifests through parliamentary hearings. The 2015 protests led to the president instructing a fee freeze at all universities and the establishment of a commission of inquiry with the following remit:

1. The feasibility of making higher education and training fee-free in South Africa, having regard to:

    1.1. the Constitution of the Republic of South Africa, all relevant higher and basic education legislation, all findings and recommendations of the various Presidential and Ministerial Task Teams, as well as all relevant educational policies, reports and guidelines;

    1.2. the multiple facets of financial sustainability, analysing and assessing the role of government together with its agencies, students, institutions, business sector and employers in funding higher education and training; and

    1.3. the institutional independence and autonomy which should occur vis-à-vis the financial funding model (The Presidency 2016).

The additional injection of R6.5 billion was welcomed by vice-chancellors of universities, although a cautionary note was sounded on the model of funding of higher education, which they articulated as a cost-sharing model with students contributing a percentage and the state the balance (Universities South Africa 2016). The 2015/2016 turbulence in the macro-political landscape in higher education may result in an increased dependency relationship between institutions and the state. It could also be argued that increased instability at universities might trigger governance reforms.

National government's oversight and accountability for the public university system is enshrined in the Higher Education Act (No. 101 of 1997), which assigns the minister of higher education and training, as the executive member responsible for higher education, a variety of responsibilities. The minister can appoint an independent assessor to a university (Chapter 6 of the Amendments to the Higher Education Act). In terms of this same chapter, the minister may place a university under administration and appoint the administrator. Significantly, ministerial appointments to university councils (the highest governance structure in a university) are also in place: 'not more than five persons appointed by the Minister' are to sit on a university council (Section 27(4)(c)).

Approval of the institutional statutes by the minister (Section 33) is a mechanism to ensure that the governance structures within universities are in place as stated in the Amendment to the Higher Education Act (No. 9 of 2016):

Institutional statutes to be approved or made by the Minister (1) Any institutional statute must be submitted to the Minister for approval, and if so approved must be published by notice in the Gazette and comes into operation on the date mentioned in such notice. (2) The Minister must table any institutional statute made under section 32 in parliament as soon as reasonably practicable after it has been published as contemplated in subsection (1). (3) The Minister must make a standard institutional statute, which applies to every public higher education institution that has not made an institutional statute, until such time as the Council of such public higher education institution makes its own institutional statute under section 32.

The increasingly complex university reporting requirements are set out in sections 41(2) and (3) of the Higher Education Act (No. 101 of 1997):

(2) The council of a public higher education institution must, in respect of the preceding year and by a date or dates and in the manner determined by the Minister, provide the Minister with – (a) a report on the overall governance of the public higher education institution; (b) a duly audited statement of income and expenditure; and (c) a balance sheet and cash flow statement. (3) The council of a public higher education institution must provide the Minister with such information, in such format, as the Minister may reasonably require.

Government funding of public universities (Section 39 of the Act) is addressed as follows:

(1) The Minister must, after consulting the CHE and with the concurrence of the Minister of Finance, determine the policy on the funding of public higher education, which must include appropriate measures for the redress of past inequalities, and publish such policy by notice in the Gazette. (2) The Minister must, subject to the policy determined in terms of subsection (1), allocate public funds to public higher education on a fair and transparent basis. (3) The Minister may, subject to the policy determined in terms of subsection (1), impose (a) any reasonable condition in respect of an allocation contemplated in subsection (2); and (b) different conditions in respect of different public higher education institutions, different instructional programmes or different allocations, if there is a reasonable basis for such differentiation. (4) The policy referred to in subsection (1) may discriminate in

> a fair manner between students who are not citizens or permanent residents of the Republic and students who are citizens or permanent residents of the Republic.

Despite the submission of annual reports to the DHET between the years 1994 and 2016, several institutions have required interventions because of maladministration, poor governance and financial problems. There are more than 12 institutions that have had assessors appointed, and in nine instances administrators have also been appointed for varying lengths of time. Against this backdrop, the fundamental governance structures of the public university in South Africa have to follow the prescripts of the new accountability demands in the most recent Regulations for Reporting by Public Higher Education Institutions (DHET 2014). The aim and objective of the new accountability requirements are to provide a measure of 'real-time' monitoring of institutions and to serve as an early trigger for proactive measures to support institutions in crisis, especially regarding financial problems.

FUNDING

'Follow the money' is synonymous with understanding the way in which decisions are made, and the impact of those decisions. The government in South Africa is still largely the prime funder of universities. Governance decisions happen within the context of defined resources, possibilities and restraints. This section illustrates the current funding approach of government for universities in South Africa and how this could either support or pervert good governance within the system.

The most important source of funding for South Africa's public universities is the state. It is important to point out that the inequities of our institutional landscape have a direct bearing on the dependency of institutions on state funding as opposed to other income streams. However, the degree of dependence varies, with some universities receiving slightly more than 30 per cent of their total income from government while others receive 65 per cent of their total revenue from this source (Wangenge-Ouma and Cloete 2008). On average, the South African university derives slightly more than 25 per cent from third-stream sources, with the average historically white university (HWU) earning about 40 per cent from this source, and the average university of technology (UoT) about 12 per cent (Duncan 2009). The Duncan (2009) study also shows that the proportion of institutional revenue received from the state (the 'first stream' of income) has declined on average from 62 per cent in 1986 to 41 per cent in 2007. Second-stream income in the form of tuition fees increased from 15 per cent to 32 per cent, and third-stream income, from other sources including research, consultancies, investment income, and so on, increased from 23 per cent to 27 per cent during the same period (Duncan 2009).

In the African context, the South African HE funding system has some interesting, innovative and rare features. First, the system has always had a fee-paying component. In fact, tuition fees have always comprised a significant component of institutional revenue. Second, higher education institutions are free to generate 'third stream' income through, inter alia, research and other entrepreneurial activities. Third, an interesting feature of this aspect of financing is that unlike some other African countries, higher education institutions are not penalised through receiving lower state funding if they raise third-stream income. Fourth, there is a close link between planning (at both the institutional and system levels) and funding. Higher education institutions are required to submit three-year enrolment plans to the government as part of the state's planning and Medium Term Expenditure Framework (MTEF) budgeting process. Institutions are required to propose institutional targets against the national target of enrolments. In developing these targets, institutions must consider the following:

- Areas of growth, capacity and efficiency;
- Racial and gender equity imperatives; and
- Quality aspects such as institutional audits and programme review.

Fifth, a key component of the HE financing framework is that it is underpinned by a funding formula. The funding framework proposed in the White Paper (DoE 1997a) reconceptualised the relationship between institutional costs and government expenditure on higher education. This new funding framework is viewed as a distributive mechanism – a way of allocating government funds to individual institutions in accordance both with the budget made available by government and with government's policy priorities. The new framework recognises that institutional costs tend to be functions of income, and of what is available to be spent. Government funds for higher education institutions are not designed to meet specific kinds or levels of institutional cost, but are intended rather to pay institutions for delivering the teaching-related and research-related services specified by government-approved plans.

In terms of the higher education funding framework, higher education institutions receive the following:

- Block funds, which are undesignated amounts made available to each institution and which consist of
  - research funds generated by approved outputs;

- teaching funds generated by: a) planned full-time equivalent (FTE) student enrolments, and b) approved teaching outputs;
- institutional factor funds to address equity.
- Earmarked funds, which are designated for specific purposes (e.g. capital expenditure).

The funding framework developed for higher education in South Africa has a number of important implications for equity and efficiency which include predictability, recognition, promoting institution autonomy and efficiency and equity. Implementing a formula-driven approach ensures a level of predictability, particularly with regard to 'certainty of revenue'. Institutions are aware of the factors driving the formula and will know, within certain parameters, the magnitude of resources that will flow to them over a certain period. Such certainty undoubtedly enhances institutional planning. The new funding framework takes place in the context of the recognition of a hard budget constraint and is driven by the availability of public resources for higher education, rather than by the costs of provision. The various mechanisms in the framework come into operation only after government has determined: a) the total amount of public funds that should be spent in a given year on higher education; and b) what services should be delivered by the higher education system. Promoting institutional autonomy and equity is achieved by using a mixture of block and earmarked grants. Block grants confer a degree of freedom with respect to how the funds are used by institutions, while earmarked grants by definition are directed towards the attainment of specific goals such as equity – for example, in research development, and through foundation programmes for historically disadvantaged students. The formula-driven framework provides for efficiency incentives in a number of ways. The block grant rewards efficiency of outcomes in research. Grants are based on the output of publications and of master's and doctoral graduates. Research grants are based not on a predetermined monetary amount but against benchmarks based on academic capacity. Inadequate research performance by the system as a whole will result in surpluses of funds allocated for research. These funds provide a further incentive to stimulate output in that they are distributed on a pro-rata (output) determined basis. The formula is designed to reward the output of certain categories of graduates more than it does others (for example, professional bachelor's degrees as against other bachelor's degrees). Such a funding mechanism enables the government to stimulate the development of skills that are in short supply. As with research, teaching output funds are determined not by pre-set amounts of funding but are developed through a set of benchmark graduation rates, based on the National Plan for Higher Education (DoE 2001). In line with this, the formula promotes differential funding in line with the country's human development needs (for example, agriculture and health sciences as against librarianship and psychology). Finally, through institutional factor funding, the framework promotes economies of scale and thus lower institutional unit costs.

Equity is enhanced by the funding process in a number of ways. Funding is earmarked for, inter alia, capacity building, research development and foundation programmes for the historically disadvantaged. Institutional factoring for students from historically advantaged backgrounds and for small institutions, especially those in rural, areas ensures a more balanced funding for those institutions. For rural-based universities such as Venda and Fort Hare, earmarked funding would, for example, open opportunities for these institutions to procure better teaching and learning capacity, which in turn would lead to better success rates.

South Africa has reached a relatively high level of sophistication in the development of its higher education funding mechanisms, particularly with the close link between the planning and budgeting processes, and the implementation of a relatively simple funding formula. The system has also benefited from always having had a fee-paying system, so no new cost-sharing mechanisms have had to be developed. Finally, there is also a strong systemic thrust towards greater equity exemplified in both the funding formula and the student loan scheme. However, South Africa continues to face enormous challenges with respect to quality and efficiency. The apartheid legacy of differentiated systemic quality and efficiency continues, except that the main determinant is no longer race, but socio-economic status and region.

More recently, serious questions have been raised about the adequacy of the instruments within the funding formula to promote inter-institutional equity. It is argued that the funding mechanism currently in place may be serving to entrench and even accentuate inequalities between previously advantaged and previously disadvantaged institutions. This occurs in at least three ways. First, the formula rewards research outputs, but most universities of technology or former historically disadvantaged institutions do not have research capacity and, in light of heavy teaching burdens, are not likely to develop this capacity in the short to medium term. Second, although capital expenditure has been increasing substantially in the past few years, it still falls short of the requirements in light of increased access. Third, and finally, the earmarked grants provided for in the funding formula have not been adequate to address the equity challenge. What is clear, however, is that the funding mechanisms available permit the state to steer the ways in which universities make decisions and thus influence the governance practices of public universities. This may well be further heightened in the light of the 2015/2016 protests at universities.

ACCESS

Access is a key imperative for the state and it is noteworthy that the public university system has more than doubled in size since 1994. As a priority for the state, the question of access to higher education has been central to the debates within the governance structures of universities. The state has conventionally managed access through admission requirements, enrolment planning and student financial aid.

Admissions – one of the primary goals of national government is to increase access to higher education. Government has used a number of instruments to achieve this goal, including both policy and funding. Policies to this effect include the Minimum Admission Requirements for Entry into a Higher Certificate; Diploma and Bachelor Degree Studies requiring the National Senior Certificate; Minimum Admission Requirements for Entry into a Higher Certificate; and Diploma and Bachelor Degree Studies requiring the National Certificate Vocational at NQF Level 4. One contentious matter in relation to the admissions criteria for academic programmes at universities is that of Section 37 of the Higher Education Act (No. 101 of 1997). This section provides for universities to set additional requirements over and above the minimum criteria determined by the state in the aforementioned policies.

Enrolment planning is an established practice that forms part of the planning and funding functions of government through the Department of Higher Education and Training. The DHET, using historical data against capacity of the universities, negotiates the *n* year enrolment plans (normally three years linked to the MTEF) with each of the universities.

Student financial aid – a prime barrier of access to higher education is affordability. The state responded to this through the establishment of the National Student Financial Aid Scheme (NSFAS), which is governed by the National Student Financial Aid Scheme Act (No. 56 of 1999) and subsequent amendments, and the Public Finance Management Act (PFMA) (No. 1 of 1999), in terms of which NSFAS is listed as a public entity. The Act sets out the functions of NSFAS:

a) allocate funds for loans and bursaries to eligible students;
b) develop criteria and conditions for the granting of loans and bursaries to eligible students in consultation with the Minister;
c) raise funds as contemplated in section 14(1);
d) recover loans;
e) maintain and analyse a database and undertake research for the better utilisation of financial resources;
f) advise the Minister on matters relating to student financial aid; and perform any other functions as assigned to it by the Act or by the Minister.

The ANC conference in Polokwane in 2007 laid the ground for a renewal of the cry for 'free education' by adopting a formal resolution that speaks of the 'progressive intro-duction of free education until undergraduate level' (ANC 2007). In 2009, the minister of higher education and training proclaimed by gazette the terms of reference for the review of NSFAS (DHET 2009). The overall purpose of the review of the NSFAS was:

a) to assess the strengths and shortcomings of current scheme;
b) to advise the Minister on the short-, medium- and long-term needs in order for student financial aid to promote the twin goals of equity of access and pro-viding free undergraduate education to students from working class and poor communities, who cannot afford further or higher education.

The review report made several recommendations, especially in relation to higher education. Relevant to the discussion on widening of access and provision of free education is the following recommendation:

[...] a higher education student financial aid model that progressively provides free higher education to undergraduate level for students from poor and working class communities. The model also provides student loans on favour-able terms to higher education students from lower middle-income families.

The review report made several insightful recommendations based on the findings of students on NSFAS loans for whom the burden of debt was untenable, especially changes to the interest regime for loans. Between 2010 and 2012, several changes were made that gave life to the recommendations of the review committee and provided a rough roadmap for the realisation of free undergraduate education. One major change directly addresses the 'burden of debt' problem and it is simply that as of 1 April 2011, a student registered for full-time studies would not be charged interest on loans, and interest would only accrue a year after completion of the degree (NSFAS 2011, 2012). A second radical shift in policy was the Final Year Programme of the NSFAS that worked on the principle that if a student on a NSFAS loan successfully completes the requirements for the degree, then the amount owing for the final year would be converted into a bursary (NSFAS 2011, 2012). The events of 2015/2016 have also propelled further injections into NSFAS with an additional allocation to the R10 billion that was allocated in the 2016/17 financial year. In total, the budget that was to be administered by NSFAS in 2016 came to R14.582 billion (NSFAS 2016).

The announcement by President Jacob Zuma, on the eve of the 54th conference of the ANC in 2017, that higher education will be free for those whose combined family income is less than R350 000 – in the absence of a clear policy document (specifically in relation to implementation) – has added additional confusion amongst the university management (and councils), further straining the governance environment on many campuses around South Africa (Quintal 2017).

QUALITY ASSURANCE AND ACCREDITATION

The third leg of the state's steering mechanism of HE other than funding and planning is that of quality assurance and accreditation. A robust and intensive quality assurance and accreditation regime has been established and embedded in the South African HE system since the mid-1990s. One of the catalysts for this revolutionary development may be ascribed to the need to unify a highly fragmented system resulting from a history of colonialism and apartheid.

The first education law passed in the newly democratic South Africa was the South African Qualifications Authority (SAQA) Act (No. 58 of 1995) (RSA 1995). The Act established the mandate of SAQA to develop and implement the National Qualifications Framework (NQF). Through this piece of legislation, the government signalled its intention for a single, integrated qualifications framework not delinked from the broader socio-economic realities of South Africa. This included the need to redress past unfair discrimination in education, training and development, as well as facilitating access to, and mobility and progression within, education, training and career paths. Another central objective of the Act provided for the imperative to 'enhance the quality of education and training'. The NQF Act (No. 67 of 2008) (RSA 2008) repealed the SAQA Act, but continued to provide for the existence of SAQA to oversee the further development and implementation of the NQF, and retained the original objectives under the SAQA Act, namely:

- create a single integrated national framework for learning achievements;
- facilitate access to, and mobility and progression within, education, training and career paths;
- enhance the quality of education and training; and
- accelerate the redress of past unfair discrimination in education, training and employment opportunities.

The NQF Act regulated the Council on Higher Education as the Quality Council for Higher Education responsible for quality assurance in the higher education sector as stated in Section 27(i) where it must

(i)   develop and implement policy for quality assurance;
(ii) ensure the integrity and credibility of quality assurance;

(iii) ensure that such quality assurance as is necessary for the sub-framework is undertaken.

Following the SAQA Act in 1995 was the Higher Education Act (No. 101 of 1997), which provided for the Council on Higher Education (CHE), established in 1998, and the Higher Education Quality Committee as a permanent committee of the CHE responsible for quality assurance matters.

A National Qualifications Framework, with eight NQF levels, was developed and implemented with effect from 1998, with a revised ten-level NQF following the implementation of the NQF Act in 2009. A Higher Education Qualifications Framework (2007); Framework and Criteria for Programme Accreditation (2004); Framework and Criteria for Institutional Audits (2004); Framework for Institutional Quality Enhancement in the Second Period of Quality Assurance (2012); and Criteria for National Reviews (Master of Business Administration (2002–2004), Teacher Education Programmes (2005–2006), and Social Work Programmes (2014–2015)); Higher Education Qualifications Sub-Framework (2014); and (Draft) Qualification Standards for the Master of Business Administration (MBA), Bachelor of Laws (LLB), Bachelor of Social Work (BSW), Bachelor in Engineering (BEng and BSc in Engineering), and Diploma in Engineering (2015) – all developed very rapidly following the establishment of entities such as SAQA in 1996 and the CHE in 1998 respectively. These policy developments consolidated the quality assurance and accreditation regime pertinent to the higher education sector in South Africa. Both the CHE and SAQA account to the minister of higher education and training, and to parliament. From the state's perspective, it could be argued that quality is a means to an end – the end being accountability. Quality – in its various dimensions of assurance, management, enhancement and control – is an instrument used by the state to ensure that accountability is built into the system.

CONCLUSION

The governance of higher education continues to change form rapidly as the reforms and restructuring of higher education systems are underpinned by the constant need for the re-interrogation of the objectives of higher education. The challenges faced by higher education institutions and the societies they are located in are perennial, and higher education is clearly not impervious to national, regional and global challenges. In the South African context, government has exercised its control over the sector in terms of governance and fiscal accountability. There is documented evidence of extensive interference and intervention within universities prior to 1994, especially concerning the racial profile of admissions policies and practices, institutional statutes, research activities, and so on. Since 1994, there have been rumblings at various stages due to the restructuring of higher education, the introduction of PQMs (Programme Qualification Mix), enrolment planning, the performance-based funding formula, and the introduction of multiple levels of reporting to the DHET as recently as in 2014. The student uprisings of 2015, whether in the form of the #RhodesMustFall or #FeesMustFall campaigns, brought into sharp focus the role of the state in relation to universities. Thus, while the state's control of public institutions has been formalised through the different regulatory mechanisms of the government department, the DHET, the student unrest called into question the powers of the state to regulate fee increases and to support the call for free higher education. Although at this stage it is unclear what the long-term impact will be on universities, it was unprecedented. The result is that the Office of the President intervened and announced on 23 October 2015 that there would be a zero per cent tuition fee hike despite the fact that fee setting has long been the function of the council of a university. This was followed up when Zuma announced free higher education on the eve of the 54th conference of the ANC in December 2017. The consequences and sustainability of this pronounce-ment, in a policy void, are yet to be manifested.

South African reform measures in higher education, when subjected to detailed policy analysis, have revealed ambiguity: ambivalence, inaction and compromises on one hand, and firmness, clear agenda setting and goal-driven processes on the other. The vacillation between the two extremes is evident and poses challenges to those on the ground to interpret and enact in a highly subjective way. Levin (2001: 8) argued that reform, by its very nature, is political and that 'one finds a high level of ambiguity and contingency in every aspect of the political process'. It is important to recognise that these contrary features are not unique to this country, but are characteristics of policymaking processes globally. The radical intervention approach was evident in China, which declared that higher education had to be expanded radically in the 1990s. Despite some problems, such as an increase in tuition fees, social exclusion of the poor and uneven development of institutions, participation grew from 0.4 million to 3.4 million between 1978 and 1998 (Li, Whalley, Zhang and Zhao 2008: 4). This combination of resourcing and planning achieved specific goals for China, like massification of higher education, even though it has had unin-tended consequences, like graduate unemployment, differential quality and inequit-able access to higher education. The model adopted in China was that of direct intervention and not gentle steering of the higher education system.

It is not clear what the impact of the extraordinary measure of state interventions in the fee crisis will be, or the reverberations for future state interventions in rela-tion to a domain that is clearly university-demarcated. It is unlikely that there will be a loosening of the state's appetite to maintain its hold on the way in which public universities are governed. This is evident in the suite of amendments to the Higher Education Act (Higher Education Amendment Act [No. 9 of 2016], January 2017). The amendments instead seek to strengthen the minister of higher education and training's authority to intervene decisively in the event of mismanagement and poor governance. The amended Act provides for the voices of multiple stakeholders to be heard prior to an intervention.

The political model of governance is the core driving force of governance in the South African public institutions of higher learning. It is influenced by aspects of the bureaucratic model through rules imposed by the regulatory governance structures, as well as those negotiated by institutional role players; and by aspects of the collegial model, where professional values influence the nature of political engagement and agency.

The key questions to be raised relate to the initial questions asked in the introduction: What will the impact on the balance of power between the state and the universities be? And finally, what level of state intervention in higher education is palatable?

NOTES

[1] 'I hate that phrase "the real world". Why is an aircraft factory more real than a university? Is it?' (Hugo 1992).

[2] Some parts of this chapter derive directly from Menon (2014).

[3] #FeesMustFall began in mid-October 2015, at the University of the Witwatersrand. It is a student protest movement that was triggered by the increase in tuition fees at South African universities. It also called for an end to outsourcing of services at universities. The movement gained momentum and was taken up at other universities throughout 2016.

[4] The Report of the Working Group on Fee Free University Education for the Poor in South Africa (DHET 2012) outlines the political and policy imperatives underpinning the fee-free debates.

[5] 'to progressively introduce free higher education for the poor until undergraduate level' (ANC 2007).

[6] Statutory bodies like the Council on Higher Education (CHE) and the South African Qualifications Authority (SAQA).

[7] Extracts from Menon 2014.

REFERENCES

African National Congress (ANC). 2007. 52nd ANC National Conference: Resolutions, 20 December. http://www.anc.org.za/show.php?id=2536 (accessed 10 October 2012).

Austin, A.E. 1994. Understanding and assessing faculty cultures and climates. *New Directions for Institutional Research* 84: 47–63.

Baldridge, J.V. 1971. *Power and Conflict in the University: Research in the sociology of complex organizations.* New York: Wiley.

Cedras, J.P. 2013. Policy Targeting as a Strategy to Increase Access to Higher Education. *African Journal of Public Affairs* 6(4): 43–58.

Cloete, N. 2012. Higher education and economic development in Africa. In: Vukasović, M., Maassen, P., Nerland, M., Pinheiro, R., Stensaker, B. & Vabo, A. (eds) *Effects of Higher Education Reforms: Change Dynamics*: 137–152. Rotterdam: Sense Publishers.

Department of Education (DoE). 1997a. Education White Paper 3: A programme for the transformation of higher education. Pretoria: Department of Education.

Department of Education (DoE). 1997b. Higher Education Act (No. 101 of 1997). Pretoria: Government Printers.

Department of Education (DoE). 2001. National Plan for Higher Education. Pretoria: Department of Education.

Department of Higher Education and Training (DHET). 2009. Review of the National Student Financial Aid Scheme: *Government Gazette* 32917. Pretoria: Government Printers.

Department of Higher Education and Training (DHET). 2011a. Ministerial Review of University Funding: *Government Gazette* 34347. Pretoria: Government Printers.

Department of Higher Education and Training (DHET). 2011b. Report of the Ministerial Committee on the Review of the National Student Financial Aid Scheme. Pretoria: Government Printers.

Department of Higher Education and Training (DHET). 2012. Report of the Working Group on Fee Free University Education for the Poor in South Africa. October.

Department of Higher Education and Training (DHET). 2013. Report of the Ministerial Committee for the Review of the Funding of Universities. Pretoria: Department of Education.

Department of Higher Education and Training (DHET). 2014. Regulations for Reporting by Public Higher Education Institutions. *Government Gazette* 37726. Pretoria: Government Printers.

Department of Higher Education and Training (DHET). 2017. Amendment to the Higher Education Act (No. 9 of 2016). Pretoria: Government Printers.

Duncan, J. 2009. *Third Stream Income at South African Universities.* Grahamstown: Centre for Higher Education Research, Teaching and Learning, Rhodes University.

Hall, M., Symes A. & Luescher, T.M. 2002. *Governance in South African Higher Education Research Report.* Pretoria: Council on Higher Education (CHE). http://www.che.org.za/documents/d000006/Governance Research_Report.pdf) (accessed 24 March 2017).

Hugo, R. 1992. *The Triggering Town: Lectures and Essays on Poetry and Writing.* New York: W.W. Norton & Company.

Jansen, J.D. 2001. Rethinking education policy making in South Africa: Symbols of change, signals of conflict. In: Kraak, A. & Young, M. (eds) *Education in Retrospect: Policy and implementation since 1990*: 41–57. Pretoria: Human Sciences Research Council.

Levin, B. 2001. Conceptualizing the Process of Education Reform from an International Perspective. *Education Policy Analysis Archives* 9(14). http://epaa.asu.edu/epaa/v9n14.html (accessed 22 August 2006).

Li, Y., Whalley, J., Zhang, S. & Zhao, X. 2008. *The Higher Educational Transformations of China and its Global Implications.* Working Paper 13849, March. Cambridge: National Bureau of Economic Research.

Makoni, M. 2014. Higher education is not cheap. *University World News*, 24 October. http://www.universityworldnews.com/article.php?story=2014102313130139 (accessed 28 March 2017).

Menon, K. 2014. Exclusion and access in higher education policies. Unpublished PhD thesis. Johannesburg: University of the Witwatersrand. wiredspace.wits.ac.za/./Exclusion%20and%20Access%20in%20Higher%2 (accessed 26 January 2015).

Millett, J.D. 1962. *The Academic Community: An Essay on Organisations.* New York: McGraw-Hill.

Mortimer, K.P. & McConnell, T.R. 1978. *Sharing Authority Effectively.* San Francisco, CA: Jossey-Bass.

National Commission on Higher Education (NCHE). 1996. An Overview of a New Policy Framework for Higher Education Transformation. Pretoria: National Commission on Higher Education.

National Student Financial Aid Scheme (NSFAS). 2011. Annual Report 2011. http://www.nsfas.org.za/content/reports/annualreport2011.pdf (accessed 19 February 2019).

National Student Financial Aid Scheme (NSFAS). 2012. Annual Report 2012. http://www.nsfas.org.za/content/reports/annualreport2012.pdf (accessed 19 February 2019).

National Student Financial Aid Scheme (NSFAS). 2016. Statement on 2016 funding allocation and implementation of the announcement by the President of the Republic of South Africa on short-term funding solutions. Press release, 21 January. http://www.dhet.gov.za/SiteAssets/Media/Statements/NSFAS%20Media%20Statement%20on%202016%20budget%20allocations.pdf-1.pdf (accessed 28 March 2016).

Osborne, D. & Gaebler, T. 1992. *Reinventing Government: How the Entrepreneurial Spirit is Transforming Government.* Reading, MA: Addison-Wesley.

Quintal, G. 2017. Zuma announces free higher education. *Business Day*, 16 December. https://www.businesslive.co.za/bd/national/education/2017-12-16-zuma-announces-free-higher-education/ (accessed 9 January 2018).

Republic of South Africa (RSA). 1995. South African Qualifications Authority Act (No. 58 of 1995).

Republic of South Africa (RSA). 1999. National Student Financial Aid Scheme Act (No. 56 of 1999).

Republic of South Africa (RSA). 2008. National Qualifications Framework Act (No. 67 of 2008).

Republic of South Africa (RSA). 2017. Higher Education Amendment Act (No. 9 of 2016).

Riley, G.L. & Baldridge, V.J. 1977. *Governing Academic Organisations: New problems, new perspectives.* Berkeley, CA: McCutchan.

The Presidency. 2016. President Zuma announces commission of inquiry into Higher Education funding and other issues. Press release, 14 January. http://www.dhet.gov.za/SiteAssets/Latest%20News/January%202016/PRESIDENT%20ZUMA%20ANNOUNCES%20COMMISSION%20OF%20.pdf (accessed 10 February 2016).

Universities South Africa. 2015. Reflections on Higher Education Transformation: Discussion paper prepared for the second national Higher Education Transformation Summit. www.dhet.gov.za/summit/docs/2015 (accessed 10 February 2015).

Universities South Africa. 2016. Joint statement from the Vice-chancellors, Principals and Rectors of Universities in South Africa. Press release, 10 January. http://www.usaf.ac.za/universities-sa-statement-february-2016/ (accessed 20 February 2016).

Wangenge-Ouma, G. & Cloete, N. 2008. Financing Higher Education in South Africa: Public Funding, Non-government Revenue and Tuition Fees. *South African Journal of Higher Education* 22(4): 906–919.

Weber, M. 1947. *The Theory of Social and Economic Organization.* New York: The Free Press.

12

Decolonisation and Governance at South African Universities: Case study of the Green Leadership Schools

Darlene Miller, Nomalanga Mkhize, Rebecca Pointer and Babalwa Magoqwana

INTRODUCTION

Resistance by the national #FeesMustFall students' movement in South Africa placed the governance of university spaces at the centre of public discourse and university policies in 2015/2016. At the outset, this phase of student resistance in South Africa involved a fierce symbolic struggle to remove the statue of colonial imperialist Cecil John Rhodes at the University of Cape Town. The man and his chair were finally dismantled and moved by crane in 2015. The historical hangover of colonial culture in an African university space, so many years after African independence from colonial rule, points to wider problems of governance at South African universities. Spaces of learning are organised under the gaze of white men and the postcolonial patriarchy. Transformation in higher education has not fundamentally disrupted hegemonic and racialised structures of governance at South African universities.

This chapter focuses on the importance of space and power, and how alternative approaches to higher education learning spaces – the physical organisation of learning, dominant knowledge systems, and the integration of the environment – may allow greater freedom for black Africans in university learning spaces. The premise is that the present university system still constrains the growth of black intellectuals and professionals. We present a radical alternative based in a grounded research method, in which a number of workshops called Green Leadership Schools (GLS) were run by the authors of this chapter. Key social problems and theories made up the curriculum of the GLS – land, gender and leadership – and these were related to crucial environmental issues such as climate change and indigenous knowledge(s).

The format and foci of the different GLS, organised over a two-year period as four residential workshops in 2014 and 2015, experimented with a different kind of learning space that stepped outside the modernist structures of the university learning space. The GLS initiative predated and then overlapped with the #FeesMustFall national students' movement. The concerns for radical university transformation by these students intersected with the radical pedagogies envisaged by the GLS. The final (and fourth) GLS was organised as a writing workshop for these students. Themes of indigenous environmentalism, matriarchal leadership and green learning spaces informed our idea of green leadership, and were explored in various ways at the schools. While only workshops, the thinking behind them endeavoured to introduce an epistemic shift in which African women intellectuals led the discussion on environmentalism and university transformation; hence their designation as 'schools'.

Indigeneity and endogeneity were flagged as relevant concepts for framing our environmental discussions. Endogeneity links to notions of local self-reliance, advanced by Samir Amin and others during the period of the New International Economic Order (NIEO) in the 1970s and 1980s, in which local resources and strengths are marshalled for development (Tickner 1986). Indigeneity has been theorised as Indigenous Knowledge Systems (IKS) (Claxton 2010). One of the challenges with IKS is the political association with patriarchal systems, such as traditional systems of governance which oppress women and LGBTIAQ+. As we explore indigeneity in our work, we are keen to find approaches that draw on indigenous knowledge in a way that restores the centrality of African matriarchal systems of leadership and knowledge prevalent in African precolonial societies.

Drawing on the work of human geographers, we argue that the way that space is organised serves to reproduce social power, including the spaces of learning at the university. The theoretical framework examines learning spaces as social spaces (Bourdieu 1990), and utilises the metaphor of colour (brown and green) to infuse these learning spaces with social meanings. The green metaphor – and green leadership by extension – invokes the soil literally and figuratively as a space of indigeneity and a source of alternative knowledge about leadership. Being rooted in or closer to the soil is advocated as an important component of green leadership and green governance.

Informed by Paulo Freire's (1970) radical pedagogy, the Green Leadership Schools set out to learn by doing in a different and green environmental context rather than the brown, modern and Westernised structures of the South African university. Our radical experiment placed our workshops (schools) on private and cooperative farms, and at a hotel where rolling hills meet the ocean (Coffee Bay).

This chapter chronicles the GLS's radical green governance experiment. The first part of the chapter provides a theoretical framing for the learning initiative embodied in the GLS, pointing to the important relationship between the production of power and the decolonisation of learning spaces. Decolonisation has been examined from various angles, but for the purposes of this chapter, we focus on space – spaces of formal education, local spaces as a site of indigenous learning, spaces of healing and spaces of ritual. We argue for a shift from overemphasising equity in transformation objectives to focus on the context and decolonisation of learning spaces at South African universities. The second part of the chapter explores the key objectives and approaches in the GLS initiative and provides a brief overview of the schools' activities. The conclusion, in short, argues that decolonisation of university governance requires a radical interrogation of universities as spaces of learning. The GLS proposed a template for a new decolonised campus.

POWER AND DECOLONISATION OF HIGHER EDUCATION SPACES

In South Africa today we are experiencing a radical epistemic conjuncture. The current education crisis (especially the #FeesMustFall movement of 2015/2016) placed decolonisation in education curricula as a priority. The overarching influence of Western knowledge systems and white scholarship of the global north still prevails in our academic curricula. While there have been policy shifts in the demographic requirements for South African universities to reflect transformation, curriculum and spatial transformation has lagged behind. Awareness about the need for ongoing post-apartheid transformation has been lacking in many learning contexts, particularly in tertiary education.

Radical resistance at universities often revolves around visible historical vestiges of power, such as language, symbols and the demographics of those in power. The histories of power are routinely scrutinised by colonial subjects: paintings and sculptures of old white men have to come down, and universities are under pressure to include black faculty. What is less visible in the postcolonial machinery of the African university is the way that the *physical organisation* of the university reproduces a white and colonial imagery – the rolling lawns introduced by British settlers in Africa; the imposing imperial architecture imitating the pillars of Greek pantheons; the modernist square buildings where support staff beaver (or while) away their time; the quarantined laboratory spaces where shadowy lab-coated figures mystically glide around. The physical structures of these university spaces thus embody a Westernised learning context. Although the hallowed spaces of the university lecture hall and quiet libraries may hark back to precolonial Africa, they have also come to typify Western learning spaces, which may not be appropriate to decolonial learning. It is important to remember that the precolonial African university system did not have the mass audiences found in undergraduate university classes today. As we will argue in this chapter, new spaces of university learning such as the garden and yoga rooms offer opportunities for postcolonial learning, beyond precolonial and colonial spaces of learning.

Architectural form and design follows function: the modern university has adapted to the functional needs of the university in the twenty-first century. Mass tertiary education dictates the use of space to accommodate large numbers of students, faculty and support staff. Lecture halls need to hold hundreds or, in some cases, over a thousand students. But there is more to the physical organisation of university learning than mere function, as the heated discourse around symbols and statues at South African universities demonstrates. Why is the current university system entrenched as the optimal space of learning? Is the current system of learning Westernised and, if so, why? What makes our modes of learning and knowledge production Westernised, and if colonial learning systems are deeply ensconced in Westernised systems of learning, what do we need to change to obtain liberation in our higher education systems?

Drawing on human geography, we argue that space represents and reproduces power relations. In many ways, our social spaces at South African universities reinforce colonial power in the physical organisation of our buildings and learning spaces. For example, faculties, departments and disciplines are grouped and housed in separate buildings, limiting the possibilities for cross-disciplinary learning.

Even though universities, especially at the postgraduate level, are increasingly moving away from lectures as primary spaces of learning, and embracing tutorials, seminars and colloquia, learning still takes place within the confines of Western architectural spaces that have not been much refurbished to accommodate new styles of learning. Given class sizes at undergraduate level, lectures still form the basis of mass education; in our efforts to break with a racialised and colonial past, transformation initiatives in higher education focus on equity and emphasise the demographics of the professorial elite.

The hierarchical system of learning elevates recognised professors as the bearers of scientific knowledge. If this professorial elite is mainly white and male – and to a lesser extent white and female – in the South African context, it is to be expected that we will focus on these overt features of colonial racialisation of our higher education system, leading to an overemphasis on demographics and less emphasis on curriculum content and epistemology.

Echoing this overemphasis on equity in the project of university decolonisation, Pumla Gqola in *Reflecting Rogue* (2017: 94) argues:

> Most studies of institutional culture focus on its inadequacies as far as equitable representation of Black people and/or women in the academic staff are concerned, or on the limited resources even when employed by universities. To the extent that universities are visible towers in/of knowledge production, the nature of this knowledge or systems of knowledge, should be unpacked and subject to scrutiny. This is particularly so given that power is institutionally defined.

Why would it be necessary to organise the university as a hierarchical system of learned dons, as is currently the approach? The answer to this question is power. We have long recognised the role of universities in reproducing society's power arrangements, since they are part of endorsing hierarchy and power in societies. Finding alternatives to Westernised knowledge is not easy given the historical ruptures that have occurred in Africa. We face an epistemic challenge to find our way back to the beauty of indigeneity rather than the reaction of traditionalism. Drawing on Henri Lefebvre (1992) in *The Production of Space*, we believe that our spaces of representation (the ways in which we physically organise ourselves and symbolically represent ourselves) are in an epistemic collusion with Western rationalism. Discipline is an important way to manufacture acquiescence to power structures, and forms of organisation of social space or workspace at universities (and elsewhere) have important consequences for the way that power unfolds.

These systems of discipline are organised into the very organisation of *space and time* at universities:

- fragments of knowledge presented bite-size in lectures;
- the lectern as the site of privileged knowledge;

- the cultural mode of teaching in English (or Afrikaans) with specialised professional languages;
- linear time slots for learning instruction;
- books, articles and reports written by an alien elite with little experience of working-class realities and the life of the people; and
- a highly specialised professoriate often lacking breadth of cultural, political and social knowledge and experience.

All these features of university mass education conspire to produce a disciplined learning subject (as Michel Foucault [1977] argues in *Discipline and Punish*). This discipline is disrupted during times of resistance, and space is then organised differently in response to such radicalisation. As such radical rupture recedes, disillusionment and pragmatism take hold. With an emphasis on discipline, the learning opportunities offered by rebellion are quelled. Untidy spillovers from one discipline to another are prevented, producing disciplined students confined to the disciplines of faculties and departments. This means, for example, that racism and gender oppression in scientific laboratories is seen as being outside the discipline of science, and outside of what science students must learn about. #FeesMustFall has attempted to rupture these confines, only to be subjected to the discipline of police and punishment. Since addressing racism and gender oppression are not at the core of most learning, for many students, learning in university spaces is alienating.

As such, transformation cycles in university spaces succumb to wounded institutional life, or brown spaces. We call existing spaces of learning 'brown spaces' because the architectural design and forms of learning instruction mirror the epistemic foundations of colonial and commodified learning spaces. South African higher education spaces are located within this context of cultural wounding and dispossession. As we enter these learning spaces, we are at risk of new wounds being inflicted along old lines. In the next section, we elaborate on our understanding of brown and wounded spaces.

Brown spaces and wounded spaces

Given the contestations in South African higher education, it is important to look at the political and social terrain in which higher education takes place. In South Africa today, even left-wing political spaces (that push for equity-oriented societal change) can be characterised as brown spaces due to several compounding factors. These include a history of cultural wounding as a result of colonialism and apartheid; formal and informal patriarchal structures and ideologies (Kearney

2014); and compassion fatigue as a result of successful or unsuccessful service to causes and people. Apart from the extreme atrocities of apartheid such as murder and torture, apartheid left indelible marks on the psyches of most South Africans because it was not only physically violent, but also 'a constant, psychically persistent, pervasive and invasive presence in the minds of black South Africans' (Gagiano 2012: 220).

Political spaces (and in South Africa, most spaces are political spaces) are marked by cultural wounds. As described by Hoosain (2013), most South Africans are the walking wounded, carrying apartheid trauma that is then transmitted from one generation to the next. Apartheid has resulted in 'disenfranchised grief, silence, socialisation in institutional racism and shame' (Hoosain 2013: v); as well as 'intimate partner violence and substance abuse and community violence in the form of gang violence' (Hoosain 2013: v); male interpersonal violence (Lazarus, Tonsing, Ratele and Van Niekerk 2009); or in 'displaced modes, in differing forms of chauvinism, xenophobia and bigotry' (Hook 2011: 72). In most cases, South Africans have not received support to recover from and 'interrupt the trauma transmission' (Hoosain 2013: vi), so the violence and dehumanisation continues postapartheid (Hook 2011).

Globally, South Africa has a disproportionate level of violence, HIV and Aids, suicide, and injury rates (Ratele 2014). At the same time, since race-based social inequality persists, South Africans are precluded from 'exiting racial thinking or even thinking about race differently; race is still the most significant factor in post-apartheid identities' (McKinney 2007: 216). Apartheid's racism is also linked to ongoing domination and marginalisation in social, political and economic processes (Hook 2004), with current leadership models mimicking patterns of apartheid domination and marginalisation, and encouraging authoritarian systems of control.

As already mentioned, apartheid impacted not only on race relations, but also on gender relations. Although South Africa has an above average incorporation of women in its national legislature, political spaces are still male-dominated and hostile to women (Goetz 1998). For example, the leading trade union council, the Congress of South African Trade Unions (Cosatu), has resisted 'quotas for women in leadership' (Meer 2005: 39). In political spaces, patriarchy is acted out in terms of 'unwanted sexual advances, male domination at meetings, male abuse of power, male devaluation of women's contribution, the ignoring of women's concerns, and side-lining of women' (Meer 2005: 44). While different masculinities coexist in South Africa, power and privilege is bestowed on men through the domination and control they need in order to be seen as men (Morrell 1998).

Therefore, we contend that our social and political spaces are spaces of woundedness – brown spaces in which disillusionment has taken hold. The zeitgeist of neo-liberal capitalism is that there is no alternative to the self-gratifying and individualistic ethos of a profit-driven society. Pragmatism and 'reason' prevail in institutional life and in political choices. The tyranny of pragmatism as a counterpoint to revolutionary idealism allows bureaucratisation in society to be compacted into a political sediment that is difficult to dislodge, limiting the scope of possible action (Deleuze and Guattari 2004). In this disenchanted context, any form of imagination or idealism is dismissed as foolish and quixotic.

Reflecting this dominant global disposition, in the 2000s, South Africa entered political life with an aversion for radical change; activists campaigning against privatisation were characterised by the ANC Youth League (2001) as ultra-left and quislings. Institutional life became a dowdy, routine affair, devoid of the courage, enthusiasm, and sincerity that characterised the struggle of the 1970s and 1980s. Layered into this burden of pragmatism, the history of woundedness contributed to governance spaces that are increasingly toxic and corrupt. The toxicity extends to our learning spaces as universities succumbed to pragmatism by increasingly commodifying knowledge (Sawyerr 2004). Disillusionment, pain and disenchantment have reinforced the brown spaces of institutional life, since universities have not comprehensively addressed the racial experience of black pain and alienation (Luckett 2016). Until the recent student protests, demands for transformation had stalled (Haupt 2014; Legoabe 2011; Mangcu 2014; Sesanti 2014), so it is now imperative to reignite the push for transformation, and reconnect with local knowledge and the enchanted condition of idealism in order to create a conducive terrain for social and educational change.

Green spaces as indigenous spaces of healing

Recognising this condition of disenchantment and the commodification of tertiary education, the GLS set out to reconnect with a radical indigeneity. This section discusses our understandings of the importance of African ontologies, a key component of indigeneity, in our GLS curriculum. In South Africa, ongoing Eurocentrism in our education system 'ignores and even contradicts much of what is important in traditional African values and learning of South Africa's black majority' (Botha 2010: 35). For example, African values and knowledge emphasise that survival depends on the world as an interconnected reality, with human beings, plants, animals, and the universe as one interconnected whole (Ntuli 2002). When we are ensconced in the global Eurocentric worldview, the specificity of local knowledge and local ecologies becomes invisible. To move towards a green consciousness and green leadership, we need to make the local variances visible and work closely with the local environment and local climate, rediscovering valuable indigenous knowledge. Scientifically relevant indigenous knowledge includes local economic strategies related to agriculture, fishing, forest management, astronomy, climatology, architecture, engineering, medicine, nursing, veterinary science and pharmacology (Hewson 2012).

Decolonisation requires that we turn to knowledge traditions that are generated locally and across Africa, but which have been suppressed through colonialism. Recentring indigenous knowledge is thus one component of decolonising education. Colonial and postcolonial domination have privileged external academic and knowledge traditions, so it is important for university education to shift towards more emphasis on African content, drawing on African teaching and learning to transform pedagogies, and creating time and space for African academics to undertake research and writing to generate new indigenous knowledge. How, then, do we bring our ontologies back home, closer to our soil? How do we engage with vernacular approaches to learning and life that bring an end to the violence of learning systems that alienate and disadvantage our black and indigenous students?

Within this decolonisation drive, environmental consciousness and awareness is imperative to grounding knowledge, not only for experts in the field but for all knowledge practitioners, whether a lecturer in history or a professor of epidemiology. Socially aware academics need to engage with ontological shifts related to, firstly, our understandings of nature and the environment; and, secondly, to the place of indigenous knowledge within these ontologies. While the GLS at the outset mainly focused on understanding climate change, food, land, and the body, our quest was for an indigenous environmentalism that aspired to African ways of knowing.

Accessing indigenous knowledge is about the approach to learning as well as the product (Adeyemi and Adeyinka 2003). In many African traditions, teaching and learning can include playing games, cooking, farming, dancing, music and critical thinking. Learning takes place in multiple environments including the home, in the fields, communal meetings, and ritual spaces. Turning to local indigenous knowledge is not only about ancient traditions, but also about creating new indigenous knowledges as we work with local circumstances, in local environments, developing local solutions to local problems. In this sense, this knowledge is endogenous, created within our own national and local spaces and contexts. Nevertheless, in creating our own green spaces, we also honour some ancient traditions, because our history is part of what makes us who we are, and part of what brought about our current social forms; hence, indigenous. The rituals undertaken at GLS sought to connect what is useful in ancient knowledge to the imperatives of South Africa now; in particular, we focused on rituals as a way to create spaces of healing.

Through healing, then, traditional rituals connect the past with the possibility of creating new futures. The space of 'ritual has a political integrative function, often serving as a vehicle for solidarity in the face of heightening social and public conflict' (Urbasch 2002: 11). Rituals are also an 'important means to (re)produce both locality and local subjects participating in that locality' (Postel 2010: 108). Drawing on and adapting ancient rituals can help heal the social distance created between different social groups by our wounding. Traditional healing, for example, sees the self as embedded in social connections (Jonker 2008). However, indigenous rituals can also have coercive and repressive possibilities. The persecution of 'witches' in South Africa and elsewhere is one example of the gendered consequences of rituals based on superstition and the containment of women (Federici 2004). Drawing on indigenous practices thus needs to distinguish itself from African patriarchal systems of oppression, whether these systems are embedded in traditionalism or in colonial and apartheid ideology. The African approach to healing and recovery involves connecting with one's community, recognising that one's illness is not just in oneself but also part of the social field (Urbasch 2002). The idea of connecting with one's community suggests directions for decolonisation of the university space by fostering a community which encourages engagement, not just in the classroom, or with the formal structures of Student Representative Councils (SRCs), but also in configuring different types of spaces for different types of engagement.

Because of the infection of brown spaces with the wounds of racism, hierarchy, patriarchy, and the effects of compassion fatigue, it is necessary to create new political spaces. Governance systems require overhauling. Political and public spaces need to be sites of healing, growth, rejuvenation and regeneration – green spaces. But in talking about healing, one healer is not taking the lead in dispensing healing to broken others. Instead, healing involves a relay, with different people taking the lead at different times: a person can move between being a healer–leader and a patient, recognising shared injuries among the group, and striving to restore inner and outer harmony. A different approach to leadership is thus envisaged in this healing endeavour. The healing journey involves ritual, reconnecting with the body, reconnecting with human processes of food production through planting, (re)connecting with the 'collective aspect of our existence' (Washington 2010: 33), creativity and play, as well as deep thinking and immersion in a green body of knowledge.

Green leadership and transformation/social justice

Rather than only focusing on red, green and the various conceptions of brown spaces in relation to green leadership, we added the dimension of indigeneity, a conceptualisation that we are aware requires further in-depth investigation. We proposed in the GLS that green leadership combines three kinds of indigenous and endogenous (as in local) knowledge traditions:

1. Feminists/matriarchs within the social justice tradition;
2. Green social activists; and
3. Indigenous social activists.

All three traditions are endogenous to South Africa. While some theorists (Coetzee 2001; Barnard 2006) argue that traditional and indigenous knowledge, ritual and practice are full of problematic gender dynamics, as explained by Gqola (2015), much of the *violence* of gender dynamics in black South African communities is a direct result of colonialism and apartheid, which inscribed black men with racialised, patriarchal violence.

The GLS therefore employed a radical pedagogy, incorporating gender and indigeneity into the complex of new knowledges and endogeneity. We aimed to shift awareness from human-centred perspectives to planetary-centred awareness, and generate a conception of green leadership informed by indigenous notions of the environment (and climate change). Green leadership, in our understanding, was about using feminism as a guiding compass for building knowledge around sustainability, drawing on the three traditions cited above:

1. Red knowledge for ethics and social justice;
2. Green knowledge for deep ecological living and being; and
3. Indigenous knowledge for rootedness and/or endogeneity.

Social transformation and environmentalism have often been disconnected in social justice movements in South Africa (Burkett 1999), posing some challenges for their combination. The integration of environmental awareness into university curricula within transformative educational agendas is also affected by these divides. Red critiques of environmentalism contend that green concerns do not address basic needs such as infrastructure and jobs; and green issues are mostly championed by white and middle-class southern Africans who can afford alternative lifestyles.

This disconnect is characterised by David Harvey (1996) as a tension between the objective of self-actualisation and the limits of structural conditions. The GLS facilitated a discussion between red and green agendas: 'red agendas' refers to the socialist, communist and/or economic transformation programmes that have been an integral part of southern Africa's political change agenda since independence from colonial rule. The agendas of mass-based organisations (such as unions) in southern Africa are often informed by the daily needs and exigencies of working-class communities. In southern Africa, survival and mobilisation are clustered around immediate and urgent material needs that relate to fundamental aspects of human dignity such as health, housing, and food.

However, the rationale guiding the agenda of many unions and community organisations based in poor communities centres on human needs without integrating environmental or planetary concerns and objectives into such red agendas. The green agenda is often associated with middle-class elites (Khan 2000) who can, for example, afford to buy green products and demand that green spaces remain untouched to allow for tourism, but not for traditional life-sustaining activities such as hunting, grazing animals, and gathering indigenous plants for medicines. An example of this is the push against the right of a poor rural community to stay in the state-owned Dukuduku Forest in the St Lucia Nature Reserve in KwaZulu-Natal (Khan 2000).

Poorer communities and African elites often express concern that the environmental agenda denies less developed nations the material comforts long enjoyed in more developed nations (Schlosberg 2009). Job creation through industrialisation is often offered as a remedy for poverty, regardless of the resulting environmental damage. For example, Saldanha Steel was commissioned in 1998 and despite organisations such as Earthlife highlighting environmental concerns, the project went ahead with the support of poor local communities because the investors argued the project would create jobs (Khan 2000). Poor communities in Africa, whose livelihoods depend on using natural resources, are often at loggerheads with environmentalists who want to create conservation areas and block access to those same natural resources. For example, the enclosure of land for the Kgalagadi Transfrontier Park has led to indigenous populations being pushed off the agricultural land and losing hunting rights (Thondhlana, Shackleton and Muchapondwa 2011).

In her prescient paper, 'Connecting the red, brown and green', Jacklyn Cock (2004: 3) points to the diversity of environmental struggles in South Africa, with 'no common understanding shared by all members even within a single organisation or campaign'. In these analyses of the environmental movements, brown and various shades of green are used to connote different kinds of environmentalism (Sklair quoted in Cock 2004: 2). Cock (2004: 20) conjectures that the South African environmental movement is bridging ecological and social justice issues, forging strong connections between the red, the green and the brown. Such connections between red and green struggles are also evident today.

A precursor to the GLS was The Red Tent research project (Miller 2013b), based on focus group discussions about the aims of the Rondebosch Common land occupation in Cape Town in January 2012. Local women leaders from Manenberg in Cape Town involved in the Proudly Manenberg social movement conducted a land protest on Rondebosch Common in Cape Town as part of the Occupy movement sweeping through various countries in 2011/2012 (Miller 2012, 2013a). The Manenberg women articulated thoughtful notions of the green spatial futures they imagined for their children. The women critiqued the densification of their coloured township and the continued apartheid geographies that bequeathed confined social spaces to them and their families. They yearned for greener spaces for themselves, their children and the township youth. They greened their organisation's plot of land in Manenberg by growing vegetables and planting a garden to beautify the spot (which they call 'the Waterfront' in a satiric reference to the opulent and elite Waterfront development in Cape Town's Foreshore area).

The ability of the Manenberg women to link their immediate social justice struggles and their longing for a spatially green future is a concrete example of how red and green agendas could be productively synthesised. Their environmentalism embodied all the contradictions of an African context: an oppressive masculine leadership in their organisation; a resource-challenged environment; an adjacent (chemical) factory pumping effluents into the township's soil and water; and a racially excluded and poverty-stricken coloured community. They also longed to be near the shopping malls to which they felt white and middle-class elites (and African immigrants) had easy geographic access.

Activists have made some inroads in relation to environmental concerns among community groups and social movements (biofuels, GMOs, solar energy) (Cock and Fig 2000). Such concerns reflect enhanced environmental awareness in local communities. Much more can be done, however, to find a complementary relationship between red and green agendas. Many academic, community-based and social movement local leaders have a dismissive attitude at worst, and an ambivalent attitude at best, to green agendas. Since local leaders are involved in tackling social justice issues, they are an important constituency in southern Africa. Academic leaders influence students who are future corporate, political and social leaders; social movement leaders influence the course of resistance and engagement around local community struggles; NGOs may often be self-serving but are still important sites of information-sharing and training for local communities. Because the environmental understanding among such local leaders is important, they were targeted to facilitate and participate in the GLS. The GLS thus sought to combine social justice approaches, key policy issues and environmental awareness in the curriculum of the schools.

CASE STUDY OF THE GREEN LEADERSHIP SCHOOLS – BRIEF OVERVIEW

Environmentalism in South Africa has often been problematically embedded within racialised structures and learning practices, such that green initiatives and curricula are dominated by a white professoriate, white practitioners and white activists. These white, middle-class environmentalists often espouse a class morality at variance with poor communities and African ways of being. In this context, the GLS strove to explore a more indigenous environmentalism, in which predominantly black academics and NGO leaders tried to link their specific knowledge areas (the environment, food, land and the body) to key global problems such as climate change and social justice. Our first systemic challenge was to provide a green space of learning, in contrast to the brown spaces of production, in order to break down the discipline of Westernised learning. So we headed for peri-urban, green learning spaces.

In the context of the growing call for curriculum transformation, we initiated four workshops over a period of 18 months (July 2015–October 2016), organised from the University of Western Cape (UWC). These workshops were called Green Leadership Schools (GLS) and were organised with the assistance of a number of women academics (four of whom are co-authors of this chapter) and administrators. The schools were five-day, in-residence workshops. A key aim of the GLS was to step outside of the formal physical environment of the university. This stepping-out inductively tested how being liberated from the constraints of the colonial university context could alter the learning experience. In a pedagogic initiative that invited nature (non-built environment) into the learning space, we employed a grounded theory approach in this learning experiment. While the GLS ran as workshops, the expanded notion captured in the idea of a school relates to our desire to build a new 'school of thought' around indigenous environmentalism and specific ontological shifts linked to the critique of anthropocentrism (human-centred thinking).

The objective of the GLS was to contribute to a radical break with structures of university power by literally stepping outside of the physical institutional structures. Based on a Lefebvrian (Lefebvre 1992) understanding of the reproduction of power through the production of space, the GLS sought to decolonise the learning experience by shifting the physical space of learning into a green environment. All environments are part of our social relations *within* nature as we are not separate from nature (Costanza, Graumlich, Steffen, Crumley, Dearing, Hibbard, Leemans, Redman and Schimel 2007). However, some environments are more built-up than others (in other words, less 'natural' than others). The green of trees and hills, and the blues of the ocean and even sky – nature's *luhlaza*[1] – are removed from much of the built environment of South African universities. Where there are forests, such as Newlands Forest near the University of Cape Town, they are on the margins of the university, exiled from the spaces of learning. Our historically black universities, built in the later decades of modern education, are often brown expanses of flat buildings and cheaper materials, creating a cultural desert for the primarily black and coloured students who attend these universities.

In 2014 and 2015, four Green Leadership Schools were organised in Stellenbosch, Western Cape, and Coffee Bay, Eastern Cape, in South Africa. The concepts of enchantment and disenchantment framed our search for radical pedagogies, so cultural activities in beautiful locales were an important aesthetic objective. The GLS wanted the large, open expanses of farms and fields, and the rocky edges of the turbulent ocean trapped in a bay, as the canvas for our disruption of educational norms. Starting in the contained farm spaces of white-dominated Stellenbosch, we adventured as far as the hills of Coffee Bay by the third GLS.

The workshops are called 'schools' because they pursue an integrated peda-gogy in which connecting one's body with the soil was an essential component of the learning environment and experience. The GLS were subtitled 'Changing the "Climate" in SA', a reference to how the emphasis on environmental awareness and knowledge of key issues such as climate change could be a focus in undergraduate and postgraduate training; learning could also improve the South African political climate through personal healing and revitalisation, to create generations of healthy political leaders – green leaders.

South African universities face the ongoing challenge of transformation, as the new, black-led student movements at historically white universities nationally have demonstrated by challenging the slow transformation of institutional cul-ture, demographics and curricula. The fourth GLS was a Writing Workshop for #FeesMustFall students, hosted under the auspices of the UWC Department of Sociology. Seventeen student participants attended, with five academic facilitators and a number of additional presenters. The students at this GLS were drawn from the #FeesMustFall movement at three different campuses (two historically white universities and one historically black university). Two natural sciences students were included as the beginnings of cross-disciplinary learning interactions between natural and social scientists. The central learning objective of the fourth GLS in 2015 was to create a writing and learning opportunity for tertiary students to write their own stories. A short monograph was generated, which we still hope to publish.

The fourth GLS was given an isiXhosa name, the Luhlaza Leadership Initiative (LLI), which reflected the desire to indigenise the schools as well as to frame discussions of environmental issues such as food, land and politics within an indigenous context. The goal of the LLI 2015 was to develop alternative educational materials, which could be used by universities as indigenous intellectual resources. The writing opportunity at the LLI 2015 aimed to help students achieve intellectual self-clarification and to broaden environmental awareness drawing on the African context. Knowledge production often involves those who are not affected by a social problem or crisis appropriating and retelling the stories of others. Therefore, the LLI provided the opportunity for those affected by social ills (the students who supported transformation at universities) to write their own histories.

The fourth GLS also aimed to interrogate the ways in which indigenous forms of knowledge and artistic production could help social scientists to Africanise their research methods. What are the ways in which gathering and presenting knowledge would help to free us of underlying Eurocentric assumptions, some of which we are not even aware? The LLI created a moment of cultural interaction in the GLS learning setting by transporting participants away from the GLS workshop setting (a hall with tables for laptops and overhead projectors), to a beautiful residence in a plant nursery at Zevenwacht, close to the venue of the Stellenbosch GLS. Here, we organised a 'Green Carpet' (an 'earthwalk' runway) for an alternative fashion show, in which each of the sixteen students ramped their identity and showed how their clothing related to their political identities. Urban cool sweats, bright African beads and t-shirts, cheap retro vintage as a nod to anti-commodification, and bits of gold in ears, noses and navels as a statement to start reclaiming Africa's gold were all creative ways in which these mostly young women expressed their many selves, sprinkled with laughter and joy at the unusual opportunity afforded by a tribute to their individual styles.

After the earthwalk, an artist presented an exposition of his work. This visual album created lively engagement between two different sets of identities: one, a gay white Afrikaner man; the other, a black woman university student (Miller 2015).

What we learned from the Green Leadership Schools

We learned many different things from our Green Leadership Schools. We encountered the university's lack of interest in initiatives generated by junior staff who lacked senior positions or stellar research records, particularly in relation to a transformation-from-below initiative. The neo-liberal turn in universities globally, and in South Africa in particular, emphasises competition and collaboration at the peak research level in highly visible (global) spaces. Local and endogenous initiatives like ours were not supported by the university, and were seen as an imposition on the institution as the GLS was an independent autonomous initiative. Meetings with representatives such as the dean elicited a dismissive and even punitive response, with a reminder not to give ourselves any special titles attached to the Green Leadership Schools. The head of the research unit where the schools took place was neutral, waiting to see what these schools could do, and somewhat resentful that the labour of the research and administrative staff was not being channelled to the unit's star academic performers. Because the schools were externally funded, however, UWC did not prevent their organisation, even though the alternative learning activity was mostly frowned upon. These responses demonstrate South African universities' ambivalent relationship with transformation, supporting transformation initiatives led from the top with senior management approval, while suppressing or stifling initiatives led from below.

The injunction of the GLS to create 'spaces of enchantment' had mixed success. At a guest farm closer to the city, students criticised the contradictions of our learning environment for its replication of apartheid colonial relations:

> Invading the landscape, settlers architecture […] I feel my humanity and dignity encounter with the curio-shop racist which posits the requirement of high-tea discipline served with buttered cucumber-encumberment sandwiches […] The interior design is kitsch. This is the ironic site of exposition of the Curio-Shop Racist. The curtains have been designed with the ethos of corporate social responsibility; they are draped and layered in Earth tones. Adjacent to this is of course a big leafy plastic pot plant. This is truly the settlers' guest farm. The owner feels the need to explain that she has a deep need to help the community and that's why she doesn't have paved roads. I might have been hallucinating. However, I felt her voice resonated with resentment against those bodies who have held her back from the nice things she could have had (Faye Crankshaw, LLI participant, 2015).

Being in residential accommodation, however, did allow participants to rest up and recover their energies, so a boisterous and playful atmosphere often prevailed at the various schools, despite the contradiction of the setting. The further away we moved from the city centre, and deeper into hauntingly beautiful environments such as the

Coffee Bay setting at the edge of the ocean, the more conducive the environment seemed for a rethinking exercise that demanded a different kind of connection with nature, and a new mindfulness of our place within nature. Awakening planetary awareness as a component of environmentalism came more organically in Coffee Bay's lush green setting with the waves crashing against great rock formations on the coastline. In a deeply industrialised society that has forgotten its connections with the earth in its haste to 'pave paradise', a pristine environment can help to remind us of our duties as stewards of the Earth. Feedback from various participant evaluations (including the fireside evaluation) provided evidence of this awareness of humanity's place within the Earth and planetary systems.

The child-like activities of play through group painting; the disciplined approach to the gardening when properly guided; the cultural infusion of the balletic forms of classical belly dancing that harked back to Persian civilisation; the young male fire-eater, whose charm and lithesome form beguiled everyone; the sonorous voice and plaintive guitar of the *xhopera*[2] singer and player who, true to their indigenous sounds and connected with their lineage, provided an example of cultural authenticity that used the *uhadi*, the indigenous isiXhosa bow instrument, to reclaim a receding authenticity based on these artists' (Mthwakazi) quest for truth in a journey extending both backwards and forwards: all these moments of play were far removed from the self-interested promotions of neo-liberal and professionalised academia, and intimately linked to a quest for beauty that recalled the original purpose of universities as a space of deeper understanding and philosophical enquiry, entirely contrary to the shallow pursuits of quantitative performance measures that now govern the university space.

A greater ease in the body while learning was ensured through the daily practice of yoga. Many workshops and teaching contexts tie the student to a bench for hours on end, followed by further hours of study and sitting at home or at libraries. This produces a deeply unnatural state for the body, in which we are hunched in the same writing or typing position for hours on end. The spatial containment in education's institutional organisation becomes a disciplining tool that is not always optimal for the free disposition necessary to creative thought and enquiry. Liberating ourselves from these physical spaces becomes an important component of an emancipatory learning environment.

The creation of food gardens, or cooperation with local food cooperatives, created a sense of purpose and achievement in the learning endeavour. At the end of the workshop, the gardens were handed over to the workers on the farms for their use, which often delighted the receiving workers. Where we were able to follow up afterwards, we found that some gardens endured and grew well. However, the food cooperative in the rural area of Coffee Bay collapsed, which has been typical of cooperatives in South Africa and elsewhere, for various reasons. But the wisdom in cooperative gardening was the way in which it brought together South African trade unionists from competing factions. Instead of focusing on their political differences, these unionists drew on the agricultural knowledge they had gained from continued connections with customary land and rural areas in South Africa. They chose the most difficult terrain to break open for the planting of calabash seeds. The vision was that these seeds would grow into the pumpkin-like bowl that anchors the *uhadi* instrument, which could then be sold to local schools to help them revive their school music programmes: a beautiful vision. It was encouraging to see these participants working together, hoes in hand, figuring out how to efficiently till the soil.

The Rosa Luxemburg Foundation representative, Arndt Hopfmann, was dismayed at the techniques (or lack thereof) of the food NGO representative from Johannesburg who led the gardening. Arndt promptly set out to show school participants how we should proceed with sowing the seedlings we had bought and brought for the Makande Cooperative. Quick resolution of problems was a garden trademark. When the #FeesMustFall group displayed their trademark rebellion to the LLI horticultural facilitator in Stellenbosch, for example, they were quickly pulled into line by her. They ended up singing, harmonising and happily working in the food garden that they had created on the first morning. Different sides of each urban personality showed through in the gardening initiatives.

Green leadership was confounded by black leadership. The African black and coloured black women who made up the core leadership of the school differed from one another in multiple ways, and different kinds of tensions emerged. The black African women had mixed responses to the belly dancing, on occasion loving it and at other times being totally dismissive. Black student leaders resented the cultural appropriations of sangoma identities by a white woman sangoma-in-training and her enactment of the isiXhosa cleansing ceremony; yet others accepted her with openness but decried her lack of commitment to the process which they believed showed through. Rotational women's leadership floundered when some women were unable to lead from the front, allowing ill-discipline to creep into a highly variegated schedule. Virtual lectures, filmed in earlier schools, with live-stream Skyping of video-recorded facilitators created the opportunity for live discussions and questions with participants, incorporating blended learning methods.

South African society, despite the political revolution of 1994, observes the 'housewifisation' of women brought about through colonialism (Mies 2009); the southern African region is known for the oppression and high levels of rape of women, deep homophobia and lesbian murder. The right to choose an abortion by pregnant women is taboo, even though this is enshrined in the Constitution. Post-democracy activists have been vilified and stigmatised as society's 'losers', in the pervasive neo-liberal thinking and sentiment. The multiple forms of experimentation with learning techniques and contexts through the different GLS could only be the offshoot of free thinkers in a society that has a good store of conservatism and resistance to everyday social change. What our classes without walls (Mbembe 2015) taught us was that the green leadership we aspire to is not a 'nanny-leadership' of thin, scolding environmentalists who find fault with the Caliban ways of naughty natives who insist on littering and eating *shisanyama* (barbecued meat). Our educational objectives are to understand the nexus of money, sex and power, and to generate a planetary awareness within the contradictory African context of conspicuous consumption, urban food cultures and the desire for endogeneity: the quest to reconnect with what is ours, despite our evisceration as a people, and the subordination and invisibility of our cultural practices within 'civilised' contexts.

CONCLUSION – DECOLONISATION AS AN EDUCATIONAL OBJECTIVE

Decolonisation can proceed in various ways. The students of the #FeesMustFall movement sought to disrupt the daily reproduction of the university's learning. They wanted to stop the clock on the reproduction of learning with a colonial past. They utilised various techniques of resistance such as marches and sit-ins to secure this clock-stopping initiative. If all colonisation debases and violates through stripping the colonial subject – of land, resources, heritage, identity – the project of colonised learning rests on the act of decontextualisation, in which the learning subject has no historical or ontological attachment to the learning material.

In Africa, for example, spirituality is deeply ingrained through indigenised memory or religious practices. The act of dis-embedding the colonial student therefore has to reinforce the evisceration and destruction of non-secular belief systems in the practice of knowledge dissemination and production. Simply stated, spirituality has to be exiled from the colonised (or invaded) learning space. The physical organisation of the learning space; the endorsement of elders or professors who profess; the recognised learning materials and modes of instruction; the systems of evaluating and testing; the spatial location of the university and its layout; the designation of the university as a limited public space through which only recognised members may walk, not just any citizen – all of these higher education learning contexts serve to create a colonised system of learning.

The GLS project asked: what would happen if we freed ourselves from these colonial impositions and returned to a more indigenous learning environment, in which the earth and the sea are willing partners? Would this change the way that we learned? How could moving from brown spaces to green spaces help embody an African indigenous green leadership? Would this release us from the gaze of colonial patriarchy if we stepped outside a physically encaged, modernised system of learning? Would this be the pedagogic equivalent of learning by doing?

Various attempts have been made to decolonise university spaces, including:

- renaming buildings to enshrine indigenous history;
- rebranding academic presentations such as Unisa's 'calabash conversations', and
- 'tolerance' of African ululation at graduation ceremonies.

However, the physical integrity of colonial and modernist architecture of our learning spaces remains mostly untouched, despite these efforts to integrate indigenous cultural practices into the rituals and architecture of university spaces. The patriarchal leadership of these spaces of the dons has not significantly altered the pedagogies of the colonial space, despite these important and not insignificant efforts at Africanisation. Such initiatives as rebranding and renaming, however, only skirt the edges of the way in which space and power are mutually constituted in the environs of the university.

Global and national governance systems highlight innovation as a driver of growth. However, innovation and newness are insufficient to ensure economic prosperity: we need to shift the relationship between people and the planet we inhabit. Ecological sustainability requires a radical transformation in our ways of being and doing, to a transformative state of being. This transformative state of being needs to embed itself within a new form of leadership which brings about healing and a reconnection with lost knowledge (indigenous knowledge) that could inform a new way of life and new models of leadership. We termed the leadership that promotes green spaces a form of green leadership that is premised on greater environmental consciousness. While the GLS were short-lived and transient, the questions posed by the GLS remain. The challenges presented to academics to re-envision their learning material in the wake of urgent environmental issues highlighted the need to rethink and restructure our learning spaces in our ongoing decolonisation endeavours.

The GLS provided one possible template for a new decolonised and de-commodified campus. The Green Leadership Schools began to develop a closer link between humanities topics (land, leadership, environment, indigeneity) and the local food production agenda, with discussions on the possibilities of diversification of food gardens. A range of different vegetables (and some fruit) were chosen for growing at the food cooperative in Coffee Bay, including calabash seeds for traditional musical instruments (the *uhadi*). Workers at La Provence farm in Stellenbosch (GLS 1 and 2) and the women's cooperative in Coffee Bay (GLS 3) were cooperative owners of the food gardens. They have sent us photographs to show that the gardens are growing well. Planning and presenting four schools in 18 months (July 2015–October 2016) was exhausting given that the team could not work full-time on this activity. The GLS team took a lot of strain. Some administrative capacity was provided by the university, but mostly the GLS team were viewed as mavericks and upstarts by university management. Our team managed to stay united, despite the difficult workload, and we completed the schools with a measure of success. Participants were eager for the Green Leadership Schools to be rolled out for social movements, trade unions, and university academics and postgraduates, building on a potential research internship programme in the humanities. This is still our dream.

NOTES

[1] The isiXhosa word for blue *and* green, which are not seen as separate colours in the isiXhosa colour spectrum.

[2] A blend of traditional isiXhosa and operatic singing.

REFERENCES

Adeyemi, M.B. & Adeyinka, A.A. 2003. The principles and content of African traditional education. *Educational Philosophy and Theory* 35: 425–440. https://doi.org/10.1111/1469-5812.00039 (accessed 1 October 2018).

ANC Youth League (ANCYL). 2001. The President's political report to the 21st National Congress.

Barnard, I. 2006. The language of multiculturalism in South African soaps and sitcoms. *Journal of Multicultural Discourses* 1(1): 39–59. https://doi.org/10.1080/10382040608668531 (accessed 19 June 2018).

Botha, L.R. 2010. Indigenous knowledge as culturally-centred education in South Africa. *Africa Education Review* 7(1): 34–50. https://doi.org/10.1080/18146627.2010.485804 (accessed 1 March 2015).

Bourdieu, P. 1990. *The Logic of Practice*. Redwood City, CA: Stanford University Press.

Burkett, P. 1999. *Marx and Nature: A Red and Green Perspective*. New York: St Martin's Press.

Claxton, M. 2010. Indigenous knowledge and sustainable development. Third Distinguished Lecture, The Cropper Foundation UWI, St Augustine, Trinidad and Tobago.

Cock, J. 2004. Connecting the red, brown and green: The environmental justice movement in South Africa (Case study for the Globalisation, Marginalisation and New Social Movements in Post-Apartheid South Africa project). Durban: Centre for Civil Society, University of KwaZulu-Natal.

Cock, J. & Fig, D. 2000. From colonial to community based conservation: Environmental justice and the national parks of South Africa. *Society in Transition* 31: 22–35. https://doi.org/10.1080/21528586.2000.10419008 (accessed 1 October 2018).

Coetzee, D. 2001. South African education and the ideology of patriarchy. *South African Journal of Education* 21(4): 300–304.

Costanza, R., Graumlich, L., Steffen, W., Crumley, C., Dearing, J., Hibbard, K., Leemans, R., Redman, C. & Schimel, D. 2007. Sustainability or collapse: What can we learn from integrating the history of humans and the rest of nature? *AMBIO: A Journal of the Human Environment* 36: 522–527. https://doi.org/10.1579/0044-7447(2007)36[522:SOCWCW]2.0.CO;2 (accessed 1 October 2018).

Deleuze, G. & Guattari, F. 2004. *A Thousand Plateaus*. New York, London: Continuum.

Federici, S. 2004. *Caliban and the Witch: Women, the Body and Primitive Accumulation* (1st edn). New York: Autonomedia.

Foucault, M. 1977. *Discipline and Punish: The Birth of the Prison*. New York: Vintage Books.

Freire, P. 1970. *Pedagogy of the Oppressed* (trans. M.B. Ramos). New York: Continuum.

Gagiano, A. 2012. Re-examining apartheid brokenness – *To Every Birth its Blood* as a literary testament. In: Mengel, E. & Borzaga, M. (eds) *Trauma, Memory, and Narrative in the Contemporary South African Novel: Essays*: 217–237. Amsterdam, New York: Rodopi.

Goetz, A.M. 1998. Women in politics & gender equity in policy: South Africa & Uganda. *Review of African Political Economy* 25: 241–262. https://doi.org/10.1080/03056249808704312 (accessed 2 March 2015).

Gqola, P.D. 2015. *Rape: A South African Nightmare*. Johannesburg: MF Books Joburg.

Gqola, P.D. 2017. *Reflecting Rogue – Inside the Mind of a Feminist*. Johannesburg: MF Books Joburg.

Harvey, D. 1996. *Justice, Nature and the Geography of Difference* (1st edn). Cambridge, MA: Blackwell.

Haupt, A. 2014. Black professors stalled by policy. *City Press*, 13 November.

Hewson, M.G. 2012. Traditional healers' views on their indigenous knowledge and the science curriculum. *African Journal of Research in Mathematics, Science and Technology Education* 16(3): 317–332. https://doi.org/10.1080/10288457.2012.10740748 (accessed 1 March 2015).

Hook, D. 2004. Racism as Abjection: A Psychoanalytic Conceptualisation for a Post-Apartheid South Africa. *South African Journal of Psychology* 34: 672–703. https://doi.org/10.1177/008124630403400410 (accessed 5 March 2015).

Hook, D. 2011. Narrative form, 'impossibility' and the retrieval of apartheid history. *Psychoanalysis Culture & Society* 16(1): 71–89. https://doi.org/10.1057/pcs.2010.43 (accessed 3 March 2015).

Hoosain, S. 2013. The transmission of intergenerational trauma in displaced families. Unpublished PhD thesis (Social Work). Cape Town: University of the Western Cape.

Jonker, I. 2008. A study of how a sangoma makes sense of her 'sangomahood' through narrative. Unpublished MA dissertation (Counselling Psychology). Pretoria: University of Pretoria.

Kearney, A. 2014. Ethnicity, cultural wounding and the 'healing project': What happens when the wounded survive? *Ethnicities* 14(5): 597–614. https://doi.org/10.1177/1468796814526398 (accessed 3 March 2015).

Khan, F. 2000. Environmentalism in South Africa: A sociopolitical perspective. *Macalester International* 9(11): 156–181.

Lazarus, S., Tonsing, S., Ratele, K. & Van Niekerk, A. 2009. *Conceptual framework for understanding male interpersonal violence in South Africa. An exploratory study into theoretical frameworks for investigating the risk and protective factors to male interpersonal violence.* Research Report. Cape Town: Medical Research Council.

Lefebvre, H. 1992. *The Production of Space.* Malden, MA: Wiley-Blackwell.

Legoabe, R. 2011. Lack of transformation at the University of Pretoria. Higher Education Transformation Network, Pretoria, South Africa.

Luckett, K. 2016. Curriculum contestation in a post-colonial context: A view from the South. *Teaching in Higher Education* 21: 415–428. https://doi.org/10.1080/13562517.2016.1155547 (accessed 1 October 2018).

Mangcu, X. 2014. Black academics must unite. *City Press*, 22 October.

Mbembe, A. 2015. Decolonizing knowledge and the question of the archive. Lecture. Wits Institute for Social and Economic Research (WISER), University of the Witwatersrand, Johannesburg.

McKinney, C. 2007. Caught between the 'old' and the 'new'? Talking about 'race' in a post-apartheid university classroom. *Race, Ethnicity and Education* 10: 215–231. https://doi.org/10.1080/13613320701330734 (accessed 5 March 2015).

Meer, S. 2005. Freedom for women: Mainstreaming gender in the South African liberation struggle and beyond. *Gender & Development* 13: 36–45. https://doi.org/10.1080/13552070512331332285 (accessed 2 March 2015).

Mies, M. 2009. Housewifisation – globalisation – subsistence-perspective. In: Van der Linden, M. & Roth, K.H. (eds) *Beyond Marx: Theorising the Global Labour Relations of the Twenty-first Century*: 209–237. Brill, Leiden, The Netherlands: Historical Materialism Book Series.

Miller, D. 2012. The Red Tent: Regional dispositions and women's leadership in post-apartheid Southern Africa. In: Initiative for Equality, Waiting to Be Heard: IFE Equity Report for the Rio+20 Summit. Initiative for Equality, Rio de Janeiro, Brazil.

Miller, D. 2013a. The Red Tent: Rough Diamonds – Who's Got Your Back? Cape Town: Human Sciences Research Council.

Miller, D. 2013b. *The Red Tent: Understanding 'Regionality' – hidden 'democratic dispositions' and women's leadership in post-apartheid Southern Africa.* Final project report. Cape Town: Human Sciences Research Council.

Miller, D. 2015. Luhlaza exhibition by Mtini (YouTube). Cape Town: Department of Anthropology and Sociology, University of the Western Cape.

Morrell, R. 1998. Of boys and men: masculinity and gender in Southern African studies. *Journal of Southern African Studies* 24: 605–630. https://doi.org/10.1080/03057079808708593 (accessed 2 March 2015).

Ntuli, P. 2002. Indigenous knowledge systems and the African Renaissance: Laying the foundation for the creation of counter-hegemonic discourses. In: Hoppers, C.A.O. (ed.) *Indigenous Knowledge and the Integration of Knowledge Systems: Towards a Philosophy of Articulation*: 53–66. Cape Town: New Africa Books.

Postel, G. 2010. Media, mediums and metaphors: The modern South African Sangoma in various texts. *Current Writing: Text and Reception in Southern Africa* 22: 107–122. https://doi.org/10.1080/1013929X.2010.9678337 (accessed 1 March 2015).

Ratele, K. 2014. Currents against gender transformation of South African men: Relocating marginality to the centre of research and theory of masculinities. *International Journal for Masculinity Studies* 9: 30–44. https://doi.org/10.1080/18902138.2014.892285 (accessed 5 March 2015).

Sawyerr, A. 2004. Challenges facing African universities: Selected issues. *African Studies Review* 47(1): 1–59. https://doi.org/10.1017/S0002020600026986 (accessed 10 January 2018).

Schlosberg, D. 2009. *Defining Environmental Justice: Theories, Movements, and Nature.* Oxford: Oxford University Press.

Scsanti, S. 2014. Black academics must move the centre. *City Press,* 31 October.

Thondhlana, G., Shackleton, S. & Muchapondwa, E. 2011. Kgalagadi Transfrontier Park and its land claimants: A pre- and post-land claim conservation and development history. *Environmental Research Letters* 6(2): 1–12. https://doi.org/10.1088/1748-9326/6/2/024009 (accessed 10 January 2018).

Tickner, J.A. 1986. Local self-reliance versus power politics: Conflicting priorities of national development. *Alternatives* 11: 461–483. https://doi.org/10.1177/030437548601100402 (accessed 6 August 2018).

Urbasch, M. 2002. *Representations and Restitutions of African Traditional Healing Systems.* Working Paper No. 2. Paris: Institut Français d'Afrique du Sud.

Washington, K. 2010. Zulu traditional healing, Afrikan worldview and the practice of Ubuntu: Deep thought for Afrikan/Black psychology. *Journal of Pan African Studies* 3: 24–39.

13

Low-hanging Fruit or Deep-seated Transformation? Quality of life and governance in Gauteng, South Africa

David Everatt

INTRODUCTION

The core challenge facing South Africa after the transition to democracy in 1994 was to meet the basic needs of the majority denied by apartheid, and simultaneously restore people's dignity by undoing the psychosocial damage through more deep-seated transformation. In engaging these imperatives, could the new democratic state offer to focus overwhelming attention on service delivery and ignore the precarious social fabric? Did the state have the capacity needed to repair the social fabric, even if only under the rubric of building a 'rainbow nation' or the 'new South Africa'? Substantively, could the state afford *not* to prioritise visible and tangible delivery over more opaque social transformation initiatives?

The state needed to be democratised, laws repealed, new structures put in place, together with meeting the massive delivery backlog of the decades-long denial of basic needs for the majority of citizens. These were primarily bricks-and-mortar matters, and hence the low-hanging fruit of post-apartheid liberation where important and visible gains could easily be made. With respect to people's dignity, continuing racial and ethnic animosities and their accumulated pain and anger, the focus was primarily on establishing a Truth and Reconciliation Commission (TRC), and putting in place affirmative action measures for better economic and institutional representation. Underlying the dominant approach was the hope that people's dignity would be restored by service delivery: by giving people decent houses, sanitation, tarred roads, potable water, health services, education, and so on. The logic was that the rest of the complex, distinctly human mess left by apartheid would somehow self-repair. Services would restore dignity, as would the (expected) availability of jobs and opportunities. Expressed bluntly, there was little reflection or action related to what to do with the messy stuff of 'ordinary' people and their psychosocial make-up, behaviours and interactions.

Using data from the 'Quality of Life' surveys conducted by the Gauteng City-Region Observatory (GCRO), this chapter argues that the 'low-hanging fruit' or 'bricks-and-mortar' approach represented a significant failure of the postcolonial imagination, compounded by failures of governance.

Quality of life is measured using an admixture of over 50 indicators. The measurement tool includes objective indicators on service provision and subjective indicators that look at interiority. The approach is in contrast to the dominant post-1994 assumption that service access alone will adequately measure quality of life. The overall argument here is that the interior life of the people using those services matters just as much as the services themselves. As will be demonstrated through the data, delivering hard services, such as water, sewerage and houses, tends to score high on the Quality of Life index, reflecting government's prioritisation. The failure to do so is evident in the fact that virtually all social indicators are in a consistent downward trend.

The natural allure of reaching for the low-hanging fruit of service delivery arose from a post-apartheid necessity, but the failure of deep-seated economic redistribution, combined with no substantial intervention in the complex realm of the individual or social relations, has defined post-apartheid South Africa. It is an approach which may have fundamentally compromised the possibility of a deep-seated transformation of society as a whole.

From the vantage point granted by hindsight, it has become de rigueur in some quarters to write off the 1994 settlement as a 'sellout' (Bond 2000; Marais 2001). It is widely cited as a loss of courage; a weak or self-serving capitulation to gung-ho capitalism; or an unseemly rush for personal privilege by a new political elite at the expense of 'the masses'. To use just one example, the Nelson Mandela Foundation (NMF), charged with maintaining and deepening the legacy of the former president, released a 'Position Paper' in 2015 that effectively wrote off the Mandela government (1994–1999) as a failure because of the adoption of what was seen as a neo-liberal economic policy, and a concomitant failure to adopt a black consciousness stance towards race. The latter would have emphasised black individualism and pride and rejected dominant white and/or Western values in place of what the NMF paper chose to portray as an infantile 'colour-blind' non-racialism (Hatang and Harris 2015).

To contemplate the notion that the African National Congress (ANC), in its moment of victory, would jettison decades of support for non-racialism which it created, and adopt the rival black consciousness approach in its place, is both naïve and a-contextual. The base argument of the NMF seems to be that a less aggressively capitalist economic policy may have presaged greater economic redistribution and equality, which in turn would have assisted with tackling racial mistrust. Alternatively, it suggests that a more muscular approach to race may have signalled a more deep-seated transformation. Both are attractive propositions, but fail to grasp fully the nettle of a deeply divided and damaged society and populace, and the need to tackle multiple issues on numerous fronts.

Although the NMF's paper seems set to critically analyse both objective (economic policy) and subjective (race and identity) issues simultaneously, it fails. It offers a sideswipe at the Growth, Employment and Redistribution (Gear) strategy (adopted in 1996, when Mandela was president), seen as 'either setting or being closely aligned to a global neoliberal agenda', and then focuses almost entirely on race. According to the authors of the paper, race 'is still a critical fault line in South Africa's social landscape', and public discourse on race is 'dominated by expressions of denial, alienation, obfuscation and even self-hatred'. The Mandela government, in their view, had three strategies for transformation: nation-building; interventions geared at redress; and longer-term societal restructuring. The authors conclude that these projects have failed as '[…] the state […] has had little success in shifting apartheid-era socio-economic patterns', which has led to ongoing white privilege and ongoing racial hatred (Hatang and Harris 2015: 3). But the conclusion seems to be that if only the Mandela government had put race at centre stage, not service delivery, all would be better.

Less inequality and greater redistribution are self-evidently worth pursuing in and of themselves. The NMF provides no clarity as to how greater black economic wealth would in itself deal with centuries of settler colonialism and decades of apartheid, with all the violent racism these visited on black South Africans, and the psychosocial damage they did to all South Africans, in very different ways. Government chose service delivery as key to restoring dignity, and thus healing. The NMF prefers a focus on race that, somehow, leads to healing. Both hoped that more and decent jobs for black South Africans would be the elixir that provided the magic remedy. Neither provides a compelling narrative or analytic frame. A Manichean preference for one or the other explanatory variable, in place of an integrated approach, seems to be a common feature; it is an approach that quality of life, as used here, very firmly rejects.

The 1994 Reconstruction and Development Programme (RDP), the blueprint for governing produced by the ANC and its allies, claimed to be a 'people-driven process', and set the tone for successive major policy statements by claiming that '[d]evelopment is not about the delivery of goods to a passive citizenry', and talked to the need for 'active involvement and growing empowerment' (ANC 1994: 5).

Fast-forward to the National Development Plan (NDP), almost two decades later in 2011, and we find talk of a 'mobilised, active and responsible citizenry' (National Planning Commission [NPC] 2011: 415). Again, however, this nod towards what animates 'the active citizen' is the final 19-page chapter in a 430-page report, prefaced by the 'real' business of government (economic management, service delivery, foreign policy, rural development, human settlements, sustainability, and so on). The chapter gestures in the direction of the responsibilities of social and sectoral agencies – family, the media, the courts – but, as with the RDP, has seemingly no idea that the state can or should play any role (even a coordinating one) in this sphere, nor what that role might comprise. That, however, did not stop the chapter from making the remarkable assertion that '[t]he end of apartheid restored the dignity of all South Africans' (NPC 2011: 411). The RDP at least acknowledged the scale of the psychosocial crisis facing South Africa, with considerable trepidation, although, as we have seen, it was premised on the hope that meeting basic needs would 'open up previously suppressed economic and human potential [which were …] essential if we are to achieve peace and security for all' (ANC 1994: 6–7). The NMF (and others) have bemoaned the failure to grapple with issues of race and racial inequality. The NDP, on the other hand, seemed to prefer the whole messy business wished away, in the absence of any ideas about how to tackle growing marginalisation, alienation, xenophobia, gender-based violence, rape, and multiple other signs of deepening social collapse.

In sum, there seems to be consensus that South Africa continues to face severe challenges. For some, these are overwhelmingly economic, and the failure is laid at the door of a pro-capitalist ANC. For others, South Africa's woes derive overwhelmingly from the failure to confront race head-on and thus to permit the longevity of 'whiteliness', laid at the door of an ANC bewitched by the historical halo of non-racialism. For others, race remains the fault line, but this in turn is divisive: it is ascribed to a generational (young, black) obsession with whites and whiteliness, where a United States-derived narrative about critical race theory has seen people revise their 'position on non-racialism and replace it with a simmering resentment about a perceived white cultural and financial domination that has replaced formal apartheid' (Haffajee 2015: 5).

Governance is often implicated when South Africa's past and present are being analysed, though 'governance' and 'government' are often misliterated. The challenge, as many authors in this volume attest, is that there is a proliferation of definitions of governance, whether proffered by different institutions or applied to different sectors (environmental governance, private/public governance, corporate governance, etc.). Governance, whose original meaning differed little from 'government' and derived from the same Greek verb for 'to steer', was given new life as a term to describe the exercise of power by government; and then later, to analyse the exercise of power wherever it is located in society, with all the attendant influences and actors.

If governance identifies the points where power is located and used (and abused), it feeds into the multilateral and donor institution discourse of 'good governance', just as it feeds into those using a more grounded approach which accepts that power is impacted on by politics, media, all (relevant) sectors of society, and so on, rather than leaving it as a rather anaemic matter of 'public administration', somehow hermetically sealed off from these actors and agencies. The media and commentators commonly focus on overt rent-seeking and corruption as failures of governance – and of those who staff the structures of government – and they seem to have a consistent supply of targets at which to aim. This chapter argues that we face a deeper failure of governance: the continuum, from RDP to NDP, to develop a genuinely integrated response to the multiple challenges bequeathed to South Africa by its violent past. Uni-focal arguments provide good sound bites, whether about race or inequality or corruption; but none of these, in and of themselves, can resolve the integrated set of challenges facing South Africa and South Africans.

APPROACH AND THEORY

A quality of life approach is not a measuring instrument that tries to answer the question, 'how far have we come?' by bean counting. This is a common approach – reeling off numbers of houses built, or water connections made, or roads tarred – and not surprising, given the focus of RDP and NDP on service delivery. By the same token, it makes no a priori valorisation of one variable or set of variables above another. Extreme racial views, for example, comprise part of the index – but this variable is not weighted above others, and nor are service delivery measures. The approach tries to find the right way to ask, and offer possible answers to, the question: are Gautengers (who live in the smallest province with the greatest population share and largest economy) attaining all-round quality of life?

This chapter is located within the discipline of social indicators research, using an approach that relies on survey-generated data – with all the flaws and pitfalls that such reliance can generate (Babbie 1995: 273–274). It is an approach that searches for hypotheses by analysing data, rather than testing hypotheses through data analysis. These reverse-engineered hypotheses are usually generated through qualitative analysis, as grounded theory might do, but this is a quantitative attempt to discover whether the South African approach of meeting basic needs has contributed to improving the overall well-being of South Africans, especially black South Africans, using multivariate analysis.

The hypothesis, it can be argued, was proposed by the RDP: provide the basic service delivery requirements for human dignity, and healing will follow. This was not stated as a hypothesis but is the foundation on which a basic needs approach (especially in the RDP) rests; how it might operate in a recently democratised, post-authoritarian, racially divided society is entirely unknown. It is difficult to find comparable quality of life studies, given that no other society has recently democratised after 400 years of settler colonialism and white supremacy, with legalised racial discrimination (and attendant violence) in every facet of life.

LOCALE

This chapter focuses on residents (regardless of nationality or citizenship status) of Gauteng, the smallest province but contributing some 35 per cent of national gross domestic product (GDP) (GCRO 2014). The province forms part of the broader Gauteng City-Region (GCR), a constellation of urban nodes within a radius of 175 kilometres from the centre of Johannesburg. With a population of some 13 million people and contributing some 40 per cent of national GDP (the vast bulk of which comes from the province of Gauteng itself), the GCR is a major player nationally, regionally and continentally. The nodes are intimately linked through daily commuting, intense economic interaction, and shared bulk infrastructure and services, but the Quality of Life surveys have tended (after the first in the series) to gather data only within Gauteng's provincial boundaries, and thus Gauteng is the spatial focus.

Gauteng, which enjoys just 1.4% of national land cover in South Africa, contains a fifth of South Africa's population, which is expected to rise to a quarter (16 million people) by 2020, if migration patterns remain at the level measured across censuses in 1996, 2001 and 2011. Given that services are provided to households not individuals, it is notable that there was an annual average growth in household numbers of 3.6% between 2001 and 2011, with 2.9 million households in Gauteng by 2011.

As a result of apartheid, Gauteng's settlements have been developed on the principle of a hard separation in space between the wealthy and the poor. All cities have some spatial separation between rich and poor areas, as the vicissitudes of property development drive the poor into lower-value areas. But nowhere in the world are the distinctions as clearly marked as in South African cities, nor as starkly based on racial grounds. The wealthier parts of Gauteng's cities provide a standard of urban infrastructure and a quality of life that matches those to be found in the world's most developed cities. The poorer areas, in contrast, are located far from work and educational opportunities, often buffered by major highways, industrial parks, and the like. Apartheid created literal, physical boundaries between races, and thus between classes, since race and class were so closely correlated under apartheid.

When apartheid barriers to movement began to crumble in the 1980s, and were formally eradicated in the 1990s, a pent-up demand for urban life and opportunities led to a massive wave of urbanisation. This process of correction in population distribution continues today. For Gauteng, huge inflows of largely poor people have been and remain difficult to manage. The new in-migrants add daily to the pre-existing challenge of addressing service backlogs for the African residents who were already living in underserviced townships in the province, continually challenging the basis of government's approach of service delivery as the cornerstone of dignity and healing. The result was a burgeoning of large informal settlements, the growth of informal dwellings in the backyards of formal houses, and overcrowding of historical points of first access into the city such as inner-city areas.

Both provincial and local government in Gauteng moved quickly to address service backlogs and accommodate new arrivals. Significant progress has been made in housing provision, but often with perverse outcomes: the price of land and a limited government budget meant that hundreds of thousands of RDP houses have been built in large housing estates in peripheral areas. Because of the speed of housing delivery, urban amenities such as schools, crèches, libraries and clinics were often only added later (if at all). The implications for variations in quality of life – even if it is 'better than apartheid' – are self-evident.

That said, in many ways delivery in Gauteng since 1994 has been a success story, if measured as government sees it. According to the 2011 census produced by Statistics South Africa (StatsSA 2011), the proportion of people with no formal education has dropped from 10 per cent in 1996 to 4 per cent in 2011, and half of those have migrated into the province from elsewhere. Census 2011 tells us that where 75 per cent of Gautengers lived in formal dwellings in 1996, that figure has now risen – despite the massive population growth above – to 80 per cent. While 11 per cent still live in informal dwellings, 98 per cent of people now have access to piped water, 96 per cent have access to a flush toilet, and 87 per cent access the national grid for lighting energy.

Critics will correctly ask about quality and affordability – but these are still impressive figures, whether measured absolutely or as an achievement over time. The basic needs approach seems to have been very successful – though it simulta-neously, through its very success, continues to draw in many thousands of migrants (South African, African, East European, and others) who join the queue of those needing their basic needs met. But bricks and mortar may not be 'healing through dignity', when we recall that the province of Gauteng has witnessed more social protest – often referred to as 'service delivery protests' – than any other province in South Africa. Relative deprivation – having received some services but the desire for more – seems to be widespread (Quintal 2014).

If poor (overwhelmingly African) people have been housed in large estates, the same has happened at the other end of the scale. Many suburbs formerly zoned for whites have become near-impenetrable lifestyle estates, gated communities and the like, with electronic booms controlling entry, backed up with extensive security and armed guards. Apartheid socio-spatial design has effortlessly adapted itself to accommodate class – black middle-class families now live in those same estates, cheek by jowl with white middle-class families, all safely walled off from 'the poor'. As such, apartheid geography has proved remarkably difficult to eradicate or even ameliorate.

QUALITY OF LIFE

'Quality of life' is a phrase often used by policymakers and planners, but less often understood conceptually, defined or unpacked. Take, for example, the following headline from an article on the *South Africa: The Good News* website: 'Quality of life improves, but inequality widens' (2008). The article that follows makes no fur-ther mention of quality of life, but does go on to report on issues such as income, poverty, housing, basic services, inequality and national pride. Quality of life is thus merely adjectival, and not at all analytical.

The term 'quality of life' is typically used to describe (not always to analyse) the general well-being of individuals and societies, actual or imputed. The term is used in a wide range of contexts, including the fields of international development, health care, psychosocial services and political science. Quality of life and national (or regional or local) well-being had emerged before the move away from standard of living, and have become more popular than GDP as the best measure of how well a society is performing. Where the earlier approaches only included economic indicators – and thus only measured economic performance (but, for example, ignored the environmental damage caused by that economic performance) – standard indicators of the quality of life include not only wealth and employment, but also the built environment, physical and mental health, education, recreation and leisure time, and social belonging.

There is an unexpectedly strong history of exploring quality of life in the South African context, stretching back into the apartheid era. The South African Quality of Life Trends Study has data that go back to the early 1980s (Møller 1998). While the focus of the study (and the reports emanating from it) has shifted with time, it has concentrated on the issue of quality of life across a number of different areas: global satisfaction, family life, personal life, food, health, sociopolitical issues, housing, education, community facilities, work and income, and social security. The data, as with the data reported below, are generated through surveys that ask respondents for their level of satisfaction across a variety of indicators within each of these areas, relying on subjective responses to gauge quality of life. To that extent, there is a convergence of approaches.

However, the key challenge in South African work on quality of life, despite its long history, has been the failure to create a compelling composite index that speaks to multiple audiences, from citizens to policymakers, and to multiple domains of life without selecting this or that set of variables for additional weighting or emphasis. This requires restraint on the part of quality of life researchers, who in the past have valorised one variable above others (Everatt 2017). The 1994 'South African miracle' saw some academics selecting single indicators from the South African Quality of Life Trends Study– such as black attitudes to freedom and democracy – at the expense of other variables, because of their global interest, contextual significance as well as the large 'jump' in the data. A brief 'headline' can take the place of analysing other conditions required to attain fuller quality of life in a holistic and long-term manner.

If quality of life researchers, in a society undergoing a fundamental transition such as occurred in South Africa between 1990 and 1994, face the (understandably seductive) danger of selecting one or two variables because of the exigencies and global fascination of the historical moment, quality of life studies located in sub-national areas face other dangers. For example, Boddy and Parkinson (2004: 242) argue that quality of life – more or less clearly defined – is merely a tool that contributes to the competitiveness (or not) of large cities, to be used in making investment decisions or marketing locations for future investment. Ranking 'world cities' is a global fad, and one that easily absorbs quality of life studies into a broader marketing exercise for those seeking to influence investment decisions. In this approach, quality of life studies are merely a flag to wave so as to garner attention and investment as a 'natural' part of globalisation, with little value to the citizens being studied, or those seeking to govern them.

Worse, quality of life can be seen as separating the worthy from their less worthy brethren in the cut-and-thrust world of globalised capitalism. With globalisation seen as a modern form of social Darwinism, the logic is fairly simple: the better-educated and well-off citizens of a city or city-region will do well, and those less well-off will inevitably fall by the wayside, the unavoidable victims of market forces. The positive and negative impacts of globalisation on quality of life are regarded by some authors as 'two sides of the same coin' rather than the trade-offs and negative social costs of 'progress' (Hack, Barkin and LeRoyer 1996: 2).

Thus we are in a strange situation where city-level discourse is predominantly focused on economic indicators, co-opts the language of 'quality of life' as part of its discourse, but (mis)uses it for economic reasons. Quality of life deliberately veers away from economic reductionism to try to understand far more complex and subtle nuances of life in the city. The rise of quality of life indicators beyond the economic, in tandem with the growth of studies of well-being, does suggest that greater convergence may lie ahead.

QUALITY OF LIFE MEASURES IN SOUTH AFRICA

In South Africa, measuring quality of life of citizens has been a subject of robust debate among policymakers and academics alike. Different writers, following different theoretical traditions, have deployed a range of indicators of life satisfaction and (latterly) happiness. Broadly speaking, literature on measuring quality of life for the citizens of South Africa has followed two theoretical trajectories, namely: a) that life satisfaction and happiness are a function of material conditions linked to the individual; or b) that expression of life satisfaction or dissatisfaction is the projected expression of personal well-being. This is not an approach favoured here, since the distinction is a false one, and only by combining 'interior' variables with material measurements will we open a window on quality of life.

Research on the material aspect of quality of life commands more appeal. Beginning in the early 1980s, the academics who initiated the Quality of Life Trends Project argued that they were developing cross-cultural quality of life methodologies for a heterogeneous society (Møller 1998). To date, a corpus of literature generated by this project contains many important insights on quality of life. Valerie Møller's work (1998, 2007; Møller and Dickow 2002) is important in this area and has focused principally on tracking the satisfaction and happiness of South Africans against the background of changing socio-economic and political circumstances before and after 1994.

However, as occurs with other quality of life researchers, Møller often cannot resist focusing on specific components rather than overall index scores. For example, in examining what she terms the 'trendiness' of subjective life satisfaction indicators versus objective quality of life indicators (at a national level), Møller reviewed contrasting approaches to quality of life in black and white communities in South Africa over different periods of time, both before and after the dawn of democratic rule. Her principal observation was that post-1994 election data have shown that attaining freedom in 1994 was not the only determinant of happiness and satisfaction among South Africans. A shift of focus is evident once the afterglow of 1994 fades: to a closer examination of the influence of different phenomena impacting on substantive democracy, such as service delivery, crime and unemployment, as differentially experienced by South Africa's different racial groups. South Africa offers researchers a too-easy racial fixation, given the massive material and attitudinal differences between races; the danger is that issues such as gender, age (a more recent focus of the project) and other key social variables may be submerged in the drama of racial differentiation.

South Africa is known for, inter alia, racial division and inequality – so many researchers go looking for, and find, that these matter. Thus some researchers suggest that there is a large gap between the life satisfaction of black and white South Africans because (they argue, not wrongly) race is a reasonable proxy for income and access to resources – a single factor which explains the highest proportion of variance of satisfaction with life and domain satisfaction. At one level, this is both true and obvious. At another, however, it is reductionist and misleading – the burgeoning black middle class (probably the most important social change occurring in the society) is swallowed by macro-level black/white differences, as well as other intra-racial differences (both subjective and objective). The real question is: what is happening *beneath* the surface?

Some post-apartheid governments have embraced quality of life measurements. For example, in 1998, the eThekwini Metropolitan Municipality (including the port city of Durban) began conducting annual surveys to monitor the changes in the quality of life of Durban's people. The available reports reflect on areas including service delivery, individual sense of well-being, crime, HIV prevalence, and the like. The hypothesis we are seeking to either test or develop – the interrelationship between objective and subjective indicators, between meeting basic needs and enhancing psychosocial health – would not be adequately serviced by this (otherwise robust) model, which is heavily loaded with objective and rather light on subjective indicators, designed as it is for policymakers. Moreover, the eThekwini study makes no attempt to create an aggregate score within each broad area (of which there are nine), nor, more importantly, across the different areas, in order to generate an overall quality of life index. Data are merely reported for each indicator and, on occasion, disaggregated by variables such as race.

This chapter argues strongly for the creation of a quality of life index and then using it to look beneath the surface of society, rather than picking 'easy' variables such as race and making judgements accordingly. Higgs proposed one such model, which he called 'Everyday Quality of Life' (EQL) (Higgs 2003: 11). Higgs' EQL model operates across 15 broad areas, ranging from genetics to diet to socio-economic status, and so on. Although it appears to be a fairly comprehensive model, it is unclear whether the resultant survey instrument adequately covers each area within the model or how the model is put together, since the paper ends before an overall EQL score is computed.

In short, many South African academics and researchers have been working in the broad domain of quality of life, but few if any seem to have taken the key step: moving beyond a description of specific variables or analytic categories (many of which, such as race, politics and inequality, are deeply alluring) to creating and analysing a composite index. The drivers behind the overall scores must of course be analysed – but as drivers behind an index, not proxies for it. As has been argued elsewhere, any adequate measure of quality of life must be a plural measure, recognising a number of distinct components that are irreducible to one another (Nussbaum and Sen 1993: 3).

Quality of life in Gauteng[1]

The Gauteng City-Region Observatory (GCRO) completed its third Quality of Life survey in 2013 (the first took place in 2009, the second in 2011). Samples grew from an initial 6600 to 17 000 to 27 490. This allows some sense of change over time, although three points in time barely make reliable trend analyses possible.

In order to measure quality of life, the GCRO surveys include some 200 questions across a wide range of areas, and 54 of those (see Table 13.1) are variables used to construct the Quality of Life index. These include subjective and objective indicator questions. Both are combined into ten 'dimensions' of quality of life – again, to try to measure both overall quality of life, and the 'drivers' behind quality of life either rising or falling, while trying to steer clear of one particular variable receiving too much attention.

The history of the current Quality of Life index began with a multivariate index created in 1991, to try to understand the impact of apartheid and resistance to it, on youth – the 'marginalised youth' project. (Everatt and Orkin 1993). This was a survey that collected data on subjective and objective indicators, used factor analysis to identify typologies, and correspondence analysis to identify correlations between categories and variables, such as age cohort, race, sex, and others. The emphasis in this early outing was more on subjective than objective indicators, given that apartheid laws were still in place and the survey took place in 1991, one year after the transition to democracy began. The focus was on trying to understand and measure youth marginalisation; and the subjective components remain key to current quality of life measurement in South Africa.

The project was further developed into a 2001 Quality of Life index used to assess the impact of service delivery on deep rural communities, including the use of control areas where no delivery had occurred, to assess whether quality of life improved because of service delivery (Jennings and Everatt 2001). The conclusion was that objective indicators rose – predictably – driving the overall index higher, but with little impact on psychosocial issues. This was an early warning that the RDP approach was not working: that service delivery did not equate with dignity, and that 'healing' did not necessarily follow on from delivery.

These early attempts at defining quality of life have since been developed and refined, resulting in an index comprising the following broad dimensions: life satisfaction ('global')/'headspace', family, community and sociopolitical, all of which are heavily loaded (see Table 13.1) with subjective indicators as well as objective indicators; and then education and connectivity, health, housing, infrastructure, security and work.

These ten dimensions comprise a series of subjective indicators and – except in the life satisfaction/'headspace' dimension (which includes alienation, anomie, extreme racial views, and so on) – objective indicators. The use of objective indicators as well as multiple subjective indicators is important as it seeks to limit (although not negate) the influence that a bad experience or event in the preceding hours, days or months before being interviewed may have on the attitudes of the interviewees. The indicators used are set out in Table 13.1. (Please note that some indicators are themselves derived from multiple individual questions – thus 'decent work', for example,

Table 13.1: Objective and subjective indicators used to construct the Quality of Life index

Broad areas	Subjective indicators (level of satisfaction)	Objective indicators (measured to RDP standard*)
Global/ 'headspace'	• Life satisfaction • Alienation • Anomie • Country going in right direction	
Family	• Marriage/relationship • Family life • Time available for family • Leisure time	• Ability to feed children/self in year prior to interview
Community	• Trust community (social capital) • Friends • Important to look after environment	• Membership of clubs, organisations, societies (across 21 civil society organisations)
Health	• Health affects work • Health affects social activities	
Housing-dwelling	• Rating of dwelling • Rating of area/place	• Dwelling structure • Dwelling ownership • Overcrowding (more than two households sharing one room excluding kitchen/bathroom)
Infrastructure	• Perceived improvement in community • Water cleanliness (self-reported)	• Sanitation access • Water access • Electricity • Refuse removal • Cut-offs/evictions for non-payment of bills
Education & connectivity	• Press is free (Likert item)	• Highest level of education attained • Telephone/cellphone ownership • Radio/television ownership • Internet connection
Work	• Amount of money available • Household status (self-described class position) • Standard of living • Working conditions (decent work index)	• Employment status • Household income • Absence of debt *(Continued)*

Broad areas	Subjective indicators (level of satisfaction)	Objective indicators (measured to RDP standard*)
Security	• Safety in area during day • Safety in area during night • Safety at home • Crime situation improved	• Victim of crime (self-reported)
Sociopolitical	• Politics is waste of time (Likert) • Elections are free and fair (Likert) • Judiciary is free (Likert) • Trust between races (Likert) • Foreigners are taking benefits meant for locals • Government performance rating • Government officials live up to Batho Pele principles (i.e. 'People First' principles of the South African public service)	• Public participation (in a range of government/community initiatives such as local development fora, school governing bodies, etc.) • Voted in most recent election • Have been asked for a bribe by officials/police

Source: GCRO Quality of Life index

*The RDP set standards for service delivery, such as clean water piped into dwellings, into yards, or being available within 200 metres; acceptable types of sanitation; and so on.

is one variable in the 'work dimension' but is itself a score derived from a 12-part index of questions about conditions of service.) In all, there are 54 indicators, across the ten dimensions of quality of life.

For each indicator, a score of 0 or 1 was allocated to each individual respondent in order to compute an overall score for the area. For each dimension, the score was then scaled out of 1. For each dimension, a maximum score of 1 was possible (working on the same 0–1 basis as the Gini coefficient). A score of 1 would reflect extremely high levels of quality of life; a score of 0, the reverse. When the dimensions are added, perfect quality of life would be represented by 10 (out of 10), where a respondent scores 1 out of 1 on every dimension: this is a simple matter of adding together the scores from the ten dimensions. Therefore, the higher the score, the higher the level of quality of life. The mean scores for each dimension, for the three years, are shown in Figure 13.1, and immediately reflect quite significant changes.

No variables or dimensions in the index were weighted, an approach that can be challenged, most obviously in post-apartheid Gauteng – it is reasonable to ask, should specific variables or entire dimensions be weighted above others? For example, given the extended unemployment crisis that has beset South Africa for decades (and mainly affected black South Africans), should unemployment – part of the 'work' dimension – not be weighted more than, say, membership of a civil society organisation, or satisfaction with respondent's dwelling, and so on? Or should attitudes to race and xenophobia be treated differently? These are legitimate questions, but when Principal Component Analysis (PCA) was used to analyse the 2009 and 2011 surveys to see whether or not PCA – which applies weights to key variables as they emerge from the analysis – generated results that were significantly different from the unweighted approach (Greyling 2011), the simple answer was 'no', and treating all variables as equal seems to work well.

One obvious headline is the rise in the mean score across all ten dimensions of quality of life, starting at 6.24 in 2009, dipping in 2011 as the global financial crisis really impacted South Africa (later than much of the world) to 6.1, but rising again to 6.28 in 2013. It is impossible to say how this compares with other parts of South Africa, since the index is not used elsewhere. Very few respondents scored *very* badly – no one scored below 1.75 (out of 10) at all, suggesting that while there are challenges in the social domain, they are balanced against important tangible benefits. Put simply, delivery of services may not be transforming the mindset of respondents, but is nonetheless having a positive impact on their overall quality of life. However, it is also apparent that there is enormous inequality in the GCR, given that there are respondents scoring just below 10 on the index. While there is a positive aggregation of respondents in the 4–8 midpoints, there remains a very broad range, reflecting inequalities within the system.

The scores, as represented in Figure 13.1, show that virtually no respondents scored below 2/10, while at the positive end of the scale, scores do approach the 'perfect quality of life' score of 10/10. A provincial mean of 6.28 is very positive: the majority of citizens are enjoying a quality of life at the higher end of the scale. This is not meant to and should not obscure the work that is needed to lift those between 2–5/10, but also suggests that despite population growth at an annualised 2.6% per annum, Gauteng has done well in its seeking to meet the needs of its residents. The question is, of course, which needs? Are residents receiving an appropriately balanced range of services that meet their various and differing needs, or is government sticking to its service delivery targets at the expense of concerns over social cohesion, social capital, and the like?

The answer is clear as soon as one looks across the ten dimensions (which contain the 54 variables) making up the Quality of Life index. Looking across the ten dimensions for 2009, 2011 and 2013 (Figure 13.2), it is immediately apparent that

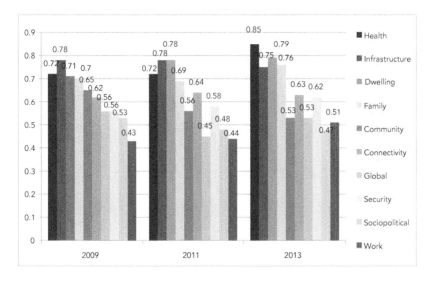

Figure 13.2: Scores for all dimensions of Quality of Life surveys 2009, 2011 and 2013

the highest scorings are those primarily related to service delivery – 'infrastructure' (subjective perceptions of improvement in respondents' community and cleanliness of water, but dominated by key RDP delivery items including water, sanitation, electricity, and so on); 'dwelling' (subjective measures of quality of place but dominated by objective measures of delivery of houses, ownership of dwelling, and so on); and 'health', which is not reflecting delivery but rather self-reported health assessments.

The fourth dimension, with scores in the 0.7 range, is 'family', comprising one objective measure (those who could not afford to feed their children in the year before interview), is dominated by satisfaction with partner, family, time for leisure, and so on. This is the only 'soft' indicator set that scores high. 'Infrastructure' remained constantly high across the three surveys, joined by the 'dwelling' dimension in the last two surveys. 'Health' had scored above 0.7 and rose by 2013, while 'family' started from a lower base (0.67 to 0.69 between 2009 and 2011), and moved above 0.7 only in 2013. 'Connectivity', which includes accessing communication devices as well as mechanisms (internet connection at home, radio, TV, cellphone) and reflects a mixture of service delivery and the explosion in affordable and accessible electronic communication, has also scored steadily high, from 0.62 to 0.64, and dropping back to 0.62 in 2013. 'Security' scores predictably lower, given the ongoing crime rate – but has remained largely constant at 0.56, and then 0.58 for 2011 and 2013, respectively. This includes measures of both incidence of crime and subjective perceptions of security.

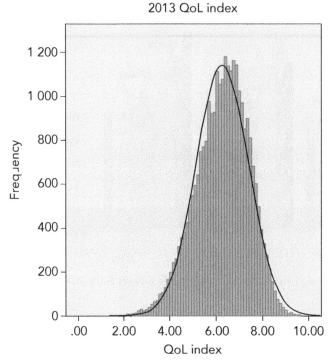

Figure 13.1: Histogram of Quality of Life scores 2013

Source: GCRO Quality of Life data (2013)

At one level, this pattern may seem fine. From a government perspective, from the RDP to the NDP, the emphasis has been on delivering infrastructure, and here we can see the extent to which service delivery is driving the overall Quality of Life index upwards (high scores are good news). From the non-infrastructure side, it seems that only the 'family' dimension is strong enough to score as high as infrastructure/service delivery-related dimensions. The positive spin that can be given is true until we look at those dimensions that are low, and those that are declining.

It is notable that 'work' – which includes (un)employment status, a decent work index as well as satisfaction with work indicators – remains consistently among the weakest dimensions across all three surveys. With a strict unemployment rate (which only measures 'active work-seekers' as unemployed) of 29 per cent and a broader rate (which includes all people who can work but are out of work) closer to 36 per cent in Gauteng, this is not surprising. That said, the marginal increases over the three surveys may provide a glimmer of hope – but should be seen in context, as the worst-performing dimension despite the fact that both the RDP and NDP note that jobs are the key elixir needed to transform the post-apartheid landscape.

It is of deep concern that by 2013, the most recent iteration of the survey at the time of writing, the 'sociopolitical' dimension became the lowest-scoring for 2013, having dropped from 0.53 to 0.48 to 0.47 over the period being studied – and by 2013 was the worst-performing dimension, lower even than 'work'. It is particularly concerning when we recall that this dimension speaks to 'the active citizen', invoked in the RDP and especially the NDP as a key partner in realising the goals of both documents. The citizen, it would appear, is not playing their role.

'Sociopolitical' as a dimension includes a series of attitude questions (Likert items), including the notion that politics is a waste of time, freedom of electoral and judicial systems, racial trust, attitudes to foreigners and to public officials performing well. On the objective side, it includes participation in appropriate fora (school governing bodies, local development initiatives, etc.), voting, and so on. This is the home of the active and engaged citizen – and by 2013, had dropped from 0.53 in 2009 to 0.47 in 2013. The index does not provide for causality: readers can draw their own conclusions from the clustering of variables and the low scores across them all. It does appear, however, that there is a deep-seated – and worsening – political malaise in Gauteng, where residents are alienated from the political process, hold public officials in low esteem, and participate in low numbers. This is our first, very clear signal that the hoped-for synergy between service delivery by government in partnership with the 'engaged citizen' is failing to materialise. Service delivery is up, but alienation from the political domain is the reverse. Something seems to be going very wrong.

This is confirmed when we look at the 'global' dimension. The 'global' refers to an overall sense of well-being, and the dimension includes measures of (the presence or absence of) anomie, alienation, overall life satisfaction and a sense that South Africa is heading in the right (or wrong) direction. Alienation and anomie both score excessively high as individual variables, perhaps reflecting a society in transition (as Durkheim [1951] had originally outlined his understanding of anomie. Some four in ten respondents regard themselves as anomic ('I am unable to influence developments in my community') or alienated ('No one cares about people like me'). Perhaps more worryingly, these scores have risen consistently across the three Quality of Life surveys, suggesting that the transition to a post-apartheid South Africa is taking a considerable toll on the citizenry.

This is confirmed when we examine the steady decline, over time, of the 'community' dimension. This includes membership of civil society organisations (the objective indicator) as well as social capital, having reliable friends and

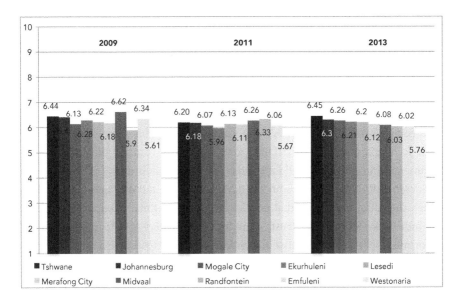

Figure 13.3: Quality of Life by municipality 2009, 2011 and 2013

environmental awareness. The dimension was ranked fifth in 2009 with a score of 0.62 – this had dropped by more than a full point to 0.53 by 2013 – and the dimension was tied as third worst-performing with 'global', discussed above. The concerns remain twofold: firstly, the very low scores across the board, barring 'family' for social indicators and dimensions; and, secondly, their steady decline over time. The only social dimension to buck this trend is that of 'family', which speaks very much to the life of the individual, not the individual within a social setting.

By analysing the data spatially, at sub-provincial level, it is also clear that the overall scores mask some differences within Gauteng (Figure 13.3). The overall pattern is consistent: 2009 scores are followed by a dip in 2011, as the global financial crisis hits, and then lift again in 2013. What is clear is that over time, the three big cities – Tshwane, Johannesburg and then Ekurhuleni – have edged ahead of the smaller municipalities. It seems that while smaller, and poorer, municipalities managed to perform reasonably during the financial crisis, this seems to be based more on funding received from the national sphere than local performance. The municipality with the consistently lowest quality of life score, Westonaria, has virtually no tax base, and relies on equitable share and conditional grant funds. But it seems that the low-hanging fruit, referred to earlier – service delivery, especially in areas such as Gauteng, which present few challenges to delivery (such as natural barriers like mountains or far-flung rural communities) – are becoming more scarce.

With service delivery – admittedly, of basic services such as water, sanitation, and so on – sitting very close to universal in Gauteng, it throws into stark contrast the difference between the bricks-and-mortar delivery (which is positive and which drives up overall quality of life scores) and the 'soft' dimensions, those dealing with interiority, social life, psychosocial issues, public participation, civil society membership, social capital, trust in the state, and so on. Houses, taps, water connections, and so on are being built not in a silo, but for the same people who show that the transition continues to take an extraordinary psychological toll on them. The recrudescence of racism, xenophobia, gender-based violence, high crime rates, and so on all bear testimony to the fact.

This may help explain why so many protests are violent, and also why protesters may turn on the very services being delivered, be it a library or a clinic or a railway station. In sum: at an aggregate level, receiving services has not restored dignity, and has not healed people damaged by apartheid and/or by the first 21 years of democracy. Despite having the power – political and budgetary – to tackle the transition in totality, government has chosen the easier path of hard service delivery above all else. Despite widespread awareness and discussion around the need, for example, for community-level therapy to aid healing in the period immediately before and after the 1994 elections, government failed to follow through on any such 'soft' service (to 'ordinary people', not extreme cases requiring medical assistance), and simultaneously civil society underwent a mass exodus of staff into government while funds were also directed away from non-governmental organisations to government.

Twenty-one years later, the data suggest that we are now reaping the results of this approach. At precisely the point where the ANC's electoral power seems to be slipping,[2] it is also reaching the limit of affordable low-hanging fruit (i.e. basic needs service delivery to urban and peri-urban areas), and (assuming the Quality of Life surveys are accurate) people are losing faith in the state and its machinery – and in each other. The ubiquity of media reports and legal cases against politicians and officials for acts of corruption merely underscores what surveys suggest people are thinking anyway – that South Africa is no longer 'heading in the right direction', and that rent-seeking behaviour has instead replaced the wished-for solidarity of the 'rainbow nation'.

CONCLUSION

Quality of life as measured here seeks to provide a holistic reflection of society. It does so by combining objective and subjective indicators, in the belief that real quality of life must include both access to goods and services and robust psychosocial values and attitudes.

What the index suggests is that many of the areas of delivery in which local, provincial and national government work have improved, but many of the 'softer' social dimensions of quality of life have deteriorated. This strongly suggests that the hoped-for transformative power of meeting basic needs to somehow restoring dignity (let alone the notion that the elections of 1994 were sufficient to restore dignity), and in turn psychosocial healing, is misplaced. People are receiving goods and services, and are happy about those services; but they remain deeply scarred about race, cenophobia, deeply alienated and anomic, mistrustful of friends and neighbours, isolated and withdrawn from civil society.

Without direct intervention in these more intricate areas, however complex, the future is bleak: and it is so because of governance failure: namely, the inability or unwillingness to use the massive electoral dominance (and thus power to determine budgets) of the ruling party to embrace the full ambit of transformation. Precisely by sticking to bricks-and-mortar issues – but exclusively so – government (in all spheres) has allowed the social fabric to be stretched to what appears to be close to breaking point. The issue is not to find a stick with which to beat government, but to point to the obvious strategic error made – and repeated in every five-year electoral cycle – in their use of power to transform the country. Providing services, of all types, is the normal business of government, but with an accepted urgency given what apartheid did to black South Africans. However, apartheid also damaged all South Africans psychologically, whether at individual or communal levels. Providing services, but not providing the assistance needed to undo the psychological damage wrought by apartheid, is short-termist – quite the opposite of what the ANC government should have embarked on, given its electoral might in the first 21 years of democracy.

NOTES

[1]   This chapter does not provide detailed statistical analysis by demographic, or other variable or cross-segment. For more on this, please read successive iterations of State of the GCR at http://www.gcro.ac.za/data-gallery/state-of-the-gcr/. See also Everatt 2013, 2014, 2017.

[2]   See, for example, Schulz-Herzenberg 2014.

REFERENCES

African National Congress. 1994. *The Reconstruction and Development Programme.* Johannesburg: Ravan Press.

Babbie, E. 2007. *The Practice of Social Research* (7th edn). Belmont, CA: Wadsworth Publishing Company.

Boddy, M. & Parkinson, M. 2004. Competitiveness, cohesion and urban governance. In: Boddy, M. & Parkinson, M. (eds) *City matters: Competitiveness, cohesion and urban governance.* Bristol, UK: Policy Press.

Bond, P. 2000. *Elite Transition: From Apartheid to Neoliberalism in South Africa.* London: Pluto Press; Pietermaritzburg: UKZN Press.

Constitution of the Republic of South Africa, 1996 (No. 108 of 1996).

Durkheim, E. 1951. *Suicide: A study in sociology.* New York: The Free Press.

Everatt, D. 2013. Quality of Life in the Gauteng City-Region: A steady ship on a global sea of change? *Focus* (Helen Suzman Foundation journal) (Special issue on Future of our cities) 69 (June): 5–16.

Everatt, D. 2014. Poverty and Inequality in the Gauteng City-Region. In: Todes, A., Wray, C., Gotz, G. & Harrison, P. (eds) *Changing Space, Changing City: Johannesburg after apartheid.* Johannesburg: Wits University Press.

Everatt, D. 2017. Quality of Life in the Gauteng City-Region, South Africa. *Social Indicators Research* 130(1): 71–86.

Everatt, D. & Orkin, M. 1993. 'Growing up tough': a national survey of South African youth, submitted to the second national conference on Marginalised Youth, convened by the Joint Enrichment Project, Broederstroom, March.

Gauteng City-Region Observatory (GCRO). 2014. State of the Gauteng City-Region. http://legacy.gcro.unomena.net/regional-economy (accessed 6 January 2016).

Greyling, T. 2011. *Measuring and understanding the well-being of the Gauteng City-Region's population.* Working Paper, Gauteng City-Region Observatory.

Hack, G., Barkin, D. & LeRoyer, A. 1996. Global City Regions: Searching for Common Ground. *LandLines* (Newsletter of the Lincoln Institute of Land Policy) 8(1): 1–7.

Haffajee, F. 2015. *What if there were no whites in South Africa?* Johannesburg: Picador Africa.

Hatang, S. & Harris, V. 2015. Position Paper on Race and Identity in 2015. Mimeo. April. Johannesburg: Nelson Mandela Foundation.

Higgs, N. 2003. Beyond wealth and poverty: a new model – measuring well-being and everyday quality of life: how people live. *Proceedings of 2003 Market Research Society Conference,* Market Research Society, London.

Jennings, R. & Everatt, D. 2001. *Evaluation of the 1998/99 Community Based Public Works Programme: Consolidated Report.* Johannesburg: Strategy & Tactics.

Marais, H. 2001. *South Africa: Limits To Change: The Political Economy of Transition.* London and New York: Zed Books; Cape Town: UCT Press.

Møller, V. 1998. Quality of life in South Africa – Post-apartheid trends. *Social Indicators Research* 43(1–2): 27–68.

Møller, V. 2007. Quality of life in South Africa – the first ten years of democracy. *Social Indicators Research* 81(2): 181–201.

Møller, V. & Dickow, H. 2002. The Role of Quality of Life Surveys in Managing Change in Democratic Transitions: The South African Case. *Social Indicators Research* 58(1): 267–292.

National Planning Commission (NPC). 2011. National Development Plan: Vision for 2030. Pretoria: National Planning Commission.

Nussbaum, M. & Sen, A. 1993. *The Quality of Life*. Oxford: Oxford University Press.

Quintal, G. 2014. South African Press Association press release on protest statistics. Johannesburg, 5 February.

Schulz-Herzenberg, C. 2014. Trends in electoral participation, 1994–2014. In: Schulz-Herzenberg, C. & Southall, R. (eds) *Election 2014 South Africa:* 23–26. Johannesburg: Jacana.

South Africa: The Good News. 2008. *Quality of life improves, but inequality widens.* http://www.sagoodnews.co.za/benchmarking_progress/quality_of_life_improves_but_inequality _widens.html (accessed 20 August 2017).

StatsSA. 2011. *Census 2011: Preliminary findings.* Pretoria: Statistics South Africa.

Caryn Abrahams is a senior lecturer at the Wits School of Governance.

Patrick Bond is a distinguished professor, and teaches Political Economy and Political Ecology at the Wits School of Governance.

Susan Booysen is professor emeritus and visiting professor at the Wits School of Governance. She is also director of research at the Mapungubwe Institute for Strategic Reflection.

Jody Cedras is the registrar and regulatory affairs officer for the Pearson Institute of Higher Education.

David Everatt is head of the Wits School of Governance.

William Gumede is associate professor in the Wits School of Governance, and course leader in the School of Public Policy, Central European University, Budapest.

Salim Latib is a PhD candidate in African Multilateralism in Governance, at the Wits School of Governance.

Babalwa Magoqwana is a senior lecturer in the Sociology, Anthropology and History Department at Nelson Mandela University.

Kirti Menon is the senior director in charge of Academic Planning and Academic Staff Development at the University of Johannesburg (UJ), and research associate in the Faculty of Education at UJ.

Darlene Miller is a senior lecturer at the Wits School of Governance. She is principal investigator in a research project on food governance and new food movements.

Nomalanga Mkhize is associate professor in History at Nelson Mandela University. She currently holds an NIHSS Sam Moyo Postdoctoral Fellowship at Rhodes University.

Chelete Monyane, an advocate of the High Court, is a senior lecturer at the Wits School of Governance.

Mike Muller is a professional engineer and visiting adjunct professor at the Wits School of Governance.

Bongiwe Ngcobo Mphahlele is a PhD candidate at the University of Pretoria.

Pundy Pillay is professor of Economics and Public Finance, and research director at the Wits School of Governance.

Rebecca Pointer is a PhD candidate at Wits School of Governance.

Anthoni van Nieuwkerk is associate professor and teaches Security Studies at the Wits School of Governance.

Printed and bound by CPI Group (UK) Ltd, Croydon, CR0 4YY

16/04/2025

14658440-0004